STUDIES IN THE SERMON ON THE MOUNT

STUDIES IN
THE SERMON
ON THE MOUNT

by
D. Martyn Lloyd-Jones

VOLUME TWO

WM. B. EERDMANS PUBLISHING COMPANY
GRAND RAPIDS, MICHIGAN

CONTENTS

Volume Two: Matthew vi and vii

PREFACE

As this volume consists of a continuation of the Studies in the Sermon on the Mount begun in Volume I, it does not call for any special word of introduction. All that was said in the Preface to that volume applies here and, from my standpoint, it is important that it should be borne in mind.

Each chapter is a sermon in and of itself and yet each can be understood only in the light of the whole.

The fact that there are thirty sermons in this volume, as in the previous one, is quite accidental and not planned nor contrived. It has never been my custom to divide up a portion of Scripture into a number of parts and then to issue a syllabus announcing what will be done each week. That seems to me to limit the freedom of the act of preaching, quite apart from the fact that in actual practice I sometimes find that I succeed in doing only about half of what I had planned and purposed. In other words expository preaching must always be *preaching* and not merely mechanical exposition.

It was never my intention to preach sixty sermons on the Sermon on the Mount; I just went on from Sunday to Sunday and this turned out to be the result. I can but hope and pray that God will bless it.

I would again thank all whom I mentioned in Volume I for their invaluable help and encouragement.

D. M. LLOYD-JONES

Westminster Chapel,
Buckingham Gate,
London, S.W.1.
August, 1960

CHAPTER ONE

LIVING THE RIGHTEOUS LIFE

OUR consideration of this Sermon on the Mount began with an analysis and division of its contents.[1] We saw that here in chapter vi we come to a new section. The first section (v. 3–12) contains the Beatitudes, a description of the Christian as he is. In the next section (v. 13–16), we find this Christian man, who has thus been described, reacting to the world and the world reacting to him. The third (v. 17–48) deals with the relationship of the Christian to the law of God. It gives a positive exposition of the law and contrasts it with the false teaching of the Pharisees and scribes. It ends with the great exhortation in the closing verse: 'Be ye therefore perfect, even as your Father which is in heaven is perfect.'

We come now to quite a new section, and it runs right through this sixth chapter. Here we have what we may well call a picture of the Christian living his life in this world in the presence of God, in active submission to God, and in entire dependence upon Him. Read this sixth chapter and you will find that this reference to God the Father keeps on recurring. We have been looking at this Christian man who has been told something of his characteristics, who has been told how he is to behave in society, and who has been reminded of what it is that God expects of him and demands from him. Here we have a picture of him going on to live that life in this world; and the great thing that is ever emphasized is that he does it all in the presence of God. That is something of which he should constantly be reminded. Or, to put it in another way, this section presents a picture of the children in relationship to their Father as they wend their way on this pilgrimage called life.

The chapter reviews our life as a whole, and it considers it under two main aspects. This is something very wonderful, for in the last analysis the life of the Christian in this world has two sides, and both of them are covered here. The first one is dealt with in verses 1 to 18; the second from verse 19 to the end of the chapter. The first is what we may call our religious life, the culture and nurture of the soul, our piety, our worship, the whole

[1] See *Studies in the Sermon on the Mount*, Vol. I, p. 25.

religious aspect of our life, and everything that concerns our direct relationship to God. But of course that is not the only element in the life of the Christian in this world. He is reminded by it that he is not of this world, that he is a child of God and a citizen of a kingdom that cannot be seen. He is but a journey-man, a sojourner, a traveller in this world. He is not a worldling and does not belong to this world as other people do; he is in this unique relationship to God. He is walking with Him. Neverthe-less he is in this world, and though he is not of it any longer this world keeps doing things to him, and he is in many senses subject to it. And, after all, he does have to walk through it. So that the second picture is that of the Christian in his relationship to life in general, not so much as a purely religious being now, but as a man who is subject to 'the slings and arrows of outrageous fortune', a man who is concerned about food and drink, clothing and shelter, who may have a family and children to bring up, and who therefore is subject to what is called in the Scriptures 'the cares of this world'.

Those are the two great divisions of this chapter, the directly religious part of the Christian life, and the mundane. Both these aspects are taken up by our Lord and dealt with in considerable detail. In other words, it is vital for the Christian that he should be absolutely clear about both these matters, and he needs instruction about both. There is no greater fallacy than to imagine that the moment a man is converted and becomes a Christian, all his problems are solved and all his difficulties vanish. The Christian life is full of difficulties, full of pitfalls and snares. That is why we need the Scriptures. They would have been unnecessary but for that. These detailed instructions given by our Lord and in the Epistles would be unnecessary were it not for the fact that the life of the Christian in this world, as John Bunyan and others have been very careful to point out in their great Christian classics, is a life beset by problems. There are pitfalls associated with our practice of the Christian life, and associated also with our living our lives in this world together with other people. You will find as you analyse your own experience, and still more as you read the biographies of God's people, that many have got into difficulties, and many have for the time being found themselves in great misery and unhappiness and have lost their experience of joy and happiness in the Christian life, because of their neglect of one aspect or the other. There are some people who are wrong in their religious life as we shall see; and there are others who seem to be all right in that respect, but who, because they are tempted in a very subtle manner on the more practical side, tend to go wrong in that way. So we have to face both these matters. Here, in the teaching of our Lord, they are dealt with right down to the minutest detail.

We may as well realize at the outset that this chapter vi is again a very searching one; indeed, we can go further and say that it is a very painful one. I sometimes think that it is one of the most uncomfortable chapters to read in the entire Scriptures. It probes and examines and holds a mirror up before us, and it will not allow us to escape. There is no chapter which is more calculated to promote self-humbling and humiliation than this particular one. But thank God for it. The Christian should always be anxious to know himself. No other man truly wants to know himself. The natural man thinks he knows himself, and thereby reveals his basic trouble. He evades self-examination because to know one's self is ultimately the most painful piece of knowledge that a man can ever acquire. And here is a chapter that brings us face to face with ourselves, and enables us to see ourselves exactly as we are. But, I repeat, thank God for it, because it is only the man who has truly seen himself for what he is who is likely to fly to Christ, and to seek to be filled with the Spirit of God who alone can burn out of him the vestiges of self and everything that tends to mar his Christian life and living.

Here, as in the previous chapter, the teaching is given, in a sense, partly by way of contrast with that of the Pharisees. You remember there was a kind of general introduction to this when our Lord said: 'Except your righteousness shall exceed the righteousness of the scribes and Pharisees, ye shall in no case enter into the kingdom of heaven.' There we were looking at and contrasting the teaching of the Pharisees and scribes, and the teaching that should govern the life of the Christian. Here the emphasis is not so much on teaching as on practical living, including piety, and our whole religious demeanour and behaviour.

As we come to this first section, we find that verse 1 is an introduction to the message of verses 2 to 18. It is indeed astounding to notice the perfect arrangement of this Sermon. Those who are musical, and are interested in the analysis of symphonies, will see that there is something still more wonderful here. The theme is stated, then comes the analysis, after which the particular themes and sections—the various 'leit motifs', so

called—are taken up, until eventually all is drawn together and
gathered up in a final statement. Our Lord employs a similar
method here. In the first verse He lays down the general principle
governing the religious life of the Christian. Having done that,
He goes on to give us three illustrations of that principle, in the
matters of almsgiving, praying and fasting. There, ultimately, is
the whole of one's religious life and practice. If we analyse the
religious life of a man we find that it can be divided into these
three sections, and into these three sections only: the way I do
my almsgiving, the nature of my prayer life and contact with
God, and the way in which I should mortify the flesh. Again we
must point out that the three are but illustrations. Our Lord
illustrates what He lays down as a general principle exactly as
we found Him doing in His exposition of the law in chapter v.

The fundamental principle is laid down in the first verse. Here
there is no doubt at all but that the Revised Version is, at this
point, superior to the Authorized Version which reads like this:
'Take heed that ye do not your alms before men.' It should be:
'Take heed that ye do not your righteousness (or, if you prefer it,
your piety) before men, to be seen of them: else ye have no
reward with your Father which is in heaven.' This again is just a
question of a textual difference in the manuscripts. Without
doubt the second is the better version, and all good commentators are agreed in saying that this word should be 'righteousness'
rather than 'alms'. Almsgiving is one of the particular illustrations, whereas in this first verse our Lord is concerned to lay
down a general principle. The word 'righteousness' governs the
three aspects of righteous living. We look first at piety itself and
then come to consider the various manifestations of piety. The
general principle is this: 'Take heed that ye do not your
righteousness before men, to be seen of them: else ye have no
reward with your Father which is in heaven.' Let us consider
this in the form of a number of subsidiary principles.

The first of these is this—*the delicate nature of the Christian life.*
The Christian life is always a matter of balance and poise. It is a
life that gives the impression of being self-contradictory, because
it seems to be dealing at the same time with two things which are
mutually exclusive. We read the Sermon on the Mount and we
come across something like this: 'Let your light so shine before
men, that they may see your good works, and glorify your
Father which is in heaven.' Then we read, 'Take heed that ye do
not your righteousness before men, to be seen of them: else ye

have no reward with your Father which is in heaven.' And a man looking at that says, 'Well, what am I to do? If I am to do all these things in secret, if I am not to be seen of men, if I am to pray in my closet having locked the door, if I am to anoint my face and wash myself, thus giving the appearance that I am not fasting, how can men know I am doing these things, and how can they possibly see this light which is shining in me?'

But, of course, that is obviously only a superficial contradiction. You notice how the first statement puts it: 'Let your light so shine before men, that they may see your good works, and glorify your Father which is in heaven.' In other words there is no contradiction here, but we are called to do both these things at one and the same time. The Christian is to live in such a way that men looking at him, and seeing the quality of his life, will glorify God. He must always remember at the same time that he is not to do things in order that he may attract attention to himself. He must not desire to be seen of men, he is never to be self-conscious. But, clearly, this balance is a fine and delicate one; so often we tend to go to one extreme or the other. Christian people tend either to be guilty of great ostentation or else to become monks and hermits. As you look at the long story of the Christian Church throughout the centuries you will find this great conflict has been going on. They have either been ostentatious, or else they have been so afraid of self and self-glorification that they have segregated themselves from the world. But here we are called to avoid both extremes. It is a delicate life, it is a sensitive life; but if we approach it in the right way, and under the leading of the Holy Spirit, the balance can be maintained. Of course, if we just take these things as rules which we have to put into operation we shall go wrong on the one side or the other. But if we realize that what matters is the great principle, the spirit, then we shall be saved from the error on the right hand and on the left. Let us never forget this, the Christian at one and the same time is to be attracting attention to himself, and yet not attracting attention to himself. That will be seen more clearly as we proceed.

The second subsidiary principle is that *the ultimate choice is always the choice between pleasing self and pleasing God*. That may sound very elementary, and yet it seems necessary that we should emphasize it for this reason. 'Take heed that ye do not your alms before men, to be seen of them.' 'Surely, then,' we may think, 'the choice is between pleasing men and pleasing God.' I suggest that is not the choice: the ultimate choice is the choice between pleasing self and pleasing God, and that is where the subtlety of this matter comes in. Ultimately our only reason for pleasing men around us is that we may please ourselves. Our real desire is not to please others as such; we want to please them because we know that, if we do, they will think better of us. In other words, we are pleasing ourselves and are merely concerned about self-gratification. That is where the insidious character of sin is seen. What appears to be so selfless may be just a very subtle form of selfishness. According to our Lord it comes to this: man by nature desires the praise of man more than the praise of God. In desiring the praise of man, what he is really concerned about is his good opinion of himself. In the last analysis it always comes to this, we are either pleasing ourselves or else we are pleasing God. It is a very solemnizing thought, but the moment we begin to analyse ourselves and see the motives of our conduct we shall agree that it comes to that.

That brings us to the next subsidiary principle which perhaps is the most important of all. *The supreme matter in this life and world for all of us is to realize our relationship to God.* One almost apologizes for making such a statement, and yet I suggest that the greatest cause of all our failures is that we constantly forget our relationship to God. Our Lord puts it like this. We should realize that our supreme object in life should be to please God, to please Him only, and to please Him always and in everything. If that is our aim we cannot go wrong. Here, of course, we see the outstanding characteristic of the life of our Lord Jesus Christ. Is there anything that stands out more clearly in His life? He lived entirely for God. He even said that the words that He spoke were not of Himself and that the works He did were the works which the Father had given Him to do. His whole life was given to glorifying God. He never thought of Himself; He did nothing for Himself; He did not obtrude Himself. What we are told of Him is this, 'A bruised reed shall he not break, and smoking flax shall he not quench.' He did not raise His voice aloft. In a sense He seems to be there unseen and trying to hide Himself. We are told about Him that 'he could not be hid', but He seemed to be trying always to do this. There was a complete absence of ostentation. He lived entirely and always and only for the glory of God. He said constantly in various ways: 'I seek not My own honour but the honour of Him who has sent Me.' And He put it negatively in this way: 'How can ye believe, which receive honour one of another and seek not the honour that cometh from God only?' 'That is your trouble', He says in effect. 'You are so concerned about man. If only you had a single eye to the glory and honour of God, then all would be well.'

The second thing which we have to remember in this connection is that we are always in the presence of God. We are always in His sight. He sees our every action, indeed our every thought. In other words, if you believe in having texts placed before you in a prominent position on your desk or on the wall of your house, there is no better one than this: 'Thou God seest me'. He is everywhere. 'Take heed that ye do not your righteousness before men.' Why? 'Else ye have no reward with your Father which is in heaven.' He sees it all. He knows your heart; other people do not. You can deceive them, and you can persuade them that you are quite selfless; but God knows your heart. 'Ye', said our Lord to the Pharisees one afternoon, 'ye are they which justify yourselves before men; but God knoweth your hearts; for that which is highly esteemed amongst men is abomination in the sight of God.' Now this is obviously a fundamental principle for the whole of our life. I sometimes feel that there is no better way of living, and trying to live, the holy and sanctified life than just to be constantly reminding ourselves of that. When we wake up in the morning we should immediately remind ourselves and recollect that we are in the presence of God. It is not a bad thing to say to ourselves before we go any further: 'Throughout the whole of this day, everything I do, and say, and attempt, and think, and imagine, is going to be done under the eye of God. He is going to be with me; He sees everything; He knows everything. There is nothing I can do or attempt but God is fully aware of it all. "Thou God seest me".' It would revolutionize our lives if we always did that.

In a sense the many books which have been written on the devotional life all concentrate on this. You remember that famous little book of Brother Lawrence's, *The Practice of the Presence of God*. I am not recommending it, but I am recommending the principle behind it. We have to learn, if we want to live this life fully, that we have to discipline ourselves and speak to ourselves. This is the fundamental thing, the most serious thing of all, that we are always in the presence of God. He sees everything and knows everything, and we can never escape from His sight. Those men who wrote the Psalms knew all about it, and there are instances of where men have cried out in desperation: ' "Whither shall I flee from thy presence!" I cannot get away from You. You are there "if I make my bed in hell. . . . If I take the wings of the morning, and dwell in the uttermost parts of the sea. . . ." I cannot get away from You.' If we only remembered that, hypocrisy would vanish, self-adulation and all we are guilty of by way of feeling ourselves above others, would immediately disappear. It is a cardinal principle that we cannot get away from God. In this matter of the ultimate choice between self and God, we must always remember that God knows all about us. 'All things are naked and opened unto the eyes of him with whom we have to do.' He knows the thoughts and intents of the heart. And He can divide to the separating of the joint and marrow and the very soul and spirit. There is nothing hid from His sight. We have to start with that postulate.

If we were all to practise this it would be revolutionary. I am quite certain a revival would start at once. What a difference it would make to church life, and the life of every individual. Think of all the pretence and sham, and all that is unworthy in us all. If only we realized that God is looking at all, and is aware of it all, and is recording it all! That is the teaching of the Scriptures, and that its method of preaching holiness—not offering people some marvellous experience which solves all problems. No, it is just realizing that we are always there in the presence of God. For the man who starts with a true realization of that is soon to be seen flying to Christ and His cross, and pleading to be filled with the Holy Spirit.

The next subsidiary principle concerns rewards. This whole question of rewards seems to trouble people, and yet our Lord continually makes statements like those in verses 1 and 4. Here He indicates that it is quite right to seek the reward which God gives. He says, 'Otherwise ye have no reward of your Father which is in heaven.' If you do the right thing, then 'thy Father which seeth in secret himself shall reward thee openly.' There was a teaching (we do not hear so much of it now) towards the beginning of the century which used to say that one should live the Christian life for its own sake, and not for the reward. It was such a good thing in and of itself that one should not be animated by any motive such as desire for heaven or fear of hell. We should be disinterested and altruistic. The teaching was often put in the form of a story, an illustration. A poor man was walking along an Eastern road one day with a bucket of water in one hand and a bucket of fire in the other. Somebody asked him what he was going to do with these buckets, and he replied that he was going to burn heaven with the bucket of fire and drown hell with the bucket of water—he was not interested in either. But that is not the New Testament teaching. The New Testament teaching would have us see that it is a good thing to desire to see God. That is the *summum bonum.* 'Blessed are the pure in heart: for they shall see God.' It is a right and legitimate desire, it is a holy ambition. We are told this about our Lord Himself: 'Who for the joy that was set before him endured the cross, despising the shame' (Heb. xii. 2). And we are told about Moses that he did what he did because he had his eye on 'the recompence of the reward'. He was far-sighted. Why did the people whose lives we read of in Hebrews xi live the life they did? The answer is this—they saw certain things afar off, they were seeking for 'a city which hath foundations', they had their eye on that ultimate objective.

Concern about rewards is legitimate and is even encouraged by the New Testament. The New Testament teaches us that there will be a 'judgment of rewards'. There are those who shall be beaten with few stripes, and there are those who shall be beaten with many stripes. Every man's work shall be judged whether it be of wood or hay or stubble or silver or gold. All our works are going to be judged. 'We must all appear before the judgment seat of Christ; that every one may receive the things done in his body, according to that he hath done, whether it be good or bad.' We *should* be interested therefore in this matter of rewards. There is nothing wrong in it as long as the desire is the reward of holiness, the reward of being with God.

The second thing about rewards is this. There is no reward from God for those who seek it from men. This is a terrifying thought but it is an absolute statement. 'Take heed that ye do not your alms before men, to be seen of them: otherwise ye have no reward of your Father which is in heaven.' If you have your reward from men in that particular respect, you will have nothing whatever from God. Let me put it like this very bluntly. If I am concerned as I preach this gospel as to what people think of my preaching, well that is all that I will get out of it, and nothing from God. It is an absolute. If you are seeking a reward from men you will get it, but that is all you will get. Work through your religious life, think of all the good you have done in the past, in the light of that pronouncement. How much remains to come to you from God? It is a terrifying thought.

Those are the principles with regard to the general statement. Let us now consider briefly what our Lord has to say about this

particular matter with respect to almsgiving. It follows of
necessity from the principles we have been laying down. He says
there is a wrong and a right way of almsgiving. Almsgiving, of
course, means helping people, giving a helping hand in case of
need, giving money, time, anything you like which is going to
help people.

The wrong way to do this is to announce it. 'Therefore when
thou doest thine alms, do not sound a trumpet before thee.' Of
course they did not actually do that; our Lord is painting a picture. In effect they are engaging a trumpeter to go before them
to say: 'Look at what this man is doing.' The wrong way to do
these things is to proclaim them, and to draw attention to them.
We could spend much time showing the subtle ways in which
this can be done. Let me give one illustration. I remember a lady
who felt called of God to start a certain work, and she felt called
to do this on what is called 'faith lines'. There was to be no
collection or appeals for funds. She decided to inaugurate this
work by having a preaching service and I was given the privilege
of preaching at the service. Half way through the meeting, when
the announcements came, this good lady for ten minutes told
that congregation of people how this work was to be done
entirely on faith lines, how no collection was to be taken, how
she did not believe in collections or asking for money and so on.
I thought it was the most effective appeal for funds that I had
ever heard! I am not suggesting she was dishonest; I am quite
sure she was not, but she was very apprehensive. And in a spirit
of fearfulness we may likewise be doing this kind of thing quite
unconsciously. There is a way of saying that you do not announce
these things which just means that you are announcing them. O
how subtle it is! You know the sort of man who says, 'Of course
I do not believe in announcing the number of converts when I
take a mission. But, after all, the Lord must be glorified, and if
people do not know the numbers, well, how can they give glory
to God?' Or, 'I do not like these long reports in my anniversary
meeting, but if God is to be glorified how can people do that
unless . . .?' You see the subtlety. It is not always that there is an
obvious trumpeter. But when we truly come to examine our
hearts we find that there are very subtle ways in which this self-
same thing can be done. Well, that is the wrong way and the
result of that is this: 'Verily I say unto you, They have their
reward.' People praise and say, 'How wonderful, how marvell-
lous; terrific, isn't it?' They get their reward, they get their
praise. They get their names in the paper; articles are written

about them; there is a great deal of talk about them; people write
their obituary notices; they get it all. Poor men, that is all they
will get; they will get nothing from God. They receive their
reward. If that is what they wanted they have got it; and how
they are to be pitied. How we ought to pray for them, how we
ought to feel sorry for them.

What is the right way? The right way, says our Lord, is this.
'When thou doest alms, let not thy left hand know what thy right
hand doeth: that thine alms may be in secret: and thy Father
which seeth in secret himself shall reward thee openly.' In other
words, Do not announce to others in any shape or form what you
are doing. That is obvious. But this is less obvious: Do not even
announce it to yourself. That is difficult. It is not so difficult for
some people not to announce it to others. I think that any man
with even an element of decency in him rather despises a man
who advertises himself. He says it is pathetic, it is so sad to see
men advertising themselves. Yes, but what is so difficult is not to
pride yourself because you are not like that. You can despise
that kind of thing, you can dismiss it. Yes, but if that leads you
now to say to yourself: 'I thank God I am not like that', immediately you become a Pharisee. That is what the Pharisee
said, 'Thank God I am not like that, and especially like this
publican.' Note that our Lord does not stop at saying you must
not sound a trumpet before you and announce it to the world;
you do not even announce it to yourself. Your left hand must not
know what your right hand is doing. In other words, having
done it in secret you do not take your little book and put down:
'Well, I have done that. Of course I haven't told anybody else
that I have done it.' But you put an extra mark in a special
column where exceptional merit is recorded. In effect our Lord
said: 'Don't keep these books at all; don't keep spiritual ledgers;
don't keep profit and loss accounts in your life; don't write a
diary in this sense; just forget all about it. Do things as you are
moved by God and led by the Holy Spirit, and then forget all
about them.' How is this to be done? There is only one answer,
and that is that we should have such a love for God that we have
no time to think about ourselves. We shall never get rid of self by
concentrating on self. The only hope is to be so consumed by
love that we have no time to think about ourselves. In other
words, if we want to implement this teaching we must look at
Christ dying on Calvary's Hill, and think of His life and all He
endured and suffered, and as we look at Him realize what He
has done for us.

And what is the result of all this? It is glorious. This is how our Lord puts it. He says, 'You must not keep the account. God does that. He sees everything and He records it all, and do you know what He will do? He will reward you openly.' What utter fools we are to keep our own accounts, not realizing that if we do so we shall get no reward from God. But if we just forget all about it and do everything to please Him, we shall find that God will have an account. Nothing we have done will be forgotten, our smallest act will be remembered. Do you remember what He said in Matthew xxv? 'When I was in prison you visited me, when I was thirsty you gave me drink.' And they will say, 'When did we do all this? We are not aware we have done this.' 'Of course you have done it,' He will reply, 'it is there in the Book.' He keeps the books. We must leave the account to Him. 'You know,' He says, 'you did it all in secret; but I will reward you openly. I may not be rewarding you openly in this world, but as certainly as you are alive, I will reward you openly at the Great Day when the secrets of all men shall be disclosed, when the great Book shall be opened, when the final pronouncement shall be made before the whole world. Every detail of all you have done to the glory of God will be announced and proclaimed and you will be given the credit and the honour and the glory. I will reward you openly, and I will say, "Well done, thou good and faithful servant; . . . enter thou into the joy of thy lord." '

Let us keep our eyes upon the ultimate, let us remember that we are always in the presence and sight of God, and let us live only to please Him.

CHAPTER TWO

HOW TO PRAY

IN verses 5–8 we come to the second example taken by our Lord
to illustrate His teaching concerning piety or the conduct of
the religious life. This, as we have seen, is the theme which He
considers in the first eighteen verses of this chapter. 'Take heed',
He says in general, 'that ye do not your righteousness before men,
to be seen of them: else ye have no reward with your Father
which is in heaven.' Here is His second illustration of this.
Following the question of almsgiving comes the whole question of
praying to God, our communion and our fellowship with God.
Here, again, we shall find that the same general characteristic
which our Lord has already described is, alas, far too much in
evidence. This portion of Scripture, I sometimes think, is one of
the most searching and humbling in the entire realm of Scripture.
But we can read these verses in such a way as really to miss their
entire point and teaching, and certainly without coming under
condemnation. The tendency always when reading this is just to
regard it as an exposure of the Pharisees, a denunciation of the
obvious hypocrite. We read, and we think of the kind of ostentatious person who obviously is calling attention to himself, as the
Pharisees did in this matter. We therefore regard it as just an
exposure of this blatant hypocrisy without any relevance to ourselves. But that is to miss the whole point of the teaching here,
which is our Lord's devastating exposure of the terrible effects of
sin upon the human soul, and especially sin in the form of self and
of pride. That is the teaching.

Sin, He shows us here, is something which follows us all the
way, even into the very presence of God. Sin is not merely something that tends to assail and afflict us when we are far away from
God, in the far country as it were. Sin is something so terrible,
according to our Lord's exposure of it, that it will not only follow
us to the gates of heaven, but—if it were possible—into heaven
itself. Indeed, is not that the Scripture teaching with regard to
the origin of sin? Sin is not something which began on earth.
Before man fell there had been a previous Fall. Satan was a
perfect, bright, angelic being dwelling in the heavenlies; and he
had fallen before ever man fell. That is the essence of the teaching

of our Lord in these verses. It is a terrible exposure of the horrible nature of sin. Nothing is quite so fallacious as to think of sin only in terms of actions; and as long as we think of sin only in terms of things actually done, we fail to understand it. The essence of the biblical teaching on sin is that it is essentially a disposition. It is a state of heart. I suppose we can sum it up by saying that sin is ultimately self-worship and self-adulation; and our Lord shows (what to me is an alarming and terrifying thing) that this tendency on our part to self-adulation is something that follows us even into the very presence of God. It sometimes produces this result; that even when we try to persuade ourselves that we are worshipping God, we are actually worshipping ourselves and doing nothing more.

That is the terrible nature of His teaching at this point. This thing that has entered into our very nature and constitution as human beings, is something that is so polluting our whole being that when man is engaged in his highest form of activity he still has a battle to wage with it. It has always been agreed, I think, that the highest picture that you can ever have of man is to look at him on his knees waiting upon God. That is the highest achievement of man, it is his noblest activity. Man is never greater than when he is there in communion and contact with God. Now, according to our Lord, sin is something which affects us so profoundly that even at that point it is with us and assailing us. Indeed, we must surely agree on the basis of New Testament teaching that it is only there we really begin to understand sin.

We tend to think of sin as we see it in its rags and in the gutters of life. We look at a drunkard, poor fellow, and we say: There is sin; that is sin. But that is not the essence of sin. To have a real picture and a true understanding of it, you must look at some great saint, some unusually devout and devoted man. Look at him there upon his knees in the very presence of God. Even there self is intruding itself, and the temptation is for him to think about himself, to think pleasantly and pleasurably about himself, and really to be worshipping himself rather than God. That, not the other, is the true picture of sin. The other is sin, of course, but there you do not see it at its acme; you do not see it in its essence. Or, to put it in another form, if you really want to understand something about the nature of Satan and his activities, the thing to do is not to go to the dregs or the gutters of life; if you really want to know something about Satan, go away to that wilderness where our Lord spent forty days and forty nights.

That is the true picture of Satan where you see him tempting the
very Son of God.

All that comes out in this statement. Sin is something that
follows us even into the very presence of God.

Before we come to our analysis of this, I would make one other
preliminary observation which seems to me to be quite inevitable.
If this picture does not persuade us of our own utter sinfulness, of
our hopelessness as well as our helplessness, if it does not make us
see our need of the grace of God in the matter of salvation, and the
necessity of forgiveness, rebirth and a new nature, then I know of
nothing that ever can persuade us of it. Here we see a mighty
argument for the New Testament doctrine about the absolute
necessity of being born again, because sin is a matter of disposition, something that is so profound and so vitally a part of us that
it even accompanies us into the presence of God. But follow that
argument beyond this life and world, beyond death and the
grave, and contemplate yourself in the presence of God in
eternity for ever and ever. Is not the rebirth something which is a
bare essential? Here, then, in these instructions about piety and
the conduct of the religious life, we have implicit in almost every
statement this ultimate New Testament doctrine of regeneration
and the nature of the new man in Christ Jesus. Indeed we can go
on even beyond that and say that even if we are born again, and
even if we have received a new life and a new nature, we still
need these instructions. This is our Lord's instruction to Christian
people, not to the non-Christian. It is His warning to those who
have been born again; even they have to be careful lest in their
prayers and devotions they become guilty of this hypocrisy of the
Pharisees.

First, then, let us take this subject in general before coming to
a consideration of what is commonly called 'the Lord's Prayer'.
We are looking merely at what we might call an introduction to
prayer as our Lord teaches it in these verses, and I think that
once more the best way of approaching the subject is to divide it
into two sections. There is a false way of praying and there is a
true way of praying. Our Lord deals with them both.

The trouble with the false way is that its very approach is
wrong. Its essential fault is that it is concentrating on itself. It is
the concentrating of attention on the one who is praying rather
than on the One to whom the prayer is offered. That is the
trouble, and our Lord shows that here in a very graphic and

striking way. He says: 'When thou prayest, thou shalt not be as
the hypocrites are: for they love to pray standing in the synagogues and in the corners of the streets, that they may be seen of
men.' They stand in the synagogue in a prominent position, they
stand forward. You remember our Lord's parable of the Pharisee
and the publican who went into the temple to pray. He makes
exactly the same point there. He tells us that the Pharisee stood as
far forward as he could in the most prominent place, and there he
prayed. The publican, on the other hand, was so ashamed and
full of contrition that 'standing afar off' he could not even so
much as lift up his face to heaven, but just cried out, 'God be
merciful to me a sinner.' In the same way our Lord says here that
the Pharisees stand in the synagogues and in the corners of the
street, in the most prominent position, and pray in order that
they may be seen of men. 'Verily I say unto you, They have their
reward.'

According to our Lord, the reason for their praying in the
street corners is something like this. A man on his way to the
temple to pray is anxious to give the impression that he is such a
devout soul that he cannot even wait until he gets to the temple.
So he stands and prays at the street corner. For the same reason,
when he reaches the temple, he goes forward to the most
prominent position possible. Now what is important for us is
to extract the principle, so I put that as the first picture.

The second is put in the words: 'When ye pray, use not vain
repetitions, as the heathen do: for they think that they shall be
heard for their much speaking.' If we take these two pictures
together, we shall find that there are two main errors underlying
this whole approach to God in prayer. The first is that my
interest, if I am like the Pharisee, is in myself as the one who is
praying. The second is that I feel that the efficacy of my prayer
depends upon my much praying or upon my particular manner
of prayer.

Let us look at these separately. The first trouble, then, is this
danger of being interested in myself as one who prays. This can
show itself in many different ways. The first and the basic trouble
is that such a person is anxious to be known amongst others as one
who prays. That is the very beginning of it. He is anxious to have
a reputation as a man of prayer, anxious and ambitious in that
respect. That in itself is wrong. One should not be interested in
oneself, as our Lord goes on to show. So if there is any suspicion
of interest in ourselves as praying people we are already wrong,

and that condition will vitiate everything we are proposing
to do.

The next step in this process is that it becomes a positive and
actual desire to be seen praying by others. That, in turn, leads to
this, that we do things which will ensure that others do see us.
This is a most subtle matter. We saw in the matter of almsgiving
that it is not always blatant and obvious. There is a type of
person who parades himself and puts himself in a prominent
position and is always calling attention to himself. But there are
also subtle ways of doing this self-same thing. Let me give an
illustration of that.

There was a man who wrote quite a well-known book on the
Sermon on the Mount in the early days of the present century. In
dealing with this section he points out this subtle danger and
how it comes to a man without his knowing it—this demonstrative tendency even in the matter of prayer. And of course it is the
obvious comment to make. But I remember that when I was
reading the biography of this commentator, I came across this
interesting statement. The biographer, who was anxious to
show the saintliness of his subject, illustrated it like this. Nothing
was quite so characteristic of him, he said, as the way in which,
when he was walking from one room to another, he would
suddenly in the corridor fall down on his knees and pray. Then
he would get up and go on his way again. That was to the
biographer a proof of the saintliness and devoutness of this
particular man.

I do not think I need explain what I mean. The trouble with
the Pharisees was that they tried to give the impression that they
could not wait until they got to the temple; they had to stand
where they were at the street corners to pray, at once, blatant and
obvious. Yes, but if you fall down on your knees in a corridor in
a house it is rather wonderful! I want to show on the basis of our
Lord's teaching that that man would have been a greater saint if
he had not dropped on to his knees, but rather had offered up his
prayer to God as he was walking along that corridor. It would
have been an equally sincere prayer, and nobody would have
seen it. How subtle this is! The very man who warns us against
the thing is guilty of it himself. 'Let every man examine himself.'

Another very subtle form which it takes is this. A man may say
to himself, 'Of course I am not going to drop on my knees in a
corridor as I go from one room to another; I am not going to
stand at the corners of the street; I am not going to parade myself
in the temple or in the synagogue; I am going to pray always in

secret. Our Lord said, "Enter into thy closet, and . . . shut thy door." My prayer is always going to be the secret prayer.' Yes, but it is possible for a man to pray in secret in such a way that everybody knows he is praying in secret, because he gives the impression that by spending so much time there he is a great man of prayer. I am not romancing. Would to God I were. Do you not know something about this? When you are in the secret closet with the door shut, what are the thoughts that come to you, thoughts about other people who know you are there, and what you are doing and so forth? We must get rid of the notion that this only works in the blatant and obvious way of the Pharisees of old. It is the same thing, however subtle or hidden the form.

Of course we must not be over-scrupulous about these matters, but the danger is so subtle that we must always bear it in mind. I remember people talking about a man who attended certain conferences and remarking with great admiration that they noticed that he always slipped away after the meetings, climbed a high rock away from everybody else, and then got down on his knees and prayed. Well, that good man certainly did that, and it is not for me to judge him. But I wonder whether in that great effort of climbing there was not a little admixture of this very thing our Lord here denounces. Anything that is unusual ultimately calls attention to itself. If I go out of my way, meta-phorically, *not* to stand at the street corners, but become famous as the man of the lonely rock, I may be calling attention to my-self. That is the trouble; the negative becomes the positive in a very subtle manner before we realize what we are doing.

But let us follow it a little further. Another form which this takes is the terrible sin of praying in public in a manner which suggests a desire to have an effect upon the people present rather than to approach God with reverence and godly fear. I am not sure, for I have frequently debated this matter with myself, and therefore speak with some hesitancy, whether all this does not apply to the so-called 'beautiful prayers' that people are said to offer. I would question myself whether prayers should ever be beautiful. I mean that I am not happy about anyone who pays attention to the form of the prayer. I admit it is a highly debatable question. I commend it to your consideration. There are people who say that anything that is offered to God should be beautiful, and that therefore you should be careful about the phrasing and the diction and the cadence of your sentences. Nothing, they say, can be too beautiful to offer to God. I admit there is a certain force in that argument. But it does seem to me that it is entirely negatived by the consideration that prayer is ultimately a talk, a conversation, a communion with my Father; and one does not address one whom one loves in this perfect, polished manner, paying attention to the phrases and the words and all the rest. There is surely something essentially spontaneous about true communion and fellowship.

This is why I have never believed in the printing of so-called pulpit prayers. Of course it ultimately rests on very much larger issues into which we cannot now enter. I am simply raising the question for your consideration. I would suggest, however, that the controlling principle is that the whole being of the person praying should be intent upon God and should be centred upon Him, and that he should be oblivious of all other things. Far from desiring people to thank us for our so-called beautiful prayers, we should rather be troubled when they do so. Public prayer should be such that the people who are praying silently and the one who is uttering the words should be no longer conscious of each other, but should be carried on the wings of prayer into the very presence of God. I think if you compare and contrast the eighteenth and nineteenth centuries in this respect you will see what I mean. We have not many of the recorded prayers of the great evangelists of the eighteenth century; but we have many of the popular prayers of the so-called pulpit giants of the nineteenth century. I am not at all sure but that it was not just there that the change took place in the life of the Christian Church, which has led to the present lack of spirituality and the present state of the Christian Church in general. The Church became polished and polite and dignified, and the supposed worshippers were unconsciously occupied with themselves and forgetful that they were in communion with the living God. It is a very subtle thing.

The second trouble in connection with this wrong approach arises when we tend to concentrate on the form of our prayers, or on the amount or length of time spent in prayer. 'When ye pray', He says, 'use not vain repetitions, as the heathen do: for they think that they shall be heard for their much speaking.' You are familiar with what is meant by this term 'vain repetitions'. It is to be seen still in practice in many Eastern countries where they have prayer wheels. The same tendency is shown also in Roman Catholicism in the counting of beads. But again it comes to us in a much more subtle way. There are people who often attach great importance to having a set time for prayer. In a sense it is a good thing to have a set time for prayer; but if our concern is primarily to pray at the set time rather than to pray, we may as well not pray. We can get so easily into the habit of following a routine and forgetting what we are really doing. As the Mohammedan at certain hours of the day falls down on his knees, so many people who have their set time for prayer rush to God at this particular time, and often lose their tempers in doing so should anyone hinder them. They must get on their knees at this particular hour. Regarded objectively, how foolish it seems! But again, let every man examine himself.

It is not only the question of the set time, however; the subtle danger shows itself in yet another way. Great saints, for instance, have always spent much time in prayer and in the presence of God. Therefore we tend to think that the way to be a saint is to spend much time in prayer and in the presence of God. But the important point about the great saint is not that he spent much time in prayer. He did not keep his eye on the clock. He knew he was in the presence of God, he entered into eternity as it were. Prayer was his life, he could not live without it. He was not concerned about remembering the length of time. The moment we begin to do that, it becomes mechanical and we have ruined everything.

What our Lord says about the matter is: 'Verily I say unto you, They have their reward.' What did they desire? They wanted the praise of men, and they had it. And similarly today they are spoken of as great men of prayer, they are spoken of as those who offered wonderful, beautiful prayers. Yes, they get all that. But, poor souls, it is all they will get. 'Verily I say unto you, They have their reward.' Their obituary notices will refer to them as wonderful people in this matter of prayer, but, believe me, the poor heartbroken soul who cannot frame a sentence, but who has cried out in agony to God, has reached God in a way, and will have a reward, the other will never know. 'They have their reward.' The praise of man is what they wanted, and that is what they get.

Let us turn from them to the true way. There is a right way of praying, and again the whole secret is in the matter of the approach. That is the essence of our Lord's teaching. 'Thou, when thou prayest, enter into thy closet, and when thou hast shut thy door, pray to thy Father which is in secret; and thy Father which seeth in secret shall reward thee openly.   But when ye pray, use not vain repetitions, as the heathen do: for they think that they shall be heard for their much speaking. Be not ye therefore like unto them: for your Father knoweth what things ye have need of, before ye ask him.' What does it mean? Stated in terms of the essential principle it is this: the one thing that is important when we pray anywhere is that we must realize we are approaching God. That is the one thing that matters. It is simply this question of 'recollection', as it is called. If only we would realize that we are approaching God everything else would be all right.

But we need a little more detailed instruction, and fortunately our Lord gives it. He divides it up like this. First of all there is the process of exclusion. To make sure that I realize I am approaching God I have to exclude certain things. I have to enter into that closet. 'When thou prayest, enter into thy closet, and when thou hast shut thy door, pray to thy Father which is in secret.' Now what does this mean?

There are some people who would fondly persuade themselves that this is just a prohibition of all prayer meetings. They say, 'I do not go to prayer meetings, I pray in secret.' But it is not a prohibition of prayer meetings. It is not a prohibition of prayer in public, for that is taught of God and commended in the Scriptures. There are prayer meetings recorded in the Scriptures, and they are of the very essence and life of the Church. That is not what He is prohibiting. The principle is that there are certain things which we have to shut out whether we are praying in public or whether we are praying in secret. Here are some of them. You shut out and forget other people. Then you shut out and forget yourself. That is what is meant by entering into thy closet. You can enter into that closet when you are walking alone in a busy street, or going from one room to another in a house. You enter into that closet when you are in communion with God and nobody knows what you are doing. But if it is an actual public act of prayer the same thing can be done. I am referring to myself and to all preachers. What I try to do when I enter a pulpit is to forget the congregation in a certain sense. I am not praying to them or addressing them; I am not speaking to them. I am speaking to God, I am leading in prayer to God, so I have to shut out and forget people. Yes; and having done that, I shut out and forget myself. That is what our Lord tells us to do. There is no value in my entering into the secret chamber and locking the door if the whole time I am full of self and thinking about myself, and am priding myself on my prayer. I might as well be standing at the street corner. No; I have to exclude myself as well as other people; my heart has to be open entirely and only to God. I say with the Psalmist: 'Unite my heart to fear thy name. I will praise thee, O Lord my God, with all my heart.' This is of the very essence of this matter of prayer. When we pray we must deliberately remind ourselves that we are going to talk to God. Therefore other people, and self also, must be excluded and locked out.

The next step is realization. After exclusion, realization. Realize what? Well, we must realize that we are in the presence of God. What does that mean? It means realization of something of who God is and what God is. Before we begin to utter words we always ought to do this. We should say to ourselves: 'I am now entering into the audience chamber of that God, the almighty, the absolute, the eternal and great God with all His power and His might and majesty, that God who is a consuming fire, that God who is "light and in whom is no darkness at all", that utter, absolute Holy God. That'is what I am doing.' We must recollect and realize all that. But above all, our Lord insists that we should realize that, in addition to that, He is our Father. 'When thou hast shut thy door, pray to thy Father which is in secret; and thy Father which seeth in secret shall reward thee openly.' The relationship is that of Father and child, 'for your Father knoweth what things ye have need of, before ye ask him.' O that we realized this! If only we realized that this almighty God is our Father through the Lord Jesus Christ. If only we realized that we are indeed His children and that whenever we pray it is like a child going to its father! He knows all about us; He knows our every need before we tell Him. As the father cares for the child and looks at the child, and is concerned about the child, and anticipates the needs of the child, so is God with respect to all those who are in Christ Jesus. He desires to bless us very much more than we desire to be blessed. He has a view of us, He has a plan and a programme for us, He has an ambition for us, I say it with reverence, which transcends our highest thought and imagination. We must remember that He is our Father. The great, the holy, the almighty God is our Father. He cares for us. He has counted the very hairs of our head. He has said that nothing can happen to us apart from Him.

Then we must remember what Paul puts so gloriously in Ephesians iii: He 'is able to do exceeding abundantly above all that we ask or think.' That is the true notion of prayer, says Christ. You do not go and just turn a wheel. You do not just

count the beads. You do not say: 'I must spend hours in prayer,
I have decided to do it and I must do it.' You do not say that the
way to get a blessing is to spend whole nights in prayer, and that
because people will not do so they cannot expect blessing. We
must get rid of this mathematical notion of prayer. What we have
to do first of all is to realize who God is, what He is, and our
relationship to Him.

Finally we must have confidence. We must come with the
simple confidence of a child. We need a child-like faith. We need
this assurance that God is truly our Father, and therefore we must
rigidly exclude any idea that we must go on repeating our
petitions because it is our repetition that is going to produce the
blessing. God likes us to show our keenness, our anxiety and our
desire over a thing. He tells us to 'hunger and thirst after
righteousness' and to seek it; He tells us to 'pray and not to
faint'; we are told to 'pray without ceasing'. Yes; but that does
not mean mechanical repetitions; it does not mean believing
that we shall be heard for our 'much speaking'. It does not mean
that at all. It means that when I pray I know that God is my
Father, and that He delights to bless me, and that He is much
more ready to give than I am to receive and that He is always
concerned about my welfare. I must get rid of this thought that
God is standing between me and my desires and that which is
best for me. I must see God as my Father who has purchased my
ultimate good in Christ, and is waiting to bless me with His own
fullness in Christ Jesus.

So, we exclude, we realize, and then in confidence we make
our requests known to God, knowing He knows all about it before
we begin to speak. As a father delights that his child should come
repeatedly to ask for a thing rather than that the child should
say, 'Father has always done this', as the father likes the child to
keep on coming because he likes the personal contact, so God
desires us to come into His presence. But we must not come with
doubtful minds; we must know that God is much more ready to
give than we are to receive. The result will be that 'thy Father
which seeth in secret shall reward thee openly.'   O the blessings
that are stored at the right hand of God for God's children.
Shame on us for being paupers when we were meant to be
princes; shame on us for so often harbouring unworthy, wrong
thoughts of God in this matter. It is all due to fear, and because
we lack this simplicity, this faith, this confidence, this knowledge
of God as our Father. If we but have that, the blessings of God
will begin to fall upon us, and may be so overwhelming that

with D. L. Moody we shall feel that they are almost more than our physical frames can bear, and cry out with him, saying, 'Stop, God.'

God is able to do for us exceeding abundantly above all that we can ask or think. Let us believe that and then go to Him in simple confidence.

CHAPTER THREE

FASTING

WE turn now to consider the third illustration given by our Lord of the way in which we should conduct ourselves in this matter of personal righteousness. In chapters IV and V we shall return to our detailed study of His teaching concerning prayer, especially as it is given in what is commonly called 'The Lord's Prayer'. But before doing that, it seems to me that we should have these three particular illustrations of personal righteousness clearly in our minds.

You remember that in this section of the Sermon on the Mount our Lord is talking about the question of personal righteousness. He has already described the Christian in his general attitude to life—his thought life, if you like. Here, however, we are looking more at the Christian's conduct. Our Lord's general statement is this: 'Take heed that ye do not your righteousness (or your piety) before men, to be seen of them: else ye have no reward with your Father which is in heaven.'

We have already pointed out how our Lord shows that our Christian lives can be divided up into three main sections. There is that aspect or portion of our lives in which we do good to others—almsgiving. Then there is the question of our intimate personal relationship with God—our prayer life. The third is the one we shall look at now as we consider verses 16–18—the question of personal discipline in one's spiritual life, considered especially in terms of fasting. It is important, however, that we should realize that what our Lord says here about fasting is equally applicable to the whole question of discipline in our spiritual lives. I have my contacts with men and women; I have my contact with God; and I have also my contact with myself. Or we can put this threefold division in terms of what I do with others, what I do with God, what I do with myself. The last is the subject which our Lord takes up in this short paragraph.

We cannot approach this statement about fasting without making a few general preliminary remarks. I think we must all be struck at once by the fact that there is constantly a need of variation of emphasis, not only in our preaching of the gospel, but also in our whole approach to the gospel and in our thinking about it. Though truth is one and always the same, nevertheless, because of its many-sided character, and because human nature is what it is as the result of sin, particular eras in the history of the Church need a special emphasis on particular aspects of truth. This principle is found in the Bible itself. There are those who would have us believe that there is a great quarrel in the Old Testament as between the priests and the prophets, those who emphasized works and those who emphasized faith. The truth is, of course, that there is no quarrel as such, there is no contradiction. There were people who gave a false emphasis to particular aspects of truth, and they needed correction. The point I am making is that at a time when the priestly emphasis has been much in vogue, what is needed especially is the emphasis on the prophetic element. Or, at other times, when the emphasis has been excessively on the prophetic, then it is time to redress the balance and to remind people of, and to emphasize, the priestly.

You find the same thing occurring in the New Testament. There is no ultimate contradiction between James and Paul. It is a particularly superficial view of the New Testament which says that these two men contradict each other in their teaching. They do not; but each one, because of certain circumstances, was led by the Holy Spirit to put a certain emphasis upon the truth. James is evidently dealing with people who tended to say that, as long as you say you believe on the Lord Jesus Christ, all is well, and you need not worry about anything else. The only thing to say to such people is: 'Faith without works is dead.' But if you are dealing with people who are always drawing attention to what they do, and who put their stress upon works, then you have to emphasize to them this great aspect and element of faith.

I am reminded of all that in this context because, particularly for Evangelicals, this whole question of fasting has almost disappeared from our lives and even out of the field of our consideration. How often and to what extent have we thought about it? What place does it occupy in our whole view of the Christian life and of the discipline of the Christian life? I suggest that the truth probably is that we have very rarely thought of it at all. I wonder whether we have ever fasted? I wonder whether it has even occurred to us that we ought to be considering the question of fasting? The fact is, is it not, that this whole subject seems to have dropped right out of our lives, and right out of our whole Christian thinking.

There is no difficulty in tracing the cause of that. It is obviously a reaction against the Catholic teaching, so-called, in all its various forms. The Catholic teaching, whether it be Anglo-, or Roman-, or anything else, always does give great prominence to this question of fasting. And Evangelicalism is not only something in and of itself; it is always, in addition, a reaction against Catholic teaching. The tendency of a reaction is always to go too far. In this instance, because the false Catholic emphasis on fasting is disliked, we tend to swing to the other extreme and to leave fasting out of account altogether. Is not that why the vast majority of us have never seriously even considered this question of fasting? But I have observed certain indications that it is a subject which is gradually coming back into consideration amongst Evangelicals. I cannot say that I have noticed it hitherto in the evangelical religious literature of Great Britain; but certainly in evangelical literature that comes from across the Atlantic there is increased prominence being given to this whole question of fasting. As men and women are beginning to consider the days and the times through which we are passing with a new seriousness, and as many are beginning to look for revival and reawakening, the question of fasting has become more and more important. You will probably find that our attention is going to be directed increasingly to this subject, so it is a good thing for us to face it together. Quite apart from that, however, here it is in the Sermon on the Mount; and we have no right to pick and choose with Scripture. We must take the Sermon on the Mount as it is, and here is the question of fasting confronting us. So we must consider it.

Our Lord at this point was primarily concerned with only one aspect of the subject, and that was the tendency to do these things in order to be seen of men. He was concerned about this exhibitionist aspect, which we must therefore of necessity consider. But I feel that, in view of the neglect of the subject amongst us, it is right and profitable for us also to consider it in a more general manner, before we come to this particular point which our Lord emphasizes.

Let us approach it in this way. What is really the place of fasting in the Christian life? Where does it come in according to the teaching of the Bible? The answer is roughly like this. It is something that is taught in the Old Testament. Under the law of Moses the children of Israel were commanded to fast once a year, and this was binding upon that nation and people for ever. Further on we read that, owing to certain national emergencies, the people themselves appointed certain additional fasts. But the only fast that was directly commanded by God was that one great, annual fast. When we come to New Testament times, we find that the Pharisees fasted twice in the week. They were never commanded to do so by God, but they did so, and made it a vital part of their religion. It is always the tendency of a certain type of religious person to go beyond the Scriptures; and that was the position with the Pharisees.

When we come to look at our Lord's teaching we find that though He never taught fasting directly, He certainly taught it indirectly. In Matthew ix we are told that He was asked a question specifically about fasting. They said to Him, 'Why do we and the Pharisees fast oft, but thy disciples fast not? And Jesus said unto them, Can the children of the bridechamber mourn, as long as the bridegroom is with them? but the days will come, when the bridegroom shall be taken from them, and then shall they fast.' It seems to me that there, quite clearly, is implicit teaching of, and almost an advocacy of fasting. It is clear, at any rate, that He never prohibited it. Indeed, in this teaching which we are now considering, His approval of it is obviously implied. What He says is, 'when thou fastest, anoint thine head, and wash thy face;' so that quite clearly it was something that was regarded by our Lord as right and good for Christian people. And we remember that He Himself fasted for forty days and forty nights when He was in the wilderness being tempted of the devil.

Then, going on beyond our Lord's teaching and practice to that of the early Church, we find it was something that was practised by the apostles. The church at Antioch, when it sent out Paul and Barnabas on their first preaching tour, did so only after a period of prayer and of fasting. Indeed, on any important occasion, when faced with any vital decision, the early Church always seemed to give themselves to fasting as well as to prayer, and the apostle Paul, in referring to himself and his life, talks about being 'in fastings oft'. It was clearly something that was a regular part of his life. Now those who are interested in matters of textual criticism will remember that in Mark ix. 29, where our Lord is reported as saying, 'This kind can come forth by nothing, but by prayer and fasting,' it is probably true to say that 'fasting' should not be there according to the best documents and manuscripts, but that is quite immaterial as regards the general question because there is all this other teaching which shows quite clearly that the New Testament definitely teaches the rightness and the value of fasting. And when we enquire into the subsequent history of the Church we find exactly the same thing. The saints of God in all ages and in all places have not only believed in fasting, they have practised it. It was true of the Protestant Reformers, it was certainly true of the Wesleys and Whitefield. I admit that they tended to do it more before they were truly converted than they did afterwards; but they did nevertheless continue to fast after their conversion. And those of you who are familiar with the life of that great Chinese Christian, Pastor Hsi of China, will remember how Pastor Hsi, when confronted by some new or exceptional difficulty or problem, invariably had a period of fasting as well as of prayer. God's people have felt that fasting is not only right, but is of great value and of great importance under certain conditions.

If, then, that is the historical background, let us approach it a little more directly and ask this question. What exactly is fasting? What is its purpose? There can be no doubt that ultimately it is something which is based upon an understanding of the relationship between the body and the spirit. Man is body, mind and spirit, and these are very intimately related to one another and interact very closely upon one another. We distinguish them because they are different, but we must not separate them because of their inter-relationship and inter-action. There can be no question whatever but that physical bodily states and conditions do have a bearing upon the activity of the mind and of the spirit, so that the element of fasting must be considered in this peculiar relationship of body, mind and spirit. What fasting really means, therefore, is abstinence from food for spiritual purposes. That is the biblical notion of fasting which must be separated from the purely physical. The biblical notion of fasting is that, for certain spiritual reasons and purposes, men and women decide to abstain from food.

This is a very important point, so we must put it also in a negative form. I was reading recently an article on this subject, and the writer referred to that statement of the apostle Paul in I Corinthians ix. 27 where he says: 'I keep under my body'. The apostle says that he does this in order that he may do his work more efficiently. The writer of the article said that this is an illustration of fasting. Now I suggest that, of necessity, it has nothing whatsoever to do with fasting. That is what I would call a part of man's general discipline. You should always keep under your body, but that does not mean you should always fast. Fasting is something unusual or exceptional, something which a man does now and again for a special purpose, while discipline should be perpetual and permanent. I therefore cannot accept such texts as: 'I keep under my body', and 'Mortify your members that are upon the earth', as being a part of fasting. In other words, moderation in eating is not fasting. Moderation in eating is a part of discipline of the body, and it is a very good way of keeping the body under; but that is not fasting. Fasting means an abstinence from food for the sake of certain special purposes such as prayer or meditation or the seeking of God for some peculiar reason or under some exceptional circumstance.

To make the matter complete, we would add that fasting, if we conceive of it truly, must not only be confined to the question of food and drink; fasting should really be made to include abstinence from anything which is legitimate in and of itself for the sake of some special spiritual purpose. There are many bodily functions which are right and normal and perfectly legitimate, but which for special peculiar reasons in certain circumstances should be controlled. That is fasting. There, I suggest, is a kind of general definition of what is meant by fasting.

Before we come to consider the ways in which we fast, let us consider how we are to regard and approach the whole question. Here again the division is simple, for finally we have but the wrong and the right way. There are certain wrong ways of fasting. Here is one of them. If we fast in a mechanical manner, or merely for the sake of doing so, I suggest that we are violating the biblical teaching with regard to the whole matter. In other words, if I make fasting an end in itself, something of which I say, 'Well now, because I have become a Christian, I have to fast on such a day and at such a time in the year because it is part of the Christian religion', I might as well not do it. The special element in the act goes right out of it when that is done.

This is something which is not peculiar to fasting. Did we not see exactly the same thing in the matter of prayer? It is a good thing for people, if they can, to have certain special times for prayer in their lives. But if I make up my programme for the day and say that at such and such an hour every day I must pray, and I just pray in order to keep to my programme, I am no longer praying. It is exactly the same with regard to the question of fasting. There are people who approach it in precisely that way. They become Christians; but they rather like to be under a kind of law, they rather like to be under instruction. They like to be told exactly what they must or must not do. On one particular day in the week they must not eat meat, and so on. It is not the thing to do in the Christian life; you do not eat on a particular day. Again at a certain period of the year you abstain from food, or you eat less, and so forth. Now there is a very subtle danger in that. Anything we do merely for the sake of doing it, or as a matter of rule or rote, is surely an entire violation of the scriptural teaching. We must never regard fasting as an end in itself.

But we must add to that something at which I have already hinted, and which can be put in this form: we should never regard fasting as a part of our discipline. Some people say it is a very good thing that on one day in the week we should not eat certain things, or that at a given period in the year we should abstain from certain things. They say that it is good from the standpoint of discipline. But discipline is surely something which must be permanent, discipline is something which is perpetual. We should always be disciplining ourselves. That is something about which there can be no discussion at all. We should always keep our body under, we should always be holding the reins tightly upon ourselves, we must always be in a disciplined condition in every respect. So it is wrong to reduce fasting merely to a part of the process of discipline. Rather is it something that I do in order to reach that higher spiritual realm of prayer to God, or meditation, or intense intercession. And that puts it into an entirely different category.

Another false way of regarding fasting I would put like this. There are some people who fast because they expect direct and immediate results from it. In other words they have a kind of mechanical view of fasting; they have what I have sometimes called, for lack of a better illustration, the 'penny in the slot' view of it. You put your penny in the slot, then you pull out the drawer, and there you have your result. That is their view of fasting. If you want certain benefits, they say, fast; if you fast you will get the results. This attitude is not confined to the question of fasting. We saw earlier in dealing with prayer that there are many people who regard prayer in that way. They read accounts of how certain people at one time decided to have an all-night prayer meeting, how they went on praying right through the night, and how, as a result of that, a revival broke out. So they decide that they will have an all-night prayer meeting, and they expect a revival to follow. 'Because we pray, revival must come.' Or you can find it in connection with holiness teaching. Certain people say that if you only obey certain conditions you will get a blessing, that there will be an immediate and direct result. Now I never find that anywhere in the Bible, in connection with fasting or anything else. We must never fast for the sake of direct results.

Let me put it even more pointedly like this. There are people who advocate fasting as one of the best ways and methods of obtaining blessings from God. Some of this recent literature to which I have referred, I regret to say, seems to be guilty of that. People write an account of their life and they say, 'You know, my Christian life was one which always seemed to be "bound in shallows and in miseries"; I was never truly happy. My life seemed to be a series of ups and downs. I was a Christian but I did not seem to have what certain other people whom I knew seemed to possess. I was like that for years. I had gone the round of all the Conventions, I had read the prescribed books on this subject, but I never seemed to get the blessing. Then I happened to come across teaching which emphasized the importance of fasting, and I fasted and I received the blessing.' Then the exhortation is: 'If you want a blessing, fast.' That seems to me to be a most dangerous doctrine. We must never speak like that about anything in the spiritual life. These blessings are never automatic. The moment we begin to say, 'Because I do this, I get that', it means that we are controlling the blessing. That is to insult God and to violate the great doctrine of His final and ultimate sovereignty. No, we must never advocate fasting as a means of blessing.

Let us consider another illustration of this point. Take the question of tithing. Here we have another subject that is coming back again into prominence. Now there is very good scriptural basis for tithing; but there are many who tend to teach the question of tithing like this. A man writes an account of his life. Again he says that his Christian life was unsatisfactory. Things did not go well with him; indeed he was having financial troubles in his business. Then he came across the teaching of tithing and he began to tithe. At once great joy flooded his life. Not only that, but his business also began to be successful. I have read books which actually go so far as to say this: 'If you really want to be prosperous, begin tithing'. In other words, 'You do the tithing, and the result is bound to follow; if you want the blessing— tithe'. It is exactly the same as with fasting. All such teaching is quite unscriptural. Indeed it is worse than that; it derogates from the glory and the majesty of God Himself. Therefore we should never advocate, indulge in, or practise fasting as a method or a means of obtaining direct blessing. The value of fasting is indirect, not direct.

The last thing to consider under this heading is that we must obviously be very careful not to confuse the physical with the spiritual. We cannot consider this fully now, but, having read some accounts of people who have practised fasting, I do feel that they cross the border line from the physical to the spiritual in this way. They describe how, after the preliminary physical misery of the first three or four days, and after the fifth day especially, a period of unusual mental clarity comes in; and sometimes some of these friends describe this as if it were purely spiritual. Now I cannot prove that it is not spiritual; but I can say this, that men who are not Christian at all and who undergo a period of fasting, invariably testify to the same thing. There is no doubt whatsoever that fasting, purely on the physical and bodily level, is something which is good for one's physical frame as long as it is done properly; and there is no doubt that clarity of mind and brain and understanding does result from it. But we must always be very careful that we do not attribute to the spiritual what can be adequately explained by the physical. Here again is a great general principle. It is what some of us would say to those who make claims in the matter of faith and holiness, as also to those who are over-ready to claim something as miraculous when it is not certainly or unmistakably so. We do harm to the cause of Christ if we claim as miraculous something which can be easily explained on a natural level. The same danger is present in this question of fasting—a confusion between the physical and the spiritual.

Having considered, then, some of the false ways of viewing this matter of fasting let us now look at the right way. I have already suggested it. It should always be regarded as a means to an end, and not as an end in itself. It is something that a man should do only when he feels impelled or led to it by spiritual reasons. It is not to be done because a certain section of the Church enjoins fasting on a Friday, or during the period of Lent, or at any other time. We should not do these things mechanically. We must discipline our lives, but we must do so all the year round, and not merely at certain stated periods. I must discipline myself at all times, and must fast only when I feel led by the Spirit of God to do so, when I am intent on some mighty spiritual purpose, not according to rule, but because I feel there is some peculiar need of an entire concentration of the whole of my being upon God and my worship of Him. That is the time to fast, and that is the way to approach the subject.

But let us come to the other aspect. Having looked at it in general, let us look at the way in which it is to be done. The wrong way is to call attention to the fact that we are doing it. 'When ye fast, be not, as the hypocrites, of a sad countenance: for they disfigure their faces, that they may appear unto men to fast.' Of course, when they did it in this way, people saw they were undergoing a fasting period. They did not wash their faces or anoint their heads. Some of them went even further; they disfigured their faces and put ashes upon their head. They wanted to call attention to the fact that they were fasting, so they looked miserable and unhappy and everybody looked at them and said, 'Ah, he is undergoing a period of fasting. He is an unusually spiritual person. Look at him; look at what he is sacrificing and suffering for the sake of his devotion to God.' Our Lord condemns that root and branch. Any announcing of the fact of what we are doing, or calling attention to it, is something which is utterly reprehensible to Him, as it was in the case of prayer, and of almsgiving. It is exactly the same principle. You must not sound a trumpet proclaiming the things you are going to do. You must not stand at the street corners or in a prominent place in the synagogue when you pray. And in the same way you must not call attention to the fact that you are fasting.

But this is not only a question of fasting. It seems to me that this is a principle which covers the whole of our Christian life. It condemns equally the affecting of pious looks, it condemns equally the adoption of pious attitudes. It is pathetic sometimes to observe the way in which people do this even in the matter of singing hymns—the uplifted face at certain points and the rising on tiptoe. These things are affected, and it is when they are affected that they become so sad.

May I put a question for your consideration and for your interest at this point? Where does the question of dress come into all this? To me this is one of the most baffling and perplexing things in connection with our Christian lives, and I find myself halting between two obvious opinions. There is much in me that not only understands, but likes, the practice of the early Quakers who used to dress differently from other people. Their idea was that they wanted to show the difference between the Christian and the non-Christian, between the Church and the world. They said that we must not even look like the world; we must look different. Now in every Christian there must be something that heartily says 'Amen' to that. I cannot understand the Christian who wants to look like the typical, average, worldly person in appearance, in dress or in anything else—the loudness, the vulgarity, the sensuality of it all. No Christian should want to look like that. So there is something very natural about this reaction against it and this desire to be quite different.

But that, unfortunately, is not the only aspect of the subject. The other aspect is that it is not of necessity true that 'the apparel doth proclaim the man' in this respect. The dress does proclaim the man up to a point, but not completely so. The Pharisees wore a particular dress and 'made broad their phylacteries', but it did not guarantee true righteousness. Indeed, the Bible teaches that ultimately that is not the way in which the Christian is differentiated from the non-Christian. It seems to me that it is what I *am* that shows the difference. If I myself am right, the rest is likely to follow. So that I do not proclaim that I am a Christian by dressing in a particular way so much as by being what I am. But think it out. It is an interesting and a very fascinating question. I think probably the truth is that both statements are right. As Christians we should all desire to be unlike those worldlings, and yet at the same time we must never get into the position of saying that it is our dress that truly proclaims what we are. There, then, is the wrong way of doing it; and the reward is still the same as it is with all those false methods—'Verily I say unto you, They have their reward.' People think that those who fast in that way are very spiritual and that they are exceptionally holy people. They will get the praise of men but that is all the reward they will get, for God seeth in secret. He sees the heart and 'that which is highly esteemed amongst men is abomination in the sight of God'.

What then is the right way? Let us begin by putting it negatively. The first thing is that it does not mean going out of our way to be as unlike the Pharisees as possible. Many think that, because our Lord says, 'But thou, when thou fastest, anoint thine head, and wash thy face; that thou appear not unto men to fast, but unto thy Father which is in secret.' They say that we must not only not disfigure our faces but that we must go out of our way to conceal the fact that we are fasting, and even give the opposite impression. But this is a complete misunderstanding. There was nothing exceptional about washing the face and anointing the hair. That was the normal, usual procedure. What our Lord is saying here is, 'When you fast be natural'.

We can apply that in this way. There are some people who are so afraid of being regarded as miserable because they are Christians, or afraid of being called foolish because they are Christians, that they tend to go to the other extreme. They say that we must give the impression that to be a Christian is to be bright and happy, and so, far from being dowdy in dress, we must go to the opposite extreme. So they go out of their way not to be drab, and the result is they are quite as bad as those who are guilty of dowdiness. Our Lord's principle is always this: 'Forget other people altogether.' In order to avoid looking sad, don't put a grin on your face. Forget your face, forget yourself, forget other people altogether. It is this interest in the opinions of other people that is so wrong. Don't worry about the impression you are making; just forget yourself and give yourself entirely to God. Be concerned only about God and about pleasing Him. Be concerned only about His honour and His glory.

If our great concern is to please God and to glorify His name, we shall be in no difficulty about these other things. If a man is living entirely to the glory of God, you need not prescribe for him when he has to fast, you need not prescribe the sort of clothes he has to put on or anything else. If he has forgotten himself and given himself to God, the New Testament says that man will know how to eat and drink and dress because he will be doing it all to the glory of God. And thank God the reward of such a man is safe and certain and assured, and it is mighty— 'Thy Father which seeth in secret himself shall reward thee openly.' The one thing that matters is that we be right with God and concerned about pleasing Him. If we are concerned about that, we may leave the rest to Him. He may withhold the reward for years: it does not matter. We shall receive it. His promises never fail. Even though the world may never know what we are, God knows, and at the great Day it will be announced before the whole world. 'Thy Father which seeth in secret himself shall reward thee openly.'

> 'Men heed thee, love thee, praise thee not:
> The Master praises: what are men?'

CHAPTER FOUR

'WHEN YE PRAY'

WE return now to a consideration of our Lord's teaching concerning prayer. In Matthew vi, you remember, we have our Lord's treatment of the whole question of Christian piety. He divides up the subject into three sections which really cover the whole of our righteousness or religious living. First of all comes the question of almsgiving—our charity towards others, then the question of prayer and our relationship to God, and finally the question of personal discipline which He considers under the general heading of fasting. We have already considered those three aspects of the religious life, or the life of piety, separately; and when considering the subject of prayer, we said that we would return again to a study of what is commonly known as the Lord's Prayer. For our Lord clearly found it necessary not only to warn His followers against certain dangers in connection with prayer, but also to give them positive instruction.

He has already warned them, you remember, not to be as the hypocrites, who pray standing in the synagogues and on street corners in order to be seen of men. He has told them that vain repetitions in and of themselves have no value, and that the mere bulk or quantity of prayer will produce no special benefit. He has also told them that they must pray in secret, and that they must never be concerned about men or what men might think of them, but that what is vital and essential in this matter of prayer is not only that they should shut out other people, but that they should shut themselves in with God, and concentrate upon Him and their relationship to Him. But, as we have said, He clearly feels that a general warning is not sufficient, and that His disciples need more detailed instruction. So He goes on to say, 'After this manner therefore pray ye', and He proceeds to give them this instruction with regard to the method of prayer.

We are face to face here with one of the most vital subjects in connection with our Christian life. Prayer is beyond any question the highest activity of the human soul. Man is at his greatest and highest when, upon his knees, he comes face to face with God.

Not that we desire to indulge in vain comparisons. Almsgiving is excellent; it is a noble activity, and the man who feels led, and who responds to the leading, thus to help his fellow-men in this world is a good man. Again, fasting in various forms is a very high and noble activity. The man of the world knows nothing about this, nor about self-discipline. He just yields to every impulse, gives himself over to lust and passion, and lives more or less like an animal in a mere mechanical response to the instincts that are within him. He knows nothing about discipline. The man who disciplines himself stands out and has the mark of greatness upon him; it is a great thing for a man to discipline his life at all times, and occasionally to take exceptional measures for his spiritual good.

These things, however, pale into insignificance when you look at a man engaged in prayer. When a man is speaking to God he is at his very acme. It is the highest activity of the human soul, and therefore it is at the same time the ultimate test of a man's true spiritual condition. There is nothing that tells the truth about us as Christian people so much as our prayer life. Everything we do in the Christian life is easier than prayer. It is not so difficult to give alms—the natural man knows something about that, and you can have a true spirit of philanthropy in people who are not Christian at all. Some seem to be born with a generous nature and spirit, and to such almsgiving is not essentially difficult. The same applies also to the question of self-discipline—refraining from certain things and taking up particular duties and tasks. God knows it is very much easier to preach like this from a pulpit than it is to pray. Prayer is undoubtedly the ultimate test, because a man can speak to others with greater ease than he can speak to God. Ultimately, therefore, a man discovers the real condition of his spiritual life when he examines himself in private, when he is alone with God. We saw in chapter II that the real danger for a man who leads a congregation in a public act of prayer is that he may be addressing the congregation rather than God. But when we are alone in the presence of God that is no longer possible. And have we not all known what it is to find that, somehow, we have less to say to God when we are alone than when we are in the presence of others? It should not be so; but it often is. So that it is when we have left the realm of activities and outward dealings with other people, and are alone with God, that we really know where we stand in a spiritual sense. It is not only the highest activity of the soul, it is the ultimate test of our true spiritual condition.

Another way of putting that is this. You will find that the
outstanding characteristic of all the most saintly people the
world has ever known has been that they have not only spent
much time in private prayer, but have also delighted in it. We
cannot read the life of any saint without finding that that has
been true of him. The more saintly the person, the more time
such a person spends in conversation with God. Thus it is a
vital and all-important matter. And surely there is a greater
need for guidance at this point than at any other.

This has been true in the experience of God's people throughout the centuries. We find it recorded in the Gospels that John
the Baptist had been teaching his disciples to pray. They
obviously had felt the need of instruction, and they had asked
him for instruction and guidance. And John had taught them
how to pray. Our Lord's disciples felt exactly the same need.
They came to Him one afternoon and said, in effect, 'John the
Baptist taught his disciples how to pray; Lord, teach us how to
pray.' Undoubtedly the desire arose in their hearts because they
were conscious of this kind of natural, instinctive, initial difficulty of which we are all aware; but it must also have been greatly
increased when they watched His own prayer life. They saw
how He would arise 'a great while before dawn' and go up into
the mountains to pray, and how He would spend whole nights
in prayer. And sometimes, I have no doubt, they said to themselves: 'What does He talk about? What does He do?' They may
also have thought, 'I find after a few minutes in prayer that I
come to the end of my words. What is it that enables Him to be
drawn out in prayer? What is it that leads to this ease and
abandonment?' 'Lord', they said, 'teach us how to pray.' They
meant by this that they would like to be able to pray as He
prayed. 'We wish we knew God as You know Him. Teach us
how to pray.' Have you ever felt that? Have you ever felt dis-
satisfied with your prayer life, and longed to know more and
more what it is truly to pray? If you have, it is an encouraging
sign.

There is no question but that this is our greatest need. More
and more we miss the very greatest blessings in the Christian life
because we do not know how to pray aright. We need instruction
in every respect with regard to this matter. We need to be taught
how to pray, and we need to be taught what to pray for. It is
because it covers these two things in a most amazing and
wonderful manner that we must spend some time in a consideration of what has become known amongst us as 'The Lord's

Prayer'. It is a perfect synopsis of our Lord's instruction on how to pray, and what to pray for.

Now I must make it quite clear at this point that that is all I propose to do. The subject of prayer is a very great and large one, which might indeed engage us for a long time. However, we must not allow it to do so because we are actually working our way through the Sermon on the Mount, and therefore it would be wrong to digress over-much on this one particular question. All I intend to do is to explain our Lord's teaching in this prayer, and I am not going to do even that in any great detail. I simply intend to underline and emphasize what seem to me to be the great central principles which our Lord was obviously anxious to inculcate.

There are certain general matters with regard to this prayer that certainly need a word or two of comment. 'The Lord's Prayer', as we call it, has often been the subject of much controversy. There are many people who, for various reasons, refuse to recite it in an act of public worship. There are some who seem to object to it on doctrinal grounds, and who feel that it belongs to the realm of law rather than of grace, and that it has nothing to do with Christian people. They stumble over the petition with regard to the forgiveness of sins. We shall deal with that in detail when we come to it, but I am simply mentioning now certain of the preliminary difficulties that various friends experience. They say that forgiveness here seems to be conditional upon our forgiving, and that, they maintain, is law not grace, and so on. It is necessary therefore that we should make a number of preliminary observations.

The first is that this prayer is undoubtedly a pattern prayer. The very way in which our Lord introduces it indicates that. 'After this manner therefore pray ye.' Now, says our Lord in effect, when you come to pray to God, this is the kind of way in which you are to pray. And the amazing and extraordinary thing about it is that it really covers everything in principle. There is a sense in which you can never add to the Lord's Prayer; nothing is left out. That does not mean, of course, that when we pray we are simply to repeat the Lord's Prayer and stop at that, for that is obviously something that was not true of our Lord Himself. As we have already seen, He spent whole nights in prayer; many times He arose a great while before day and prayed for hours. You always find in the lives of the saints that they have spent hours in prayer. John Wesley used to say he held a very poor view of any Christian who did not pray for at least four hours every day.

To say that this prayer is all-inclusive, and is a perfect summary, simply means, therefore, that it really does contain all the principles. We might say that what we have in the Lord's Prayer is a kind of skeleton. Take, for instance, this act of preaching. I have certain notes before me; I have not a complete sermon. I merely have headings—the principles which are to be emphasized. But I do not stop at a mere enunciation of principles; I expound and work them out. That is the way in which we should regard the Lord's Prayer. The principles are all here and you cannot add to them. You can take the longest prayer that has ever been offered by a saint, and you will find that it can all be reduced to these principles. There will be no additional principle whatsoever. Take that great prayer of our Lord's which is recorded in John xvii—our Lord's High Priestly prayer. If you analyse it in terms of principles, you will find that it can be reduced to the principles of this model prayer.

The Lord's Prayer covers everything; and all we do is to take these principles and employ and expand them and base our every petition upon them. That is the way in which it is to be approached. And as you look at it in that way, I think you will agree with St. Augustine and Martin Luther and many other saints who have said that there is nothing more wonderful in the entire Bible than the Lord's Prayer. The economy, the way in which He summarizes it all, and has reduced everything to but a few sentences, is something that surely proclaims the fact that the speaker is none other than the very Son of God Himself.

Let us go on to another observation, which is one that we have been emphasizing right through our consideration of this Sermon. It is that this prayer is obviously meant not only for the disciples, but for all Christians in all places and at all times. When we were dealing with the Beatitudes we constantly repeated that they are applicable to every Christian. The Sermon on the Mount was not meant only for the disciples at that time and for the Jews in some coming kingdom age; it is meant for Christian people now and at all times, and has always been applicable. Exactly as we have had to judge ourselves by the teaching of the fifth chapter with respect to the relationship of the Christian to the law, so we come face to face with this prayer, and with what our Lord says in this matter: 'After this manner therefore pray ye.' He speaks to us today exactly as He spoke to the people who were about Him at that particular time. Indeed, as we have already seen, unless our prayer corresponds to this particular pattern and form, it is not true prayer.

There may be questions in the minds of many with regard to reciting the Lord's Prayer as an act of public worship. That is a point for legitimate debate, a point for legitimate difference of opinion. It seems to me, however, that we can never remind ourselves too frequently of this particular form; and, for myself, I have always been comforted by this thought, that whatever I may forget in my own private prayers, as long as I pray the Lord's Prayer I have at any rate covered all the principles. On condition, of course, that I am not merely mechanically repeating the words, but am really praying from my heart and with my mind and with my whole being.

The next point is that there are some people in trouble about the Lord's Prayer because it does not say 'for Christ's sake', or because it is not offered specifically in Christ's name. They say that it cannot be a prayer for Christian people because Christians should always pray in the name of Christ. The answer to this is, of course, that our Lord, as we have seen, was simply laying down principles which must always govern man's relationship to God. He was not concerned to say everything about that relationship at this point. But He was concerned to say this; that whoever comes into the presence of God must always realize these things. Later on in His life and teaching He will teach them explicitly about praying in His name. But it is surely clear that even in the Lord's Prayer, praying in Christ's name is implicit. No man can truly say 'Our Father which art in heaven', save one who knows the Lord Jesus Christ and who is in Christ. So it is implicit even at the very beginning. But, in any case, that does not affect the principles which our Lord teaches here so plainly.

Concerning the particular difficulty with regard to forgiveness, we shall deal with that in detail when we come to that petition in our consideration of the prayer.

Let us then sum up our general remarks by repeating that there is nothing more exalted, and more elevating, than this wonderful prayer which the Lord Jesus Christ taught His people. Let us also remember that He taught it, not that they might just repeat it mechanically for the rest of their lives, but rather that they should say to themselves, 'Now there are certain things I must always remember when I pray. I must not rush into prayer; I must not start speaking at once without considering what I am doing. I must not merely be led by some impulse and feeling.

There are certain things I must always bear in mind. Here are
the headings for my prayer; here is the skeleton which I have to
clothe; these are the lines along which I must proceed.' I trust
therefore that none of us will think that it is the hall-mark of true
Evangelicalism to speak rather disparagingly of the Lord's
Prayer. I trust also that none of us will be guilty of that spiritual
pride, not to say arrogance, which refuses to recite the Lord's
Prayer with others. Let us rather realize that our Lord here was
really telling these people how He Himself prayed, that that was
His own method, that these were the things He always had in
mind, and that therefore we can never do anything greater or
higher than to pray along the lines of the Lord's Prayer. We shall
never exceed this prayer if we pray truly, so we must never
dismiss it as legalism, and imagine that because we are in the
dispensation of grace we have gone beyond that. We shall find
as we analyse this prayer that it is full of grace. Indeed the law of
God was full of grace, as we have already seen. Our Lord has
been expounding the law of Moses and has shown that, when
spiritually understood, it is full of the grace of God, and that no
man can understand it truly unless he has the grace of God in
his heart.

Let us now look briefly at this subject of how to pray and what
to pray for. With regard to the first matter we remind ourselves
again of the vital importance of the right approach, for this is the
key to the understanding of successful prayer. People so often
say, 'You know, I prayed and prayed but nothing happened. I
did not seem to find peace. I did not seem to get any satisfaction
out of it.' Most of their trouble is due to the fact that their
approach to prayer has been wrong, that somehow or other they
did not realize what they were doing. We tend to be so self-
centred in our prayers that when we drop on our knees before
God, we think only about ourselves and our troubles and perplexities. We start talking about them at once, and of course
nothing happens. According to our Lord's teaching here we
should not expect anything to happen. That is not the way to
approach God. We must pause before we speak in prayer.

The great teachers of the spiritual life throughout the centuries,
whether Roman Catholic or Protestant, have been agreed about
this, that the first step in prayer has always been what they call
'Recollection'. There is a sense in which every man when he
begins to pray to God should put his hand upon his mouth. That
was the whole trouble with Job. In his wretchedness he had been

talking a great deal. He felt that God had not been dealing kindly with him, and he, Job, had been expressing his feelings freely. But when, towards the end of the book, God began to deal with him at close quarters, when He began to reveal and manifest Himself to him, what did Job do? There was only one thing for him to do. He said, 'Behold, I am vile; what shall I answer thee? I will lay mine hand upon my mouth.' And, strange as it may seem to you, you start praying by saying nothing; you recollect what you are about to do.

I know the difficulty in this. We are but human, and we are pressed by the urgency of our position, the cares, the anxieties, the troubles, the anguish of mind, the bleeding heart, whatever it is. And we are so full of this that, like children, we start speaking at once. But if you want to make contact with God, and if you want to feel His everlasting arms about you, put your hand upon your mouth for a moment. Recollection! Just stop for a moment and remind yourself of what you are about to do. We can put it in a phrase. Do you know that the essence of true prayer is found in the two words in verse 9, 'Our Father'? I suggest that if you can say from your heart, whatever your condition, 'My Father', in a sense your prayer is already answered. It is just this realization of our relationship to God that we so sadly lack.

Perhaps we can put it in another way like this. There are people who believe it is a good thing to pray because it always does us good. They adduce various psychological reasons. That of course is not prayer as the Bible understands it. Prayer means speaking to God, forgetting ourselves, and realizing His presence. Then again, there are others, and sometimes I think they would claim for themselves an unusual degree of spirituality, who rather think that the hallmark of true prayer life, of ease and facility in prayer, is that one's prayer should be very brief and pointed, and one should just simply make a particular request. That is something which is not true of the teaching of the Bible concerning prayer. Take any of the great prayers which are recorded in the Old Testament or in the New. None of them is what we might call this 'business-like' kind of prayer which simply makes a petition known to God and then ends. Every prayer recorded in the Bible starts with invocation. It does not matter how desperate the circumstance; it does not matter what the particular quandary might be in which those who pray find themselves. Invariably they start with this worship, this adoration, this invocation.

We have a great and wonderful example of this in the ninth

chapter of Daniel. There the prophet, in terrible perplexity, prays to God. But he does not start immediately with his petition; he starts by praising God. A perplexed Jeremiah does the same thing. Confronted by the demand that he should buy a plot of land in a seemingly doomed country, Jeremiah could not understand it; it seemed all wrong to him. But he does not rush into the presence of God for this one matter; he starts by worshipping God. And so you will find it in all the recorded prayers. Indeed, you even get it in the great High-Priestly prayer of our Lord Himself which is recorded in John xvii. You remember also how Paul put it in writing to the Philippians. He says, 'in nothing be anxious; but in everything by prayer and supplication with thanksgiving let your requests be made known unto God' (Phil. iv. 6, RV). That is the order. We must always start with invocation, before we even begin to think of petition; and here it is once and for ever put to us so perfectly in this model prayer.

It would take too long to expound as I should like the meaning of this statement, 'Our Father'. Let me put it like this, therefore, in what may appear to be a dogmatic form. It is only those who are true believers in the Lord Jesus Christ who can say, 'Our Father'. It is only the people of whom the Beatitudes are true who can say with any confidence, 'Our Father'. Now I know that this is an unpopular doctrine today, but it is the doctrine of the Bible. The world today believes in the universal Fatherhood of God and the universal brotherhood of man. That is not found in the Bible. It was our Lord who said to certain religious Jews that they were 'of their father the devil', and not children of Abraham, not children of God. It is only to 'as many as receive him' that He gives the right (the authority) 'to become the sons of God'.

'But,' says someone, 'what did Paul mean when he said, "we are also his offspring"? Does not that mean we are all His children and He is the universal Father?' Well, if you analyse this passage, you will find that Paul is speaking there, in Acts xvii, of God as the Creator of all things and all people, that God in that sense has given life and being to everybody throughout the world. But that is not the meaning of God as Father in the sense in which Paul uses it elsewhere of believers, nor the sense in which, as we have seen, our Lord Himself uses it. The Bible draws a very sharp distinction between those who belong to God and those who do not. You notice it in the Lord's High Priestly prayer in John xvii. 9. He said, 'I pray for them: I pray not for the world, but for them which thou hast given me; for they are thine.' It is an utter, absolute distinction; it is only those who are in the Lord Jesus Christ who are truly the children of God. We become the children of God only by adoption. We are born 'the children of wrath', 'the children of the devil', 'the children of this world'; and we have to be taken out of that realm and translated into another realm before we become the children of God. But if we truly believe on the Lord Jesus Christ, we are adopted into God's family, and we receive 'the Spirit of adoption, whereby we cry, Abba, Father'.

The man of the world does not like this doctrine. He says we are all the children of God; and yet in his heart he has a hatred towards God, and when, in desperation, he prays to God he has no confidence that he is speaking to his Father. He feels God is someone who has set Himself against him. He talks about the Fatherhood of God, but he has not received the Spirit of adoption. It is only the one who is in Christ who knows this.

So when our Lord says, 'Our Father', He is obviously thinking of Christian people, and that is why I say that this is a Christian prayer. A man may say, 'Our Father', but the question is, is he conscious of it, does he believe and experience it? The ultimate test of every man's profession is that he can say with confidence and with assurance, 'My Father', 'My God'. Is God your God? Do you know Him really as your Father? And when you come to Him in prayer, have you that sense of coming to your Father? That is the way to start, says our Lord, to realize that you have become a child of God because of what He has done for you through the Lord Jesus Christ. That is implicit in this teaching of Christ. He suggests and anticipates all that He was going to do for us, all He was going to make possible for His own. They did not understand it yet. Nevertheless, He says, that is the way to pray, that is how I pray, and you are going to pray like this.

You notice, however, that He adds immediately, 'Which art in heaven'. This is a most wonderful thing—'Our Father which art in heaven.' These two phrases must always be taken together, for this very good reason. Our ideas of fatherhood have often become very debased and have always, therefore, to be corrected. Do you notice how often the apostle Paul in his Epistles uses a most striking phrase? He talks about the 'God and Father of our Lord Jesus Christ'. That is most significant. It is simply calling attention to what our Lord says at this point. 'Our Father.'

Yes; but because of our debased conception of fatherhood, He hastens to say, 'Our Father which art in heaven', the 'God and Father of our Lord Jesus Christ'. That is the kind of Father we have.

But there are many people in this world, alas, to whom the idea of fatherhood is not one of love. Imagine a little boy who is the son of a father who is a drunkard and a wife-beater, and who is nothing but a cruel beast. That little boy knows nothing in life but constant and undeserved thrashings and kickings. He sees his father spend all his money on himself and his lust, while he himself has to starve. That is his idea of fatherhood. If you tell him that God is his Father, and leave it at that, it is not very helpful, and it is not very kind. The poor boy of necessity has a wrong idea of fatherhood. That is his notion of a father, a man who behaves like that. So our human, sinful notions of fatherhood need constant correction.

Our Lord says, 'Our Father which art in heaven;' and Paul says 'the God and Father of our Lord Jesus Christ'. Anyone like Christ, says Paul in effect, must have a wonderful Father, and, thank God, God is such a Father, the Father of our Lord Jesus Christ. It is vital when we pray to God, and call Him our Father, that we should remind ourselves that He is 'our Father which is in heaven', that we should remind ourselves of His majesty and of His greatness and of His almighty power. When in your weakness and your utter humiliation you drop on your knees before God, in your anguish of mind and heart, remember that He knows all about you. The Scripture says, 'all things are naked and opened unto the eyes of him with whom we have to do.' Remember, also, that if sometimes you rush into the presence of God and want something for yourself, or are praying for forgiveness for a sin you have committed, God has seen and knows all about it. It is not surprising that, when he wrote Psalm li, David said in the anguish of his heart, 'Thou desirest truth in the inward parts.' If you want to be blessed of God you have to be absolutely honest, you have to realize He knows everything, and that there is nothing hidden from Him. Remember also that He has all power to punish, and all power to bless. He is able to save, He is able to destroy. Indeed, as the wise man who wrote the book of Ecclesiastes put it, it is vital when we pray to God that we should remember that 'He is in heaven and we are upon the earth'.

Then remember His holiness and His justice, His utter, absolute righteousness. Let us remember, says the author of the

Epistle to the Hebrews, that whenever we approach Him we must do so 'with reverence and godly fear: for our God is a consuming fire'.

That is the way to pray, says Christ, take these two things together, never separate these two truths. Remember that you are approaching the almighty, eternal, ever-blessed holy God. But remember also that that God, in Christ, has become your Father, who not only knows all about you in the sense that He is omniscient, He knows all about you also in the sense that a father knows all about his child. He knows what is good for the child. Put these two things together. God in His almightiness is looking at you with a holy love and knows your every need. He hears your every sigh and loves you with an everlasting love. He desires nothing so much as your blessing, your happiness, your joy and your prosperity. Then remember this, that He 'is able to do exceeding abundantly above all that we ask or think'. As your 'Father which is in heaven' He is much more anxious to bless you than you are to be blessed. There is also no limit to His almighty power. He can bless you with all the blessings of heaven. He has put them all in Christ, and put you into Christ. So your life can be enriched with all the glory and riches of the grace of God Himself.

That is the way to pray. Before you begin to make any petition, before you begin to ask even for your daily bread, before you ask for anything, just realize that you, such as you are, are in the presence of such a Being, your Father which is in heaven, the Father of our Lord Jesus Christ. 'My God.' 'My Father.'

CHAPTER FIVE

PRAYER: ADORATION

WE come now to the next division of the Lord's Prayer which is that which deals with our petitions. 'Our Father which art in heaven': that is the invocation. Then come the petitions: 'hallowed be thy name. Thy kingdom come. Thy will be done in earth, as it is in heaven. Give us this day our daily bread. And forgive us our debts, as we forgive our debtors. And lead us not into temptation, but deliver us from evil.'·There has been much debating and disputing amongst the authorities as to whether you have there six or seven petitions. The answer turns on whether that last statement 'deliver us from evil' is to be regarded as a separate petition, or whether it is to be taken as part of the previous petition and to be read like this: 'Lead us not into temptation but deliver us from evil'. It is one of those points (and there are others in connection with the Christian faith) which simply cannot be decided, and about which we cannot be dogmatic. Fortunately for us, it is not a vital point, and God forbid that any of us should become so absorbed by the mere mechanics of Scripture, and spend so much time with them, as to miss the spirit and that which is important. The vital matter is not to decide whether there are six or seven petitions in the Lord's Prayer but rather to notice the order in which the petitions come. The first three—'Hallowed be thy name. Thy kingdom come. Thy will be done in earth, as it is in heaven'—have regard to God and His glory; the others have reference to ourselves. You will notice that the first three petitions contain the word '*Thy*', and all have reference to God. It is only after that that the word '*us*' comes in: 'Give us this day our daily bread. Forgive us our trespasses as we forgive those who trespass against us. Lead us not into temptation. Deliver us from evil.' That is the vital point—the order of the petitions, not the number. The first three are concerned about and look only to God and His glory.

But let us observe something else which is of vital importance, the proportion in the petitions. Not only must our desires and petitions with regard to God come first, but we must notice, too, that half the petitions are devoted to God and His glory and only the remainder deal with our particular needs and problems. Of course if we are interested in biblical numerics—an interest which is perhaps not to be entirely discouraged, though it can become dangerous if and when we tend to become too fanciful— we shall see, in addition, that the first *three* petitions have reference to God, and that three is always the number of Deity and of God, suggesting the three blessed Persons in the Trinity. In the same way, *four* is always the number of earth and refers to everything that is human. There are four beasts in the heavens in the book of Revelation, and so on. Seven, which is a combination of three and four, always stands for that perfect number where we see God in His relationship to earth, and God in His dealing with men. That may be true of this prayer, our Lord may have specifically constructed it to bring out those wonderful points. We cannot prove it. But in any case the important thing to grasp is this: that it matters not what our conditions and circumstances may be, it matters not what our work may be, it matters not at all what our desires may be, we must never start with ourselves, we must never start with our own petitions.

That principle applies even when our petitions reach their highest level. Even our concern for the salvation of souls, even our concern for God's blessing upon the preaching of the Word, even our concern that those who are near and dear to us may become truly Christian, even these things must never be given the first place, the first position. Still less must we ever start with our own circumstances and conditions.

It does not matter how desperate they may be, it does not matter how acute the tension, it does not matter whether it be physical illness, or war, or a calamity, or some terrible problem suddenly confronting us: whatever it may be, we must never fail to observe the order which is taught here by our blessed Lord and Saviour. Before we begin to think of ourselves and our own needs, even before our concern for others, we must start with this great concern about God and His honour and His glory. There is no principle in connection with the Christian life that exceeds this in importance. So often we err in the realm of principles. We tend to assume that we are quite sound and clear about principles, and that all we need is instruction about details. The actual truth, of course, is the exact reverse of that. If only we would always start in prayer with this true sense of the invocation; if only we were to recollect that we are in the presence of God, and that the eternal and almighty God is there, looking upon us as our Father, and more ready to bless and to surround us with His love than we are to receive His blessing, we should achieve more in that moment of recollection than all our prayers put together are likely to achieve without that realization. If only we all had this concern about God and His honour and glory!

Fortunately, our Lord knows our weakness, He realizes our need of instruction, so He has divided it up for us. He has not only announced the principle; He has divided it up for us into these three sections which we must proceed to consider. Let us look now at the first petition: 'Hallowed be thy name'.

We realize now that we are in the presence of God, and that He is our Father. Therefore this, says Christ, should be our first desire, our first petition: 'Hallowed be thy name'. What does that mean? Let us look very briefly at the words. The word 'Hallowed' means to sanctify, or to revere, or to make and keep holy. But why does He say 'Hallowed be thy name'? What does this term 'the Name' stand for? We are familiar with the fact that it was the way in which the Jews at that time commonly referred to God Himself. Whatever we may say about the Jews in Old Testament times and however great their failures, there was one respect, at any rate, in which they were most commendable. I refer to their sense of the greatness and the majesty and the holiness of God. You remember that they had such a sense of this that it had become their custom not to use the name 'Jehovah'. They felt that the very name, the very letters, as it were, were so holy and sacred, and they so small and unworthy, that they dare not mention it. They referred to God as 'The Name', in order to avoid the use of the actual term Jehovah. So that the 'name' here means God Himself, and we see that the purpose of the petition is to express this desire that God Himself may be revered, may be sanctified, that the very name of God and all it denotes and represents may be honoured amongst men, may be holy throughout the entire world. But perhaps in the light of the Old Testament teaching it is good for us to enlarge on this just a little. The 'name', in other words, means all that is true of God, and all that has been revealed concerning God. It means God in all His attributes, God in all that He is in and of Himself, and God in all that He has done and all that He is doing.

God, you remember, had revealed Himself to the children of Israel under various names. He had used a term concerning Himself (*El* or *Elohim*) which means His 'strength' and His 'power'; and when He used that particular name, He was giving the people a sense of His might, His dominion, and His power.

Later He revealed Himself in that great and wonderful name *Jehovah* which really means 'the self-existent One', 'I am that I am', eternally self-existent. But there were other names in which God described Himself: 'the Lord will provide' (*Jehovah-jireh*), 'the Lord that healeth' (*Jehovah-rapha*), 'the Lord our Banner' (*Jehovah-nissi*), 'the Lord our peace' (*Jehovah-Shalom*), 'the Lord our Shepherd' (*Jehovah-ra-ah*), 'the Lord our Righteousness' (*Jehovah-tsidkenu*), and another term which means, 'the Lord is present' (*Jehovah-shammah*). As you read the Old Testament you will find all these various terms used; and in giving these various names to Himself God was revealing Himself and something of His nature and being, His character and His attributes, to mankind. In a sense 'thy name' stands for all that. Our Lord is here teaching us to pray that the whole world may come to know God in this way, that the whole world may come to honour God like that. It is the expression of a burning and deep desire for the honour and glory of God.

You cannot read the four Gospels without seeing very clearly that that was the consuming passion of the Lord Jesus Christ Himself. It is found again perfectly in that great High Priestly prayer in John xvii when He says, 'I have glorified thee on the earth' and 'I have manifested thy name unto the men which thou gavest me'. He was always concerned about the glory of His Father. He said, 'I have not come to seek mine own glory but the glory of him that sent me.' There is no real understanding of the earthly life of Christ except in these terms. He knew that glory which ever belongs to the Father, 'the glory which I had with thee before the world was.' He had seen that glory and He had shared it. He was filled with this sense of the glory of God, and His one desire was that mankind might come to know it.

What unworthy ideas and notions this world has of God! If you test your ideas of God by the teaching of the Scriptures you will see at a glance what I mean. We lack even a due sense of the greatness and the might and the majesty of God. Listen to men arguing about God, and notice how glibly they use the term. It is not that I would advocate a return to the practice of the ancient Jews; I think they went too far. But it is indeed almost alarming to observe the way in which we all tend to use the name of God. We obviously do not realize that we are talking about the ever blessed, eternal, and absolute, almighty God. There is a sense in which we should take our shoes off our feet whenever we use the name. And how little do we appreciate the goodness of God, the kindness and the providence of God. How the Psalmist delighted in celebrating God as our rock, God as our peace, God as our shepherd who leads us, God as our righteousness, and God as the ever present One who will never leave us nor forsake us.

This petition means just that. We should all have a consuming passion that the whole world might come to know God like that. There is an interesting expression used in the Old Testament with regard to this which must sometimes have astonished us. The Psalmist in Psalm xxxiv invites everybody to join him in 'magnifying' the Lord. What a strange idea! 'O', he says, 'magnify the Lord with me, and let us exalt his name together'. At first sight that appears to be quite ridiculous. God is the Eternal, the self-existent One, absolute and perfect in all His qualities. How can feeble man ever magnify such a Being? How can we ever make God great or greater (which is what we mean by magnify)? How can we exalt the name that is highly exalted over all? It seems preposterous and quite ridiculous. And yet, of course, if we but realize the way in which the Psalmist uses it, we shall see exactly what he means. He does not mean that we can actually add to the greatness of God, for that is impossible; but he does mean that he is concerned that this greatness of God may appear to be greater amongst men. Thus it comes to pass that amongst ourselves in this world we can magnify the name of God. We can do so by words, and by our lives, by being reflectors of the greatness and the glory of God and of His glorious attributes.

That is the meaning of this petition. It means a burning desire that the whole world may bow before God in adoration, in reverence, in praise, in worship, in honour and in thanksgiving. Is that our supreme desire? Is that the thing that is always uppermost in our minds whenever we pray to God? I would remind you again that it should be so whatever our circumstances. It is when we look at it in that way that we see how utterly valueless much of our praying must be. When you come to God, says our Lord, in effect, even though you may be in desperate conditions and circumstances, it may be with some great concern on your mind and in your heart; even then, He says, stop for a moment and just recollect and realize this, that your greatest desire of all should be that this wonderful God, who has become your Father in and through Me, should be honoured, should be worshipped, should be magnified amongst the people. 'Hallowed be thy name.' And as we have seen, it has always been so in the praying of every true saint of God that has ever lived on the face of the earth.

If, therefore, we are anxious to know God's blessing and are concerned that our prayers should be effectual and of value, we must follow this order. It is all put in a phrase repeated many times in the Old Testament: 'The fear of the Lord is the beginning of wisdom'. That is the conclusion reached by the Psalmist. That is the conclusion, likewise, of the wise man in his proverbs. If you want to know, he says, what true wisdom is, if you want to be blessed and prosperous, if you want to have peace and joy, if you want to be able to live and die in a worthy manner, if you want wisdom with regard to life in this world, here it is, 'the fear of the Lord'. That does not mean craven fear; it means reverential awe. If, therefore, we want to know God and to be blessed of God, we must start by worshipping Him. We must say, 'Hallowed be thy name', and tell Him that, before mentioning any concern about ourselves, our one desire is that He shall be known. Let us approach God 'with reverence and godly fear: for our God is a consuming fire'. That is the first petition.

The second is 'Thy kingdom come'. You notice that there is a logical order in these petitions. They follow one another by a kind of inevitable, divine necessity. We began by asking that the name of God may be hallowed amongst men. But the moment we pray that prayer we are reminded of the fact that His name is not hallowed thus. At once the question arises, Why do not all men bow before the sacred name? Why is not every man on this earth concerned about humbling himself now in the presence of God, and worshipping Him and using every moment in adoring Him and spreading forth His name? Why not? The answer is, of course, because of sin, because there is another kingdom, the kingdom of Satan, the kingdom of darkness. And there, at once, we are reminded of the very essence of the human problems and the human predicament. Our desire as Christian people is that God's name shall be glorified. But the moment we start with that we realize that there is this opposition, and we are reminded of the whole biblical teaching about evil. There is another who is 'the god of this world'; there is a kingdom of darkness, a kingdom of evil, and it is opposed to God and His glory and honour. But God has been graciously pleased to reveal from the very dawn of history that He is yet going to establish His kingdom in this world of time, that though Satan has entered in and conquered the world for the time being, and the whole of mankind is under his dominion, He is again going to assert Himself and turn this world and all its kingdoms into His own glorious kingdom. In

other words, running right through the Old Testament, there
are the promises and the prophecies concerning the coming of
the kingdom of God or the kingdom of heaven. And, of course, at
this particular, crucial point of world history, when our Lord
Himself was here on earth, this matter was very much in the
forefront of men's minds. John the Baptist had been preaching
his message, 'Repent ye: for the kingdom of heaven is at hand'.
He called the people to be ready for it. And when our Lord began
preaching, He said exactly the same thing; 'Repent: for the
kingdom of heaven is at hand.' In this petition He obviously has
that whole idea in His mind as He teaches His disciples to offer
this particular prayer. At that immediate historical point He was
teaching His disciples to pray that this kingdom of God should
come increasingly and come quickly, but the prayer is equally
true and equally right for us as Christian people in all ages until
the end shall come.

We can summarize the teaching concerning the kingdom. The
kingdom of God really means the reign of God; it means the law
and the rule of God. When we look at it like that we can see that
the kingdom can be regarded in three ways. In one sense the
kingdom has already come. It came when the Lord Jesus Christ
was here. He said, 'If I with the finger of God cast out devils, no
doubt the kingdom of God is come upon you'. He said in effect,
'The kingdom of God is here now; I am exercising this power,
this sovereignty, this majesty, this dominion; this is the kingdom
of God'. So the kingdom of God in one sense had come then. The
kingdom of God is also here at this moment in the hearts and
lives of all who submit to Him, in all who believe in Him. The
kingdom of God is present in the Church, in the heart of all those
who are truly Christian. Christ reigns in such people. But the
day is yet to come when His kingdom shall have been established
here upon the earth. The day is yet to come when

> 'Jesus shall reign where'er the sun
> Does his successive journeys run.'

That day is coming. The whole message of the Bible looks
forward to that. Christ came down from heaven to earth to
found, to establish, and to bring in this kingdom. He is still
engaged upon that task and will be until the end, when it shall
have been completed. Then He will, according to Paul, hand it
back to God the Father, 'that God may be all in all'.

So our petition really amounts to this. We should have a great
longing and desire that the kingdom of God and of Christ may

come in the hearts of men. It should be our desire that this kingdom should be extended in our own hearts; for it is to the extent that we worship Him, and surrender our lives to Him, and are led by Him, that His kingdom comes in our hearts. We should also be anxious to see this kingdom extending in the lives and hearts of other men and women. So that when we pray, 'Thy kingdom come', we are praying for the success of the gospel, its sway and power; we are praying for the conversion of men and women; we are praying that the kingdom of God may come today in Britain, in Europe, in America, in Australia, everywhere in the world. 'Thy kingdom come' is an all-inclusive missionary prayer.

But it goes even further than that. It is a prayer which indicates that we are 'Looking for and hasting unto the coming of the day of God' (2 Peter iii. 12). It means that we should be anticipating the day when all sin and evil and wrong and everything that is opposed to God shall finally have been routed. It means that we should have longings in our hearts for the time when the Lord will come back again, when all that is opposed to Him shall be cast into the lake of burning, and the kingdoms of this world shall have become the kingdoms of our God and of His Christ.

> 'Thy kingdom come, O God;
> Thy rule, O Christ, begin;
> Break with Thine iron rod
> The tyrannies of sin.'

That is the petition. Indeed its meaning is expressed perfectly at the very end of the book of Revelation. 'Even so, come, Lord Jesus'. 'The Spirit and the bride say, Come'. Our Lord is just emphasizing here that before we begin to think of our own personal needs and desires, we should have this burning desire within us for the coming of His kingdom, that the name of God may be glorified and magnified over all.

The third petition, 'Thy will be done in earth, as it is in heaven' needs no explanation. It is a kind of logical consequence and conclusion from the second, as that was a logical conclusion from the first. The result of the coming of the kingdom of God amongst men will be that the will of God will be done amongst men. In heaven the will of God is always being done perfectly. We have only some dim and faint figures of it in the Scriptures, but we have sufficient to know that what is characteristic of heaven is that everyone and everything is waiting upon God and anxious to glorify and magnify His name. The angels, as it were,

are on the wing all ready and waiting to fly at His bidding. The
supreme desire of all in heaven is to do the will of God, and
thereby to praise and worship Him. And it should be the desire
of every true Christian, says our Lord here, that all on earth
should be the same. Here, again, we are looking forward to the
coming of the kingdom, because this petition will never be
fulfilled and granted until the kingdom of God shall indeed be
established here on earth amongst men. Then the will of God
will be done on earth as it is done in heaven. There will be 'new
heavens and a new earth, wherein dwelleth righteousness'.
Heaven and earth will become one, the world will be changed,
evil will be burned out of it, and the glory of God will shine
over all.

In these words, then, we are taught how we begin to pray.
Those are the petitions with which we must always start. We can
summarize them again in this way. Our innermost and greatest
desire should be the desire for God's honour and glory. At the
risk of being misunderstood I suggest that our desire for this
should be even greater than our desire for the salvation of souls.
Before we even begin to pray for souls, before we even begin to
pray for the extension and the spread of God's kingdom, there
should be that over-ruling desire for the manifestation of the
glory of God and that all might humble themselves in His
presence. We can put it like this. What is it that troubles and
worries our minds? Is it the manifestation of sin that we see in
the world, or is it the fact that men do not worship and glorify
God as they ought to do? Our Lord felt it so much that He put it
like this in John xvii. 25: 'O righteous Father, the world hath not
known thee: but I have known thee, and these (referring to the
disciples) have known that thou hast sent me.' 'Righteous
Father,' He said in effect, 'here is the tragedy, here is the thing
that perplexes Me, and saddens Me, that the world has not
known Thee. It thinks of Thee as a tyrant, it thinks of Thee as a
harsh Law-giver, it thinks of Thee as Someone who is opposed
to it and always tyrannizing over it. Holy Father, the world has
not known Thee. If it had but known Thee it could never think
of Thee like that.' And that should be our attitude, that should
be our burning desire and longing. We should so know God that
our one longing and desire should be that the whole world
should come to know Him too.
What a wonderful prayer this is. O the folly of people who
say that such a prayer is not meant for Christians, but that it was

meant only for the disciples then and for the Jews in some coming age. Does it not make us feel in a sense that we have never prayed at all? This is prayer. 'Our Father which art in heaven, Hallowed be thy name'. Have we arrived at that yet, I wonder? Have we really prayed that prayer, that petition, 'Hallowed be thy name'? If only we are right about that, the rest will follow. 'Thy kingdom come. Thy will be done in earth, as it is in heaven'. We need not turn to .Him and ask Him, 'Lord, teach us how to pray'. He has done so already. We have but to put into practice the principles He has taught us so plainly in this model prayer.

CHAPTER SIX

PRAYER: PETITION

ANY man who attempts to preach on the Lord's Prayer must surely find himself in great difficulties. There is a sense in which it is almost presumption to preach on it at all. One should simply repeat these phrases and meditate upon them and consider them from the heart. For they themselves say everything, and the more I study this prayer the more I believe that if only one used these phrases as our Lord intended them to be used, there is really nothing more to be said. But, on the other hand, we are all frail and fallible, we are sinful creatures, and the result is that we need to have these things analysed and enforced.

We have been trying to do so and we come now to the last section (verses 11–15). We have already considered whether there are three petitions here, or four. On the whole, and in spite of the interesting possibility from the standpoint of biblical numerics, I would say there are *three*, and these last three petitions have reference to ourselves and our own needs and desires. It seems to me that the words our Lord uses in verse 13 really determine this: 'And', He says—that is the word that introduces each new petition—'And lead us not into temptation, but deliver us from evil'. If there were four petitions it would probably read like this: 'And lead us not into temptation, and deliver us from evil'. His use of 'but' seems to indicate that it is really one petition offered from two angles or two different sides.

Before we comment on these three petitions individually, there are two or three general statements which must be made. The first concerns the all-inclusiveness of these petitions. All our great needs are summed up in them. 'Give us this day our daily bread'. 'Forgive us our debts, as we forgive our debtors'. 'And lead us not into temptation, but deliver us from evil'. Our whole life is found there in those three petitions, and that is what makes this prayer so utterly amazing. In such a small compass our Lord has covered the whole life of the believer in every respect. Our physical needs, our mental needs and, of course, our spiritual needs are included. The body is remembered, the soul is remem-

67

bered, the spirit is remembered. And that is the whole of man, body, soul and spirit. Think of all the activities going on in the world at this moment, the organizing, the planning, the legislation and all other things; they are for the most part concerned with nothing but the body of man, his life and existence in this world of time. That is the tragedy of the worldly outlook, for there is another realm, the realm of relationships—the soul, the thing whereby man makes contact with his fellow man, the means of communication with one another and all social life and activity. It is all here. And above all, we have the spiritual, that which links man with God, and reminds him that he is something other than dust, and that as Longfellow says, 'Dust thou art, to dust returnest, was not spoken of the soul'. Man has been made this way; he cannot escape it, and our Lord has provided for it. We cannot fail to be impressed by the all-inclusiveness of these petitions. That does not mean that we should never enter into details; we must, we are taught to do so. We are taught to bring our life in detail to God in prayer; but here we have only the great headings. Our Lord gives us these and we fill in the details, but it is important for us to be sure that all our petitions should belong under one or other of the headings.

The second general comment concerns the wonderful order in which these petitions are put. How often, when we have thought about this prayer and meditated upon it, have we felt a sense of surprise that the first should be what it is? Let us look at it again in its setting: 'Our Father which art in heaven, Hallowed be thy name. Thy kingdom come. Thy will be done in earth, as it is in heaven'—a wonderful, exalted, spiritual level. We would have expected that immediately after that would come the spiritual needs of man followed in a descending order by the needs of his soul and at the very end some remembrance of the body and its needs. But that is not how our Lord puts it. Immediately after those exalted petitions about God and His glory, He says: 'Give us this day our daily bread'. He starts with the body. There is indeed something surprising about that at first sight, but the moment we stop to think about it we shall realize that the order is absolutely right. Our Lord is now considering our needs, and clearly the first thing that is necessary is that we must be enabled to continue our existence in this world. We are alive and we must be kept alive. The very fact of my existence and being are involved, so the first petition deals with the needs of our physical frame, and our Lord starts with that. He then goes on to deal with the need of cleansing from the defilement and guilt of sin; and, lastly, with the need for being kept from sin and its power. That is the true way to look at man's life. I am alive and I must be kept alive. But then I am conscious of guilt and unworthiness, and feel the need to be cleansed from that. Then I think of the future and realize that I need to be delivered from certain things that face me there.

Another way is to put it like this. Life in a physical sense, or in a biological sense, is the basis upon which all depends, so I must pray about my existence. But the moment I do so I come to realize that the physical is only one side of my life. There is another side. I remember that our Lord said, 'This is life eternal, that they might know thee the only true God, and Jesus Christ, whom thou hast sent'. He also said that He had come 'that they might have life, and that they might have it more abundantly'. Having been concerned only with my bare physical existence, I now begin to learn that what really makes life, *life*, is that I should be walking in fellowship and communion with God.

That, according to John in his First Epistle, is the real way of facing life in a world such as this. There are contradictions and difficulties; there are all sorts of things to get me down. But John said he was writing that letter in order that 'your joy may be full' in spite of it all. How is my joy to be full in such a world? By having fellowship with the Father and with His Son Jesus Christ. That is real living. But the moment I realize that, I know there are certain things that tend to interrupt that fellowship. I am sinful; therefore I need forgiveness of sins in order that I may enjoy that life of God. And when my communion with God has been restored the only other thing I need is to continue to enjoy that fellowship without interruption, without anything ever coming between me and the face of God who has become my Father in the Lord Jesus Christ.

So that is the order—daily bread; forgiveness of sins; to be kept from anything that may cast me again into sin, to be delivered from everything that is opposed to my higher interests and to my true life. The sum of it all is that ultimately there is nothing in the whole realm of Scripture which so plainly shows us our entire dependence upon God as does this prayer, and especially these three petitions. The only thing that really matters for us is that we know God as our Father. If we only knew God like this our problems would be solved already and we would realize our utter dependence upon Him and go to Him daily as children to their Father.

There, then, are our general observations. Let us now look briefly at the separate petitions in the order in which they appear. If we were interested in the mechanics of Scripture we could stay for some time considering the meaning of the term 'our daily bread'. It is said to be one of the most difficult terms in the whole of the Bible. What is the exact meaning of the expression? I am not going to weary you with all the views and theories. It must at least mean this. 'Give us this day what is necessary for us'. Some would say it should read: 'Give us this day our bread for tomorrow', which means exactly the same thing. In other words, all we are to ask for is sufficient, or what is necessary, for each day. It is a prayer for necessities. Bread is the staff of life; and I agree with those who say it should not be confined to the matter of food. It is meant to cover all our material needs, everything that is necessary for the life of man in this world.

Having said that, we must make a number of further comments. In the first place is there not something extraordinary and wonderful about the connection between this request and the previous requests? Is not this one of the most wonderful things in the whole of Scripture, that the God who is the Creator and Sustainer of the universe, the God who is forming His eternal kingdom and who will usher it in at the end, the God to whom the nations are but as 'the small dust of the balance'—that such a God should be prepared to consider your little needs and mine even down to the minutest details in this matter of daily bread! But that is the teaching of our Lord everywhere. He tells us that even a sparrow cannot fall to the ground without our Father, and that we are of much greater value than many sparrows. He says that 'the very hairs of your head are all numbered'. If only we could grasp this fact, that the almighty Lord of the universe is interested in every part and portion of us! There is not a hair of my head that He is not concerned about, and the smallest and most trivial details in my little life are known to Him on His everlasting throne. This is something you find only in Scripture. You go straight from 'Thy will be done in earth, as it is in heaven', to 'Give us this day our daily bread'. But that is the way of God, 'the high and lofty One that inhabiteth eternity, whose name is Holy'; who nevertheless, as Isaiah tells us, dwells with him also 'that is of a contrite and humble spirit'. That is the whole miracle of redemption; that is the whole meaning of the incarnation which tells us that the Lord Jesus Christ takes hold of us here on earth and links us with the almighty God of glory. The kingdom of God, and my daily bread!

It must be emphasized, of course, that all we pray for must be absolute necessities. We are not told to pray for luxuries or superabundance, nor are we promised such things. But we are promised that we shall have enough. David looking back in his old age could say, 'I have not seen the righteous forsaken, nor his seed begging bread'. The promises of God never fail. But they refer to necessities only, and our idea of necessity is not always God's. But we *are* told to pray for necessities.

Let us come, however, to another matter that is perhaps more perplexing. There are some people who see an apparent contradiction here. Our Lord asks us to make our requests; but He has just said that we are not to be like the heathen who think they shall be heard for their much speaking, because 'your Father knoweth what things ye have need of, before ye ask him'. 'Very well,' says someone; 'if God knows before we ask Him, why should we express our needs to Him? Why tell Him about things that He knows already?' This brings us to the heart of the meaning of prayer. We do not tell God these things because He is not aware of them. No, we must think of prayer more as a relationship between father and child; and the value of prayer is that it keeps us in touch and contact with God.

An illustration once used by Dr. A. B. Simpson gave me great help when I first read it, and it continues to do so in this connection. He said that so many of us tend to think that God as our Father gives us the great gift of grace in one great lump sum, and that, having received it, we just go on living on it. 'But', he said, 'it is not like that. That would be very dangerous for us. If God just gave us all His glorious gifts of grace in one lump sum, we would be in danger of enjoying the gift and forgetting all about God.' For though we cannot understand it, God wants us, and as our Father, He likes us, to speak to Him. He is like an earthly father in that respect. The earthly father is grievously wounded by the son who is content to enjoy the gift the father has given him but who never seeks his company again until he has exhausted his supplies and needs some more. No, the father likes the child to come and speak to him; and this is God's way of doing it. It is, says Dr. Simpson, exactly as though a father put a great deposit for his son into the bank, and the son can only receive a supply each time by writing a cheque. Each time he needs another instalment he has to write a cheque. And that is how God deals with us. He does not give it to us all at once. He gives it to us in instalments. God is there in grace offering His guarantee, and all we have to do is to sign our cheques and present them. That is prayer, it is presenting our cheque, just going to God and asking Him to honour it.

This, surely, is the marvellous thing, that God likes us to come to Him. The God who is self-existent, the great Jehovah, the God who is not dependent upon anybody, who is from eternity to eternity, who exists in Himself apart from all—this is the astounding thing, that because we are His children He likes us to come to Him, and likes to hear us. The God who made heaven and earth, and orders the stars in their courses, likes to hear our lisping praises, likes to hear our petitions. That is because God is love; and that is why, though He knows all about our needs, it gives Him great pleasure, if we can so put it, when He sees us coming to Him to ask for our daily bread.

But we must emphasize next another aspect: we must all realize our utter dependence upon God, even for our daily bread. If God willed it so, we should have no daily bread. He could withhold the sun and its influence; He could stop the rain; He could make our land absolutely barren so that the farmer with all his modern implements and chemicals could not raise a crop. He could blast the crop if He wanted to. We are absolutely in the hand of God, and the supreme folly of this twentieth century is the folly of thinking that because we have acquired a certain amount of knowledge of the laws of God, we are independent of Him. We cannot live for a day without Him. Nothing would continue were it not sustained and kept going by God. 'Give us this day our daily bread.' It is a good thing for us at least once a day, but the oftener the better, to remind ourselves that our times, our health, and our very existence, are in His hands. Our food and all these necessary things come from Him, and we depend upon His grace and mercy for them.

We come now to the second division, which is often a great cause of difficulty. 'And forgive us our debts, as we forgive our debtors.' There are two main difficulties about this. There are those who feel that there is no need for a Christian to ask for forgiveness, and these people are divided into two groups. Some of them say that Christians need not ask for forgiveness, because we are justified by faith, by which they mean, of course, that we are justified by faith in the presence of God. What does it mean to be 'justified by faith'? It is God's declaration that He has dealt with our sins in full in the Person of the Lord Jesus Christ, the sins we have committed and the sins we shall commit, that He has imputed to us the righteousness of Jesus Christ, and regards and declares us to be righteous in Him. That is justification by faith. In that case, they argue, if all my sins were dealt with there, what need have I to ask for forgiveness?

Others say there is no need to ask for forgiveness because of their view of sanctification. Their position is that they do not sin any longer; they are perfect. They hold the holiness theory which teaches that sin has been eradicated, and that they are perfect, and sinless. So that for them it would be wrong to pray for forgiveness of sins; neither need they do so, for they do no wrong. But the answer to this error is that our Lord tells us to pray for forgiveness of our debts, trespasses, sins (or whichever word you prefer). He is not talking about justification; He is not dealing here with the case of a sinner who has just awakened to the fact that he needs to have his sins forgiven and so comes to God and receives the gift of salvation and realizes his justification in Christ—that is not what we have here. Here, rather, is what our Lord speaks of in John xiii. You remember that as He washed the disciples' feet, Peter said to Him, 'Lord, not my feet only, but also my hands and my head'. 'No,' said Christ, 'he that is washed needeth not, save to wash his feet, but is clean every whit.' There is only one washing of the entire person—that is our justification. But having been justified, as we walk through this world we become soiled and tarnished by sin. That is true of every Christian. Though we know we have been forgiven, we need forgiveness still for particular sins and failures. It is all stated briefly in chapter i of John's First Epistle, where we see that the Christian, though walking in the life of faith, may yet fall into sin. What are we to do about it? John tells us to 'confess our sins'. And 'if we confess our sins, he is faithful and just to forgive us our sins, and to cleanse us from all unrighteousness'. John is not writing to unbelievers; it is a letter to believers. He is writing to Christians, and our Lord was speaking to believers here.

Who is the man who can pray, 'Forgive us our debts, as we forgive our debtors'? He is the man who already has a right to say, 'Our Father'. And the only man who has a right to say 'Our Father' is the one who is in Christ Jesus. It is 'The Children's Prayer'. It is not a prayer for anybody, but only for those who have become the children of God in the Lord Jesus Christ. It is the relationship of the child to the Father, and the moment we realize we have offended, or grieved or sinned against the Father, we confess it and ask to be forgiven, and we are sure that we are forgiven.

With regard to those who claim that they are so sanctified that they do not need forgiveness, we learn again from John's Epistle that 'If we say we have no sin, we deceive ourselves, and the truth is not in us'. The man who does not know the blackness of his own heart, but is simply concerned with his own theories, is a man who is not examining himself truly. The greater the saint the greater is the sense of sin and the awareness of sin within.

But let us look at the second great difficulty in connection with this petition. 'Forgive us our debts, as we forgive our debtors.' There are people who say that this prayer should never be used by Christian people, for to do so, they say, is to go back to the law. These words apply, they maintain, only to those people to whom our Lord was actually speaking, and it will apply again only to those who will live in the future 'Kingdom Age'. These alone are the people who will pray, 'Forgive me because I forgive others'. They will be back on legal ground. 'It does not say "for Christ's sake",' say these interpreters; they say, 'there is no mention of the atonement; therefore it does not apply to Christians'. What do we say to this?

The first comment is that the text does not say, 'Forgive us our debts because we forgive our debtors'; it does not say, 'Forgive us on the ground of the fact that we forgive our debtors'. It says rather 'even as', 'even as I forgive those who are my debtors'. Or let us look at it like this. Take that argument which says that because the Lord's Prayer does not say 'for Christ's sake', and because the atonement is not specifically mentioned, it contains no gospel. To be consistent they must never again use the parable of the Prodigal Son for it also does not mention the atonement. It does not say anything about 'for Christ's sake'. It just gives an amazing picture of God as Father. It simply says that the son came back and that the father freely forgave him everything and showered his love upon him. But such an attitude towards the parable and towards this petition is quite ridiculous and pathetic. As the parable is concerned to point out one great central truth, so our Lord here was simply concerned to remind us of the need for forgiveness and to assure of the fact of forgiveness. He is not so much concerned about the mechanism or the way of forgiveness here, any more than He is in the parable of the Prodigal Son. We must take our Scriptures as a whole and compare Scripture with Scripture.

Now take this idea that there was ever a time when men were forgiven on strictly legal grounds, or that there is to be some time in the future when men will be on strictly legal grounds before God, and will be forgiven even as they forgive. Do we realize what that means? It means, of course, that such people will never be forgiven. Paul says that the law condemns everybody. 'There is none righteous, no, not one.' 'All have sinned, and come short of the glory of God.' The whole world lies guilty before God, and has been condemned. And I can assure you that there will never be anyone in any coming 'Kingdom Age', or in any other age, who can ever be forgiven by God apart from the death of the Lord Jesus Christ upon the cross. How absurd is this theory that in some coming kingdom age forgiveness will be strictly on legal grounds or that at any time it has been procured on such grounds. The only way of forgiveness before Christ, after Christ and always, is through Christ and Him crucified. The way of salvation in Him was ordained 'before the foundation of the world', and that fact is implicit in this and in every similar statement everywhere in the Scriptures. We must learn to take our Scriptures together, and to compare Scripture with Scripture, and to realize that here our Lord was simply concerned about the relationship of Father and child. He could not at this point explain the doctrine of the atonement. He even said at the end of His life that there were certain truths which He had to teach them but which they could not bear then. The truth concerning the way of forgiveness is implicit here, but the great fulfilment was to come.

We must not allow ourselves to be misled in this way. What we have here is what we find so clearly taught in Matthew xviii, in the parable of the steward who would not forgive his underling although he had been forgiven by his master. It means that the proof that you and I are forgiven is that we forgive others. If we think that our sins are forgiven by God and we refuse to forgive somebody else, we are making a mistake; we have never been forgiven. The man who knows he has been forgiven, only in and through the shed blood of Christ, is a man who must forgive others. He cannot help himself. If we really know Christ as our Saviour our hearts are broken and cannot be hard, and we cannot refuse forgiveness. If you are refusing forgiveness to anybody I suggest that you have never been forgiven. 'Forgive us our debts, as we forgive our debtors.' I say to the glory of God and in utter humility, that whenever I see myself before God and realize even something of what my blessed Lord has done for me,

I am ready to forgive anybody anything. I cannot withhold it, I do not even want to withhold it. That is what our Lord is saying here. We have a right therefore to pray like that. Pray to God and say, 'Forgive me O God as I forgive others because of what Thou hast done for me. All I ask is that Thou shouldst forgive me in the same manner; not to the same degree, because all I do is imperfect. In the same way, as it were, as Thou hast forgiven me, I am forgiving others. Forgive me as I forgive them because of what the cross of the Lord Jesus Christ has done in my heart.'

This petition is full of the atonement, it is full of the grace of God. We see how important it is by the fact that our Lord actually repeats it. Having finished the prayer He goes back and says (in verses 14 and 15), 'For if ye forgive men their trespasses, your heavenly Father will also forgive you; but if ye forgive not men their trespasses, neither will your Father forgive your trespasses.' The thing is absolute and inevitable. True forgiveness breaks a man, and he must forgive. So that when we offer this prayer for forgiveness we test ourselves in that way. Our prayer is not genuine, it is not true, it is of no avail, unless we find there is forgiveness in our heart. God give us grace to be honest with ourselves, and never to repeat these petitions in the Lord's Prayer in a mechanical way.

Now just a word about the last petition, 'Lead us not into temptation, but deliver us from evil'. That is the final request and it means this. We are asking that we should never be led into a situation where we are liable to be tempted by Satan. It does not mean that we are dictating to God what He shall or shall not do. God does test His children, and we must never presume to tell God what He is or is not to do. He knows that we need much training in our preparation for glory. But though it does not mean that we are to dictate to God, it does mean that we may request of Him that, if it be in accordance with His holy will, He should not lead us into positions where we can be so easily tempted, and where we are liable to fall. It means that we should request Him to preserve us from this, and not to lead us in this way. This is what our Lord meant when He said to His disciples at the end, 'Watch and pray, that ye enter not into temptation'. There are situations which will be dangerous to you; watch and pray, always be on guard lest you fall into temptation. And coupled with that is this other aspect of the petition, that we pray to be delivered from evil. Some would say 'from the evil one', but I think that limits the meaning, for 'evil' here includes not only Satan but evil in every shape and form. It certainly includes Satan; we need to be delivered from him and his wiles. But there is evil also in our hearts, so we need to be delivered from that, and from the evil in the world as well. We need to be delivered from it all. It is a great request, a comprehensive petition.

Why should we ask that we may be kept from evil? For the great and wonderful reason that our fellowship with God may never be broken. If a man merely wants to be holy as such, there is something wrong with him. Our supreme desire should be to have a right relationship with God, to know Him, to have uninterrupted fellowship and communion with Him. That is why we pray this prayer, that nothing may come between us and the brightness and the radiance and the glory of our Father which is in heaven. 'Lead us not into temptation, but deliver us from evil.'

Then, you remember, there is a postscript: 'For thine is the kingdom, and the power, and the glory, for ever.' It is in some of the old versions; it is not in others. We do not know for certain whether our Lord did actually utter it at this point or not; but whether He did or not, it is very appropriate. What can one say after facing such a prayer, and such words? There must be a kind of final thanksgiving, there must be some sort of doxology. As we consider our needs, our dependence upon Him, our relationship to Him, we cannot stop by saying, 'Deliver us from evil'. We must end as we began, by praising Him. The measure of our spirituality is the amount of praise and of thanksgiving in our prayers. 'Thine is the kingdom, and the power, and the glory.' Our daily food is assured us, we have as our Father One who can keep us from hell, from Satan, from ourselves, from all. 'Thine is the kingdom, and the power'—And Thine must be, and, as far as we are concerned, shall be, the glory for ever and ever. Amen.

CHAPTER SEVEN

TREASURES ON EARTH AND IN HEAVEN

THE theme of this section of the Sermon on the Mount is, you remember, the relationship of the Christian to God as his Father. There is nothing more important than this. The great secret of life according to our Lord is to see ourselves and to conceive of ourselves always as children of our heavenly Father. If only we do that we shall be delivered immediately from two of the main temptations that attack us all in this life.

These temptations He puts in this way. The first is the very subtle one that comes to every Christian in the matter of his personal piety. As a Christian I have my private, personal life of devotion. In that connection our Lord says that the one thing that matters, and the one consideration for me, should always be that God's eye is upon me. I must not be interested in what people say, neither must I be interested in myself. If I give alms, I must not give them in order to be praised of men. The same is true of my prayers. I must not want to give the impression that I am 'a great man of prayer'. If I do, my prayer is useless. I must not be interested in what people think of me as a man of prayer. All that He denounces. I must pray as under God and in the presence of God. Exactly the same principles obtain with the question of fasting; and you remember how we worked it out in detail in chapter III. These considerations have brought us to the end of verse 18 of Matthew vi.

We come now to verse 19 where our Lord introduces the second aspect of this great question of the Christian living his life in this world in relationship to God as his Father, involved in its affairs and feeling its cares, its strains and its stresses. It is, in fact, the whole problem of what is so often called in the Bible, 'the world'. We frequently say that the Christian in this life has to contend with the world, the flesh and the devil; and our Lord recognizes that threefold description of our problem and conflict. In handling this question of personal piety He deals first with the temptations that come from the flesh and the devil. The devil is particularly watchful when a man is pious, and when he is engaged in the manifestations of his piety. But having dealt with that, our Lord proceeds to show that there is another problem, and that is the problem of the world itself.

Now what do the Scriptures mean by the expression 'the world'? It does not mean the physical universe, or merely a collection of people; it means an outlook and a mentality, it means a way of looking at things, a way of looking at the whole of life. One of the most subtle problems with which the Christian ever has to deal is this problem of his relationship to the world. Our Lord frequently emphasizes that it is not an easy thing to be a Christian. He Himself when He was here in this world was tempted of the devil. He was also confronted by the power and subtlety of the world. The Christian is in precisely the same position. There are attacks which come upon him when he is alone, in private. There are others which come when he goes out into the world. You notice our Lord's order. How significant it is. You prepare yourself in the secrecy of your own chamber. You pray and do various other things—fasting and almsgiving and doing your good deeds unobserved. But you also have to live your life in the world. That world will do its best to get you down, it will do its utmost to ruin your spiritual life. So you have to be very wary. It is a fight of faith, and you need the whole armour of God, because if you have not got it, you will be defeated. 'We wrestle not against flesh and blood.' It is a stern battle, it is a mighty conflict.

Our Lord teaches that this attack from the world, or this temptation to worldliness, generally takes two main forms. First of all there may be a positive love of the world. Secondly, there may be anxiety, or a spirit of anxious care with respect to it. We shall see that our Lord shows that one is as dangerous as the other. He deals with the love of the world from verses 19 to 24, and He deals with the problem of being conquered by anxiety and care with respect to the world and its life and all its affairs, from verse 25 to the end of the chapter.

Again, however, we must remember that He treats both aspects of the problem still in terms of our relationship to our heavenly Father. So, as we enter into the details of His teaching, we must never forget the great principles which govern everything. We must again be very careful that we do not reduce this teaching to a number of rules and regulations. If we do that, we shall fall immediately into the whole error of monasticism. There are some people who are so worried about the cares and the affairs of this life that for them there is only one thing to do, that is to get out of it. So they shut themselves up in monasteries and become monks, or live as hermits in their lonely cells. But that is the false view which is found nowhere in the teaching of the Bible, where we are shown how to overcome the world while living in the midst of it.

Our Lord puts His teaching first of all in the form of a blunt assertion, which is also an injunction. He lays down a law, a great principle. And having given the principle, He then, in His infinite kindness and condescension, supplies us with various reasons and considerations which will help us to carry out His injunction. As we read words like these, we must surely again be amazed and impressed by His condescension. He has a right to lay down laws and then leave us with them. But He never does that. He states His law, He gives us His principle, and then in His kindness He gives us reasons, He supplies us with arguments which will help us and strengthen us. We are not meant to rely upon them, but they are a great help, and sometimes when our faith is weak, they are of inestimable value.

First and foremost then, here is the injunction: 'Lay not up for yourselves treasures upon earth . . . but lay up for yourselves treasures in heaven'. That is the injunction, that is the exhortation. The remainder, you see, goes into the realm of reason and explanation. 'Lay not up for yourselves treasures upon earth, where moth and rust doth corrupt, and where thieves break through and steal; but lay up for yourselves treasures in heaven, where neither moth nor rust doth corrupt, and where thieves do not break through nor steal.' But look first of all at the exhortation itself. It is a twofold one—negative and positive. Our Lord puts the truth in such a way that we are left without excuse. If any of us Christian people find ourselves receiving a very poor reward when we come to the great judgment of rewards, we shall have no excuse at all.

Negatively, then, He says, 'Lay not up for yourselves treasures upon earth'. What does He mean by this? First of all we must avoid interpreting this only with respect to money. Many have done that, and have regarded this as a statement addressed only to rich people. That, I suggest, is foolish. It is addressed to all others also. He does not say, 'Lay not up for yourselves money', but, 'Lay not up for yourselves treasures'. 'Treasures' is a very large term and all-inclusive. It includes money, but it is not money only. It means something much more important. Our Lord is concerned here not so much about our possessions as with our attitude towards our possessions. It is not what a man may have, but what he thinks of his wealth, what his attitude is towards it. There is nothing wrong in having wealth in and of itself; what can be very wrong is a man's relationship to his wealth. And the same thing is equally true about everything that money can buy.

Indeed we go further. It is a question of one's whole attitude towards life in this world. Our Lord is dealing here with people who get their main, or even total, satisfaction in this life from things that belong to this world only. What He is warning against here, in other words, is that a man should confine his ambition, his interests and his hopes to this life. That is what He is concerned about, and viewed in that way, it becomes a much bigger subject than the mere possession of money. Poor people need this exhortation about not laying up treasures upon earth quite as much as the rich. We all have treasures in some shape or form. It may not be money. It may be husband, wife or children; it may be some gift we have which in actual worth and monetary value is very small. To some people their treasure is their house. That whole danger of being house proud, of living for your house and home is dealt with here. No matter what it is, or how small it is, if it is everything to you, that is your treasure, that is the thing for which you are living. This is the danger against which our Lord is warning us at this particular point.

That gives us some idea of what He means by 'treasures upon earth', and you see it is almost endless. Not only love of money, but love of honour, the love of position, the love of status, the love of one's work in an illegitimate sense, whatever it may be, anything that stops with this life and this world. These are the things of which we must be wary, lest they become our treasure.

Having said that, we come to a very practical question. How does one 'lay up' treasures on earth with respect to these things? Once more we can merely give some general indications as to what it means. It may mean living to hoard and amass wealth as wealth. Many people do that, and our Lord may have had that chiefly in mind. But surely it has a wider reference. Our Lord's injunction means avoiding anything that centres on this world only. It is, as we have just seen, all-inclusive. It applies to people who, though they may not be interested in wealth or money at all, are yet interested in other things which are entirely worldly in the last analysis. There are people who have often been guilty of sad and serious lapses in their spiritual life because of this very

II—6

thing we are considering. They cannot be tempted by money, but they can be tempted by status and position. If the devil comes and offers them some material bribe they will smile at it. But if he comes with guile, and, in connection with their Christian work, offers them some exalted position, they persuade themselves that their one interest is in the work, and they accept and receive it, and you soon begin to observe a gradual decline in their spiritual authority and power. Promotion has done endless harm in the Church of God to men who have been quite honest and sincere, but who have not been on guard against this danger. They have been laying up treasures on earth without knowing it. Their interest has suddenly been moved from that one centre of pleasing God and working for His honour and His glory, and has turned, almost without their knowing it, to themselves and their own engagement in the work.

In such ways a man can be laying up treasures on earth, and it is so subtle that even good people can be a man's greatest enemy. Many a preacher has been ruined by his congregation. Their praise, their encouragement of him as a man, has almost ruined him as the messenger of God, and he has become guilty of laying up treasures on earth. He tends almost unconsciously to be controlled by the desire to have his people's good opinion and praise, and the moment that happens a man is laying up treasures on earth. The possible examples are almost endless. I am simply trying to give you some slight indication of the realm and scope of this amazing injunction. 'Lay not up for yourselves treasures on earth.' Whatever the *form* may be, it is the *principle* that matters.

Let us look now at the positive side of the injunction, 'Lay up for yourselves treasures in heaven'. It is very important that we should be clear about this. Some people have interpreted it as meaning that our Lord is teaching that a man can achieve his own salvation. 'Treasure in heaven,' they say, 'means a man's salvation and his eternal destiny. Therefore, is not our Lord exhorting a man to spend his whole life in making sure of his eternal destiny?' Patently that is wrong. That is to deny the great central New Testament doctrine of justification by faith only. Our Lord cannot mean that, because He is addressing people of whom the Beatitudes are true. It is the man who is poor in spirit, who has nothing, who is blessed. It is the man who mourns because of his sinfulness who knows that, at the end, in spite of all he may or may not have done, he can never achieve his own salvation. That interpretation, therefore, is clearly wrong. What then does it mean? It means something that is taught in many places in the Scriptures, and two other passages will help us to understand the teaching here. The first is in Luke xvi where our Lord deals with the case of the unjust steward, the man who made a quick and clever use of his position. You remember He sums it up like this. 'Make to yourselves', He says, 'friends of the mammon of unrighteousness; that, when ye fail, they may receive you into everlasting habitations.' Our Lord teaches that the children of this world are wiser in their generation than the children of light. They make sure of their own ends. Now, says our Lord in effect, I am going to take that as a principle and apply it to you. If you have money, so use it while you are here in this world that, when you arrive in glory, the people who benefited by it will be there to receive you.

The apostle Paul expounds this in 1 Timothy vi. 17-19: 'Charge them that are rich in this world, that they be not high-minded, nor trust in uncertain riches, but in the living God, who giveth us richly all things to enjoy; that they do good, that they be rich in good works, ready to distribute, willing to communicate; laying up in store for themselves a good foundation against the time to come, that they may lay hold on eternal life.' In other words, if you have been blessed with riches, use them in such a way in this world that you will be building up a balance for the next. Our Lord says exactly the same thing at the end of Matthew xxv where He talks about the people who gave Him meat when He was hungry and who visited Him in prison. They ask, 'When saw we thee an hungred, and fed thee? . . . or in prison, and came unto thee?' And He says, 'Inasmuch as ye have done it unto one of the least of these my brethren, ye have done it unto me.' You do not realize it, but in doing these good deeds to these people, you have been building up your balance in heaven, there you will receive your reward and enter into the joy of your Lord.

That is the principle which our Lord constantly emphasizes. He said to His disciples after His encounter with the rich young ruler, 'How hard is it for them that trust in riches to enter into the kingdom of God'. It is this trusting in riches, it is this fatal self-confidence, that makes it impossible for you to be poor in spirit. Or again, as He put it to the people one afternoon when He said, 'Labour not for the meat which perisheth, but for that meat which endureth unto everlasting life'. That is the kind of thing He meant by 'laying up treasures in heaven'.

How do we do this in practice? The first thing is to have a right view of life, and especially a right view of 'the glory'. That is the principle with which we started. The great fact of which we must never lose sight is that in this life we are but pilgrims. We are walking through this world under the eye of God, in the direction of God and towards our everlasting hope. That is the principle. If we always think of ourselves in that way, how can we go wrong? Everything will then fall into position. That is the great principle taught in Hebrews xi. Those mighty men, those great heroes of the faith had but one purpose. They walked 'as seeing him who is invisible'. They said they were 'strangers and pilgrims on the earth', they were making for 'a city which hath foundations, whose builder and maker is God'. So when God called out Abraham he responded. He turned to a man like Moses who had amazing prospects in the Egyptian court and commanded him to leave it all and to become a miserable shepherd for forty years, and Moses obeyed, 'for he had respect unto the recompence of the reward'. And so with all of them. What made Abraham ready to sacrifice his beloved son Isaac? What made all the other heroes of the faith prepared to do the things they did? It was that they desired 'a better country, that is, an heavenly'.

We must always start with that great principle. If we have a right view of ourselves in this world as pilgrims, as children of God going to our Father, everything falls into its true perspective. We shall immediately take a right view of our gifts and our possessions. We begin to think of ourselves only as stewards who must give an account of them. We are not the permanent holders of these things. It matters not whether it is money, or intellect, or ourselves, or our personalities, or whatever gift we may have. The worldly man thinks he himself owns them all. But the Christian starts by saying, 'I am not the possessor of these things; I merely have them on lease, and they do not really belong to me. I cannot take my wealth with me, I cannot take my gifts with me. I am but a custodian of these things'. And, at once, the great question that arises is: 'How can I use these things to the glory of God? It is God I have to meet, it is God I have to face, it is He who is my eternal Judge and my Father. It is to Him that I shall have to render up an account of my stewardship of all the things with which He has blessed me.' 'Therefore,' the Christian says to himself, 'I must be careful how I use these things, and of my attitude towards them. I must do all the things He tells me to do in order that I may please Him.'

There, then, is the way in which we can lay up treasures in heaven. It all comes back to the question of how I view myself and how I view my life in this world. Do I tell myself every day I live, that this is but another milestone I am passing, never to go back, never to come again? I am pitching my moving tent 'a day's march nearer home'. That is the great principle of which I must constantly remind myself—that I am a child of the Father placed here for His purpose, not for myself. I did not choose to come; I have not brought myself here; there is a purpose in it all. God has given me this great privilege of living in this world, and if He has endued me with any gifts, I have to realize that, although in one sense all these things are mine, ultimately, as Paul shows at the end of 1 Corinthians iii, they are God's. Therefore, regarding myself as one who has this great privilege of being a caretaker for God, a custodian and a steward, I do not cling to these things. They do not become the centre of my life and existence. I do not live for them or dwell upon them constantly in my mind; they do not absorb my life. On the contrary, I hold them loosely; I am in a state of blessed detachment from them. I am not governed by them; rather do I govern them; and as I do this I am steadily securing, and safely laying up for myself, 'treasures in heaven'.

'But what a selfish outlook', says someone. My reply is that I am but obeying the exhortation of the Lord Jesus Christ. He tells us to lay up for ourselves treasures in heaven, and the saints have always done so. They believed in the reality of the glory that awaited them. They hoped to get there and their one desire was to enjoy it in all its perfection and in all its fullness. If we are anxious to 'follow in their train' and to enjoy the same glory we had better listen to our Lord's exhortation, 'Lay not up for yourselves treasures upon earth . . . but lay up for yourselves treasures in heaven.'

CHAPTER EIGHT

GOD OR MAMMON

IN our analysis of verses 19–24 we have seen that our Lord first of all lays down a proposition or a commandment, 'Lay not up for yourselves treasures upon earth . . . but lay up for yourselves treasures in heaven.' In other words, He tells us that we are so to live in this world, and so to use everything we have, whether our possessions, or gifts, or talents, or propensities, that we shall be laying up for ourselves treasures in heaven.

Then, having given us the injunction in that way, our Lord proceeds to supply us with reasons for doing this. I would remind you again that here we have an illustration of the wonderful condescension and understanding of our blessed Lord. He has no need to give us reasons. It is for Him to command. But He stoops to our weakness, mighty as He is, and He comes to our aid and supplies us with these reasons for carrying out His commandment. He does so in a very remarkable manner. He elaborates the reasons and presses them upon our consideration. He does not merely give us one reason; He gives us a number. He works it out for us in a series of logical propositions, and, of course, there can be no doubt at all but that He does this, not only because He is anxious to help us, but also, and still more perhaps, because of the desperate seriousness of the subject with which He is dealing. Indeed, we shall see that this is one of the most serious matters which we can ever consider together.

Again we must remember that these words were addressed to Christian people. This is not what our Lord has to say to the unbeliever out in the world; this is the warning that He gives to the Christian. We are dealing here with the subject of worldliness, or worldly-mindedness, and the whole problem of the world; but we must cease to think of it in terms of people who are in the world outside. This is the peculiar danger of *Christian* people. At this point our Lord is dealing with them and nobody else. You can argue if you like that if all this is true for the Christian, it is much more so for the non-Christian. That is a perfectly fair deduction; but there is nothing so fatal and tragic as to think that words like these have nothing to do with us because we are Christians. Indeed, this is perhaps the most urgent word that is needed by Christian people at this very moment. The world is so subtle, worldliness is such a pervasive thing, that we are all guilty of it, and often without realizing it. We tend to label worldliness as meaning certain particular things only, and always the things of which we are not guilty. We therefore argue that this has nothing to say to us. But worldliness is all-pervasive, and is not confined to certain things. It does not just mean going to theatres or cinemas, or doing a few things of that nature. No, worldliness is an attitude towards life. It is a general outlook, and it is so subtle that it can come into the most holy things of all, as we saw earlier.

We might digress here for a moment and look at this subject from the standpoint of the great political interest in this country, particularly, for example, at the time of a General Election. What, in the last analysis, is the real interest? What is the real thing that people on both sides and all sides are concerned about? They are interested in 'treasures upon earth', whether they be people who have treasures or whether they be people who would like to have them. They are all interested in the treasures; and it is most instructive to listen to what people say, and to observe how they betray themselves and the worldliness of which they are guilty, and the way in which they are laying up for themselves treasures upon earth. To be very practical (and if the preaching of the gospel is not practical it is not true preaching), there is a very simple test which we can apply to ourselves to see whether these things apply to us or not. When, at the time of a General or local Election, we are called on to make a choice of candidates, do we find ourselves believing that one political point of view is altogether right and the other altogether wrong? If we do, I suggest we are somehow or another laying up for ourselves treasures on earth. If we say that the truth is altogether on one side or the other, then if we analyse our motives we shall discover it is because we are either protecting something or anxious to have something. Another good way of testing ourselves is to ask ourselves quite simply and honestly why we hold our particular views. What is our real interest? What is our motive? What, when we are quite honest and truthful with ourselves, is really at the back of these particular political views that we hold? It is a most illuminating question if we are really honest. I suggest that most people will find if they face that question quite honestly, that there are some treasures upon earth about which they are concerned, and in which they are interested.

The next test is this. To what extent are our feelings engaged in this matter? How much bitterness is there, how much violence, how much anger and scorn and passion? Apply that test, and again we shall find that the feeling is aroused almost invariably by the concern about laying up treasures upon earth. The last test is this. Are we viewing these things with a kind of detachment and objectivity or not? What is our attitude towards all these things? Do we instinctively think of ourselves as pilgrims, and mere sojourners in this world, who of course have to be interested in these things while we are here? Such an interest is certainly right, it is our duty. But what is our ultimate attitude? Are we controlled by it? Or do we stand apart and regard it objectively, as something which is ephemeral, something which does not really belong to the essence of our life and being, something with which we are concerned only for a while, as we are passing through this life? We should ask ourselves these questions in order that we may make quite certain whether this injunction of our Lord is speaking to us. Those are some of the ways in which we can find out very simply whether we are or are not guilty of laying up for ourselves treasures upon earth, and not laying up for ourselves treasures in heaven.

When we come to consider our Lord's arguments against laying up treasures on earth, we find that the first is one which we may very well describe as the argument of common sense, or of ordinary observation. 'Lay not up for yourselves treasures upon earth.' Why? For this reason: 'where moth and rust doth corrupt, and where thieves break through and steal'. But why should I lay up treasures in heaven? For this reason: 'where neither moth nor rust doth corrupt, and where thieves do not break through nor steal'. Our Lord is saying that worldly treasures do not last; that they are transitory, passing, ephemeral. 'Change and decay in all around I see.' 'Where moth and rust doth corrupt.'

How true it is. There is an element of decay in all these things, whether we like it or not. Our Lord puts it in terms of the moth and rust that tend to lodge themselves in these things and destroy them. Spiritually we can put it like this. These things never fully satisfy. There is always something wrong with them; they always lack something. There is no person on earth who is fully satisfied; and though in a sense some may appear to have everything that they desire, still they want something else. Happiness cannot be purchased.

There is, however, another way of looking at the effect of moth and rust spiritually. Not only is there an element of decay in these things; it is also true that we always tend to tire of them. We may enjoy them for a while, but somehow or other they begin to pall or we lose interest in them. That is why we are always talking about new things and seeking them. Fashions change; and though we are very enthusiastic about certain things for a while, soon they no longer interest us as they did. Is it not true that as age advances these things cease to satisfy us? Old people generally do not like the same things as young people, or the young the same as the old. As we get older these things seem to become different, there is an element of moth and rust. We could even go further and put it more strongly and say that there is an impurity in them. At their best they are all infected. Do what you will you cannot get rid of the impurity; the moth and rust are there and all your chemicals do not stop these processes. Peter says a wonderful thing in this very connection: 'Whereby are given unto us exceeding great and precious promises; that by these ye might be partakers of the divine nature, having escaped the corruption that is in the world through lust' (2 Peter i. 4). There is corruption in all these earthly things; they are all impure.

The last fact, therefore, about these things is that they inevitably perish. Your most beautiful flower is beginning to die immediately you pluck it. You will soon have to throw it away. That is true of everything in this life and world. It does not matter what it is, it is passing, it is all fading away. Everything that has life is, as the result of sin, subject to this process—'moth and rust doth corrupt'. Things develop holes and become useless, and at the end they are gone and become utterly corrupt. The most perfect physique will eventually give way and break down and die; the most beautiful countenance will in a sense become ugly when the process of corruption has got going; the brightest gifts tend to fade. Your great genius may be seen gibbering in delirium as the result of disease. However wonderful and beautiful and glorious things may be, they all perish. That is why, perhaps, the saddest of all failures in life is the failure of the philosopher who believes in worshipping goodness, beauty and truth; because there is no such thing as perfect goodness, there is no such thing as unalloyed beauty; there is an element of wrong and of sin and a lie in the highest truths. 'Moth and rust doth corrupt.'

'Yes,' says our Lord, 'and thieves break through and steal.' We must not stay with these things, they are so obvious, and yet we are so slow to recognize them. There are many thieves in this life and they are always threatening us. We think we are safe in our house; but we find thieves have broken in and ransacked it. Other marauders are always threatening us—illness, a business loss, some industrial collapse, war and finally death itself. It matters not what it is that we tend to hold on to in this world, one or other of these thieves is always threatening and will eventually take it from us. It is not only money. It may be some person for whom you are really living, your pleasure is in that one person. Beware, my friends; there are robbers and thieves who are bound to come and eventually rob you of these possessions. Take our possessions at their highest as well as their lowest; they are all subject to these robbers, these attacks. 'The thieves break through and steal', and we cannot prevent them. So our Lord appeals to our common sense, and reminds us that these worldly treasures never last. 'Change and decay in all around I see.'

But look at the other, positive side. 'Lay up for yourselves treasures in heaven, where neither moth nor rust doth corrupt, and where thieves do not break through nor steal.' This is wonderful and full of glory. Peter puts it in a phrase. He says 'to an inheritance incorruptible, and undefiled, and that fadeth not away, reserved in heaven for you' (1 Peter i. 4). 'The things which are not seen are eternal,' says St. Paul; it is the things which are seen that are temporal (2 Corinthians iv. 18). These heavenly things are imperishable and the thieves cannot break through and steal. Why? Because God Himself is reserving them for us. There is no enemy that can ever rob us of them, or can ever enter in. It is impossible because God Himself is the Guardian. Spiritual pleasures are invulnerable, they are in a place which is impregnable. 'I am persuaded, that neither death, nor life, nor angels, nor principalities, nor powers, nor things present, nor things to come, nor height, nor depth, nor any other creature, shall be able to separate us from the love of God, which is in Christ Jesus our Lord' (Romans viii. 38, 39). Furthermore, there is nothing impure there; naught that corrupts shall enter in. There is no sin there, nor element of decay. It is the realm of eternal life and eternal light. He dwells 'in the light which no man can approach unto', as the apostle Paul puts it (1 Timothy vi. 16). Heaven is the realm of life and light and purity, and nothing belonging to death, nothing tainted or polluted can gain admission there. It is perfect; and the treasures of the soul and of the spirit belong to that realm. Lay them up there, says our Lord, because there is no moth nor rust there, and no thief can ever break through nor steal.

It is an appeal to common sense. Do we not know that these things are true? Are they not true of necessity? Do we not see it all as we live in this world? Take up your morning newspaper and look at the death column; look at all that is happening. We know all these things. Why do we not practise them and live accordingly? Why do we lay up treasures on earth when we know what is going to happen to them? And why do we not lay up treasures in heaven where we know that there is purity and joy, holiness and everlasting bliss?

That, however, is merely the first argument, the argument of common sense. But our Lord does not stop at that. His second argument is based upon the terrible spiritual danger involved in laying up treasures on earth and not in heaven. That is a general heading, but our Lord divides it into certain sub-sections. The first thing against which He warns us in this spiritual sense is the awful grip and power of these earthly things upon us. You notice the terms He uses. He says, 'Where your treasure is, there will your heart be also.' The heart! Then in verse 24 He talks about the mind. 'No man can serve two masters'—and we should notice the word 'serve'. These are the expressive terms He uses in order to impress upon us the terrible control that these things tend to exercise over us. Are we not all aware of them the moment we stop to think—the tyranny of persons, the tyranny of the world? This is not something we can think about at a distance as it were. We are all involved in this; we are all in the grip of this awful power of worldliness which really will master us unless we are aware of it.

But it is not only powerful; it is very subtle. It is the thing that really controls most men's lives. Have you seen the change, the subtle change, that tends to take place in men's lives as they succeed and prosper in this world? It does not happen to those who are truly spiritual men; but if they are not, it invariably happens. Why is it that idealism is generally associated with youth and not with middle age and old age? Why do men tend to become cynical as they get older? Why does the noble outlook upon life tend to go? It is because we all become victims of 'treasures on earth', and if you watch you can see it in the lives of men. Read the biographies. Many a young man starts out with a bright vision; but in a very subtle way—not that he falls into gross sin—he becomes influenced, perhaps when he is at college, by an outlook that is essentially worldly. Though it may be highly intellectual, he nevertheless loses something that was vital in his soul and spirit. He is still a very nice man and, moreover, just and wise; but he is not the man he was when he began. Something has been lost. Yes; this is a familiar phenomenon: 'Shades of the prison house begin to close upon the growing boy.' Do we not all know something about it? It is there; it is a prison house, and it fastens itself upon us unless we are aware of it. This grip, this power, masters us and we become slaves.

However, our Lord does not stop at the general. He is so anxious to show us this terrible danger that He works it out in detail. He tells us that this terrible thing that grips us tends to affect the entire personality; not merely part of us, but the whole man. And the first thing He mentions is the 'heart'. Having laid down the injunction He says, 'For where your treasure is, there will your heart be also.' These things grip and master our feelings, our affections and all our sensibility. All that part of our nature is absolutely gripped by them and we love them. Read John iii. 19. 'This is the condemnation, that light is come into the world, and men loved darkness rather than light, because their deeds were evil.' We love these things. We pretend that we only like them, but really we love them. They move us deeply.

The next thing about them is a little more subtle. They not only grip the heart, they grip the mind. Our Lord puts it in this way: 'The light of the body is the eye: if therefore thine eye be single, thy whole body shall be full of light. But if thine eye be evil, thy whole body shall be full of darkness. If therefore the light that is in thee be darkness, how great is that darkness!' (verses 22, 23). This picture of the eye is just His way of describing, by means of an illustration, the way in which we look at things. And according to our Lord, there are but two ways of looking at everything in this world. There is what He calls the 'single' eye, the eye of the spiritual man who sees things really as they are, truly and without any double view. His eye is clear and he sees things normally. But there is the other eye which He calls the 'evil' eye, which is a kind of double vision, or, if you like, it is the eye in which the lenses are not clear. There are mists and opacities and we see things in a blurred way. That is the evil eye. It is coloured by certain prejudices, coloured by certain lusts and desires. It is not a clear vision; it is all cloudy, coloured by these various tints and taints. That is what is meant by this statement which has so often confused people, because they do not take it in its context. Our Lord in this picture is still dealing with the laying up of treasures. Having shown that where the treasure is, the heart will be also, He says that it is not only the heart but the mind as well. These are the things that control man.

Let us work out this principle. Is it not amazing to notice how much of our thought is based upon these earthly treasures? The divisions in thought in almost every realm are almost entirely controlled by prejudice, not by pure thought. How very little thinking there is in this country at the time of a General Election for example. None of the protagonists reason; they simply present prejudices. How little thought there is on every side. It is so obvious in the political realm. But alas, it is not confined to politics. This blurring of the vision by love of earthly treasures tends to affect us morally also! How clever we all are at explaining that a particular thing we do is not really dishonest. Of course if a man smashes a window and steals jewellery he is a robber; but if I just manipulate my income tax return. . . .! Certainly that is not robbery, we say, and we persuade ourselves that all is well. Ultimately there is but one reason for our doing these things, and that is our love of earthly treasures. These things control the mind as well as the heart. Our views and our whole ethical outlook are controlled by these things.

Even worse than that, however, our religious outlook is controlled by these things also. 'Demas hath forsaken me', writes Paul. Why? 'Having loved this present world.' How often this is seen in the matter of service. These are the things that determine our action, though we do not recognize it. Our Lord says in another place: 'Take heed to yourselves, lest at any time your hearts be overcharged with surfeiting, and drunkenness, and cares of this life, and so that day come upon you unawares. For as a snare shall it come on all them that dwell on the face of the whole earth. Watch ye therefore, and pray always, that ye may be accounted worthy to escape all these things that shall come to pass, and to stand before the Son of man' (Luke xxi. 34-36). It is not only evil doing that dulls the mind and makes us incapable of thinking clearly. The cares of this world, settling down in life, enjoying our life and our family, any one of these things, our worldly position or our comforts—these are equally as dangerous as surfeiting and drunkenness. There is no doubt but that much of the so-called wisdom which men claim in this world is nothing, in the last analysis, but this concern about earthly treasures.

But lastly, these things not only grip the heart and mind, they also affect the will. Says our Lord, 'No man can serve two masters'; and the moment we mention the word 'serve' we are in the realm of the will, the realm of action. You notice how perfectly logical this is. What we do is the result of what we think; so what is going to determine our lives and the exercise of our wills is what we think, and that in turn is determined by where our treasure is—our heart. So we can sum it up like this. These earthly treasures are so powerful that they grip the entire personality. They grip a man's heart, his mind and his will; they tend to affect his spirit, his soul and his whole being. Whatever realm of life we may be looking at, or thinking about, we shall find these things are there. Everyone is affected by them; they are a terrible danger.

But the last step is the most solemn and serious of all. We must remember that the way in which we look at these things ultimately determines our relationship to God. 'No man can serve two masters: for either he will hate the one, and love the other; or else he will hold to the one, and despise the other. Ye cannot serve God and mammon.' This is indeed a very solemn thing, and that is why it is dealt with so frequently in Scripture. The truth of this proposition is obvious. Both make a totalitarian demand upon us. Worldly things really do make a totalitarian demand as we have seen. How they tend to grip the entire personality and affect us everywhere! They demand our entire devotion; they want us to live for them absolutely. Yes, but so does God. 'Thou shalt love the Lord thy God with all thy heart, and with all thy soul, and with all thy mind, and with all thy strength.' Not in a material sense necessarily, but in some sense or other He says to us all, 'Go, sell all that thou hast, and come, follow me.' 'He that loveth father or mother more than me is not worthy of me: and he that loveth son or daughter more than me is not worthy of me.' It is a totalitarian demand. Notice it again in verse 24: 'Either he will hate the one, and love the other; or else he will hold to the one, and despise the other.' It is 'either—or'; compromise is completely impossible at this point. 'Ye cannot serve God and mammon.'

This is something which is so subtle that many of us miss it completely at the present time. Some of us are violent opponents of what we speak of as 'atheistic materialism'. But lest we may feel too happy about ourselves because we are opponents of that, let us realize that the Bible tells us that all materialism is atheistic. Ye cannot serve God and mammon; it is impossible. So if a materialistic outlook is really controlling us, we are godless,

whatever we may say. There are many atheists who speak
religious language; but our Lord tells us here that even worse
than atheistic materialism is a materialism that thinks it is godly
—'if the light that is in thee be darkness, how great is that
darkness!' The man who thinks he is godly because he talks
about God, and says he believes in God, and goes to a place of
worship occasionally, but is really living for certain earthly
things—how great is that man's darkness! There is a perfect
illustration of that in the Old Testament. Study carefully
2 Kings xvii. 24–41. Here is what we are told. The Assyrians
conquered some area; then they took their own people and
settled them in that area. These Assyrians of course did not
worship God. Then some lions came and destroyed their
property. 'This', they said, 'has happened to us because we do
not worship the God of this particular land. We will get priestly
instruction on this.' So they found a priest who instructed them
generally in the religion of Israel. And then they thought that all
would be well. But this is what Scripture said about them: they
'feared the Lord, and served their graven images.'

What a terrible thing that is. It alarms me. It is not what we
say that matters. In the last day many shall say, 'Lord, Lord,
have we not done this, that and the other?' But He will say unto
them, 'I never knew you'. 'Not every one that saith unto me,
Lord, Lord, shall enter into the kingdom of heaven; but he that
doeth the will of my Father.' Whom do you serve? That is the
question, and it is either God or mammon. There is nothing in
the last analysis that is so insulting to God as to take His name
upon us and yet to show clearly that we are serving mammon in
some shape or form. That is the most terrible thing of all. It is the
greatest insult to God; and how easily and unconsciously we can
all become guilty of this.

I remember once hearing a preacher tell a story which he
assured us was simple, literal truth. It illustrates perfectly the
point which we are considering. It is the story of a farmer who
one day went happily and with great joy in his heart to report to
his wife and family that their best cow had given birth to twin
calves, one red and one white. And he said, 'You know I have
suddenly had a feeling and impulse that we must dedicate one
of these calves to the Lord. We will bring them up together, and
when the time comes we will sell one and keep the proceeds, and
we will sell the other and give the proceeds to the Lord's work.'
His wife asked him which he was going to dedicate to the Lord.
'There is no need to bother about that now,' he replied, 'we will

treat them both in the same way, and when the time comes we will do as I say.' And off he went. In a few months the man entered his kitchen looking very miserable and unhappy. When his wife asked him what was troubling him, he answered, 'I have bad news to give you. The Lord's calf is dead.' 'But', she said, 'you had not decided which was to be the Lord's calf.' 'Oh yes,' he said; 'I had always decided it was to be the white one, and it is the white one that has died. The Lord's calf is dead.' We may laugh at that story, but God forbid that we should be laughing at ourselves. It is always the Lord's calf that dies. When money becomes difficult, the first thing we economize on is our contribution to God's work. It is always the first thing to go. Perhaps we must not say 'always', for that would be unfair; but with so many it is the first thing, and the things we really like are the last to go. 'Ye cannot serve God and mammon.' These things tend to come between us and God, and our attitude to them ultimately determines our relationship to God. The mere fact that we believe in God, and call Him, Lord, Lord, and likewise with Christ, is not proof in and of itself that we are serving Him, that we recognize His totalitarian demand, and have yielded ourselves gladly and readily to Him. 'Let every man examine himself.'

CHAPTER NINE

SIN'S FOUL BONDAGE

IN our consideration of this particular passage we have so far been dealing with what we might call the direct and explicit teaching of our Lord concerning this matter of treasures upon earth and treasures in heaven. But we cannot leave it at that, because there is surely something else here. In these verses 19–24, there is indirect teaching, there is implicit teaching; and we fail to pay attention to such teaching in Scripture always at our peril. Our Lord is concerned with the practical aspect of this matter, but obviously there is something else involved as well. In warning us about this very practical matter, He also deals incidentally with most important doctrine, although He does not set out primarily to do that. We can put it like this. Why is it that these instructions are necessary? Why is it that the Bible is full of this kind of warning? It is to be found everywhere; this is only one example, but there are many others which we could take. What is it that makes it so necessary for our Lord, and the apostles afterwards, to warn us as Christian people about these things?

Surely there is only one answer to that question. All this is simply due to sin and its effects. There is a sense in which one is astounded when one reads a passage such as this. One tends to say, 'I am a Christian; I have a new view of things, and I do not need this'. And yet we see it is necessary, and we all need it. In various ways all of us are not only being attacked by this, but are being conquered by it. There is only one thing that explains that, and that is sin, the terrible power and effect of sin upon mankind. So that here we can see that, as our Lord expounds His teaching, gives His commandment and states His reasons, He is incidentally telling us a great deal about sin and what it does to man.

I

The first thing we must note is that sin is obviously something that has an entirely disturbing and upsetting effect upon the normal balance in man, and the normal functioning of his qualities. There are three parts to man. He was made by God, body, mind and spirit, or, if you prefer it, body, soul and spirit;

and the highest is the spirit. Next to that comes the soul, and next
to that the body. Not that there is anything wrong with the body,
but that is the relative order. The effect of sin is that the normal
functions of man have been entirely disturbed. There is no
doubt that, in one sense, the highest gift that God has given to
man is the gift of mind. According to the Scripture man was
made in the image of God; and a part of the image of God in
man is undoubtedly the mind, the ability to think and to reason,
especially in the highest sense and in a spiritual sense. Man,
therefore, was obviously meant to function in the following way.
His mind, being the highest faculty and propensity that he
possesses, should always come first. Things are perceived with
the mind and analysed by it. Then come the affections, the
heart, the feeling, the sensibility given to man by God. Then
thirdly there is that other quality, that other faculty, called the
will, the power by which we put into operation the things we
have understood, the things we have desired as the result of
apprehension.

That is the way in which God made man, and that is how
man was meant to function. He was meant to understand and
to be governed and controlled by his understanding. He was to
love that which he thus understood to be best and truest for
himself and for all concerned; and then he was to put all that
into practice and into operation. But the effect of the Fall and of
sin upon man has been to upset that order and balance. You
notice how our Lord puts it here. He lays down His instruction:
'Lay not up for yourselves treasures upon earth, where moth and
rust doth corrupt, and where thieves break through and steal:
but lay up for yourselves treasures in heaven, where neither moth
nor rust doth corrupt, and where thieves do not break through
nor steal. For where your treasure is, there will your heart be
also.' The heart comes first. Then He goes on to the mind and
says, 'The light of the body is the eye: if therefore thine eye be
single, thy whole body shall be full of light. But if thine eye be
evil, thy whole body shall be full of darkness.' The heart is first,
the mind second, and the will third; for 'No man can serve two
masters: for either he will hate the one, and love the other; or
else he will hold to the one, and despise the other. Ye cannot
serve God and mammon.'

We have already considered the way in which these earthly
treasures and possessions tend to master and control the entire
personality—heart, and mind, and will. Then we were not

concerned about the order; but this time we are very concerned about the order in which our Lord puts these things, for what He says here is nothing but the simple truth about us all by nature. Man, as the result of sin and the Fall, is no longer governed by his mind and understanding; he is governed by his desires, his affections and his lusts. That is the teaching of Scripture. Thus we see that man is in the terrible predicament of being no longer governed by his highest faculty, but by something else, something subsidiary.

There are many Scriptures which prove this. Take that great statement in John iii. 19: 'This is the condemnation (this is the final condemnation of mankind), that light is come (or has come) into the world.' What, then, is the matter with man? Does he not believe it? Does he not accept it? No, 'This is the condemnation, that light is come into the world, and men loved darkness rather than light, because their deeds were evil'. Man, in other words, instead of looking at life with his mind, looks at it with his desires and affections. He prefers darkness; he is controlled by his heart instead of by his head. We must be quite clear about this. This is not to say that man as God made him should not have a heart, and should not feel things. The important thing is that no man should be *governed* by his emotions and desires. That is the effect of sin. A man should be governed by his mind, his understanding.

This surely is the final answer to all those people who are not Christian, and who say they are not Christian because they think and because they reason. The simple truth about them is that they are governed, not by their minds, but by their hearts and by their prejudices. Their elaborate attempts to justify themselves intellectually is nothing but an attempt to camouflage the godlessness of their hearts. They are trying to justify the kind of life they are living by putting up an intellectual position; but the real trouble is that they are governed by desires and by lusts. They do not approach the truth with the mind, they approach it with all these prejudices which come from the heart. As the Psalmist puts it so perfectly: 'The fool hath said in his heart, There is no God.' That is what the unbeliever always says, and that is why he says it; and then he tries to find an intellectual reason to justify what his heart wants to say.

Our Lord here reminds us of this plainly. It is the heart that covets these worldly things, and the heart in sinful man is so powerful that it governs his mind, his understanding and his intellect. Man likes to think of himself as a gigantic intellect.

Scientists are often fond of claiming this; but I can assure you that scientists are sometimes the most prejudiced men you can meet. Some of them are prepared to manipulate facts in order to buttress their theory. They often start their books by saying that a certain idea is but a theory, but a few pages later you find them referring to it as a fact. That is the heart in operation and not the mind. This is one of the greatest tragedies about sin and its effects. In the first instance it upsets the order and the balance; and the greatest and supreme gift becomes subservient to the lesser. 'Where your treasure is, there will your heart be also.'

II

The second thing that sin does is to blind man in certain vital respects. Of course that follows by a kind of inevitable logic. If the mind is not always in control there is of necessity going to be a kind of blinding. The apostle Paul's way of putting it is this: 'If our gospel be hid, it is hid to them that are lost: in whom the god of this world hath blinded the minds of them which believe not' (2 Corinthians iv. 3 and 4). That is precisely what sin does and it does it through the heart. We can see how our Lord illustrates that principle in this short paragraph at which we are looking. Sin blinds the mind of man to things which are perfectly obvious; and so, though they are so obvious, man in sin does not see them.

Take this question of worldly treasures. It is a simple fact that none of them continue. There is no need to argue about that; it is the obvious truth. We looked at some of these treasures in our last chapter. People pride themselves on personal appearance. It is bound to deteriorate. They are going to be desperately ill one day and die, and decay will set in. It is bound to happen; yet people pride themselves on this, and may even sacrifice their belief in God for it. The same thing applies to money. We cannot take it with us when we die, and we are always liable to lose it. All these things pass away; they are all bound to go. If a man sits down and really faces that, he must admit that it is the simple truth; yet all people who are not Christian tend to live on the opposite assumption. They are jealous and envious of one another, they will sacrifice everything for these things—these things that are bound to come to an end and which they are bound to leave behind them. The real situation is so obvious, and yet they do not seem to see the obvious. If a man just sits down and says, 'Well, now; here I am today living in this world. But what is going to happen to me? What is my future?', he is bound to say in reply, 'I may go on living like this for a number of years, or I may not; I do not know. I may not be alive to-morrow; I may not be alive a week today; I do not know. But I know for certain that this is bound to come to an end. There will be an end to my life in this world. I have to die; and when I die I have to leave all these things. I shall have to leave my house, my loved ones, my possessions. I have to leave it all behind and go on without them.' We know that that is the simple fact. But how often do we face that fact? How often do we live in the realization of it? Is our whole life controlled by the consciousness of that obvious truth? The answer is that it is not; and the reason for this is sin which blinds the mind of man to that which is absolutely obvious. 'Change and decay in all around I see' we often sing. Yet though I do see it, I do not seem to perceive it.

In the same way sin blinds us to the relative values of things. Take time and eternity. We are creatures here in time and we are going on to eternity. There is no comparison between the relative importance of time and eternity. Time is limited and eternity is endless and absolute. Yet do we live as realizing these relative values? Is it not again a simple fact that we give ourselves to things that belong to time and entirely ignore the things that are eternal? Is it not true that all the things about which we bother so much belong to a very short span of time, and though we know that there are other things that are eternal and endless, we scarcely stop to think about them at all? That is the effect of sin—relative values are not appreciated.

Or take darkness and light. There is no real comparison between them. There is nothing more wonderful than light. It is one of the most amazing things in the universe. God Himself is light and 'in him is no darkness at all'. We know the kind of deeds that belong to darkness, the things that happen in the dark, and under the cover of night. But there will be no darkness and no night in heaven. It is all light and glory there. But how slow we are to appreciate the relative value of light and darkness. 'Men love darkness rather than light, because their deeds are evil.'

Then think again of the value of man and of God. The whole of life apart from Christianity is evaluated in terms of man. He is the one to be considered, his being and his welfare. All who are not Christian are living for man, for themselves and others like themselves. God in the meantime is being forgotten and ignored. He is told to wait until we have a little more time for Him. This is surely characteristic of the life of all mankind as affected by sin. We do not hesitate to turn our backs upon God and say, in effect,

'When I am ill, or on my deathbed I will turn to God; but now I am living for myself.' Our worldly life is being put before God. This is blindness. The mind is blind to relative values. Think of men coveting earthly wealth and earthly riches, position and status, and putting all that before becoming 'heirs of God, and joint-heirs with Christ', before becoming inheritors of the whole world! 'Blessed are the meek: for they shall inherit the earth.' But men do not consider that, and do not covet it, so intent are they upon the immediate.

Consider yet another respect in which sin and evil blind the mind of man. They blind him to the impossibility of mixing opposites. It is all here. Man is always trying to mix things which cannot be mixed. Still worse is the fact that he persuades himself that he can do it successfully. He is quite sure this compromise is possible, and yet our Lord tells us it is not. If you want it stated philosophically, you have but to turn to Aristotle and his axiom to the effect that 'there is no mean between two opposites'. Opposites are opposites, and you will never get a mean between them. Here it is. There is no possible mixing of light and darkness. It is no longer light if you do, and it is no longer darkness. Neither can you mix God and mammon, for no man can serve two masters. It is one or the other, 'for either he will hate the one, and love the other; or else he will hold to the one, and despise the other.' These are absolutes, and if we were capable of thinking clearly we should recognize them as such. They are both totalitarian. Both demand our entire allegiance, and therefore they cannot be mixed. But man in sin and in his supposed cleverness sees two things at one and the same time; and he glories in this double vision. Our Lord, however, tells us here that it cannot be done. We cannot love two opposite things at the same time. Love is exclusive; it is demanding, and always insists upon the absolute. It is either one or the other; it must be light or darkness. The eye is single or not single; it is either God or mammon.

Is not the failure to recognize this the whole trouble with the world today? I fear it is no longer the trouble with the world only. Is it not the trouble with the Church also? The Church of God for many a day has been trying to mix certain incompatibles. If it is a spiritual society, then we cannot mix the world with it in any shape or form. It does not matter what the form is. 'The world' does not mean gross sin only; it means things which are quite legitimate in and of themselves. It is this constant compromising in the life of the Church that has been her ruination ever since the days of Constantine. Once you have lost the division between the world and the Church, the Church ceases to be truly Christian. But, thank God, there have been revivals, there have been people who have seen this truth and who have refused to compromise. It is the only hope for the Church. We have been trying to sustain her by worldly methods, and it is not surprising that she is as she is. And she will continue to be like this as long as we continue to attempt the impossible. It is only when we come to realize that we are God's people, and a spiritual people, and that we live in the realm of the spirit, that we shall be blessed and shall begin to see a revival. We can introduce our worldly methods, and we may appear to be having success, but the Church will not improve. No! the Church is spiritual, and her spiritual life must be nurtured and sustained in a purely spiritual manner.

III

The next effect of sin upon man is to make him a slave of things that were meant to serve him. This is one of the terrible, tragic things about it. According to our Lord here, these earthly, worldly things tend to become our god. We serve them; we love them. Our heart is captivated by them; we are at their service. What are they? They are the very things that God in His kindness has given man in order that they might be of service to him, and in order that he may enjoy life while he is in this world. All these things that can be so dangerous to our souls because of sin were given to us by God, and we were meant to enjoy them— food and clothing, family and friends and all such things. These are all but a manifestation of the kindness and the graciousness of God. He has given them to us that we might have a happy and enjoyable life in this world; but because of sin, we have become their slaves. We are mastered by appetites. God has given us our appetites; hunger, thirst and sex are God-created. But the moment a man is dominated by them, or is mastered by them, he is a slave to them. What a tragedy; he bows down and worships at the shrine of things that were meant to be at his service. Things that were meant to minister to him have become his master. What a terrible, awful thing sin is!

IV

The last point, however, is the most serious and the most solemn of all. The final effect of sin upon mankind is that it entirely ruins man. That is the teaching of the Bible from beginning to end. This thing which came into life through the serpent in the Garden of Eden is intent upon nothing but our final ruination. The devil hates God with the whole of his being, and he has but one object and one ambition; it is to ruin and spoil all that God has made, and in which He delights. In other words, he is intent especially upon the ruination of man and of the world.

How does sin ruin man? Here is the answer as we find it in these verses. It ruins man in the sense that, having spent his lifetime in laying up certain things here on earth, he finds himself at the end with nothing. After laying up for himself treasures on earth where moth and rust doth corrupt, and thieves break through and steal, he finds himself face to face with the most powerful adversary of all which is death itself. Then this poor wretched man who has been living for these things suddenly finds himself with absolutely nothing—stripped with nothing at all but his naked soul. It is utter ruination. 'What shall it profit a man, if he shall gain the whole world, and lose his own soul?'

That is what sin eventually leads to, and there are many scriptural passages to prove this. Look at Luke xvi. 19–31. There it is perfectly; you need not go beyond that. This is a matter of understanding and common sense to which we need to apply our minds. Think of all the things for which you tend to be living at this moment, the things that really count, the things that really matter in your life. Then ask yourself this simple question: 'How many of these things will I be able to take with me when I die?' That is the test. How many of them will still be with you in the River of death and beyond the River? Sin is final ruination which leaves a man with nothing at the end.

Still worse in a sense is this, that at the end he also finds that he has been entirely and utterly wrong all his life. Our Lord puts it like this: 'The light of the body is the eye: if therefore thine eye be single, thy whole body shall be full of light. But if thine eye be evil, thy whole body shall be full of darkness. If therefore the light that is in thee be darkness, how great is that darkness!' That is a picture which means this. As we have seen, the light of the body is, in a sense, the mind, the understanding, this extraordinary faculty that God gave to man. If, as the result of sin and evil, and because of the control of the heart and of lust and passion and desire, this supreme instrument has become perverted, how great is that darkness! Is anything worse than that, or more terrible than that?

We can look at it like this. Man today, as we have been

saying, and as we know full well, not only believes he is being led by his mind; he rejects God because of his mind and under-standing. He laughs at religion, he laughs at those who denounce this worldly view of life. He lives for the present; it is the one thing that counts. And he believes that to be a rational point of view to take. He proves it to his own satisfaction and is convinced that he is led by his mind. He does not realize that the light that is in him has become dark. He does not see that his faculties have become upset because of sin. He does not see that various forces are controlling and drugging his mind which is therefore no longer operating freely and rationally. But at the end he will come to see it; at the end he will come to himself like the Prodigal Son of old. Suddenly he will see that the things in which he trusted were dark, and have misled him, and that he has lost everything—the light in him is darkness and how great is that darkness! There is nothing worse than that, to discover at the end that the very thing to which you pinned your faith is the one thing that has let you down.

All this can be seen in that picture of Dives and Lazarus in Luke xvi. That man, I am sure, justified himself day by day and said, 'It is all right'. But after he died and found himself there in hell, he suddenly saw it. He saw that he had been a fool all his life. He had done it all deliberately, and it had led him to this. He saw what a fool he had been, and he pleaded with Abraham to send somebody to his brethren who were doing the same thing. He discovered that the light that was in him was darkness and that it was great darkness. That is one of the most subtle deeds of Satan. He persuades a man that by denying God he is being rational; but, as we have seen already several times, what is really hap-pening is that he makes him a creature of lust and desire whose mind is blinded and whose eye is no longer single. The greatest faculty of all has become perverted.

If you are not a Christian do not trust your mind; it is the most dangerous thing you can do. But when you become a Christian your mind is put back in the centre and you become a rational being. There is no more pathetic illusion than for a man to think of the Christian faith as sob-stuff, the dope of the people, something purely emotional and irrational. The true view of it is stated perfectly by the apostle Paul in Romans vi. 17. You have 'obeyed from the heart that form of doctrine which was delivered you'. The doctrine was preached to them, and when they came to see it they liked it, believed it, and put it into practice. They received the truth of God first of all with the mind. Truth must

be received with the mind, and the Holy Spirit enables the mind
to become clear. That is conversion, that is what happens as the
result of regeneration. The mind is delivered from this bias of
evil and darkness; it sees the truth and loves and desires it above
everything else. That is it. There is nothing more tragic than for
a man to find at the end of his life that he has been entirely wrong
all the time.

A final word. This wretched man who is ruined by sin not only
finds he has nothing, he not only discovers that he has entirely
fooled himself and been misled by his supposed light, he finds
himself also to be outside the life of God and under His wrath.
'Ye cannot serve God and mammon.' So if a man has served
mammon in this life until he dies, he will find himself beyond
death outside God. He has not served God, so there is only one
thing to say about him, according to Scripture, and that is that
'the wrath of God abideth on him' (John iii. 36). All he has lived
for has gone; there in eternity he is a naked soul having to face
God, the God who is love and who is gracious and kind. The
Father, the One who counts the very hairs of the Christian's head,
is a stranger to him. He is without God, and not only without God
in the world but without God in eternity, without hope, facing
an eternity of wretchedness and remorse, of misery and regrets.
Sin is a total loss. If you are not living to serve Him, then that
will be your fate. You will have nothing at all, and you will
dwell in that negativity, that hopeless negativity through all
eternity. God forbid that that should be the fate of anyone
within reach of these words. If you want to avoid it, go to God
and confess to Him that you have been serving earthly things,
and laying up for yourselves treasures upon earth. Confess it to
Him, give yourself to Him, place yourself unreservedly in His
hands and above all ask Him to fill you with His Holy Spirit who
alone can enlighten the mind, clear the understanding, make the
eye single and enable us to see the truth—the truth about sin, and
the only way of salvation by the blood of Christ—the Holy Spirit
who can show us how to be delivered from the perversion and the
pollution of sin, and to become new men and women, created
after the fashion and pattern of the Son of God Himself, loving
the things of God and serving Him, and Him alone.

CHAPTER TEN

BE NOT ANXIOUS

AT verse 25 we start a new section in this consideration of
the Sermon on the Mount. It is a sub-section, in reality, of
the major theme which is being considered in this sixth
chapter, namely, the Christian walking and living in this world,
in his relationship to the Father.

There are two main aspects to be considered—what the Christian does in private, and what he does in public. You see how
practical this Sermon is. It is far from being something remote
and theoretical. It deals with the practicalities of the personal,
private life—all I do, my life of prayer, my life of attempting to
do good, my life of fasting, my personal devotion, the nurture
and culture of my own spiritual life.

But I do not spend the whole of my time in these occupations.
That would be to become a monk or a hermit. I do not segregate
myself. No; I live in the world, and am engaged in business and
in affairs, and have these multitudes of problems pressing in
upon me. Above everything else our Lord reminds us in the
second section, starting at verse 19, that the big problem that
confronts us is that of worldliness, which is always there and
always attacking us. That is the theme from verse 19 to the end of
the chapter. But we have seen that it is divided into subsidiary
sections. First of all there is the section we have already considered, consisting of verses 19–24. Here now, from verse 25 to
the end of the chapter, we come to the second section. It is still
the one theme, the danger of worldliness, the danger of mammon,
the danger of being defeated by the mind, outlook and life of this
present world.

There are perhaps two main ways of looking at the difference
between verses 19–24 and this section. One way is to say that in
the previous sub-division our Lord was chiefly emphasizing the
danger of laying up treasures upon earth, hoarding them,
amassing them, living to do that. Here, He is concerned not so
much with our laying them up, as with our worrying about them,
being anxious concerning them. And of course the two things are
different. There are many people who may not be guilty of
laying up treasures upon earth, but who nevertheless can be

very guilty of worldliness, because they are always thinking
about these things, being anxious about them and dwelling upon
them constantly. That is the main difference between these two
sub-sections. But it can be put in another way. Some people say
that in verses 19–24 our Lord was chiefly addressing rich people,
people who are well-off in this world's goods, and who therefore
are in a position to lay them up and to amass them. But they
suggest that from verse 25 to the end of the chapter He is thinking
more of people who are either actually poor, or else those who
cannot be described as rich, those who just manage to make both
ends meet, those who are face to face with the problem of making
a living and keeping things going in a material sense. To these
people the main danger is not the danger of laying up treasures,
or worshipping treasures in some shape or form, but the danger
of being burdened by these things and being anxious about them.
It does not really matter which interpretation you take. Both are
true, for it is possible for a man who is really wealthy to be worried
and burdened by these worldly matters; so we need not press the
antithesis between rich and poor. The great thing is to concentrate on this danger of being oppressed and obsessed by the
things that are seen, the things that belong to time and to this
world alone.

Here, we are reminded once more of the terrible subtlety of
Satan and of sin. It does not matter very much to Satan what
form sin takes as long as he succeeds in his ultimate objective. It
is immaterial to him whether you are laying up treasures on
earth or worrying about earthly things; all he is concerned about
is that your mind should be on them and not on God. And he
will assail and attack you from every direction. You may think
you have won this great battle against Satan because you
conquered him when he came in at the front door and talked to
you about laying up treasures on earth. But before you are aware
of it, you will find he has come in through the back door and is
causing you to have anxious concern about these things. He is
still making you look at them, and so is perfectly content. He can
transform himself into 'an angel of light'. There is no end to the
variety of his methods. His one concern is that we should keep
our minds on these things instead of centring them upon God and
holding them there. But fortunately for us, we are led by One
who knows him and his methods, and if we can say with St. Paul
that 'we are not ignorant of his devices', it is because we have
been taught and instructed by the Lord Jesus Christ Himself.
How subtle was the devil's threefold temptation of Him in the

wilderness! 'If thou be the Son of God.' We are subject to similar attacks but, thank God, our Lord has instructed us concerning it here, and His teaching is given in a very plain and explicit manner.

Our Lord continues His warning, He takes nothing for granted. He knows how frail we are; He knows the power of Satan and all his horrible subtlety, so He comes down to details. Again we shall see here, as we saw in the previous section, that He is not content merely to lay down principles or to give a command or injunction. He provides us with arguments and gives us reasons, He puts it to our common sense. We are reminded again that He puts the truth to our minds. He is not concerned to produce a certain emotional atmosphere only, He reasons with us. That is the great thing we need to grasp. So He again starts with a 'therefore'—'Therefore I say unto you'.

He is carrying on the main argument, but He is going to put it in a slightly different manner. The theme of course is still this, the need of the single eye, the need of looking centrally at the one thing. You find Him repeating it, 'Seek ye first'. That is just another way of saying that you must have the single eye, and serve God and not mammon. At all costs we must do this. He therefore puts it three times over, introducing it by means of the word 'therefore'. 'Therefore I say unto you, Take no thought for your life, what ye shall eat, or what ye shall drink; nor yet for your body, what ye shall put on. Is not the life more than meat, and the body than raiment?' Then in verse 31, He says it again: 'Therefore take no thought, saying, What shall we eat? or, What shall we drink? or, Wherewithal shall we be clothed?' Then in verse 34, He says it again finally: 'Take therefore no thought for the morrow: for the morrow shall take thought for the things of itself. Sufficient unto the day is the evil thereof.' There was never a Teacher in this world like the Lord Jesus Christ! The great art of teaching is the art of repetition; the true teacher always knows that it is not enough to say a thing once, but that it needs to be repeated. So He says it three times, but each time in a slightly different form. His method is particularly interesting and fascinating, and as we proceed to consider it we shall see exactly what it is.

The first thing we must do is to consider the terms which He uses, and particularly this expression 'Take no thought', which

people have often misunderstood, and over which many have
tripped and stumbled. The Authorized Version puts it like this:
'Take no thought for your life, what ye shall eat . . .', and it goes
on repeating that expression. But, of course, the real meaning of
'Take no thought' has changed since this Authorized Version
was introduced in 1611. If you consult the authorities, you will
find that they give quotations from Shakespeare to show that
'taking thought' was then used in the sense of 'being anxious', or
tending to worry. So that the real translation at this point should
be, 'Be not anxious', or 'Have no anxiety', or if you prefer it, 'Do
not worry', about your life, what you shall eat or what you shall
drink. That is the real meaning of the word. Indeed the actual
word that was used by our Lord is a very interesting one; it is the
word used to indicate something which divides, separates or
distracts us, a word used very frequently in the New Testament.
If you turn to Luke xii. 29, a corresponding passage to this, you
will find that the expression used there is 'neither be ye of
doubtful mind'. It is a mind which is divided into sections and
compartments, and which is not functioning as a whole. We
cannot do better therefore than say that it is not 'a single eye'.
There is a kind of double vision, a looking in two directions at
one and the same time, and therefore not really seeing anything.
That is what it means to be anxious, to be worried, to be 'taking
thought' in this sense.

A still better illustration of the meaning of the term is to be
found in the story of Martha and Mary when our Lord was in
their house (Luke x. 38–42). Our Lord turned to Martha and
rebuked her. He said, 'Thou art careful and troubled about
many things.' Poor Martha was 'distracted'—that is the real
meaning of the expression; she did not know where she was nor
what she really wanted. Mary, on the other hand, had a single
purpose, a single aim; she was not distracted by many things.
What our Lord is warning us against, therefore, is the danger of
thus being distracted from the main objective in life by care, by
this anxiety about earthly, worldly things, by looking so much at
them that we do not look at God—this danger of living
the double life, this false view, this dualism. That is what He is
concerned about.

Perhaps it is important to put in the negative at this point.
Our Lord is not teaching us here that we must not think about
these things at all. 'Taking no thought' does not mean that. Many
times in the history of the Church there have been zealous, mis-

guided people who have taken this literally, and have felt that to
live the life of faith they must not think about the future in any
sense, they must make no provision at all. They just 'live by
faith', they just 'pray to God' and do nothing about it. That is
not the meaning of 'Take no thought'. Quite apart from the
exact meaning of these words, the context alone, surely, and the
plain teaching of the New Testament elsewhere should have
saved them from that error. A knowledge of the exact meaning
of the words in the Greek is not the sole essential to true interpretation; if you read the Scriptures, and if you watch the context, you should be safeguarded from these errors. Surely the
context here, the very illustration that our Lord uses, proves
that these people must be wrong. He takes the argument of the
birds of the air. It is not true to say that they just have to perch
themselves upon the trees or upon a pole, and wait until food is
mechanically brought to them. That is not true. They search
for it busily. There is real activity in the fowls of the air, so that
the very argument our Lord uses at this point entirely precludes
the possibility of interpreting it as a kind of passive waiting upon
God and doing nothing. Our Lord never condemns farmers for
ploughing and harrowing and sowing and reaping and
gathering into barns. He never condemns that, for it was God's
command that man should live in that way, by the sweat of his
brow. So these arguments put in the form of illustrations and
including also that of the lilies of the field—how they draw their
sustenance from the earth in which they are planted—taken
especially in the light of the teaching of the Bible everywhere,
should have saved men from this ridiculous misinterpretation.
The apostle Paul put it very explicitly in his second letter to the
Thessalonians where he says that if a man 'would not work,
neither should he eat'. There were people then, misguided and
somewhat fanatical, who said, 'The Lord is going to return at
any moment; therefore we must not work; we must spend our
time waiting for His return.' So they ceased to work and imagined
they were being exceptionally spiritual. And that is Paul's
laconic remark respecting them: 'If a man will not work, neither
shall he eat.' There are certain fundamental principles governing
life, and that is one of them.

We find an exposition of this commandment in that great
saying of the apostle Paul in Philippians iv. 6, 7, where he says,
'Be careful for nothing; but in every thing by prayer and supplication with thanksgiving let your requests be made known

unto God. And the peace of God, which passeth all understanding, shall keep your hearts and minds through Christ Jesus.' Or, if you like, 'Do not be careful ('do not be full of care') about anything.' Again, that is not an injunction to idleness, it is a warning against care and anxiety, this tendency to worry that so constantly afflicts us in this life.

There can be no question at all about the real danger of this whole matter. The moment we stop to consider and examine ourselves, we shall find that we are not only open to this danger, but that we have often succumbed to it. Nothing seems to be more natural to mankind in this world than to become anxious, to become burdened and worried. It is the peculiar temptation, some would say, of women, especially of those who are responsible for the care of the home; but it is not by any means confined to them. The danger confronting the husband or father, or anyone who has responsibility towards loved ones and other people, in a world like this, is to spend the whole of life oppressed by these things, and weighed down by them. They tend to master and control us, and we go through life enslaved by them. That is the thing with which our Lord is concerned, and He is so concerned about it that He repeats this warning three times over.

First we shall look at His argument in a very general manner. Let us paraphrase what He actually says. 'Take no thought for your life, what ye shall eat, or what ye shall drink; nor yet for your body, what ye shall put on.' Here again He starts with a general statement and injunction, as He did in the previous section. There He began by laying down a law and then proceeded to give us reasons for keeping it. It is exactly the same here. There is the general statement; we are not to be anxious or worried about what we shall eat or what we shall drink, nor yet for our body what we shall put on. That of course is as comprehensive as anything can be. He is dealing with our life, our existence, our being in this body in which we live. Here we are, distinct personalities; we have this gift of life, and we live our life, in this world and through our bodies. So that when our Lord considers our life and our bodies He is, as it were, considering our essential personality and our life in this world. He puts it broadly; it is comprehensive and it includes the whole of man. He maintains that we must never be anxious either about our lives as such, or about the clothing of our bodies. It is as fully comprehensive as that, and it is very important that we should realize that, because this is a very thorough-going injunction. It does not apply only to certain aspects of our life; it takes in the whole of life, our health, our strength, our success, what is going to happen to us—that which is our life in any shape or form. And equally it takes the body as a whole, and tells us that we must not be anxious about our clothing, or any of these things that are part and parcel of our life in this world.

Having given the commandment, He then gives us a general reason for observing it and, as we shall see, having done this, He proceeds to sub-divide it and to give particular reasons under two headings. But He starts with the general reason in these words: 'Is not the life more than meat, and the body than raiment?' That takes in the life and the body. Then He sub-divides it and takes the life, and gives His argument; then He takes the body and gives His argument. But let us first look at the form of the general argument, which is very striking and important. The logicians would tell us that the argument He uses is one based upon a deduction from the greater to the lesser. He says in effect, 'Wait a minute; consider this before you become anxious. Is not your life more than meat, the sustenance, the food? Is not the body itself more important and greater than the raiment?'

What does our Lord mean by this? The argument is a very profound and powerful one; and how prone we are to forget it! He says in effect, 'Take this life of yours about which you are tending to worry and become anxious. How have you got it? Where has it come from?' And the answer, of course, is that it is a gift of God. Man does not create life; man does not give being to himself. Not one of us ever decided to come into this world. And the very fact that we are alive at this moment is entirely because God willed and God decided it. Life itself is a gift, a gift from God. So the argument which our Lord uses is this. If God has given you the gift of life—the greater gift—do you think He is now suddenly going to deny Himself and His own methods, and not see to it that that life is sustained and enabled to continue? God has His own ways of doing that, but the argument is that I need never become anxious about it. Of course I am to plough and sow and reap and gather into barns. I am to do the things that God has ordained for man and life in this world. I must go to work and earn money and so on. But all He says is that I need never be concerned or worried or anxious that suddenly there will not be sufficient to keep this life of mine going. That will never happen to me; it is impossible. If God has given me the gift of life, He will see to it that that life is kept going. But this is

II—8

the point: He is not arguing as to *how* this will be done. He is just saying that it will be.

I commend to your study, as a matter of great interest and vital importance, the frequency with which that argument is used in the Scriptures. We have a perfect illustration of it in Romans viii. 32, 'He that spared not his own Son, but delivered him up for us all, how shall he not with him also freely give us all things?' It is a very common biblical argument, the argument from the greater to the lesser, and we must always be watching for it and applying it. The Giver of the gift of life will see that the sustenance and support of that life will be provided. We must not stay now to take the argument from the birds of the air, but that is exactly what God does with them. They have to find their food, but it is He who provides it for them; He sees that it is there for them.

Exactly the same, of course, applies to the body. The body is a gift from God, and therefore we can be quite happy and certain in our minds that He will somehow or other provide the means whereby these bodies of ours can be covered and clothed. Here we come to one of His great principles, one of the great central principles of the Bible. There is nothing of which this modern generation needs to be reminded so much as just this. The main trouble with most of us is that we have forgotten first principles, and especially this vital one that the things we enjoy in this life are the gift of God. For instance, how often do we thank God for the gift of life itself? We tend to think that with our scientific knowledge we can understand the whole origin and essence of life. So we think of these things in terms of natural causes and inevitable processes. Quite apart, however, from the fact that all such theories are nothing but theories which cannot be proved, and are lacking at the most vital point, how tragic they are in the lack of understanding of biblical teaching which they reveal. Where does life come from? Read your modern scientists on the origin of life and you will find that they cannot explain it. They cannot bridge the gulf from the inorganic to the organic. They have their theories; but they are nothing more than this, and even so they disagree amongst themselves. That, however, is the fundamental problem. Where has this principle called life come from? What is its origin? If you say it started with the inorganic somehow becoming organic, I ask where did the inorganic come from? You are bound to go back to the life principle. And there is only one satisfactory answer—God is the Giver of life.

But we must not take this in just a general way. Our Lord was particularly interested in our individual case and condition, and what He is really teaching us here is that it is God who has given us the gift of life and being and existence. It is a tremendous conception. We are not merely individuals thrown up or thrown out by an evolutionary process. God is concerned about us one by one. We should never have come into this world if God had not willed it. We must take a firm hold and grasp of this great principle. There should never be a day in our lives when we fail to thank God for the gift of life and food and existence, and the marvel and the wonder of the body that He has given us. These things are solely and entirely His gift. And, of course, if we fail to realize that, we shall fail everywhere.

It may be well for us at this point to stop and meditate upon this great principle, before going on to our Lord's subsidiary argument. He sums up His central teaching in these words: 'O ye of little faith'. Faith there, as we shall see, does not mean some vague principle; He has in mind our failure to understand, our lack of comprehension of the biblical view of man and of life as it is to be lived in this world. That is the real trouble with us, and our Lord's purpose in giving the illustrations which we shall consider later, is to show us how we fail to think as we ought. He asks: 'How is it that you do not see inevitably that this must be true?' And of all the things I have mentioned which we fail to grasp and to understand truly, this preliminary, fundamental point about the nature and being of man himself is most important. Here it is in all its simplicity. It is God Himself who gives us life, and the body in which we live it; and if He has done that we can draw this deduction, that His purpose with respect to us will be fulfilled. God never leaves unfinished any work He has begun; whatever He starts, whatever He has purposed, He will most surely fulfil. And therefore we come back to this, that there is a plan for every life in the mind of God. We must never regard our lives in this world as accidental. No. 'Are there not twelve hours in the day?' Christ said one day to his timorous and frightened disciples. And we need to say that to ourselves. We can be certain that God has a plan and a purpose for our lives, and it will be carried out. So we must never be anxious about our life and about its sustenance and its support. We must not be anxious if we find ourselves in a storm at sea, or in an aeroplane, and things seem to be going wrong, or if in a railway train we suddenly remember that there was an accident on that line the previous week. That sort of thing is abolished if we really get this right view about life itself and the body as gifts of God. They are from Him and are given by Him. He does not just start a process like that and then allow it to continue anyhow, somehow. No; once He starts it He keeps it going. God who decreed all things at the beginning is carrying them out; and God's purpose for mankind and God's purpose for the individual are certain and always sure.

We cannot do better than remind ourselves again of something we have already mentioned, and that is the faith of God's people throughout the centuries. That is the faith and teaching to be found, for example, in the hymns of Philip Doddridge. A typical example is found in his great hymn:

'O God of Bethel! by whose hand
Thy people still are fed;
Who through this weary pilgrimage
Hast all our fathers led.'

That is his great argument, based ultimately upon the sovereignty of God, that God is the Ruler of the universe, and we are known to Him one by one, and are in a personal relationship to Him. It was the faith of all the great heroes of the faith described in Hebrews xi. That is what kept those men going. Quite frequently they did not understand but they said, 'God knows and God undertakes'. They had this final confidence that He who had brought them into being, and who had a purpose for them, would not leave them nor forsake them. He would surely sustain and lead them all the journey through, until their purpose in this world had been completed, and He would receive them into their heavenly habitation where they would spend their eternity in His glorious presence. 'Be not anxious about your life, what ye shall eat, or what ye shall drink; nor about your body, where-withal it shall be clothed. Is not the life more than meat, and the body than raiment?' Argue it out, start with first principles and draw the inevitable deduction. The moment you do so, care and worry and anxiety will vanish, and as a child of your heavenly Father you will walk with peace and serenity in the direction of your everlasting home.

CHAPTER ELEVEN

BIRDS AND FLOWERS

WE have been considering in these verses 25–30 our Lord's general statement concerning the terrible danger that confronts us in this life arising from our tendency to be over-interested in various ways in the things of the world. We tend to become anxious about our life, about what we shall eat, and what we shall drink, and also about our body, what we shall put on. It is appalling to notice how many people seem to live entirely within that compass; food, drink and clothing is the whole of their life. They spend the whole of their time thinking about these things, talking about them, discussing them with others, arguing about them, and reading about them in various books and magazines. And the world today is doing its utmost to get us all to live on that level. Take a casual glance at the books on the bookstalls and you will see how all these things are catered for. That is the mind of the world, and that is the circle of its interest. People live for these things, and become concerned and worried about them in all sorts of different ways. Knowing this and being aware of the dangers, our Lord first of all gives us an omnibus reason for avoiding that particular snare.

But having warned us that we must not be anxious about what we shall eat or drink, or what we shall put on, He now goes on to give each aspect of the question separate consideration. The first is considered in verses 26 and 27, and deals with our existence, the continuation and sustaining of our life in this world. Here is the argument: 'Behold the fowls of the air: for they sow not, neither do they reap, nor gather into barns; yet your heavenly Father feedeth them. Are ye not much better than they? Which of you by taking thought can add one cubit unto his stature?' Some people would say that the statement in verse 27 belongs to the following section, but it seems to me perfectly clear that it must, for reasons which will emerge in a moment, belong to this first section.

With regard to the whole question of food and drink and the maintenance of life, our Lord provides us with a double argument, or, if you like, with two main arguments. The first is derived from the birds of the air. You notice that at this point the argument is no longer from the greater to the lesser; rather is it the other way round. Having established the proposition on a lower level He then raises it to the higher level. First of all He starts by making a general observation, by calling our attention to something that is a fact of life in this world. 'Behold the fowls of the air.' Look at them. 'Behold' does not always carry the meaning of intense gazing. He is just asking us to look at something that is staring us in the face. See what is before your eyes— these birds, these fowls of the air. What is the argument we can deduce from them? It is that these birds are obviously provided with food.

There is a great deal of difference between the way the life of the birds is sustained and that of man. In the case of the birds it is provided for them. In the case of man a certain process is clearly involved. He sows the grain, and later on reaps the crop that has grown from the seed sown. Then he proceeds to gather it into barns and to put it aside until he needs it. That is man's way, and it is the right way; it was the way that God commanded man after the Fall, 'In the sweat of thy face shalt thou eat bread' (Genesis iii. 19). Away back at the beginning of history seedtime and harvest were determined by God, not by man, so that sowing and reaping and gathering into barns is absolutely right for him. He is supposed to do that, and that is how he is to live. That is why the injunction not to 'take thought' cannot mean that we are to sit down and expect our bread to arrive miraculously in the morning. That is not scriptural, and all who imagine that that is the life of faith have misunderstood the teaching of the Bible.

But man is never to be worried about these things. He must not spend the whole of his time looking at the sky, wondering what the weather is going to be, and whether he will have something to put into his barn. That is what is condemned by our Lord. Man has to sow; he is commanded by God to do so. But he is to rely upon God who alone can give the increase. Our Lord draws attention to the birds. There is nothing more obvious about them than the fact that they are kept alive and that food is provided for them in nature—worms and insects and all the things on which birds live. It is there for them. Where does it come from? The answer is that God provides it for them. There, is a simple fact of life, and He tells us to look at it. These little birds who make no provision in the sense of preparing or producing food for themselves, have it provided for them. God looks after them and takes care of them. He sees to it that there is something for them to eat. He sees to it that their life is sustained.

That is a simple statement of the fact. Our Lord now takes that fact and draws two vital deductions from it. God deals thus with the animals and the birds of the air only in and through His general providence. He is not their Father; 'Behold the birds . . . yet your heavenly Father feedeth them'. That is a very interesting statement. God is the Maker and the Creator and the Sustainer of everything in the world; and He deals with the whole world, not only man, through His general providential arrangements, and only in that way. Then you notice the subtle change, introducing the profoundest argument of all: 'your heavenly Father feedeth them'.

God is our Father, and if our Father takes this great care of the birds to whom He is related only in His general providence, how much greater, of necessity, must be His care for us. An earthly father may be kind, for instance, to the birds or to animals; but it is inconceivable that a man should provide sustenance for mere creatures and neglect his own children. If this is true of an earthly father, how much more is it true of our heavenly Father. Here is our first deduction.

You see our Lord's method of reasoning and arguing; every word is important and must be noted carefully and closely. Observe the subtle transition from God caring providentially for the birds of the air, to 'your heavenly Father'. And as we follow His argument in these verses we shall see that this is something absolutely basic and vital. As we go through life in this world we notice and observe these facts of nature as we call them. But because we are Christians we must look at them with a deeper understanding and say to ourselves, 'No; things do not just happen in nature. They have not just come into being anyhow, somehow, fortuitously, as so many modern scientists would have us believe. Not at all. God is the Creator, and God is the sustainer of all things that are. He provides even for the birds, and the birds know instinctively that it is there, and He sees to it that it is there. Very well then; but what about myself? I now remind myself that I am a child of God, that He is my heavenly Father. God is not to me merely a Creator. He is the Creator, but He is more than that; He is my God and Father in and through the Lord Jesus Christ.' We should reason thus with ourselves, according to our Lord; and the moment we do that, care and anxiety and worry are quite impossible. The moment we begin to apply these truths to our minds fear goes out immediately and of necessity.

That, then, is our first deduction from this general observation of nature, and we must hold on to it. God is our heavenly Father if we are truly Christian. We must add that, because all that we are considering applies only to Christians. Indeed we can go further and say that, although God does deal in a providential manner with the whole of mankind—as we have seen in the previous chapter where He says that God 'maketh his sun to rise on the evil and on the good, and sendeth rain on the just and on the unjust'—these specific statements of our Lord's here are for God's children only, for those who are children of their heavenly Father in and through our Lord and Saviour Jesus Christ. And it is only the man who is a Christian who knows God to be his Father. The apostle Paul in the Epistle to the Romans says that no man but a Christian can say 'Abba, Father'. No man, unless the Holy Spirit dwells in him, really knows God as his Father and can rely upon Him. But, says our Lord, if you are in that relationship, then you must realize it is a sin for you to be anxious and worried, because God is your heavenly Father, and if He takes care of the birds, how much greater will be His care for you.

Our Lord puts His second deduction in these words, 'Are ye not much better than they?' Here again is this argument from the lesser to the greater. It means, as it is put elsewhere, 'of how much greater value are you than the birds of the air'. This is the argument which derives from the true greatness and dignity of man, and especially the Christian man. Here we can only work out the mechanics of the argument. We shall have to take it on a deeper level later, but we must say now that there is nothing more remarkable in the whole of biblical doctrine than the doctrine of man, this emphasis on the greatness and dignity of man. One of the ultimate objections to the godless, sinful, unchristian life is that it is an insult to man. The world thinks that it is making much of man. It talks about human greatness and suggests that the Bible and its teaching humble and humiliate human nature. The truth is, of course, precisely the opposite. True human greatness has tended to disappear as the biblical view of man has waned, for even at its best and highest the worldly, naturalistic view of man is unworthy. Here is true greatness and dignity; man made in the image of God, and therefore in some sense like God the Master and Lord of Creation. Our Lord comes in a humble, lowly manner; but it is as you look at Him that you see the true greatness of man. Though He was born in a stable and placed in a manger it is there, not in king's palaces, that we see the true dignity of man.

The world has a false idea of greatness and dignity. To find the true conception of man you must go to Psalm viii and other places in Scripture. Above all, you must look at the Lord Jesus Christ, and look also at the New Testament picture of a man 'in Christ' made after His image. Then you will see the true relevance of this argument from the lesser to the greater—'Are ye not much better than they?' But God takes care of these birds; they have a value, they are precious in His sight. Has He not said that not one of them can fall to the ground without 'your heavenly Father' knowing? If that is true, then look at yourself and realize what you are in the sight of God. Remember that He sees you as His child in the Lord Jesus Christ, and once and for ever you will cease to be concerned and worried and anxious about these things. When you see yourself as His child, then you will know that God will inevitably care for you.

There is, however, a second argument implied in this first one, an argument based upon the uselessness and futility of worry. These are our Lord's words: 'Which of you by taking thought can add one cubit unto his stature?' This is an argument which we must follow very carefully. To begin with, we must determine what exactly the statement is saying, and here we have two main opinions. When we ask what is the meaning of this term 'stature', we find that there are two possible answers. Half the authorities say that 'stature' means height, and normally when we talk about stature we think of height. But the Greek word used for 'stature' also means length or duration of life. And it is used in both senses in scriptural as well as in classical Greek. So it is no use asking, 'What does the Greek say?' because it does not say; the word may be used in either sense. So we cannot decide it in terms of the Greek.

How then do we approach it? The context surely must determine and decide this matter. What is a cubit? It happens to be 18 inches, and bearing that in mind this mention here of 'stature' simply cannot mean height. It is quite impossible, for the reason that our Lord is again working from the lesser to the greater. Can you imagine anybody being anxiously concerned to add 18 inches to his height! The suggestion is ridiculous. It cannot refer to height; it must refer to duration of life. This is what our Lord is saying: 'How many of you by taking all this trouble and care, and by being so worried and anxious, can extend the length of your life even by a moment.' We talk about the span of life, and that is the argument which our Lord is using, for He is still concerned here about our life in this world. The original statement is, 'Take no thought for your life'. He is not considering the body, He is considering existence, the continuance of life in this world. The introduction of the idea of height into the teaching here would be a complete irrelevance. No; our Lord is referring in this verse to the duration and extension of life, and it is because of their obsession with this that so many people become worried about their bodily needs. They desire to extend their life.

Now then, says our Lord in effect, face this question; face this argument. With all that you do, with all your tremendous efforts, with all your trouble and anxiety, is there any one of you that can extend the span of life by even a moment? And the answer to that question is that we cannot. That is one of the things which are so obvious, but which we all tend to forget. We do not remind ourselves of it as we should; but it is incontrovertibly true. The fact is that we cannot extend our lives in this world though we may try to do so in various ways. The millionaire can buy all the food and drink he wants, but he cannot extend his life. We are told that 'Money is power!' Perhaps it is in many respects, but not in this. The millionaire has no advantage over the most wretched pauper in existence.

We can go further. Medical knowledge and skill cannot extend life. We think they can, but that is because we do not know. These things are all determined by God, and thus even medical men are often bewildered and frustrated. Two patients who appear to be in the same condition are given identical treatment. One recovers; the other dies. What is the answer? The answer is that 'no man can add one cubit to his duration of life'. It is a great mystery, but we cannot escape it. Our times are in the hands of God, and do what we will, with all our food and drink, and our medical profession, and all our learning and science and skill, we cannot add a fraction to the duration of a man's life. In spite of all modern advances in knowledge, our times are still in the hands of God. And so, our Lord argues, why all the fuss and bother, why all the excitement, why all this worry and anxiety? Life is a gift from God. He starts it and He determines the end of it. He sustains it, and we are in His hands. Therefore, when you tend to become worried and anxious, just pull yourself up at once and say, I cannot start, or continue or end life; all this is entirely in His hands. If that greater thing is there in His control,

I can leave the lesser also to Him. You cannot extend your life
even by one cubit; therefore recognize the utter futility and
waste of time and energy involved in worrying about these
things. Do your work; sow, reap and gather into barns; but
remember that the remainder is in the hands of God. You may
have the finest seed you can buy on the market; you may have the
best plough and everything necessary in the sowing; but if God
withheld the sun and the rain you would not have a crop. God is
ultimately behind it all. Man has his place and his work, but it is
God that giveth the increase. This is what we must always
remember, and it applies always and in all circumstances.

But we must now turn our attention to the section which
starts at verse 28. 'And why take ye thought for raiment?' Here
is the second matter—the body and its clothing. 'Consider the
lilies of the field, how they grow; they toil not, neither do they
spin: and yet I say unto you, That even Solomon in all his glory
was not arrayed like one of these. Wherefore, if God so clothe the
grass of the field, which to day is, and to morrow is cast into the
oven, shall he not much more clothe you, O ye of little faith?'
Again the argument is from the lesser to the greater. Again
we are asked to observe a fact of nature. But this time He uses
a slightly stronger term. It was 'behold the fowls'; now it is
'*consider* the lilies of the field'. He means, of course, that we
must meditate about these things and consider them on a deeper
level.
Our Lord puts the argument as before. First of all look at the
facts, the lilies of the field, the natural wild flowers, the grass. The
authorities again spend many pages in trying to decide exactly
what a 'lily' means. But surely He is referring to some common
flowers which were growing in the fields of Palestine, and with
which they were all perfectly familiar. And He says, Look at these
things—consider; these do not toil, neither do they spin, and yet
look at them. Look at the marvel, look at the beauty, look at the
perfection. Why, even Solomon in all his glory was not arrayed
like one of these. The glory of Solomon was proverbial amongst
the Jews. You can read of his magnificence in the Old Testament,
the marvellous clothing and all the wonderful vestures of the
king and his court, his palaces of cedarwood with their furniture
overlaid with gold and encrusted with precious stones. And yet,
says our Lord, all that pales into insignificance when compared
with one of these. There is an essential quality in the flowers, in
the form, in the design, in the texture and substance, and in the

colouring that man, with all his ingenuity, can never truly imitate.

> 'To me the meanest flower that blows can give
> Thoughts that do often lie too deep for tears.'

That is what *He* sees. He sees the hand of God; He sees the perfect creation; He sees the glory of the Almighty. The little flower that is never perhaps seen during the whole of its brief existence in this world, and which seemingly 'wastes its sweetness on the desert air', is nevertheless perfectly clothed by God. That is a fact, is it not? If so, draw the deduction from it. 'If God so clothe the grass of the field . . . shall he not much more clothe you, O ye of little faith?' If God does that for the flowers of the field, how much more for you?

But why is this so? Here is the argument. 'If God so clothe the grass of the field, which to day is, and to morrow is cast into the oven, shall he not much more clothe you?' What a mighty argument this is. The grass of the field is transient and passing. In ancient times they used to cut it and use it as fuel. It was the old way of baking bread. You first of all cut the grass and dried it, and then put it in the oven and set it on fire, and it generated great heat. Then you raked it out and put in the bread which you had prepared for baking. That was a common practice, and it was so in our Lord's day. So you see the powerful argument. The lilies and the grass are transient; they do not last very long. How well aware of this we are. We cannot make our flowers last; the moment we cut them they are beginning to die. They are here today with their exquisite beauty and all their perfection, but it is all gone by tomorrow. These beautiful things come and go, and that is the end of them. You, however, are immortal; you are not only a creature of time, you belong to eternity. It is not true to say that you are here today and gone tomorrow in a real sense. God hath 'set eternity' in the heart of man; man is not meant to die. 'Dust thou art, to dust returnest, was not spoken of the soul'. You go on, and on, and on. You not only have natural dignity and greatness, but you also have an eternal existence beyond death and the grave. When you realize that truth about yourself, can you believe that the God who has made you and destined you for that, is going to neglect your body while you are in this life and world? Of course not. 'If God so clothe the grass of the field, which to day is, and to morrow is cast into the oven, shall he not much more clothe you, O ye of little faith?'

CHAPTER TWELVE

LITTLE FAITH

'O YE of little faith' (Matthew vi. 30). We have here our Lord's final argument concerning the problem of anxious care. Or, perhaps, we can describe it as being our Lord's summing up of the warning not to 'take thought' about our lives as to what we shall eat or drink, or about our bodies in the matter of dress. It is the conclusion of the detailed argument which He has worked out in terms of birds and flowers. In effect, He seems to say: This is what it all amounts to. The real cause of the trouble is your failure to draw obvious deductions from the birds and the flowers. But, coupled with that, there is an obvious lack of faith. 'O ye of little faith.' That is the ultimate cause of the trouble.

The question that obviously arises is this: What does our Lord mean by 'little faith'? What is its exact connotation? He does not say, you notice, that they have no faith; He charges them with 'little' faith. It is not the absence of faith on their part that concerns Him; it is the inadequacy of that faith, the fact that they do not have sufficient faith. It is therefore a very striking phrase and our immediate reaction should be to thank God for it. What exactly does it mean? The right way to answer that question is to pay careful attention to the entire context. Who are the people whom He is describing here and against whom this charge is preferred? Once more we must remind ourselves that they are Christian people, and only Christian people. Our Lord is not speaking about everybody in the world. The Christian message really has no comfort and consolation to give to people who are not Christian. Words like these are not addressed to everybody; they are addressed only to those of whom the Beatitudes are true. They are, therefore, addressed to those who are poor in spirit, and those who mourn because of their sense of guilt and of sin, those who have seen themselves as truly lost and helpless in the sight of God, those who are meek and therefore hungering and thirsting after righteousness, realizing that it is only to be obtained in the Lord Jesus Christ. They have faith; the others have no faith at all. So it is spoken of such people only.

Further, it is spoken of people with respect to whom He can

use the term 'your heavenly Father'. God is Father only to those who are in Jesus Christ. He is the Maker and the Creator of all men; we are all His offspring in that sense. But, as the apostle John puts it, it is only those who believe on the Lord Jesus Christ who have the right and the authority to become the sons of God (see John i. 12). Our Lord, in addressing the Pharisees, spoke of 'my Father' and 'your father', and said 'you are of your father the devil'. So here. He is not teaching some vague general doctrine about the 'universal fatherhood of God' and the 'universal brotherhood of man'. No; the gospel divides people into two groups, those who are Christian and those who are not. We must assert, and more than ever at a time like this, that the gospel of Jesus Christ has only one thing to say to the non-Christian world, namely that it is under the wrath of God, that it can expect nothing in this world but misery and unhappiness, wars and rumours of wars, and that it will never know any true peace. Put positively, the Christian gospel tells the world that it must believe on the Lord Jesus Christ if it desires to be blessed of God. There is no hope for the world as such; there is only hope for those who are Christian. This is a message only for the people of whom the Beatitudes are true, those who can truly and rightly say that they are the children of God in Jesus Christ. Indeed, in the very next phrase which we shall be considering, He contrasts these people with the Gentiles—'all these things do the Gentiles seek'. There we see the division, 'the Gentiles' and those who are 'in Christ', those who are outside and those who are inside, God's people and those who are not God's people.

That, then, is the way in which we must understand this phrase. These people have faith, but it is insufficient faith. Surely, therefore, we are entitled to put it like this. Our Lord is speaking here about Christian people who have only saving faith, and who tend to stop at that. Those are the people about whom He is concerned, and His desire is that they should be led, as the result of listening to Him, to a larger and deeper faith. The first reason for this is that people who have saving faith only, and who go no further, rob themselves of so much in this life. And not only that. Because of their lack of a larger faith, they are obviously more prone to the worry and anxiety and to this killing care which attacks us all in this life. Our Lord, indeed, goes so far as to say that worry in a Christian is always due ultimately to a lack of faith, or to little faith. Worry and anxiety, being cast down and defeated, being mastered by life and its attendant circumstances, are always due, in a Christian, to lack of faith.

The thing we must aim at, therefore, is greater faith. The first step in obtaining this is to realize what is meant by 'little faith'. We shall see that this is our Lord's method in the next little section which begins at verse 31: 'Therefore take no thought, saying, What shall we eat? or, What shall we drink? or, Wherewithal shall we be clothed?' Our Lord gives us positive instruction as to how to increase our faith; but before He does that, He wants us to see exactly what is meant by little faith. You start with the negative, then go on to the positive.

What then is this condition which is described by our Lord as being 'little faith'? What sort of faith is it, and what is wrong with it? First of all, let us consider a general definition. We can say of this type of faith in general that it is one which is confined to one sphere of life only. It is faith that is confined solely to the question of the salvation of our souls, and it does not go beyond that. It does not extend to the whole of life and to everything in life. This is a common complaint among us as Christian people. On the question of the salvation of our souls we are perfectly clear. We have been awakened by the work of the Holy Spirit to see our lost estate. We have been convicted of sin. We have seen how utterly helpless we are to put ourselves right in the sight of God, and that the only way of deliverance is in the Lord Jesus Christ. We have seen that He came into the world, and died for our sins, and thereby reconciled us to God. And we believe on Him, and have that saving faith with regard to the present and to all eternity. That is saving faith, the thing that makes us Christians, and without which we are not Christian at all. Yes; but Christian people often stop at that, and they seem to think that faith is something that applies only to that question of salvation. The result is, of course, that in their daily lives they are often defeated; in their ordinary daily lives there is very little difference to be seen between them and people who are not Christian. They become worried and anxious, and they conform to the world in so many respects. Their faith is something that is reserved only for their ultimate salvation, and they do not seem to have any faith with regard to the every-day affairs of life and living in this world. Our Lord is concerned about that very thing. These people have come to know God as their heavenly Father, and yet they are worried about food and drink and clothing. Their faith is confined; it is a little faith in that way; its scope is so curtailed and limited.

We must start with that. You cannot read the Bible without seeing that true faith is a faith that extends to the whole of life.

You see it in our Lord Himself, you see it in the great heroes of the faith we read of in Hebrews xi. We can put it like this. A little faith is a faith which does not lay hold of all the promises of God. It is interested only in some of them, and it concentrates on these. Look at it in this way. Go through the Bible and make a list of the various promises of God. You will find that there are a great number, indeed an astonishing number. Peter talked about the 'exceeding great and precious promises'. It is amazing and astounding. There is no aspect of life that is not covered by these extraordinary promises of God. How guilty we all are in the light of this! We select certain of these promises and concentrate upon them, and somehow or other we never look at the others. We never lay hold of the others, and the result is that, while we triumph in certain respects, we fail so miserably in others. That is 'little faith'. It is faith, which is confined in its relationship to the promises, and does not realize that it is meant to be something that should link up with them all, and appropriate every one of them.

Let us look at it again from a slightly different angle. I once heard a man use a phrase which affected me very deeply at the time, and still does. I am not sure it is not one of the most searching statements I have ever heard. He said that the trouble with many of us Christians is that we believe on the Lord Jesus Christ, but that we do not believe Him. He meant that we believe on Him for the salvation of our souls, but we do not believe Him when He says a thing like this to us, that God is going to look after our food and drink, and even our clothing. He makes such statements as 'Come unto me, all ye that labour and are heavy laden, and I will give you rest', and yet we keep our problems and worries to ourselves, and we are borne down by them and defeated by them, and get anxious about things. He has told us to come to Him when we are like that; He has told us that if we are thirsting in any respect we can go to Him, and He has assured us that whosoever comes to Him will never thirst, and that he that eats of the bread that He shall give shall never hunger. He has promised to give us 'a well of water springing up into everlasting life' so that we shall never thirst. But, we do not believe Him. Take all these statements He made when He was here on earth, the words He addressed to the people around Him; they are all meant for us. They are meant for us today as definitely as when He first uttered them, and so also are all the astounding statements in the Epistles. The trouble is that we do not believe Him. That is the ultimate trouble. 'Little faith' does not

really take the Scripture as it is and believe it and live by it and
apply it.

So far we have been looking at 'little faith' in general. Let us
come now to the details and look at it in a more analytical
manner. We must do this in order that we may be essentially
practical, for after all this subject is a vital and practical one.
There is no greater fallacy than to regard the gospel of Jesus
Christ as just something that you think of when you are in church
or when you are spending a certain amount of time in meditation. No, it applies to the whole of life. Let us look at it like this.
To be 'of little faith' means, first of all, that we are mastered by
our circumstances instead of mastering them. That is an obvious
statement. The picture given in this entire section is of people
who are being governed by life. There they are, as it were,
sitting helplessly under a great cloud of concern about food and
drink and clothing and many other things. These things are
bearing down upon them and they are the victims of them. That
is the picture which He gives, and we know how true it is. Things
happen to us, and immediately, as we put it, we are 'bowled
over', we are mastered by them. That is something which,
according to Scripture, should never happen to a Christian. The
picture given of him everywhere in the Bible is of one who is
above his circumstances. He can even 'rejoice in tribulation', not
just stand up to it with a stoical kind of fortitude. He does not
give way or whimper; he is not simply, to use the common
phrase, 'grinning and bearing it'. No; he rejoices in the midst of
tribulation. Only one who has true faith can look down upon
life in that way, and can ever rise to such a height: but that,
according to the Bible, is possible to the Christian.

Why does the man of little faith allow things to master him and
to get him down? The answer to that question is that, in a sense,
the real trouble with 'little faith' is that it does not think. In other
words, we have to be right in our whole conception of faith.
Faith, according to our Lord's teaching in this paragraph, is
primarily thinking; and the whole trouble with a man of little
faith is that he does not think. He allows circumstances to
bludgeon him. That is the real difficulty in life. Life comes to us
with a club in its hand and strikes us upon the head, and we
become incapable of thought, helpless and defeated. The way to
avoid that, according to our Lord, is to think. We must spend
more time in studying our Lord's lessons in observation and
deduction. The Bible is full of logic, and we must never think of

faith as something purely mystical. We do not just sit down in an armchair and expect marvellous things to happen to us. That is not Christian faith. Christian faith is essentially thinking. Look at the birds, think about them, and draw your deductions. Look at the grass, look at the lilies of the field, consider them.

The trouble with most people, however, is that they will not think. Instead of doing this, they sit down and ask, What is going to happen to me? What can I do? That is the absence of thought; it is surrender, it is defeat. Our Lord, here, is urging us to think, and to think in a Christian manner. That is the very essence of faith. Faith, if you like, can be defined like this: It is a man insisting upon thinking when everything seems determined to bludgeon and knock him down in an intellectual sense. The trouble with the person of little faith is that, instead of controlling his own thought, his thought is being controlled by something else, and, as we put it, he goes round and round in circles. That is the essence of worry. If you lie awake at night for hours I can tell you what you have been doing; you have been going round in circles. You just go over the same old miserable details about some person or some thing. That is not thought; that is the absence of thought, a failure to think. That means that something else is controlling your thought and governing it, and it leads to that wretched, unhappy state called worry. So we are entitled to define 'little faith' in the second place as being a failure to think, or of allowing life to master our thought instead of thinking clearly about it, instead of 'seeing life steadily and seeing it whole'.

Little faith, if you like, can also be described as a failure to take scriptural statements at their face value and to believe them utterly. Here is a man who has suddenly found himself in trouble and tried by circumstances. What should he do? He should turn to the Bible, and then say to himself: 'I must take the statements of that Book exactly as they are'. Everything that is in us by nature, and the devil outside us, will do their utmost to prevent our doing this. They tell us that those statements were meant only for the disciples, and that they are not meant for us. Some people, as we have seen, would even relegate the whole of the Sermon on the Mount to the disciples, and to people who are going to live in some future kingdom. Others say that it was all right for the first Christians who had just passed through Pentecost but that now the world has changed. Those are the suggestions that come to us. But I reject all that. We are to read the Scriptures, and we are to say to ourselves, 'Everything I am going to read here is spoken to me; everything our Lord said to the Pharisees He says to me; and if there is anything corresponding to what He said of them in me it means that I am a Pharisee. All these promises likewise are meant for me. God does not change; He is exactly as He was two thousand years ago, and all these things are absolute and eternal.' So I must come to the Bible and remind myself of that. It means that I take it and its teaching as it is, in its context, and know that it is speaking to me. I must not dismiss it in any way. I have to learn to take Scripture at its face value. 'Little faith' means a failure to do that as we ought.

We must go on, however, to something which is still more practical. 'Little faith' really means a failure to realize the implications of salvation, and the position resulting from salvation. That is clearly our Lord's argument and reasoning here. Half our trouble is due to the fact that we do not realize to the full the implications of the doctrine of salvation which we believe. That is the argument of every New Testament Epistle. The first part consists of a doctrinal statement, which is designed to remind us of what we are and who we are as Christians. Then comes a practical second part, which is always a deduction from the first. That is why it generally starts with the word 'therefore'. That is exactly what our Lord is doing here. Here we are, worrying about food and drink and clothing! The trouble with us is that we do not realize that we are children of our heavenly Father. If only we realized that, we should never worry again. If only we had some dim, vague conception of the purposes of God with respect to us, worry would be impossible. Take, for instance, Paul's great prayer for the Ephesians. He tells them that he was praying that 'the eyes of their understanding might be enlightened'—note the word 'understanding'. To what end and for what purpose? 'That ye may know what is the hope of his calling, and what the riches of the glory of his inheritance in the saints, and what is the exceeding greatness of his power to usward who believe' (Ephesians i. 18, 19). That, according to Paul, is what they needed to know and understand. Read every Pauline Epistle and you will find that kind of statement somewhere.

The trouble with us Christian people is that we do not realize what we are as children of God, we do not see God's gracious purposes with respect to us. We saw that earlier, in passing, when we considered how He contrasted us as children with the grass of the field. The grass is here today in the field, but tomorrow it will be thrown as fuel into the oven to bake bread. But God's children are destined for glory. All the purposes and the promises of God are meant for us and designed with respect to us; and the one thing we have to do, in a sense, is just to realize what God has told us about ourselves as His children. The moment we truly grasp that, worry becomes impossible. A man then begins to apply the logic which argues: 'If, when we were enemies, we were reconciled to God by the death of his Son, much more, being reconciled, we shall be saved by his life' (Romans v. 10). That is it. Whatever happens to us, 'He that spared not his own Son, but delivered him up for us all, how shall he not with him also freely give us all things?' The mighty argument continues in Romans viii: 'Who shall lay any thing to the charge of God's elect?' . . . (Romans viii. 32 ff.).We may have to face problems and distresses and sorrow, but 'in all these things we are more than conquerors through him that loved us'. The vital thing is to see ourselves as His children. The argument follows of necessity. If God so clothe the grass how much more shall He clothe you? Your heavenly Father, who sees the birds, feedeth them. Are ye not much better than they? We have to realize what we are as God's children.

Or, to put it the other way round, we have to realize what God is as our heavenly Father. Here, again, is something which Christian people are so slow to learn. We believe in God; but how slow we are to believe and to realize that He is what He says He is, our heavenly Father. Christ talked about going 'to my Father, and your Father'. He has become our Father in Christ. And what are we to learn about Him? Here are some headings for your consideration.

Think first of the immutable purposes of God with regard to His children, and I would emphasize that word 'immutable'. The children of God have their names written in the Lamb's Book of Life before the foundation of the world. There is nothing contingent about this. It was 'before the foundation of the world' that we were elected. His purposes are immutable and changeless, and they envisage our eternal destiny and nothing less. This is constantly expressed in various ways in the Scriptures. 'Elect according to the foreknowledge of God', 'separated unto Christ Jesus', 'sanctified, set apart by the Spirit', and so on. When people believe things like that they are able to face life in this world in a very different way. That was the secret, once more, of the heroes of the faith in Hebrews xi. They understood something of the immutable purposes of God, and, therefore, whether it was Abraham or Joseph or Moses, they all smiled at calamities. They just went on because God had told them to do so, because they knew that His purposes must surely come to pass. Abraham was put to the supreme test of being asked to sacrifice Isaac. He could not understand it but he said: I will do it because I know God's purposes are sure, and though I have to slay Isaac, I know that God can raise him from the dead. The immutable purposes of God! God never contradicts Himself, and we must remember that He is always behind, beneath and everywhere round about us. 'Underneath are the everlasting arms.'

Then think of His great love. The tragedy of our position is that we do not know the love of God as we should. Paul prayed again for the Ephesians that they might know the love of God. We do not know His love to us. In a sense the whole of the first Epistle of John was written in order that we might know that. If only we knew the love of God to us, and rested in it (1 John iv. 16) our whole lives would be different. How easy it is to prove the greatness of that love in the light of what He has already done in Christ. We have already looked at those mighty arguments from the Epistle to the Romans. If while we were yet enemies He has done the greatest thing, how much more, we say it with reverence, is He bound to do the lesser things. The love of God to us!

Then we must meditate upon His concern for us. That is what our Lord is emphasizing here. If He is concerned about the birds, how much more for us? He tells us in another place that even 'the hairs of our head are all numbered'. Yet we worry about things. If only we realized God's loving concern for us, that He knows everything about us, and is concerned about the smallest detail of our lives! The man who believes that can no longer worry.

Then think about His power and His ability. 'Our God', 'my God'. Who is my God who takes such a personal interest in me? He is the Creator of the heavens and the earth. He is the Sustainer of everything that is. Read again Psalm xlvi to remind yourself of this: 'He maketh wars to cease unto the end of the earth; he breaketh the bow, and cutteth the spear in sunder'. He controls everything. He can smash the heathen and every enemy; His power is illimitable. And as we contemplate all that, we must agree with the deduction of the Psalmist when, addressing the heathen, he said: 'Be still, and know that I am God'. We must not interpret that 'Be still' in a sentimental manner. Some regard it as a kind of exhortation to us to be silent; but it is nothing of the sort. It means, 'Give up (or 'Give in') and admit that I am God'. God is addressing people who are opposed to Him and He says: This is My power; therefore give up and give in, keep silent and know that I am God.

We must remember that this power is working for us. We have seen it in Paul's prayer for the Ephesians: 'The exceeding greatness of his power' (i. 19). He 'that is able to do exceeding abundantly above all that we ask or think, according to the power that worketh in us' (iii. 20). In the light of such statements is not worry ridiculous? Is it not utterly foolish? It just means that we do not think; we do not read our Scriptures, or, if we do, we do so in a perfunctory manner, or are so controlled by prejudices that we do not take them at their face value. We must face these things and draw out our mighty deductions.

A last thought. This 'little faith', is ultimately due to a failure to apply what we know, and claim to believe, to the circumstances and details of life. I can put that in a phrase. Do you remember that famous incident in our Lord's earthly life and ministry when He was sleeping in the stern of the ship and the water began to come in? The sea had become boisterous, and the disciples became worried and anxious and said, 'Master, carest thou not that we perish?' His reply to them summarizes perfectly all we have said in this chapter. He said: 'Where, where is your faith?' (see Luke viii. 23–25). Where is it? You have it, but where is it? Or, if you like, He said: Why don't you apply your faith to this? You see it is not enough to say we have faith; we must apply our faith, we must relate it, we must see that it is where it ought to be at any given moment. It is a poor type of Christianity that has this wonderful faith with respect to salvation and then whimpers and cries when confronted by the daily trials of life. We must apply our faith. 'Little faith' does not do this.

I trust that, after looking at this mighty argument of our blessed Lord, we shall not only feel convicted, but shall also see that to be worried is an utter contradiction of our position as children of God. There is no circumstance or condition in this life which should lead a Christian to worry. He has no right to worry; and if he does he is not only condemning himself as being a man of little faith, he is also dishonouring his God and being disloyal to his blessed Saviour. 'Take no thought'; exercise faith; understand the truth and apply it to every detail of your life.

CHAPTER THIRTEEN

INCREASING FAITH

HERE, in verses 31–33, our Lord presents us with the positive approach towards 'little faith'. It is not sufficient that we should realize what it means; the great thing is to have a larger and a bigger faith. He introduces His teaching with His word 'therefore'; it follows on immediately, it is a link in a chain. 'Therefore', He says, 'in the light of all this', 'Take no thought, saying, What shall we eat? or, What shall we drink? or, Wherewithal shall we be clothed?' That is a repetition of the fundamental injunction. There are those who would have us believe that the addition of the word 'saying' means that there is a slight alteration. In the first place, you remember, He said, 'Therefore I say unto you, Take no thought'; here, they point out, He says, 'Therefore take no thought, saying'.

I do not think that it is a material difference. There is no objection to the argument that there *is* a difference, that in the first instance our Lord was giving a general warning against the tendency to worry, but that here He goes a step further and says, in effect, 'You must not even say these things; you may think them, but you must not say them.' Whether that is so or not is immaterial because the point still remains the same. Our Lord shows us here the positive way to increase our faith, and again He puts it in the form of an argument. Let us remind ourselves that His method is always very logical. He does not merely make statements and pronouncements; He reasons them out with us. What marvellous condescension! Look at that word 'for'. 'For after all these things...'; 'for your heavenly Father knoweth...'; and so on. All we have to do, therefore, is to follow His argument. At this point we observe that three main points are put for our consideration, three main principles which, if we grasp and understand them, will inevitably lead to a greater faith. The way in which our Lord handles this subject is truly remarkable.

His essential argument is that we, as Christians, are to be different from the Gentiles. That is how He starts. You notice that He puts this statement in brackets as it were: 'For after all these things do the Gentiles seek.' But what a powerful statement it is, and how important! Though negative in form, it leads to a very positive result. If you want to increase your faith, the first thing you have to realize is that to be worried and anxious about food, and drink, and clothing, and your life in this world is, in a sense, to be just like the Gentiles.

What does He mean by this? The word 'Gentile', of course, really means 'heathen'. The Jews were God's chosen people. It was they who had the oracles of God and the special knowledge of God; the others were described as heathen. So we must analyse this word and realize exactly what He means. The statement is that if I am guilty of being worried and anxious about these matters of food and drink and clothing, and about my life in this world, and certain things which I lack—if these dominate me and my life, then I am really living and behaving as a heathen. But let us try to discover the real significance of that.

The heathen were people who had no revelation from God, and who therefore had no knowledge of God. That is the great point made in the Old Testament, that is the thing that differentiated the children of Israel from all others. Paul says in his argument concerning this matter in Romans iii. 2 that 'unto them were committed the oracles of God'. God made a special revelation of Himself to the Jews not only in the call of Abraham and other individual instances, but supremely in the giving of the law and the great teaching of the prophets. The heathen knew nothing about that; they had not had this special revelation, nor did they have a knowledge of God. They did not have the Old Testament Scriptures and they were, therefore, without the means of knowing Him. That is the essential point about the heathen, they know nothing about God in a real sense, they are 'without God in the world'.

We can, of course, go further in this connection and say that the heathen know nothing about the revelation of God in Jesus Christ, and know nothing about God's way of salvation. They are entirely ignorant of the view of life which is taught in the Bible. They do not know that 'God so loved the world, that he gave his only begotten Son, that whosoever believeth in him should not perish, but have everlasting life.' They know nothing about the 'exceeding great and precious promises', or about the various pledges that God has given to His own people in this world. The heathen know nothing about that, and have not received it. They are in real darkness about life in this world and how it is to be lived and about their eternal destiny. Their view of life is entirely limited by their own thoughts, and they lack this light that is given from above.

We must not stay with this, but the heathen who hold this pagan view of life generally view the things that happen to us in one of two main ways. There are those amongst them who believe that everything in this life is accidental. That view is sometimes known as the 'theory of contingency' which teaches that things happen without rhyme or reason, and that you never know what is going to happen next. That, for instance, is the view of life in this world that is held, and is being taught and given considerable prominence at the present time by men like Dr. Julian Huxley, to whom everything is accidental and contingent. There is, they say, no purpose whatsoever in life. There is no design, order or arrangement; the whole thing is fortuitous. It is a very old view. There is nothing new about it, and there are no people in the world today who are more pathetic than those who imagine that to hold such a view is the hallmark of modernity. Half the heathen take that view of life and it is obviously going to affect in a profound sense their whole attitude towards everything that happens.

The other view, commonly called 'fatalism', is the extreme opposite of that. It teaches that what is to be will be. It does not matter what you may do or say, it is going to happen. 'What is to be will be.' Therefore it is utter folly to strive or make any effort. You just go on and trust that things will not go too badly with you, and that somehow or another you will have a fairly easy passage through this world. Fatalism teaches that you can do nothing about life, that there are powers and factors controlling you inexorably, and holding you in the grip of a rigid determinism. So there is no purpose in thought, still less in worry. But fatalism leads to worry all the same, because such people are always worrying as to what is going to happen next. 'Contingency' and 'fatalism', then, are the two main expressions of the heathen view of life.

It is important for us to bear those two views in mind because Christian people often hold one or other of them unconsciously. The Christian view, on the other hand, the one taught in the Bible, and especially at this particular point in the Sermon on the Mount, is what can be described as the doctrine of 'certainty'. Life, it says, is not controlled by blind necessity, but certain things are certain because we are in the hands of the living God. So, if you are a Christian, you put that doctrine of certainty over against the theories of contingency and fatalism. There is a great difference between these views—the Christian view and the pagan; and what our Lord is saying is that, if you are living a life full of anxiety and worry, you are virtually spiritually dead and taking the pagan view of life.

It follows of necessity that if that is our fundamental view of life in this world, it is going to determine our way of living, and to control our whole behaviour. 'As a man thinketh in his heart, so is he.' You can always tell what a man's philosophy of life is by the way in which he lives and by the way he reacts to the things that are happening round about him. That is why a time of crisis always sifts people. We always betray exactly where we stand by what we say. You remember our Lord said on one occasion that we shall be judged by every idle word we utter (see Matthew xii. 36). We proclaim a great deal about ourselves as Christians by our ordinary remarks and by our ordinary comments about life. Our view of life comes out in our every expression.

Moreover, if a man has a pagan view of life in this world, he will also have a pagan view of life in the next world. The pagan view of that life is that it is a realm of shadows. You will find that in Greek and other pagan mythologies. Everything is uncertain. If a man, therefore, has that view, this world is going to be everything to him and he is going to make the best of this life because it is the only life about which he has any knowledge. Furthermore, he is either trying to anticipate contingency, or else he is trying somehow to elude this fatalism that is gripping him. What he does is this. He says, Here I am at this moment; I am going to get the most out of this because I do not know what is going to happen next. Therefore his philosophy is 'Let us eat, drink, and be merry': let us live for the hour. I have this hour, let me extract out of it everything that I can.

That is what we are seeing all around us; that is the way in which the majority of people seem to be living today. They argue that, since you do not know what is going to happen next month or next year, the essence of wisdom is to say, 'Well; let's spend all we have; let's get the maximum pleasure out of life now.' Thus they are quite negligent of consequences and quite heedless about their eternal destiny. Our Lord sums it all up by putting it like this, 'For after all these things do the Gentiles (the heathen, the pagans) seek.' And this word 'seek' is a very strong one. It means that they seek earnestly, that they are continually seeking these things, that they really live for them. Let us say this about them. They are perfectly consistent; if that is their view of life, then they are doing the right thing. They live for these things, they seek them earnestly and continually.

From all this, however, arises the vital and important question.

Are we like that? If these things are first in our lives, says our Lord, and if they monopolize our lives and our thinking, then we are nothing better than the heathen, we are worldlings with worldly minds. This word comes to us with terrible power and significance. There are so many people who can be described as spiritual worldlings. If you talk to them about salvation they have the correct view; but if you talk to them about life in general they are worldlings. When it is a matter of the salvation of the soul they have the correct answer; but if you listen to their ordinary conversation about life in this world you will discover a heathen philosophy. They are worried about food and drink; they are always talking about wealth and position and their various possessions. These things really control them. They are made happy or unhappy by them; they are put out by them or pleased by them; and they are always thinking and talking about them. That is to be like the heathen, says Christ; for the Christian should not be controlled by these things. Whatever may be his position with respect to them, he is not finally to be controlled by them. He should really not be made unhappy or happy by these things, because that is the typical condition of the heathen, who is dominated by them in his whole outlook upon life and in his living in this world.

This is a very good way, therefore, of increasing our faith and of introducing ourselves to the biblical conception of the life of faith. God's people, God's children in this world, are meant to live the life of faith; they are meant to live in the light of that faith which they profess. I suggest, therefore, that there are certain questions which we should always be putting to ourselves. Here are some of them. Do I face the things that happen to me in this world as the Gentiles do? When these things happen to me, when there seem to be difficulties about food, or drink, or clothing, or difficulties in some relationship in life, how do I face them? How do I react? Is my reaction just that of the heathen, and of people who do not pretend to be Christian? How do I react during a war? How do I react to illness and pestilence and loss? It is a very good question to ask.

But let us go further. Does my Christian faith affect my view of life and control it in all matters? I claim to be Christian, and hold the Christian faith; the question I now ask myself is, Does that Christian faith of mine affect my whole detailed view of life? Is it always determining my reaction and my response to the particular things that happen? Or, we can put it like this. Is it clear and obvious to myself and to everybody else that my whole approach to life, my essential view of life in general and in particular, is altogether different from that of the non-Christian? It should be. The Sermon on the Mount begins with the Beatitudes. They describe people who are altogether different from all others, as different as light from darkness, as different as salt from putrefaction. If, then, we are different essentially, we must be different in our view of, and in our reaction to, everything. I know of no better question that a man can ask himself in every circumstance in life than that. When something happens to upset you, do you ask, 'Is my reaction essentially different from what it would be if I were not a Christian?' Let us remind ourselves of the teaching we have already considered at the end of the fifth chapter of this Gospel. You remember that our Lord put it like this: 'If ye salute your brethren only, what do ye more than others?' That is it. The Christian is a man who does 'more than others'. He is a man who is absolutely different. And if in every detail of his life this Christianity of his does not come in, he is a very poor Christian, he is a man 'of little faith'.

Or, let us put it in a final question like this: Do I always place everything in my life, and everything that happens to me, in the context of my Christian faith, and then look at it in the light of that context? The heathen cannot do that. The heathen has not got the Christian faith. He does not believe in God, or know anything about Him; he has not this revelation of God as his Father and himself as His child. He does not know anything about God's gracious purposes so, poor man, he turns in upon himself and reacts automatically and instinctively to what happens. But what really proves that we are Christians is that, when these things come to us, or happen to us, we do not see them just as they are; as Christians we take them and put them immediately into the context of the whole of our faith and then look at them again.

We ended the last chapter by describing faith as being essentially active. Our Lord asked His disciples, 'Where is your faith? Why are you not applying it?' This time we can put it the other way round. Something happens to us that tends to upset us. The heathen in the natural man makes him lose his temper, or become hurt and sensitive. But the Christian stops and says, 'Wait a minute. I am going to take this thing and put it into the context of everything I know and believe about God and my relationship to Him'. Then he looks at it again. Then he begins to understand what the author of the Epistle to the Hebrews means when he says, 'whom the Lord loveth he chasteneth'. Because the Christian knows that, he is able to enjoy it, in a sense, even while it is happening, because he puts it into the context of his faith. He is the only man who can do that; the heathen cannot do it, he is incapable of it. So we ask that general question. Is it evident to me and to everybody else that I am not a heathen? Is my conduct and my behaviour in life such that it shows I am a Christian? Do I show plainly and clearly that I belong to a higher realm, and that I can raise everything about me to that realm? 'After all these things do the Gentiles seek,' says our Lord. But you are not Gentiles. Realize what you are; remember who you are and live accordingly. Rise to the level of your faith; be worthy of your high calling in Christ Jesus. Christian people, watch your lips, watch your tongues. We betray ourselves in our conversation, in the things we say, in the things that come out in our unguarded moments. Such behaviour is typical of the heathen; the Christian exercises discipline and control because he sees everything in the context of God and of eternity.

The second argument is really a repetition of that which our Lord has already pressed upon us several times. He does not rush these things. He says, 'For your heavenly Father knoweth that ye have need of all these things'. He has already been telling us this in the argument about the birds and the lilies of the field. But He knows us; He knows how prone we are to forget things. So He says it again: 'Your heavenly Father knoweth that ye have need of all these things'. We can put it in this form. The second principle by which you can increase and enlarge your faith is that, as a Christian, you should have implicit faith in and reliance upon God as your heavenly Father. We have already considered it,[1] so we need only summarize it here. It means something like this. Nothing can happen to us apart from God. He knows all about us. If it is true to say that the very hairs of our head are all numbered, then we must remember that we are never in any position or situation outside God's knowledge or care. He knows it much better than we do ourselves. This is the argument of our blessed Lord Himself: 'Your heavenly Father knoweth that ye have need of all these things.' There is no more blessed statement in the whole of Scripture than that. You will never be anywhere but that He sees you; there will never be anything in the depths of your heart, in the innermost recesses of your being but that He knows all about it. The author of the Epistle to the Hebrews puts this same truth in a different con-

[1] See pp. 131 ff.

nection: 'All things are naked and opened unto the eyes of him with whom we have to do' (iv. 13). He is a discerner of the thoughts and intents of the heart. He says that in order to warn those Hebrew Christians. We must remember that we are not only to live in the fear of the Lord, but we are to live in the comfort and the knowledge of God. He not only sees what is happening to you when you are taken ill, He not only knows when you are suffering bereavement and sorrow, He knows every pang of the heart, He knows every heartache. He knows everything; there is nothing outside His omniscience. He knows all about us in every respect and He therefore knows our every need. From that our Lord draws this deduction. You need never be anxious, you must never be worried. God is with you in this state, you are not alone, and He is your Father. Even an earthly father does this in a measure. He is with his child, protecting, doing everything he can for him. Multiply that by infinity, and that is what God is doing with respect to you, whatever your circumstance.

If we were but to grasp this, it would surely cause worry and strain and anxiety to be banished once and for ever. Never allow yourself for a moment to think that you are left to yourself. You are not. You and I must learn to say what our Lord Himself said under the very shadow of the cross: 'The hour cometh, yea, is now come, that ye shall be scattered . . . and shall leave me alone: and yet I am not alone, because the Father is with me.' And that is His promise to us also: 'I will never leave thee, nor forsake thee'. But above all else rely upon this, that He knows everything about us, every circumstance, every need, every wound; and therefore we can rest quietly and confidently in that blessed and most glorious assurance.

That, in turn, brings us to the third argument, which is that we are to concentrate upon perfecting our relationship to God as our heavenly Father. We, unlike the heathen, are to rely implicitly upon our knowledge of Him as our heavenly Father, and we are to concentrate upon perfecting this knowledge and our relationship to Him. 'But seek ye first the kingdom of God, and his righteousness; and all these things shall be added unto you.' I wonder whether I dare suggest that there is an element of humour introduced at this point. It seems to me, in effect, that our Lord is saying this: He has said twice over, and then has repeated in various forms: Do not worry about food and drink and clothing; do not worry about your life in this world; do not worry as to whether God is trying you or not. And then, as it were,

He says: If you want to worry, I will tell you what to worry about. Worry about your relationship to the Father! That is the thing to concentrate on. The Gentiles are seeking these other things, and so are many of you, but 'Seek ye rather'. That is the thing to seek.

Again we should remember that 'seek' carries the meaning of seeking earnestly, seeking intensely, living for it. And He even enforces it by adding another word, 'first'. 'Seek ye first.' That means, generally, principally, above everything else; give that priority. Once more we find our Lord repeating Himself. He says: You are concerned about these other things, and you are putting them first. But you must not. What you have to put first is the kingdom of God and His righteousness. He has already said that in the model prayer which He taught these people to pray. You remember the teaching. You come to God. Of course you are interested in life and in this world; but you do not start by saying, 'Give us this day our daily bread'. You start like this: 'Our Father which art in heaven, Hallowed be thy name. Thy kingdom come. Thy will be done in earth, as it is in heaven.' And then, and only then, 'Give us this day our daily bread'. 'Seek ye first'—not 'your daily bread', but, 'the kingdom of God and his righteousness'. In other words, you must bring yourself to that position in mind and heart and desires. It must take absolute priority over everything else.

What does our Lord mean by saying: 'Seek ye first the kingdom of God'? Obviously He is not telling His hearers how to make themselves Christian; but He is telling them how to behave because they are Christian. They are in the kingdom of God, and because they are in it they are to seek it more and more. They are, as Peter puts it, to 'make their calling and election sure'. In practice it means that, as children of our heavenly Father, we should be seeking to know Him better. Now the author of the Epistle to the Hebrews puts that perfectly when he says in xi. 6, 'He that cometh to God must believe that he is, and that he is a rewarder of them that diligently seek him.' Put your emphasis on the 'diligently'. Many Christian people miss so many blessings in this life because they do not seek God diligently. They do not spend much time in seeking His face. In His courts they drop on their knees to pray, but that is not of necessity seeking the Lord. The Christian is meant to be seeking the face of the Lord daily, constantly. He takes and makes time to do so.

Furthermore, it means that we must think more about the kingdom and our relationship to God, and especially about our eternal future. It was because he did this that Paul was able to say to the Corinthians, 'Our light affliction, which is but for a moment, worketh for us a far more exceeding and eternal weight of glory; while we look not at the things which are seen, but at the things which are not seen: for the things which are seen are temporal; but the things which are not seen are eternal' (2 Corinthians iv. 17, 18). Notice that 'while'. The apostle only rejoices in spite of these things—'while', 'as long as'. He puts it as a positive exhortation and injunction to the Colossians when he says, 'Set your affection on things above, not on things on the earth'. That is the meaning of seeking the kingdom of God.

But He says, 'Seek ye first the kingdom of God, and his righteousness'. Why the addition of this 'righteousness'? Again, this is a very important addition. This means holiness, the life of righteousness. You are not only to seek the kingdom of God in the sense that you set your affections on things above; you must also positively seek holiness and righteousness. Once more we get the repetition of 'Blessed are they which do hunger and thirst after righteousness: for they shall be filled.' Yes, that is it. The Christian is seeking righteousness, seeking to be like Christ, seeking positive holiness and to be more and more holy, growing in grace and in the knowledge of the Lord. This is the way to increase your faith. It works like this. The more holy we are, the nearer we shall be to God. The more holy we are, the greater will be our faith. The more sanctified and holy we are, the greater will be our assurance and therefore our claims and our reliance upon God. This is experience, is it not? Have you not known this many times? Suddenly something goes wrong in your life and you turn to God in prayer; and the moment you do so you are reminded of your slackness in the past weeks or months. Something says within you, 'Surely you are behaving just like a cad? How many days and weeks and months have passed when you have not sought the face of God? You have said your prayers mechanically; but now you are seeking God, you are making time to look for Him. But you have not done that regularly.' You feel condemned, and you have lost confidence in your prayers. There are absolute rules in this spiritual life, and it is the man who seeks the kingdom of God and His righteousness who has the greatest confidence in Him. The nearer we live to God the less we are aware of the things of this life and this world, and the greater our sense of assurance about Him. The more holy we are, the better we shall know God. We shall know Him as our Father, and then nothing that happens to us will upset our equanimity, because our relationship to Him is so close.

We can paraphrase our Lord's words thus: If you want to seek anything, if you want to be anxious about anything, be anxious about your spiritual condition, your nearness to God and your relationship to Him. If you put that first, worry will go; that is the result. This great concern about your relationship to God will drive out every lesser concern about food and clothing.

The man who knows himself to be a child of God and an heir of eternity has a very different view of things in this life and world. This is true of necessity, and the greater that faith and knowledge, the smaller will these other things become. Moreover he has a definite specific promise. Let us lay hold on this promise and grasp it firmly. The promise is that, if we do truly seek these things first and foremost, and almost exclusively, these other things shall be added unto us, they will be 'thrown into the bargain'. The heathen does nothing but think about these things. There are spiritual worldlings also who are praying about these things and nothing else, but they never find satisfaction. The man of God prays about and seeks the kingdom of God, and these other things are added unto him. It is a specific promise of God.

You have a perfect illustration of this in the story about Solomon. Solomon did not pray for riches and length of days; he prayed for wisdom. And God said in effect: Because you have not prayed for these other things I will give you wisdom; and I will give you these other things as well. I will give you riches and length of days into the bargain (see 1 Kings iii). God always does that. It is not an accident that the Puritans of the seventeenth century, especially the Quakers, became wealthy people. It was not because they hoarded wealth, it was not because they worshipped mammon. It was just that they were living for God and His righteousness, and the result was that they did not throw away their money on worthless things. In a sense, therefore, they could not help becoming wealthy. They held on to the promises of God and incidentally became rich.

Put God, His glory and the coming of His kingdom, and your relationship to Him, your nearness to Him and your holiness in the central position, and you have the pledged word of God Himself through the lips of His Son, that all these other things, as they are necessary for your well-being in this life and world, shall be added unto you. That is the way to increase your faith. Be unlike the heathen; remember that God knows all about you as your Father, and is watching over you. Therefore seek to be more like Him and to live your life nearer to Him.

WORRY: ITS CAUSES AND CURE

IN Matthew vi. 34 our Lord brings to a conclusion the subject
with which He has been dealing in this entire section of the
Sermon on the Mount, namely, the problem which is created
for us by our relationship to the things of this world. It is a
problem that confronts us all. It does so in different ways as we
have seen. Some people are tempted to be governed by worldly
possessions in the sense that they want to hoard and amass them.
Others are troubled by them in the sense that they are worried
about them; it is not the problem of superabundance in their
case, but the problem of need. But, essentially, according to our
Lord, it is one and the same problem, the problem of our
relationship to the things of this world, and of this life. As we
have seen, our Lord takes great trouble to work out the argument
with respect to this matter. He deals with both aspects of the
problem and analyses both.

Here, in this verse, He brings this consideration to an end and
He puts it in this particular form. Three times over He uses this
expression, 'Take therefore no thought'. It is so important, that
He deliberately states it like that three times, and in particular
with regard to the question of food and drink and clothing; and
He works out the argument, you remember, with regard to these
matters. Here is the conclusion of the whole subject, and I am
sure that many, when they first read this verse in its context, must
have felt almost a sense of surprise that our Lord should have
added it. He seems to have reached such a wonderful climax in
the previous verse, the thirty-third, where He has concentrated
His positive teaching in the memorable words, 'Seek ye first the
kingdom of God, and his righteousness; and all these things
shall be added unto you.' That seems like one of those final statements to which nothing can be added, and at first sight the verse
at which we are now looking seems to be almost an anti-climax.
You cannot imagine anything higher than, 'Seek ye first the
kingdom of God, and his righteousness.' Be right about that,
says our Lord, and then you have no need to worry about these
other things; they shall be added unto you. You are to be right
with God and God will look after you. But then He goes on to say,

Do not be anxious about the morrow—the future: for the morrow shall take thought for the things of itself: 'Sufficient unto the day is the evil thereof.'

It is always good when we face a problem like this to ask a question. We can be quite certain that this is not an anti-climax; there is some very good reason for this addition. Our Lord never utters words merely for the sake of doing so. Having given us this wonderful positive teaching He returns to it and puts it in this negative form. He ends on the negative and that is, at first sight, what constitutes the problem. Why did He do that? The moment you face the fact and begin to question it, you will see at once why our Lord did so. It is because this is really an extension of His teaching. It is not mere repetition, or just a summary; it is that, but it is more than that. In adding this He carried the teaching one step further. So far, He has been looking at this problem as it concerns us in the immediate present; now here He takes it on and covers the future also. He extends it, and applies it, to cover the whole of life. And here, if one may use such language and such an expression with regard to our blessed Lord, He shows His profound understanding of human nature and of the problems with which we are confronted in this life. All must agree that you will not find anywhere in any textbook a more thorough analysis of worry, anxiety, and the anxious care that tends to kill man in this world, than you find in this paragraph which we have been considering in detail.

Here our Lord shows His final understanding of the condition. Worry, after all, is a definite entity; it is a force, a power, and we have not begun to understand it until we realize what a tremendous power it is. We so often tend to think of the condition of worry as one which is negative, a failure on our part to do certain things. It is that; it is a failure to apply our faith. But the thing we must emphasize is that worry is something positive that comes and grips us and takes control of us. It is a mighty power, an active force, and if we do not realize that, we are certain to be defeated by it. If it cannot get us to be anxious and burdened and borne down by the state and condition of things that are actually confronting us, it will take this next step, it will go on into the future.

We must have discovered this in ourselves, or perhaps when we have tried to help to deliver other people who are suffering from a condition of worry. The conversation starts with the particular thing that has brought them to you. You then provide the answers and show how unnecessary worry is. You will find, however, that almost invariably they go on and say, 'Yes, but . . . ' That is typical of worry, it always gives the impression that it does not really want to be relieved. The person wants to be relieved, but the worry does not; and we are entitled to draw that distinction. Our Lord does it Himself when He talks about the morrow taking thought for the things of itself. That is personalizing worry; He is regarding it as a power, almost a person, that takes hold of you, and in spite of yourself keeps arguing with you and saying one thing and then another. It leads to that curious perverse condition in which one almost desires not to be relieved and not to be delivered: and it often works in the particular form we are considering together now. When you have brought out all the answers and given a full explanation to such persons, then they say, 'Ah yes, that is all right for now; but what about tomorrow? what about next week? what about next year?' And on and on it goes, into the future. In other words, if it cannot work up its case on the facts it has before it, it does not hesitate to conjure up facts. Worry has an active imagination, and it can envisage all sorts and kinds of possibilities. It can envisage strange eventualities, and with its terrible power and activity it can transport us into the future and into a situation that is yet to come. And there we find ourselves worried and troubled and borne down by something which is purely imaginary.

We need not go further into the matter because we all know exactly what it is. But the key to the understanding of how to treat the subject is to realize that we are dealing with a very vital force and power. I do not want to exaggerate it too much. There are cases where this condition is undoubtedly the result of the work of evil spirits; we can see clearly that there is another personality at work. But even short of direct possession we must recognize the fact that our adversary, the devil, does in various ways, through using a lowered physical condition or taking advantage of a natural tendency to over-anxiety, thus exercise a tyranny and power over many. We have to understand that we are fighting for our lives against some tremendous power. We are up against a powerful adversary.

Let us see how our Lord deals with this problem, this worry and anxiety about the future. The first thing we must remember, is that what He says now is in the context of His previous teaching. Here again it is fatal to take this statement right out of its context.

We must remember all He has been telling us, for it is all still applicable. We continue from that to the further argument that He uses here, where He shows us the folly of being anxious. He shows it for the foolish thing it is as He asks in effect: Why do you allow yourself to be worried thus about the future? 'The morrow shall take thought for the things of itself. Sufficient unto the day is the evil thereof.' If the present is bad enough as it is, why go to meet the future? To go on from day to day is enough in and of itself; be content with that. But not only that. Worry about the future is so utterly futile and useless; it achieves nothing at all. We are very slow to see that; yet how true it is. Indeed we can go further and say that worry is never of any value at all. This is seen with particular clarity as you come to face the future. Apart from anything else, it is a pure waste of energy because however much you worry you cannot do anything about it. In any case its threatened catastrophes are imaginary; they are not certain, they may never happen at all.

But above all that, says our Lord, can you not see that, in a sense, you are mortgaging the future by worrying about it in the present? Indeed, the result of worrying about the future is that you are crippling yourself in the present; you are lessening your efficiency with regard to today, and thereby you are reducing your whole efficiency with regard to that future which is coming to meet you. In other words, worry is something that is due to an entire failure to understand the nature of life in this world. Our Lord seems to picture life like this. As the result of the Fall and sin there is always a problem in life, because when man fell, he was told that henceforward he was going to live and eat his bread 'by the sweat of his brow'. He was no longer in Paradise, he was no longer just to take the fruit and live a life of ease and enjoyment. As the result of sin, life in this world has become a task. Man has to labour and must meet trials and troubles. We all know that, for we are all subject to the same tribulations and trials.

The great question is, how are we to face them? According to our Lord, the vital thing is not to spend every day of your life in adding up the grand total of everything that is ever likely to happen to you in the whole of your life in this world. If you do that, it will crush you. That is not the way. Rather, you must think of it like this. There is, as it were, a daily quota of problems and difficulties in life. Every day has its problems; some of them are constant from day to day, some of them vary. But the great thing to do is to realize that every day must be lived in and of itself and as a unit. Here is the quota for today. Very well; we must face that and meet it; and He has already told us how to do so. We must not go forward and tack tomorrow's quota on to today's, otherwise it may be too much for us. We have to take it day by day. You remember how our Lord turned upon His disciples when they were trying to dissuade Him from going back to unfriendly Judaea to the house where Lazarus lay dead? They pointed out to Him the possible consequences, and how it might shorten His life. His answer to them was 'Are there not twelve hours in the day?' You have to live twelve hours at a time and no more. Here is the quota for today; very well, face that and deal with that. Do not think of tomorrow. You will have tomorrow's quota, but then it will be tomorrow, and not today.

It is very easy to deal with this matter solely on that level and very tempting to do so. That is what you might call, if you like, psychology. Not the so-called new psychology but the old psychology of life which has been practised by mankind from the very beginning. And it is very profound psychology; it is the essence of common-sense and wisdom, purely on the human level. If you want to go through life without crippling yourself and burdening yourself and perhaps losing your health and the control of your nerves, these are the cardinal rules. Do not carry yesterday or tomorrow with you; live for today and for the twelve hours you are in. It is very interesting to notice as you read biographies how many men have failed in life because they have not done that. Most men who have been successful in life have been characterized by this wonderful capacity for forgetting the past. They have made mistakes. 'Well,' they say, 'I have made them and I cannot undo them. If I meditated upon them for the rest of my life, it would make no difference. I am not going to be a fool, I will let the dead past bury its dead.' The result is that when they make a decision they do not spend the night worrying about it afterwards. On the other hand, the man who cannot help referring back keeps himself awake saying, 'Why did I do that?' And so he saps his nervous energy, and wakes up after poor and broken sleep feeling tired and unfit. As a consequence he makes more mistakes, completing the vicious circle of worry by saying, 'If I am making these mistakes now, what about next week?' The poor man is already down and defeated.

Here is our Lord's answer to all that. Do not be foolish, do not waste your energy, do not spend your time thus in worrying over what has passed, or about the future; here is today, live to the maximum today. But of course we must not stop at that level. Our Lord does not. We must take this statement in the whole context of this teaching. So, having reasoned it out on a natural line, and having seen the essential wisdom of that, we go on to see that we must learn not only to rely on God in general, but also in particular. We must learn to realize that the God who helps us today will be the same God tomorrow, and will help us tomorrow.

This is perhaps the lesson which many of us need to learn, that not only must we learn to divide up our life in this world into these periods of twelve or twenty-four hours; we must divide up our whole relationship to God in exactly the same way. The danger is that, while we believe in God in general, and for the whole of our life, we do not believe in Him for the particular sections of our life. Thereby many of us go wrong. We must learn to take things to God as they arise. Some people fail very grievously in this matter because they are always trying to anticipate God; they are always sitting down, as it were, and asking themselves, 'Now I wonder what God is going to ask me to do tomorrow or in a week's time or in a year? What is God going to ask of me then?' That is utterly wrong. Never try to anticipate God. As you must not anticipate your own future, do not anticipate God's future for you. Live day by day; live a life of obedience to God every day; do what God asks you to do every day. Never allow yourself to indulge in thoughts such as these, 'I wonder when tomorrow comes whether God will want me to do this or to do that.' That must never be done, says our Lord. You must learn to trust God day by day for every particular occasion, and never try to go ahead of Him.

There is a sense in which we commit ourselves to God once and for ever; there is another sense in which we have to do it every day. There is a sense in which God has given us everything in grace once and for ever. Yes; but He gives grace to us also in parts and portions day by day. We must start the day and say to ourselves, 'Here is a day which is going to bring me certain problems and difficulties; very well, I shall need God's grace to help me. I know God will make all grace to abound, He will be with me according to my need—"as thy days, so shall thy strength be".' That is the essential biblical teaching with regard to this matter; we must learn to leave the future entirely in God's hands.

Take, for instance, that great statement of it in Hebrews xiii. 8. The Hebrew Christians were passing through troubles and trials, and the author of that Epistle tells them not to worry, and for this reason: 'Jesus Christ the same yesterday, and to day, and for ever.' In effect he says you need not worry, for what He was yesterday, He is today, and He will be tomorrow. You need not anticipate life; the Christ who takes you through today will be the same Christ tomorrow. He is changeless, everlasting, always the same; so you must not think about tomorrow; think instead about the changeless Christ. Or consider the way in which Paul puts it in 1 Corinthians x. 13: 'There hath no temptation taken you but such as is common to man: but God is faithful, who will not suffer you to be tempted above that ye are able; but will with the temptation also make a way to escape'. That is certain with regard to the whole of your future. There will be no trial that will come to you but that God will always provide that way of escape. It will never be above your strength; there will always be the remedy.

We can sum it all up by saying that, as we learn in wisdom to take our days one by one as they come, forgetting yesterday and tomorrow, so we must learn this vital importance of walking with God day by day, of relying upon Him day by day, and applying to Him for the particular needs of each day. The fatal temptation to which we are all prone is that of trying to store grace against the future. That means lack of faith in God. Leave it with Him; leave it entirely with Him, confident and assured that He will always be going before you. As the Scripture puts it, He will 'prevent' you. He will be there before you to meet the problem. Turn to Him and you will find that He is there, that He knows all about it, and knows all about you.

That, then, is the essence of the teaching. But if we are to explain it honestly and fully, we are compelled at this point to consider a problem. Ordinary people reading this verse have always tended to ask two questions. 'Take therefore no thought for the morrow: for the morrow shall take thought for the things of itself. Sufficient unto the day is the evil thereof.' Is it wrong, therefore, they ask, for a Christian to save, to save money, to put something by, as we say, for a rainy day? Is it right or is it wrong for a Christian to take out an insurance policy? The answer is exactly the same as it was when we dealt with the first part of this section. There we saw that the answer is that 'take no thought' does not literally mean that you should not think at all, but that you are not to worry. This should always be translated as 'Do not be anxious about', 'do not be agitated about', 'do not worry about' tomorrow. We saw, you remember, that our Lord does not tell us that, because the birds of the air are fed without

ploughing and sowing and reaping and gathering into barns,
therefore man should never plough or sow, and should never reap
and gather into barns. That is to make the thing ridiculous,
because it is God Himself who ordained seedtime and harvest.
And the farmer when he ploughs is in fact taking proper thought
for the morrow because he knows that his crop is not going to
grow automatically. He has to plough the earth and to look after
it, and eventually he reaps and gathers into his barn. In a sense
that is all a preparation for the future, and of course that is not
condemned by the Scriptures. On the contrary, it is even commended by Scripture. That is how man is to live his life in this
world according to the ordinance of God Himself. So this verse
must not be taken in that foolish and ridiculous sense. We are not
just to sit and wait for food and clothing to come to us; that is to
ridicule the teaching.

That entitles us, I think, to take the next step and to say that
our Lord's teaching throughout is that we are to do that which is
right, that which is reasonable, that which is legitimate. But—
and this is where the teaching of this verse comes in—we are
never to take so much thought about these things, or to be so
concerned about them, as to allow them to dominate our life, or
limit our usefulness, in the present. That is the point at which we
cross the line from reasonable thought and care to anxious care
and worry. Our Lord is condemning not the man who ploughs
the earth and sows the seeds, but the man who, having done that,
sits down and begins to get worried about it and has his mind
always centred on it, the man who is obsessed by the problem of
life and living, and by fear of the future. That is the one thing He
condemns, for not only is that man limiting his usefulness in the
present, not only is he crippling the present with fears for the
future, but above all he is allowing these cares to dominate his
life. Every man in this life, as the result of sin and the Fall, has
his problems. Problems are inevitable; existence in itself is a
problem. I shall therefore have to meet and face problems but I
am not to allow myself to be dominated and crushed by that
thought. The moment I am dominated by a problem I am in this
state of worry and anxiety which is wrong. So I may take
reasonable thought and care, and make reasonable provision,
and then think no more about it. Even necessary affairs must not
become my life. I must not spend all my time with them, and
they must not always be occupying my thought.

We must go a step further still. I must never allow thought

with regard to the future to inhibit in any way my usefulness in the present. Let me explain. There are various good causes in this world that need our help and assistance, and they have to be kept going from day to day. And there are certain people who are so concerned about how they are going to be able to live in the future that they have no time to help the causes which are in need at this moment. That is what is wrong. If I allow my concern about the future to cripple me in the present, I am guilty of worry; but if I make reasonable provision, in a legitimate manner, and then live my life fully in the present, all is well. Furthermore there is nothing in the Scripture which indicates that it is wrong to save or to be insured. But if I am always thinking about this insurance, or my bank balance, or as to whether I have saved enough and so on, then that is something which our Lord is concerned about and condemns. This could be illustrated in many different ways.

The danger with this text is for people to take one of two extreme positions. There are those who say that the Christian should live his life fully but should make no provision at all for the future. In the same way there are those who say that it is wrong to take up a collection in a church service, that these things should be done by faith. But it is not quite as simple as that because the apostle Paul teaches the members of the church at Corinth not only to take up collections, but he even tells them to put it aside on the first day of the week. He gives them detailed instructions; and there is much in the New Testament about the collection for the saints.

There must be no misunderstanding at this point; the teaching of Scripture is perfectly clear and explicit. There are two ways of maintaining God's work, and what applies to God's work applies to all our lives as Christians in this world. There are some men who are undoubtedly called to a special ministry of faith. Read for instance 1 Corinthians xii, and amongst the gifts that the Holy Spirit dispenses according to His own will to man you will find there is the so-called gift of faith. It is not the gift of miracles; it is the gift of faith, it is a special gift. What is this faith then? It is not saving or believing faith, for all Christians have that. What then is it? It is clearly the sort of faith that was given, for instance, to George Müller and Hudson Taylor. Those men were given a special gift by God in order that God might manifest His glory through them in that particular way. But I am equally certain that God called Dr. Barnardo to do the same sort of work and told him to take up collections and make appeals. The same God works in sanctified men in different ways; but both methods are obviously equally legitimate. Or take another illustration. It would be very difficult to find two holier or more dedicated men than George Müller and George Whitefield. Müller was definitely called to found an orphanage which was to be supported by faith and prayer, while Whitefield was called to start his orphanage in America and to keep it going by direct appeals for money to God's people.

That is clearly the truth concerning the conduct of the life of the Church as taught in the Scriptures; and we should apply exactly the same principles to our own personal lives. There are certain people who may be definitely called of God to live that particular kind of life which manifests that gift of faith. There are certain people for whom to put money aside or to take out an insurance policy would be quite wrong. But to say that anybody who takes up an insurance policy or who saves is therefore not a Christian is error. 'Let every man be fully persuaded in his own mind'; let every man examine himself in this matter; let not one condemn the other. All we must say is this; the Scripture certainly does allow this reasonable care, unless you are certain that God has called you to live your life in the other way. It is, therefore, quite wrong, and unscriptural, to condemn saving and insurance in the light of this text. But on the other hand, we must always be careful to maintain and preserve this balance.

Let us now summarize this teaching by putting it in the form of a number of general principles.

The first is this: All the things we have been dealing with in the last four or five chapters apply only to Christians. Somebody once said to me, 'How can that teaching about God's care for men be true? With all the need and poverty that exists in the world, with all the suffering of homeless and displaced men, women and children, how can you assert that?' The answer is that the promises are only to Christian people. What is the commonest cause of poverty? Why are the children ragged and without food? Is it not usually because of the sins of the parents? The money had been spent on drink or squandered on vain or evil things. Analyse the cases of poverty and you will find the results illuminating. These promises are made only to Christian people; they are not universal promises to everybody. Take that great statement of David, 'I have been young, and now am old; yet have I not seen the righteous forsaken, nor his seed begging bread.' Applied to the righteous I think this is literally true; but

let us be careful that we recognize the meaning of the word
'righteous'. He does not say, 'I have never seen a professing
Christian forsaken, nor his seed begging bread.' He says the
'righteous'. I suggest if you examine your experience you will
have to agree with David that you have never seen the righteous
man forsaken nor his seed begging bread. Now the important
word there is 'seed'. How far does it extend? Does it extend to the
posterity and the seed of this man for ever and for ever? I do not
think so. I think it extends only to his immediate seed, because
the grandson may be a profligate and an unrighteous man;
therefore the promise does not hold good. God does not say that
He is going to bless a man who is living an ungodly life. It is to the
righteous and his seed—that is the promise—and we can
challenge anybody to give us an example to the contrary. These
promises are only to God's people. They are always based on full
Christian doctrine; if you do not believe the doctrine they do not
apply to you.

   Secondly; worry is always a failure to grasp and apply our
faith. Faith does not work automatically. How often have we
seen that during these studies. Never think of faith as something
put inside you to work automatically; you have to apply it.
Faith does not grow automatically either; we must learn to talk
to our faith and to ourselves. We can think of faith in terms of a
man having a conversation with himself about himself and about
his faith. Do you remember how the Psalmist puts it in Psalm
xlii? Look at him turning to himself and saying, 'Why art thou
cast down, O my soul? and why art thou disquieted within
me?' That is the way to make faith grow. You must talk to
yourself about your faith. You must question yourself as to what
is the matter with your faith. You must ask your soul why it is
cast down, and wake it up! The child of God talks to himself; he
reasons with himself; he shakes himself and reminds himself of
himself and of his faith, and immediately his faith begins to grow.
Do not imagine that because you became a Christian all you
have to do is to go on mechanically. Your faith does not grow
mechanically, you have to attend to it. To use our Lord's
analogy, you have to dig round and about it, and pay attention
to it. Then you will find it will grow.

   Finally, a large part of faith, especially in this connection,
consists of just refusing anxious thoughts. That to me is perhaps
the most important and the most practical thing of all. Faith
means refusing to think about worrying things, refusing to think
of the future in that wrong sense. The devil and all adverse cir-

cumstances will do their utmost to make me do so, but having faith means that I shall say: 'No; I refuse to be worried. I have done my reasonable service; I have done what I believed to be right and legitimate, and beyond that I will not think at all.' That is faith, and it is particularly true with regard to the future. When the devil comes with his insinuations, injecting them into you—all the fiery darts of the evil one—say, 'No; I am not interested. The God whom I am trusting for today, I will trust for tomorrow. I refuse to listen; I will not think your thoughts.' Faith is refusing to be burdened because we have cast our burden upon the Lord. May He, in His infinite grace, give us wisdom and grace to implement these simple principles and thereby rejoice in Him day by day.

CHAPTER FIFTEEN

'JUDGE NOT'

WE come now to the last major section of the Sermon on the Mount. There is much disagreement as to the right way of approaching it. Some would regard chapter vii of Matthew's Gospel as just a collection of aphoristic statements with very little internal connection between them. But it seems to me that that is quite a mistaken view of this section of the Sermon, because there is quite clearly an underlying theme in the entire chapter, that of judgment. It is the theme that constantly recurs as our Lord proceeds with His teaching, and which He puts in different ways.

It is not difficult to trace the connection between this section and the previous one. Indeed, as we have seen repeatedly, it is very important that we should always regard the Sermon as a whole before we attempt a particular interpretation of any section, or any statement in a section. So it is good for us to review the whole again very hurriedly. First we get the description of the Christian man, his character. Then we are shown the effect upon him of all that happens in the world in which he lives and his reaction to that world. Then he is reminded of his function in the world as the salt of the earth and as a light set for all to see, and so on. Then, having thus described the Christian as he is and in his setting, our Lord goes on to give him particular instructions with regard to his life in this world. He starts with his relationship to the law. That was especially necessary because of the false teaching of the Pharisees and scribes. That is the theme of that long section in chapter v in which our Lord, in terms of six main principles, enunciates His view and interpretation of the law over against that of the Pharisees and scribes. So the Christian man is taught how he is to behave in general, how the law applies to him, and what is expected of him.

Having done that, in chapter vi our Lord looks at this Christian man who has thus been described, living his life in this world, and living it, especially, in fellowship with his Father. He has to remember always that the Father is looking upon him. He has to remember this when he is in private and when he is deciding what good he is going to do—his almsgiving, his prayer, his fasting, everything designed to bring about the growth and nurture and culture of his inner spiritual life and being. It has always to be done as realizing that the Father's eye is upon him. There is no value or merit in it if we do not realize that; if we are out to please ourselves or to impress others we may as well do nothing.

Then we come to another section, in which our Lord shows us the danger of the impact of the life of this world upon us, the danger of worldliness, the danger of living for the things of this life and this world, whether we have too much or too little, and especially the subtlety of that danger.

Having dealt with all that He now comes to this final section. And here, it seems to me, He is enforcing again the all-importance of our remembering that we are walking under the Father's eye. The particular subject He handles is one which is mainly concerned with our relationship with other people; but still the important thing to realize is that our relationship to God is the fundamental matter. It is as if our Lord were saying that the final thing which matters is not what men think of us, but what God thinks of us. In other words, we are reminded all along that our life here is a journey and a pilgrimage, and that it is leading on to a final judgment, an ultimate assessment, and the determination and proclamation of our final and eternal destiny.

All must agree that this is something of which we constantly need to be reminded. Half our troubles are due to the fact that we live on the assumption that this is the only life and the only world. Of course we know that is not true; but there is a great difference between knowing a thing and really being governed and guided by that knowledge in our ordinary life and outlook. If we were questioned and asked whether we believe that we go on living after death, and that we shall have to face God in judgment, we would undoubtedly say 'yes'. But as we live from hour to hour are we mindful of that? We cannot read the Bible without coming to the conclusion that the thing that really differentiates God's people from all others is that they have always been people who walk in the consciousness of their eternal destiny. The natural man does not care about his eternal future; to him this is the only world. It is the only world he thinks about; he lives for it and it controls him. But the Christian is a man who should walk through this life as conscious that it is but transient and passing, a kind of preparatory school. He should always know that he is walking in the presence of God, and that he is going on to meet God; and that thought should determine and control the whole of his life. Our Lord is at pains to show us here, as He was in the last section, that we ever need to be reminded of that, and that we need to be reminded of it in detail. We have to remember this fact in every part of our lives; we must remember that every section of our existence must be brought into that relationship. We are undergoing a process of judgment the whole time, because we are being prepared for the final judgment; and as Christian people we should do all things with that idea uppermost in our minds, remembering that we shall have to render an account.

That is the controlling theme in this chapter. Our Lord handles it in various ways, leading up to the great climax in that striking picture of the two houses. These represent two men listening to these things; one puts them into practice and the other does not. Once more we are reminded of the greatness of this Sermon on the Mount, its searching character, the profundity of its teaching, indeed its truly alarming character. There never has been such a Sermon as this. It finds us all somehow, somewhere. There is no possibility of escape; it searches us out in all our hiding-places and brings us out into the light of God. There is nothing, as we have seen several times before, which is so unintelligent and fatuous as the statement of those who are fond of telling us that what they really like in the New Testament is the Sermon on the Mount. They dislike the theology of Paul and all this talk about doctrine. They say, 'Give me the Sermon on the Mount, something practical, something a man can do himself.' Well here it is! There is nothing that so utterly condemns us as the Sermon on the Mount; there is nothing so utterly impossible, so terrifying, and so full of doctrine. Indeed, I do not hesitate to say that, were it not that I knew of the doctrine of justification by faith only, I would never look at the Sermon on the Mount, because it is a Sermon before which we all stand completely naked and altogether without hope. Far from being something practical that we can take up and put into practice, it is of all teaching the most impossible if we are left to ourselves. This great Sermon is full of doctrine and leads to doctrine; it is a kind of prologue to all the doctrine of the New Testament.

Our Lord opens His consideration of this great question of our walking in this world under a sense of judgment in terms of the particular matter of judging one another. 'Judge not'. Our Lord still uses, you notice, the same method that He has used right through this Sermon. He makes an announcement and then gives reasons for it; He lays down a principle and then reasons with us concerning it, or puts it to us in a more logical manner in detail. That is His method. It has been His method with regard to worldliness; and here again He comes back to it. He makes His deliberate pronouncement—'Judge not'.

We are confronted here by a statement which has often led to a great deal of confusion. Admittedly it is a subject that can be very easily misunderstood, and it can be misunderstood on two sides and from two extremes, as is almost invariably the case with truth. The question is, what exactly does our Lord mean when He says, 'Judge not'—Don't judge? The way to answer this question is not to seek a dictionary. Merely to look at the word 'judge' cannot satisfy us at this point. It has many different meanings so it cannot be decided in that way. But it is of vital importance that we should know exactly what it means. Never, perhaps, was a correct interpretation of this injunction more important than at this present time. Different periods in the history of the Church need different emphases, and if I were asked what in particular is the need of today, I should say that it is a consideration of this particular statement. This is so because the whole atmosphere of life today, and especially in religious circles, is one that makes a correct interpretation of this statement quite vital. We are living in an age when definitions are at a discount, an age which dislikes thought and hates theology and doctrine and dogma. It is an age which is characterized by a love of ease and compromise—'anything for a quiet life', as the expression goes. It is an age of appeasement. That term is no longer popular in a political and international sense, but the mentality that delights in it persists. It is an age that dislikes strong men because, it says, they always cause disturbance. It dislikes a man who knows what he believes and really believes it. It dismisses him as a difficult person who is 'impossible to get on with'.

This can easily be illustrated, as I have suggested, in the political sphere. The man who is now acclaimed and almost idolized in Great Britain is the man who, before the war, was severely criticized as being an impossible person. He was excluded from office because he was said to be an individualist who had extreme views and with whom it was impossible to work. The same mentality that led to such treatment of Winston Churchill in the thirties is in control in the realm of Christian affairs and in the realm of the Christian Church today. There have been ages in the history of the Church when men were praised because they stood for their principles at all costs. But that is not so today. Such men today are regarded as being difficult, self-assertive, non-co-operative and so on. The man who is now glorified is the man who can be described as being in 'the middle of the road', not at one extreme or the other, a pleasant man, who does not create difficulties and problems because of his views. Life, we are told, is sufficiently difficult and involved as it is, without our taking a stand on particular doctrines. That surely is the mentality today, and it is not unfair to say that it is the controlling mentality. It is very natural in a sense, because we have experienced so much trouble, so many problems, and disasters. It is only natural, also, that people should be ready to turn away from men with principles who know where they stand, and should seek ease and peace. Just cast your minds back to the twenties and the thirties of this century in the political and international spheres and you will see exactly what I am describing. The cry was for tranquillity and ease; and evasion of problems followed naturally and inevitably. Eventually, peace at almost any price, even that involving the humiliation and betrayal of others, became the controlling idea.

At a time like this, then, it is of the utmost importance that we should be able to interpret correctly this statement concerning judging, because there are many who say that 'judge not' must be taken simply and literally as it is, and as meaning that the truly Christian man should never express an opinion about others. They say that there must be no judging whatsoever, that we must be easy, indulgent and tolerant, and allow almost anything for peace and quiet, and especially unity. This is not a time for these particular judgments, they say; what is needed today is unity and fellowship. We must all be one together. This is often argued in terms of the danger of Communism. Some people are so alarmed at Communism that they say that, at all costs, all who in any sense use the name Christian should be accepted. We should all agree because of that common danger and common enemy.

The question arises therefore as to whether that is a possible interpretation. I suggest, in the first instance, that it cannot be; and it cannot be, quite clearly, because of Scripture teaching itself. Take the very context of this statement and you will surely see at once that that interpretation of 'judge not' is quite impossible. Look at verse 6, 'Give not that which is holy unto the dogs, neither cast ye your pearls before swine, lest they

trample them under their feet, and turn again and rend you'.
How can I put that into practice if I do not exercise judgment?
How do I know which kind of person can be described as a 'dog'
in this way? In other words, the injunction that immediately
follows this statement about judging at once calls upon me to
exercise judgment and discrimination. Then again, take the
more remote connection in verse 15: 'Beware of false prophets,
which come to you in sheep's clothing, but inwardly they are
ravening wolves.' How is that to be taken? I cannot 'beware of
false prophets' if I am not to think, and if I am so afraid of
judging that I never make any assessment at all of their teaching.
These people come 'in sheep's clothing'; they are very in-
gratiating and they use Christian terminology. They appear to
be very harmless and honest and are invariably 'very nice'. But
we are not to be taken in by that kind of thing—beware of such
people. Our Lord also says, 'Ye shall know them by their fruits';
but if I am not to have any standard or exercise discrimination,
how can I test the fruit and discriminate between the true and the
false? So, without going any further, that cannot be the true
interpretation which suggests that this just means being 'free and
easy', and having a flabby and indulgent attitude towards
anybody who vaguely uses the designation Christian. That is
quite impossible.

This view, however, is held so tenaciously that we must not
even leave it at that. We must go further and put it like this: the
Scripture itself teaches us that judgment has to be exercised
in connection with affairs of State. It is Scripture which teaches
us that judges and magistrates are appointed of God and that a
magistrate is called upon to deliver and pronounce judgment,
that it is his duty to do so. It is part of God's way of restraining
evil and sin and their effects in this world of time. So, if a man
says he does not believe in police courts he is contradicting
Scripture. It does not always mean the use of force, but judgment has to be exercised, and for a man not to do so, or to be
unprepared to do so, is not merely to fail in fulfilling his duty, it is
to be unscriptural.

But you also find the same teaching in the Scriptures with
regard to the Church. They show very clearly that judgment is
to be exercised in the realm of the Church. This is worthy of an
entire study on its own, because, owing to our flabby ideas and
notions, it is almost true to say that such a thing as discipline in
the Christian Church is non-existent today. When did you last

hear of a person being excommunicated? When did you last hear
of a person being kept back from the Communion Table? Go
back to the history of Protestantism and you will find that the
Protestant definition of the Church is, 'that the Church is a place
in which the Word is preached, the Sacraments are administered,
and discipline is exercised'.

Discipline, to the Protestant Fathers, was as much a mark of
the Church as the preaching of the Word and the administration
of the Sacraments. But we know very little about discipline. It is
the result of this flabby, sentimental notion that you must not
judge, and which asks, 'Who are you to express judgment?' But
the Scripture exhorts us to do so.

This question of judging applies, also, in the matter of doctrine.
Here is this question of false prophets to which our Lord calls
attention. We are supposed to detect them and to avoid them.
But that is impossible without a knowledge of doctrine, and the
exercise of that knowledge in judgment. Paul writing to the
Galatians says, 'But though we, or an angel from heaven, preach
any other gospel unto you than that which we have preached
unto you, let him be accursed.' That is a clear pronouncement.
Then you remember what the apostle has to say in 1 Corinthians
xv about those people who were denying the resurrection. He
says the same thing in 2 Timothy ii when he says that some deny
the resurrection, saying it is past already, 'of whom is Hymen-
aeus and Philetus'; and he again expresses judgment with
regard to that and exhorts Timothy to do so. In writing to Titus
he says, 'A man that is an heretick after the first and second
admonition reject.' How do you know whether a man is a heretic
or not if your view is that, as long as a man calls himself a
Christian, he must be a Christian, and you do not care what he
believes? Then go on to John's Epistles, John 'the apostle of love'.
In the First Epistle he gives his instructions with regard to the
false teachers and the anti-Christs who were to be avoided and
rejected. Indeed, in his second Epistle, he puts it very strongly in
these words: 'If there come any unto you, and bring not this
doctrine, receive him not into your house, neither bid him God
speed: for he that biddeth him God speed is partaker of his evil
deeds.' You see what the apostle is saying. If a man comes to you
who does not hold the true doctrine, you must not receive him
into your house, you must not bid him God speed and provide
him with money to preach his false doctrine. But today it would
be said that that is a lack of charity, that it is being over-punctil-

ious and censorious. This modern idea, however, is a direct contradiction of the Scripture teaching with regard to judging.

Then you find the same thing in our Lord's words to the Jews elsewhere: 'Judge not according to the appearance, but judge righteous judgment' (John vii. 24). He looks at the Pharisees and says, 'Ye are they which justify yourselves before men; but God knoweth your hearts: for that which is highly esteemed among men is abomination in the sight of God' (Luke xvi. 15). You remember His injunction as to what we are to do if our brother trespass against us; we are to go to our brother and tell him his fault 'between thee and him alone'. If he will not listen we are to take witnesses, that in the mouth of two or three witnesses every word may be established; but if he still does not listen then we are to take it to the Church, and if he will not listen to the Church we are to regard him as a heathen man and a publican. We are to have nothing more to do with him. In 1 Corinthians v and vi you will find that Paul gives exactly the same teaching. He tells the Corinthians not to keep company with a man who is an idolater, but to withdraw themselves. That is judgment the whole time. The simple question is thus: how can we put all these injunctions into practice if we are not exercising judgment, if we are not thinking, if we have not a standard, if we are not prepared to make an assessment? These are a few selections out of a large number of Scriptures which we could quote, but they are sufficient to prove that our Lord's statement cannot be interpreted as meaning that we must never judge, never arrive at conclusions and apply them.

If, then, it does not mean that, what does it mean? Surely our Lord's emphasis is this. He is not telling us that we are not to make these assessments based on judgment, but He is very concerned about the matter of condemning. In trying to avoid this tendency to condemn, people have swung right over to the other extreme, and so again they are in a false position. The Christian life is not quite as easy as that. The Christian life is always one of balance. There is a great deal to be said for the point of view that to walk by faith means to walk on a knife edge. You can fall on this side or that; you have to keep on the dead centre of truth, avoiding the error on the one side and on the other. So that while we say that it does not mean the refusal to exercise any discrimination or thought or judgment, we must hasten to say that what it does warn against is the terrible danger of condemning, of pronouncing judgment in a final sense.

The best way to illustrate this is to think of the Pharisees. In this Sermon on the Mount our Lord had the Pharisees in His mind most of the time. He was telling His own people to be very careful not to become like the Pharisees in their view of the law and in their way of living. They misinterpreted the law. They were boastful and demonstrative in their giving of alms; they were demonstrative in their praying at the street corners and in making broad their phylacteries; and they announced that they were fasting. They were, at the same time, mercenary and materialistic in their outlook with regard to the things of this world. Now our Lord has them in His mind at this particular point also. You remember the picture which He gives in Luke xviii. 9–14 of the Pharisee and the publican who both went up to the temple to pray. The Pharisee said, 'God, I thank thee, that I am not as other men . . . or even as this publican.' It was that judging and condemning attitude of the Pharisees towards others that was so wrong.

But the New Testament makes it painfully clear that that attitude was not confined to the Pharisees. It was something that constantly troubled the early Church; and it has been troubling the Church of God ever since. It is something that troubles the Church of God today, and as we approach this subject we should remember our Lord's statement in this connection when He said: 'He that is without sin among you, let him first cast a stone.' I suppose there is nothing in the whole of the Sermon on the Mount that comes to us with such a sense of condemnation as this statement which we are studying. How guilty we all are in this respect! There is a tendency for this thing to spoil all our lives and to rob us of our happiness! What havoc it has made, and does make, in the Church of God! It is a word to every one of us; it is a painful subject, but a very necessary one. This Sermon comes and speaks to us, and we ignore it, as our Lord reminds us here, at our peril. It is so important a subject that we must analyse it still further, though it is going to be painful. The way to treat a wound is not just to ignore it or to give it some superficial treatment; the right treatment is to probe it. It is painful, but it has to be done. If you want it to be cleansed and purified and healthy you have to apply the probe. Let us therefore probe this wound, this putrefying sore that is in the soul of every one of us, in order that we may be cleansed.

What is this danger against which our Lord is warning us? We can say first of all that it is a kind of spirit, a spirit which manifests itself in certain ways. What is this spirit that condemns? It is a self-righteous spirit. Self is always at the back of it, and it is always a manifestation of self-righteousness, a feeling of superiority, and a feeling that we are all right while others are not. That then leads to censoriousness, and a spirit that is always ready to express itself in a derogatory manner. And then, accompanying that, there is the tendency to despise others, to regard them with contempt. I am not only describing the Pharisees, I am describing all who have the spirit of the Pharisee.

It seems to me, further, that a very vital part of this spirit is the tendency to be hypercritical. Now there is all the difference in the world between being critical and being hypercritical. True criticism is an excellent thing. Unfortunately there is very little of it. But true criticism of literature, or art, or music, or anything else, is one of the highest exercises of the human mind. Criticism in a true sense is never merely destructive; it is constructive, it is appreciation. There is all the difference in the world between exercising criticism and being hypercritical. The man who is guilty of judging, in the sense in which our Lord uses the term here, is the man who is hypercritical, which means that he delights in criticism for its own sake and enjoys it. I am afraid I must go further and say that he is a man who approaches anything which he is asked to criticize expecting to find faults, indeed, almost hoping to find them.

The simplest way, perhaps, of putting all this is to ask you to read 1 Corinthians xiii. Look at the negative of everything positive which Paul says about love. Love 'hopeth all things', but this spirit hopes for the worst; it gets a malicious, malign satisfaction in finding faults and blemishes. It is a spirit that is always expecting them, and is almost disappointed if it does not find them; it is always on the look-out for them, and rather delights in them. There is no question about that, the hypercritical spirit is never really happy unless it finds these faults. And, of course, the result of all this is that it tends to fix attention upon matters that are indifferent and to make of them matters of vital importance. The best commentary in this connection is found in Romans xiv where Paul tells the Romans at great length to avoid judging one another in matters like food and drink, and regarding one day above another. They had been exalting these matters to a supreme position, and judging and condemning in terms of these things. But Paul tells them that that is all wrong. 'The kingdom of God is not meat and drink; but righteousness, and peace, and joy in the Holy Ghost', he says (Romans xiv. 17).

One may observe one day, and another, another. 'Let every man be fully persuaded in his own mind.' But the thing to remember, he says, is that you are all being judged by God. The Lord is the Judge. Furthermore, you do not decide whether a man is a Christian or not by regarding his views on matters such as these, which are unimportant, and matters of indifference. There are essential matters in connection with the faith, matters about which there must be no doubt, while others are matters of indifference. We must never elevate the latter into matters of vital importance.

That is more or less the spirit of the man who is guilty of judgment. I am not applying all this as we go along. I trust that the Holy Spirit is enabling us to do so. If we ever know the feeling of being rather pleased when we hear something unpleasant about another, that is this wrong spirit. If we are jealous, or envious, and then suddenly hear that the one of whom we are jealous or envious has made a mistake and find that there is an immediate sense of pleasure within us, that is it. That is the condition which leads to this spirit of judgment.

But look at it in practice. It shows itself in a readiness to give judgment when the matter is of no concern to us at all. How much of our time do we spend in expressing our opinion about people who really have no direct dealings with us? They are nothing to us, but we experience a malicious pleasure in doing so. That is part of the way in which it shows itself in practice.

Another manifestation of this spirit is that it puts prejudice in the place of principle. We are to judge in terms of principle, because otherwise we cannot discipline the Church. But if a man takes his own prejudices and puts them up as principles, he is guilty of this spirit of judgment.

Another way in which it shows itself is in its tendency to put personalities in the place of principles. We all know how easy it is for a discussion to drift to persons or personalities and away from principles. It is true to say that people who object to doctrine are generally those who are most guilty at this particular point. Because they do not have a grasp and understanding of doctrine they can talk only in terms of personalities; so the moment a man stands for principles or doctrine, they begin to say that he is a difficult person. The person is obtruded into the place where principle should come, and that, in turn, leads to the tendency to impute motives. Because they cannot understand why another man stands for principles, motives are

imputed to him; and to impute motives is always a manifestation
of this spirit of judgment.

A further way in which we may know whether we are guilty
of this, is to ask if we habitually express our opinion without a
knowledge of all the facts. We have no right to pronounce any
judgment without being aware of these facts, without going to
the trouble of becoming acquainted with them. We should search
for all the facts and then judge. To do otherwise is to be guilty of
this Pharisaical spirit.

Another indication of it is that it never takes the trouble to
understand the circumstances, and is never ready to excuse; it is
never ready to exercise mercy. A man who has a charitable spirit
possesses discrimination and is ready to exercise it. He is prepared
to listen and to see if there is an explanation, if there is an excuse,
to discover if there may be mitigating circumstances. But the
man who judges says, 'No, I require nothing further'. Therefore
he rejects any explanation, and does not listen to argument or
reason.

But perhaps we can end the description and bring it to its
awful revolting climax by putting it like this: This spirit really
manifests itself in the tendency to pronounce final judgment upon
people as such. This means that it is not a judgment so much on
what they do, or believe, or say, as upon the persons themselves.
It is a final judgment upon an individual, and what makes it so
terrible is that at that point it is arrogating to itself something
that belongs to God. You remember how, when our Lord sent
messengers into the villages of the Samaritans to make ready for
His arrival, and they would not receive them, that James and
John hearing this said: 'Lord, wilt thou that we command fire
to come down from heaven, and consume them?' That is it; they
wanted to destroy those Samaritans. But our Lord turned and
rebuked them and said, 'Ye know not what manner of spirit ye
are of. For the Son of man is not come to destroy men's lives, but
to save them.' They were guilty of forming and passing a final
judgment on those people and proposing to destroy them. There
is all the difference in the world between doing that and expressing an enlightened, intelligent criticism of a man's views
and theories, his doctrine, his teaching or his mode or manner of
life. We are called upon to do the latter; but the moment we
condemn and dismiss the person we are assuming a power that
belongs to God alone and to no-one else.

It is a painful subject, and so far we have looked only at the injunction. We have not yet considered the reason which our Lord adds to the injunction. We have just taken the two words, and I trust we shall always remember them. 'Judge not'. As we do so let us thank God that we have a gospel which tells us that 'while we were yet sinners, Christ died for us', that not one of us stands in his own righteousness, but in the righteousness of Christ. Without Him we are damned, utterly lost. We have condemned ourselves by judging others. But then God the Lord is our Judge, and He has provided a way whereby we pass 'from judgment unto life'. The exhortation is that we should live our lives in this world as people who have passed through the judgment 'in Christ', and who now live for Him and live like Him, realizing that we have been saved by His wondrous grace and mercy.

CHAPTER SIXTEEN

THE MOTE AND THE BEAM

WE have already considered the meaning of our Lord's
command 'Judge not' and what it involves in practice.
Now we come, in verses 1–5, to the reasons which He
gives for not judging. Again we cannot but feel, as we look at
them, that His case is unanswerable, His logic inevitable. At the
same time we shall feel our sinfulness and see the ugliness of sin.

Let us look at His reasons. The first is: 'Judge not, that ye be
not judged.' Do not judge, in order that you yourselves may not
be judged. That is a very practical and personal reason, but what
exactly does it mean? There are those who would have us believe
that it means something like this. Do not judge other people if
you dislike other people judging you. Do not judge other people
if you do not wish to be judged yourself by them. They say that
what this really means is that, as you do to others, they will do to
you, or, as the phrase puts it, you will be paid back in your own
coin. They say that it amounts to this, that the person who is
always critical and censorious of others, is always a person who
is likely to bring criticism upon himself. And of course that is
true and perfectly right. It is further true to say that there are no
people who are more sensitive to criticism than those who are
always criticizing others. They dislike it and complain when it
happens to them; but they never seem to remember this when
they do it with respect to others. We must agree, then, that that
statement is true, that the kind of person who is always criticizing
is criticized in turn, and that therefore, if they wish to avoid this
painful criticism, they must be less critical and censorious of
others. And, on the other hand, it is true to say that the person
who is less critical is appreciated by others, and is not subject to
criticism in the same way as that more critical kind of person.

But surely it is quite wrong to interpret this statement as
meaning that and that alone. While we must accept that in
general, it seems that our Lord goes very much further. We say
this, not only on the basis of what we have in this entire chapter,
which, as we have seen, is meant to hold us face to face with the
judgment of God, but also because of other statements in
Scripture which are parallel to this, and which explain and

therefore reinforce it. Surely it means this: 'Judge not, that ye be not judged'—by God. There are many evangelical Christians who immediately react against such an exposition in terms of the great teaching of the Scripture with regard to justification by faith only. They point out that John v. 24 teaches that, if we believe on the Lord Jesus Christ, we have passed through judgment or from judgment unto life. They add that the first verse of Romans viii says, 'There is therefore now no condemnation to them which are in Christ Jesus.' Surely, they say, this means that because we are Christians we are taken entirely outside the realm of judgment. There is no longer any judgment, they argue on the basis of such teaching, for the man who is a true Christian.

This criticism calls for attention and a reply, and we do so in this way. We remind ourselves again that the words we are considering are addressed to believers, not to unbelievers. They are addressed to people of whom the Beatitudes are true, to those who are the children of God and born again of the Spirit. It is quite clear, therefore, that in some respect such people are still subject to judgment.

But, in addition to that, we must approach the question also in terms of the parallel teaching of Scripture elsewhere. Perhaps the best way to deal with it is to put it like this. In the Scriptures we are taught that there are three types or kinds of judgment, and it is the failure to isolate and distinguish these that causes this confusion. We should be concerned about this subject for many reasons. One is that many of us who claim to be evangelical Christians are not only guilty of glibness in these matters, but are also curiously lacking in what used to be called the 'fear of God'. There is a lightness, a boisterousness, a superficiality about many of us which seems to me to be far removed from the character of truly Christian, godly people as it is to be seen in the Bible and in the Church throughout the centuries. In our anxiety to give the impression that we are happy, we are often lacking in reverence and what the Scripture means by 'reverence and godly fear'. The whole idea of 'the fear of the Lord' and of godliness somehow or other has become lost amongst us. That is partly due to this failure to realize the scriptural teaching with regard to judgment. We are so anxious to assert the doctrine of justification by faith only, that very often we are guilty of minimizing the other doctrines of Scripture which are equally a part of our faith and therefore equally true. So it is important for us to understand this doctrine with regard to judgment.

First of all there is a judgment which is final and eternal; that is the judgment which determines a man's status or his standing before God. This determines the great separation between the Christian and the non-Christian, the sheep and the goats, those who are going on to glory and those who are going to perdition. That is a kind of first judgment, a basic judgment which establishes the great dividing line between those who belong to God and those who do not. That is clearly taught everywhere in Scripture from beginning to end. That is the judgment which determines and settles man's final destiny, his eternal condition, whether he is to be in heaven or in hell.

But that is not the only judgment which is taught in the Scriptures; there is a second, which I would call the judgment to which we are subject as God's children, and because we are God's children.

In order to understand this we should read 1 Corinthians xi, where Paul expounds the doctrine concerning the Communion Service. He says, 'Whosoever shall eat this bread, and drink this cup of the Lord, unworthily, shall be guilty of the body and blood of the Lord. But let a man examine himself, and so let him eat of that bread, and drink of that cup. For he that eateth and drinketh unworthily, eateth and drinketh damnation to himself, not discerning the Lord's body' (verses 27–29). Then—'For this cause many are weak and sickly among you, and many sleep (which means 'many have died'). For if we would judge ourselves, we should not be judged. But when we are judged, we are chastened of the Lord, that we should not be condemned with the world' (verses 30–32).

That is a most important and significant statement. It indicates clearly that God judges His children in this way, that if we are guilty of sin, or of wrong living, we are likely to be punished by Him. The punishment, says Paul, may take the form of sickness or illness. There are those who are sick and ill because of their wrong living. It does not mean of necessity that God has sent sickness upon them, but it probably means that God withholds His protection from them and allows the devil to attack them with illness. You have the same statement in the same Epistle where he talks about handing a man over to Satan in order that he may correct him in that way (chapter v). It is a most serious and important doctrine. Indeed, Paul goes further and says that some of those Corinthians had died because of their wrong living; judgment had come upon them in that way. He is talking of the judgment of God, and therefore we can

interpret it thus, that God allows Satan, who controls the power
of death, to remove these people because of their refusal to judge
themselves and to repent and turn back to God. His exhortation,
therefore, is that we should examine ourselves, we should judge
ourselves and condemn that which is wrong in ourselves in order
that we may escape this other judgment. So it is very wrong for
the Christian to trip lightly through life saying that he believes in
the Lord Jesus Christ and that therefore judgment has nothing
to do with him, and all is well. Not at all; we must walk warily
and circumspectly, we must examine ourselves and search
ourselves lest this kind of judgment descend upon us.

All this is confirmed in Hebrews xii, where the doctrine is put
in this form: 'Whom the Lord loveth he chasteneth, and
scourgeth every son whom he receiveth.' The argument at that
point is designed to comfort and encourage those Hebrew
Christians in the difficult times through which they were passing.
It is this: We must be careful to look at trials in the right way. In
a sense a man ought to be more frightened if nothing ever goes
wrong with him in this world than if things do go wrong, because
'whom the Lord loveth he chasteneth'. He is bringing His sons,
His children, to perfection, and He therefore disciplines them in
this world. He judges their sins and their blemishes in this world
in order to prepare them for the glory. Those who are not saints—
well, they are 'bastards' and He allows them to flourish. You find
the same thing again in Psalm lxxiii, where we find the Psalmist
very perplexed by this fact. He says: 'I do not understand God's
ways. Look at those ungodly, evil people. Their eyes stand out
with fatness; there are no bands in their death; they always seem
to be flourishing. Verily I have washed my hands in vain.' But
he came to see that this way of thinking was very wrong, for it
was viewing the life of the ungodly only in this world. They may
have their enjoyment in this life; but that is all they get, and
judgment will suddenly descend upon them, and it will be final
and eternal. God judges His people in this world in order to
spare them from that. 'If we judge ourselves,' says Paul, 'we shall
not be condemned with the world.' That, then, is the second way
of looking at judgment, and it is a very important way. We are
all along under the eye of God, and God is watching our lives and
judging our sinfulness, all for our benefit.

But we must look at the third kind of judgment taught in
Scripture, the judgment which is often referred to as 'the judgment of rewards'. Whether that is a true designation or not does

not matter, but that there is a judgment for God's people after death is very clearly taught in the Scriptures. You find it in Romans xiv where he says, 'We shall all stand before the judgment seat of Christ.' Do not judge another man or another man's servant about these questions of observing particular days, and eating particular meats, and so on, says the apostle, for every man will have to bear his own judgment, and is responsible to God— 'for we shall all stand before the judgment seat of Christ'. You have exactly the same thing in the Corinthian Epistles. There is the passage in 1 Corinthians iii where he says: 'Every man's work shall be made manifest' and 'the day shall declare it'. Whatever a man has built upon the foundation—gold, silver, precious stones, wood, hay, stubble—it will all be judged by fire. Some of it will be entirely destroyed, the wood, hay, stubble, etc., but the man himself shall be saved, 'yet so as by fire'. But it all indicates a judgment, a judgment of our work since we have become Christian, and, particularly in this passage, of course, the preaching of the gospel and the work of ministers in the Church.

Then, in 2 Corinthians v, the judgment is clearly not only for ministers but for all—'For we must all appear before the judgment seat of Christ; that every one may receive the things done in his body, according to that he hath done, whether it be good or bad.' 'Knowing therefore', says Paul, 'the terror of the Lord, we persuade men.' That is not addressed to unbelievers; it is addressed to Christian believers. Christian believers will have to appear before this judgment seat of Christ, and there we shall be judged according to what we have done in the body, whether good or bad. This is not to *determine* our eternal destiny; it is not a judgment which decides whether we go to heaven or to hell. No, we have passed through that. But it is a judgment which is going to *affect* our eternal destiny, not by determining whether it is heaven or hell, but by deciding what happens to us in the realm of glory. We are not given any further details about this in Scripture, but that there is a judgment of believers is very clearly and specifically taught.

You find it again in Galatians vi. 5: 'Every man shall bear his own burden'. That is a reference to the same judgment. 'Bear ye one another's burdens, and so fulfil the law of Christ.' But also 'Every man shall bear his own burden'; every one of us is responsible for his own life, his own conduct and behaviour. It does not, let me emphasize again, determine my eternal destiny, but it is going to make a difference to me, it is a judgment of my life since I have become a Christian. And then there is that

moving statement in 2 Timothy i. 16–18 where, in referring to
Onesiphorus, Paul thanks God for this man who had been so kind
to him when he was in prison. This is what he prays for him: 'The
Lord grant unto him that he may find mercy of the Lord in that
day'; in that day when judgment is going to be exercised, may the
Lord have mercy upon him. And in Revelation xiv. 13 there is
the statement about all those that die in the Lord: 'Blessed are the
dead'which die in the Lord . . .; and their works do follow them.'
Our works follow us.

The chief reason, then, why Christian people must not judge,
is that we be not judged ourselves by the Lord. We shall see Him
as He is; we shall meet Him, and this judgment will take place.
If we do not want to be ashamed, as John puts it (1 John ii. 28),
on that occasion, let us be careful now. If we would have 'bold-
ness in the day of judgment', then we must be careful as to how
we live in the here and now. If we judge, we shall be judged
in terms of that very judgment. Here, therefore, is something of
which we must never lose sight. Though we are Christians, and
are justified by faith, and have an assurance of our salvation, and
know we are going to heaven, we are yet subject to this judgment
here in this life, and also after this life. It is the plain teaching of
the Scripture, and it is summarized here in this first statement by
our Lord in this section of the Sermon on the Mount: 'Judge not,
that ye be not judged.' It is not simply that if you do not want
other people to say unkind things you must not say unkind things
about them. That is all right; that is quite true. But much more
important is the fact that you are exposing yourself to judgment,
and that you will have to answer for these things. You do not lose
your salvation, but you are evidently going to lose something.

That brings us to the second reason for not judging which is
adduced by our Lord. It is in the second verse: 'For with what
judgment ye judge, ye shall be judged: and with what measure
ye mete, it shall be measured to you again.' We can put that in the
form of a principle. The second reason for not judging is that, by
so doing, we not only produce judgment for ourselves, we even
set the standard of our own judgment—'With what measure ye
mete, it shall be measured to you again.' Once more, this does
not merely indicate what other people may do to us. We say a
man is always 'paid back in his own coin', and that is perfectly
true. Men who have been so careful to scrutinize and examine
others, and to talk about minor blemishes in them, are often

amazed when those same people judge them. They cannot understand it, but they are being judged by their own yard-stick and
their own measure.

But we cannot leave this statement at that; we must go beyond
it, because Scripture does so. Our Lord is really declaring that
God Himself, in this judgment which I have been describing,
will judge us according to our own standards. Let us look at some
scriptural authority for this interpretation. Consider our Lord's
statement as recorded in Luke xii, where He talks about being
'beaten with many stripes' or 'with few stripes', and says 'unto
whomsoever much is given, of him shall be much required: and
to whom men have committed much, of him they will ask the
more' (verse 48). He teaches that God acts on that principle.
Then read the statement in Romans ii. 1, 'Therefore thou art
inexcusable, O man, whosoever thou art that judgest: for
wherein thou judgest another, thou condemnest thyself; for thou
that judgest doest the same things.' You are proving, says Paul,
by your judging of others that you know what is right; so, if you
do not do that which is right, you are condemning yourself.

But perhaps the clearest statement of this is given in James
iii. 1, a verse which is of vital importance, but which is frequently
ignored because we do not like the Epistle of James, imagining
as we do that he does not teach justification by faith only. This is
how he puts this particular matter: 'My brethren, be not many
masters, knowing that we shall receive the greater condemnation.' In other words, if you set yourself up as an authority, if you
become a master, if you are thus acting as masters and authorities,
remember you will be judged by your own authority; by the very
claim you make, you yourself will be judged. You are setting
yourself up as an authority? Very well; that will be the very
standard applied to you in your own judgment.

Our Lord puts it here plainly in the words we are considering:
'With what judgment ye judge, ye shall be judged: and with what
measure ye mete, it shall be measured to you again.' It is one of
the most alarming statements in the whole of Scripture. Do I
claim that I have exceptional knowledge of the Scripture? If I do
I shall be judged in terms of the knowledge that I claim. Do I
claim that I am a servant who really knows these things? Then I
must not be surprised if I am beaten with many stripes. We
should be very careful, therefore, how we express ourselves. If
we sit as an authority in judgment upon others, we have no right
to complain if we are judged by that very standard. It is quite
fair, it is quite just, and we have no ground whatsoever for com-

plaint. We claim we have this knowledge; and if we have that knowledge we must show it by living up to it. By the claim that I myself make, I myself shall be judged. If, therefore, I am careful in my scrutiny of other people and their lives, that very standard comes back upon myself, and I have no ground at all for complaining. The answer to me if I complain would be this: You knew it, you were able to exercise it with regard to others, why did you not exercise it in your own case? It is a very surprising and alarming thought. There is nothing I know of that is so likely to deter us from the sinful practice of condemning others and from that foul and ugly spirit that delights in doing so.

That brings us in turn to the last reason with which our Lord supplies us. He puts it in verses 3–5: 'And why beholdest thou the mote that is in thy brother's eye, but considerest not the beam that is in thine own eye? Or how wilt thou say to thy brother, Let me pull out the mote out of thine eye; and, behold, a beam is in thine own eye? Thou hypocrite, first cast out the beam out of thine own eye; and then shalt thou see clearly to cast out the mote out of thy brother's eye.' Was there ever such sarcasm? Was there ever a more perfect example of irony? How richly we deserve it. We can summarize the argument in this way in the form of a number of principles. Our Lord is teaching us that the third reason for our not judging others is that we are incapable of judgment. We cannot do it. Therefore, as we cannot do it properly, we must not try to do it at all. He says that our spirit is such that we are not entitled to judge. Not only must we remember that we ourselves shall be judged and that we determine the standards of that judgment, but furthermore He says: Stop a moment; you cannot judge because you are incapable of judging.

Our Lord proves it in this way. He first of all points out that we are not concerned about righteousness and true judgment at all, because if we were, we should deal with it in ourselves. We like to persuade ourselves that we are really concerned about truth and righteousness, and that that is our only interest. We claim that we do not want to be unfair to people, that we do not want to criticize, but that we are really concerned about truth! Ah, says our Lord in effect, if you were really concerned about truth, you would be judging yourself. But you do not judge yourself; therefore your interest is not really in truth. It is a fair argument. If a man claims that his only interest is in righteousness and truth, and not at all in personalities, then he will be as critical of himself as he is of other people. A really great artist is always the severest critic of himself. It matters not what walk of life it is, whether it is singing, or acting, or painting, or anything else, a really great artist and true critic is as critical of himself as he is of the work of other people, perhaps more so, because he has an objective standard. But you, says our Lord, have no objective standard. You are not interested in truth and righteousness, otherwise you would never pass yourselves, as you are doing, and only criticize others. That is the first statement.

Then we can take it further and say that He also shows that such people are not concerned about the principles as such but simply about persons. The spirit of hypercriticism, as we have seen, is one which is concerned with personalities rather than with principles. That is the trouble with many of us in this respect. We are really interested in the person we are criticizing, not in the particular subject or principle; and our real desire is to condemn the person, rather than to get rid of the evil that is in the person. That, of course, at once renders us incapable of true judgment. If there is bias, if there is personal feeling and animus, we are no longer true examiners. Even the law recognizes this. If it can be proved that there is some connection between any member of a jury and the person on trial, that member of the jury can be disqualified. What is desiderated in a jury is impartiality. There must be no prejudice, there must be nothing personal; it must be unbiased, objective judgment. The personal element must be entirely excluded before there can be true judgment. If we apply that to our judgment of other people, I fear we shall have to agree with our Lord that we are quite incapable of judgment, because we are so interested in the person or the personality. There is so often an ulterior motive in our judgment; so often we fail to differentiate between the person and his action.

But let us follow our Lord in His analysis. His next argument is in verse 4: 'How wilt thou say to thy brother, Let me pull out the mote out of thine eye; and, behold, a beam is in thine own eye?' That is sarcasm at its highest. He says that our own condition is such that we are quite incapable of helping others. We affect to be very concerned about these people and their faults, and we try to give the impression that we are concerned only about their good. We say that we are troubled about this little blemish that is in them, and that we are anxious to get rid of this mote. But, says our Lord, you cannot do it, because it is such a delicate

process. This beam that is in your own eye makes you incapable
of doing so.

I once read a very acute remark which put this perfectly. It
said that there is something very ridiculous about a blind person
trying to lead another blind person, but that there is something
much more ridiculous than that, and that is a blind oculist. A
blind oculist cannot possibly remove a speck out of another
man's eye. If a blind man in general is useless in helping others,
how much more useless is a blind oculist? That is what our Lord
is saying at this point. If you want to be able to see clearly to
remove this minute speck out of the sensitive eye of that other
person in whom you affect an interest, make certain your own
eye is quite clear. You cannot be a help to another while you are
blinded by the beam in your own eye.

Finally, He actually condemns us as hypocrites. 'Thou hypocrite, first cast out the beam out of thine own eye; and then shalt
thou see clearly to cast out the mote out of thy brother's eye.'
How true it is. The fact of the matter is that we are not really
concerned about helping this other person; we are interested
only in condemning him. We pretend to have this great interest;
we pretend that we are very distressed at finding this blemish.
But in reality, as our Lord has already shown us (and this is the
horrible part), we are really glad to discover it. It is hypocrisy.
One person goes to another as a would-be friend and says, 'It is
such a shame that this defect is in you.' But oh, the malice that is
often displayed by such action, and the pleasure that such a
person often enjoys! No, says our Lord, if you really want to help
other people, if you are genuine and true in this matter, there are
certain things you have to do yourself. First—and we must notice
this—first cast the beam out of thine own eye, and then thou
shalt see clearly to cast out the mote out of thy brother's eye.

That can be interpreted in this way. If you really do want to
help others, and to help to rid them of these blemishes and faults
and frailties and imperfections, first of all realize that your spirit
and your whole attitude has been wrong. This spirit of judging
and hypercriticism and censoriousness that is in you is really
like a beam, contrasted with the little mote in the other person's
eye. 'You know,' says our Lord in effect, 'there is no more
terrible form of sin than this judging spirit of which you are
guilty. It is like a beam. The other person may have fallen into
immorality, some sin of the flesh, or may be guilty of some little
error here and there. But that is nothing but a little mote in the
eye when compared with this spirit that is in you, which is like a

beam. Start with your own spirit,' He says in other words; 'face yourself quite honestly and squarely and admit to yourself the truth about yourself.' How are we to do all this in practice? Read 1 Corinthians xiii every day; read this statement of our Lord's every day. Examine your attitude towards other people; face the truth about yourself. Take the statements you make about another person; sit down and analyse them, and ask yourself what you really mean. It is a very painful and distressing process. But if we examine ourselves and our judgments and our pronouncements honestly and truly, we are on the high road to getting the beam out of our eye. Then having done that we shall be so humbled that we shall be quite free from the spirit of censoriousness and hypercriticism.

What a wonderful piece of logic this is! When a man has truly seen himself he never judges anybody else in the wrong way. All his time is taken up in condemning himself, in washing his hands and trying to purify himself. There is only one way of getting rid of the spirit of censoriousness and hypercriticism, and that is to judge and condemn yourself. It humbles us to the dust, and then it follows of necessity that, having thus got rid of the beam out of our own eyes, we shall be in a fit condition to help the other person, and to get out the little mote that is in his eye.

The procedure of getting a mote out of an eye is a very difficult operation. There is no organ that is more sensitive than the eye. The moment the finger touches it, it closes up; it is so delicate. What you require above everything else in dealing with it is sympathy, patience, calmness, coolness. That is what is required, because of the delicacy of the operation. Transfer all that into the spiritual realm. You are going to handle a soul, you are going to touch the most sensitive thing in man. How can we get the little mote out? There is only one thing that matters at that point, and that is that you should be humble, you should be sympathetic, you should be so conscious of your own sin and your own unworthiness, that when you find it in another, far from condemning, you feel like weeping. You are full of sympathy and compassion; you really do want to help. You have so enjoyed getting rid of the thing in yourself that you want him to have the same pleasure and the same joy. You cannot be a spiritual oculist until you yourself have clear sight. Thus, when we face ourselves and have got rid of this beam, and have judged and condemned ourselves and are in this humble, understanding, sympathetic, generous, charitable state, we shall then be able, as the Scripture puts it, to 'speak the truth in love' to another and thereby to help him. It is one of the most difficult things in life, it is one of the last things to which we attain. God have mercy upon us. But there are people, thank God, who can 'speak the truth in love', and when they have spoken it to you, you not only know they are speaking the truth, you thank them for it. There are other people who tell you the same truth, but in such a manner as to lead you to defend yourself at once, and to hate them for doing so. It is because they have not 'spoken the truth in love'. Let every man, therefore—again I quote James—'let every man be swift to hear, slow to speak, slow to wrath' (James i. 19).

'Judge not' for these three reasons. God have mercy upon us. How good it is that we can face such a truth in the light of Calvary and the shed blood of Christ. But if you want to avoid chastisement in this life, and the suffering of loss—that is the scriptural statement—in the next life, judge not, except you judge yourself first.

CHAPTER SEVENTEEN

SPIRITUAL JUDGMENT AND DISCRIMINATION

IN Matthew vii. 6 our Lord brings to an end what He has to say concerning the difficult and involved subject of punishment. The Authorized Version puts this verse in a special paragraph on its own; but I suggest that that is not right. It is not a statement on its own with no connection with what precedes it. It is rather the conclusion of that matter, the final statement in that connection.

It is an extraordinary statement and one which generally comes with a great shock of surprise to people. Here our Lord has been telling us in the most solemn manner not to judge, and that we should cast the beam out of our own eye before we begin to think about the mote that is in our brother's eye; He has been warning us that with what judgment we judge, we shall be judged. Then suddenly He says, 'Give not that which is holy unto the dogs, neither cast ye your pearls before swine, lest they trample them under their feet, and turn again and rend you.' It seems incongruous; it seems to come as an entire contradiction of all that we have been considering. And yet, if our exposition of the first five verses has been right, it is not surprising at all; indeed, it follows as an almost inevitable corollary. Our Lord tells us that we must not judge in the sense of condemning; but He reminds us here that that is not the total statement with regard to this matter. In order to have a right balance and a complete statement on the subject, this further observation is essential.

If our Lord had finished His teaching with those first five verses, it would undoubtedly have led to a false position. Men and women would be so careful to avoid the terrible danger of judging in that wrong sense that they would exercise no discrimination, no judgment whatsoever. There would be no such thing as discipline in the Church, and the whole of the Christian life would be chaotic. There would be no such thing as exposing heresy and pronouncing judgment with regard to it. Because everybody would be so afraid of judging the heretic, they would turn a blind eye to the heresy; and error would come into the Church more than it has done. So our Lord goes on to make this further statement here, and we cannot fail, once more, to be impressed by the wonderful balance of scriptural teaching, its amazing perfection. That is why I am never tired of pointing out that a detailed, microscopic study of any one section of Scripture is generally much more profitable than a telescopic view of the whole Bible; because if you make a thorough study of any one section, you will find that you will meet all the great doctrines sooner or later. We have done so in considering this Sermon on the Mount. It shows the importance of looking at the details, of paying attention to everything, for as we do so, we discover this wonderful balance which is to be found in Scripture. We go to extremes and become unbalanced because we are guilty of isolating statements instead of taking them in their context. It is because they forget this addition to our Lord's teaching on judging that so many people show a lack of discrimination and are ready to praise and recommend anything that is put before them which vaguely claims the name Christian. They say that we must not judge. That is regarded as a friendly and charitable spirit, and so men and women fall unchecked into grievous errors and their immortal souls are thrown into jeopardy. But all that is avoided if we just take the Scripture as it is, and remember that in it this perfect balance is always to be found.

Take this statement which seems, when looked at superficially, to be so surprising in view of what our Lord has just been saying. How do we reconcile these two things? The simple answer is that, while our Lord exhorts us not to be hypercritical, He never tells us not to be discriminating. There is an absolute difference between these two things. What we are to avoid is the tendency to be censorious, to condemn people, to set ourselves up as the final judge and to make a pronouncement on persons. But that, of course, is very different from exercising a spirit of discrimination, to which Scripture is ever exhorting us. How can we 'prove' and 'test the spirits', how can we, as we are exhorted to do later, 'beware of false prophets', if we do not exercise our judgment and our discrimination? In other words, we are to recognize the error, but we are to do so, not in order to condemn, but in order to help. And it is just there that we find the connecting link between this statement and what has preceded it. Our Lord has been dealing with the question of helping our brother to get rid of the mote that is in his eye. If we wish to do that in the right way, and He has already told us the right way, then, of course, we must have a spirit of discrimination. We must be able to recognize motes and beams and to discriminate between person and person.

Our Lord now proceeds to instruct us with regard to the whole question of dealing with people, handling them, and discriminating between person and person. And He does it in these words: 'Give not that which is holy unto the dogs, neither cast ye your pearls before swine, lest they trample them under their feet, and turn again and rend you.' What does He mean by this? Obviously He is referring to the truth, which is holy, and which can be likened to pearls. What is this holy thing, this pearl to which He is referring? It is clearly the Christian message, the message of the kingdom, the very thing about which He is speaking Himself in this incomparable Sermon. What, then, does He mean? Are we here exhorted not to present the Christian truth to unbelievers? What kind of persons can those be who are described as being dogs and swine? What extraordinary terminology to use! The dog was not regarded in Palestine as we are accustomed to do in this country; it was the scavenger of the village, its very name a term of opprobrium; not the domestic pet to which we are accustomed, but a fierce and dangerous, half-wild animal. While the swine in the Jewish mind stood for all that was unclean and outside the pale.

And these are the two terms our Lord uses in teaching us how to discriminate between people and people. We have to recognize that there is a class of person who, with respect to the truth, can be described as a 'dog' or as belonging to the 'swine'. 'Does He mean', asks someone, 'that this is to be the attitude of Christian people to unbelievers, to those who are outside the kingdom?' Clearly it cannot mean that, for the good reason that you could never convert the unconverted if you are not to present truth to them. Our Lord Himself went out preaching to such people. He sent out His disciples and apostles to preach to them, He sent the Holy Spirit upon the early Church in order that she might testify and preach the truth to them. So it clearly cannot mean that.

What, then, does it mean? The best way to approach the problem is to look at it first of all in the light of our Lord's own practice. What did He Himself do? How did He Himself implement this particular teaching? The answer of Scripture is that He very clearly differentiated between person and person and type and type. If you read the four Gospels you will see that

He does not handle any two people in exactly the same way. Fundamentally it is the same, but on the surface it is different. Take His way of handling Nathanael, and Nicodemus, and the woman of Samaria. At once you see certain differences. Look at the entire difference in His manner and method when He was confronting the Pharisees and when He was confronting the publicans and sinners. See the difference in His attitude towards the self-righteous, proud Pharisee and the woman caught in sin. But perhaps one of the best illustrations of all is the one that we encounter in Luke xxiii. When examined by Pilate, our Lord answered; but when He was questioned by Herod, who should have known better, and who just had a morbid, unhealthy curiosity and was looking for signs and wonders, He answered him nothing, He just would not speak to him (see verses 3 and 9). Thus you see that our Lord, when dealing with people in terms of the same truth, dealt with them in different ways and accommodated His way of teaching to the person. He did not vary the truth, but He varied the particular method of presentation, and that is what you will find as you read the four Gospels.

Then when you come on to the practice of the apostles, you will find that they do precisely the same as their Lord, and carry out the injunction that is given here. Take, for instance, that statement in Acts xiii. 46, where Paul was preaching at Antioch in Pisidia and meeting the jealousy and envy and opposition of the Jews. We read that Paul and Barnabas were bold and said, 'It was necessary that the word of God should first have been spoken to you: but seeing ye put it from you, and judge yourselves unworthy of everlasting life, lo, we turn to the Gentiles.' Paul is not going to preach to them any longer; he is not going to continue presenting this holy thing to them. But then you find exactly the same thing in his conduct at Corinth. This is what we read in Acts xviii. 6: 'And when they opposed themselves, and blasphemed, he shook his raiment, and said unto them, Your blood be upon your own heads; I am clean: from henceforth I will go unto the Gentiles.' Here, you see, are people to whom the truth has been presented; but they did the very thing our Lord prophesied. As dogs and swine, they turned again and they opposed, they blasphemed, and they stamped the truth under their feet. The reaction of the apostle is to turn away from them; he no longer presents the gospel to them. He turns his back upon the Jews who thus reject and show their inability to appreciate the truth, and he turns to the Gentiles and becomes the great apostle to the Gentiles.

There, it seems to me, is the right way to approach this statement which at first sight is somewhat perplexing. But we cannot leave it at that. Let us pursue the exposition a little more in detail, because we must remember that this statement is made to us. It is not something that was relevant only to that particular time, or to some future kingdom. We have seen that it is meant, like the whole of the Sermon, for Christians now, and it is therefore an exhortation to us. We are told: 'Give not that which is holy unto the dogs, neither cast ye your pearls before swine, lest they trample them under their feet, and turn again and rend you.' How do we interpret this? What does it mean to us?

First and foremost it means that we must recognize the different types and persons, and we must learn to discriminate between them. There is nothing so pathetic or so unscriptural as a mechanical way of testifying to others. There are some Christians who are guilty of that. They witness and testify, but they do it in a thoroughly mechanical way. They never really consider the person with whom they are dealing; they never try to assess the person, or to discover exactly what his position is. They fail completely to implement this exhortation. They present the truth in exactly the same way to all and sundry. Quite apart from the fact that their testifying is generally quite useless, and that the only thing they achieve is a great feeling of self-righteousness, it is utterly unscriptural.

There is no higher privilege in life than to be a witness for Jesus Christ. I understand that in these days men who would become commercial travellers generally have to attend a course of training in the psychology of salesmanship. It is felt to be necessary and important, if they are to sell their particular commodity, that they should know something about people. They must know how to approach people. We are all so different, and the same thing must be presented to different people in correspondingly different ways. Although the commodity is the same, they have discovered that it is important that the salesman should know something about people and the psychology of salesmanship. It is not for us to pronounce judgment as to whether such a course is necessary, but we can use it to emphasize the fact that the New Testament has always taught the necessity for preparation. Not that we need a course in psychology! No; but we need to know our New Testament. If we know our New Testament we know that people are all different; and if we really are concerned about winning souls, and not simply anxious to bear our own witness and testimony, then we shall realize the importance of discriminating and understanding. We must not say, 'Well; I am like this, and this is my temperament, and this is my way of doing things.' No; with the apostle Paul we must become 'all things to all men' that we may by all means save some. To the Jew he became as a Jew, to the Gentile as a Gentile, to them that were under the law as under the law, to this end.

That is the first point, and we must surely agree that we often fall into this trap with regard to witnessing. It tends to be mechanical, and it may even be that we are almost pleased when somebody does behave with us in the manner of the dog and the swine, for then we feel we have been persecuted for Christ's sake, when in reality it is not that at all, but simply that we have not known our Scriptures and have not witnessed in the right way.

The second principle is that we must not only learn to distinguish between one type and another; we must also become expert in knowing what to give to each type. You do not handle a Pilate and a Herod in exactly the same way; you answer the questions of a Pilate, but you say nothing to a Herod. We must see people as they are and be sensitive to them. We have taken the beam out of our own eye, we have got rid of everything that is censorious, and we really are concerned about helping the other. In that spirit, we try to find precisely the right thing for that person. It is curious to note how readily we become slaves to words. I have known people who, when they preach on the text about becoming 'fishers of men', are always careful to say that we must know which bait to use; but when they come to a text like this they seem to be oblivious of the fact that the same principle applies, and is equally true, here. We must know what is appropriate for each person in each particular situation. That is one reason why it is difficult for a raw convert to be a good witness. We can understand more clearly in the light of this teaching why Paul says that no novice must be given a prominent position in the Church. How far we have departed in our practice from the New Testament! Our tendency is to lay hands on the raw convert and immediately put him into some prominent position. But Scripture tells us not to push a man into prominence at once. Why? Partly for this reason, that the novice may not be an expert in the things we are considering.

Our third principle is that we should be very careful as to the way in which we present the truth. Apart from the truth itself the method of presentation must vary from person to person. We must learn to assess people. There are some to whom certain things are offensive though they are not offensive to others. We must be careful not to put truth in a way that is likely to be offensive to any type of person. For instance, to go to every unbeliever and say, 'Are you saved?' is not the scriptural method. There is a type who, if you say that to him, will take offence at it, and will not be led on to the truth. The effect of such a question on him will be to produce this response that our Lord is describing, the reaction of the dog and the swine, the trampling and the rending, the blasphemy and the cursing. And we must always be careful not to give anyone cause to blaspheme or to curse. There are those, of course, who will do that however perfect our method. Then we are not responsible and we can say with Paul, 'Your blood be upon your own heads.' But, if the offence is in us, God have mercy upon us. A man who is preaching the truth can be guilty of preaching the truth in an unworthy manner. You and I must never be the cause of antagonism; we must always preach the truth in love, and if we cause offence, it should always be 'the offence of the cross', not anything offensive in the preacher. Our Lord was teaching that.

There is one final principle under this heading. It is that we must learn to know which particular aspect of the truth is appropriate in particular cases. This means that in the case of an unbeliever we should never present to him anything but the doctrine of justification by faith only. We should never discuss any other doctrine with an unbeliever. He will often be anxious to discuss other doctrines, but we must not allow it. The account given in John iv of our Lord's interview with the woman of Samaria is a perfect illustration of this point. She wanted to discuss various matters, such as the Being of God, how and where to worship, and the differences which separated the Jews and the Samaritans. But our Lord would not allow it. He kept bringing her back to herself, to her sinful life, to her need of salvation. And we must do the same thing. To discuss election and pre-destination, and the great doctrines of the Church, and the present need of the Church, with a man who is an unbeliever is obviously quite wrong. The man who is not born again can-not understand these other doctrines and therefore you must not consider them with him. It is for us to decide what to discuss with him.

But this applies not only to unbelievers; it applies also to
believers. Paul tells the church at Corinth that he cannot give
them strong meat; he had it, but he could not give it to them
because they were still babes. He says that he had to feed them
with milk because they were not yet fit for meat. 'We speak
wisdom', he says, 'among them that are perfect.' To give this
perfect wisdom of God to a babe in spiritual understanding
is obviously ridiculous, so we are called upon to exercise this
discrimination in all directions. If we really are to be witnesses
and presenters of the truth we must pay some attention to these
things.

We should now draw some general deductions from all these
considerations. If you consider the implications of this verse you
will find that they are of grave importance. Do you notice the
first obvious implication on the surface? There is not a single
statement in Scripture that gives a more awful picture of the
devastating effect of sin upon man as this verse. The effect of sin
and evil upon man as the result of the Fall is to make us, with
respect to the truth of God, dogs and swine. That is the effect of
sin upon man's nature; it gives him an antagonism to truth. 'The
carnal mind', says the apostle Paul, 'is enmity against God', the
nature of the dog and the swine. Sin makes man hate God and
also, 'hateful (or full of hate), and hating one another,' says Paul
in Titus iii. 3. Yes, God-haters and 'not subject to the law of
God, neither indeed can be'. 'Enemies and aliens,' outside the
kingdom, at enmity with God. What a terrible thing sin is! You
can see the same reactions in the world today. Present the truth
to certain people and they snarl at it. Talk about the blood of
Christ, and they laugh and make jokes about it, and spit upon it.
That is what sin does to man; that is what it does to his nature,
that is how it affects his attitude towards the truth. It is something that gets into the very depths and vitals of man's being, and
turns him into something that is not only hateful, but utterly
opposed to God, and purity, to cleanness, and holiness, and
truth.

I emphasize this because I feel that we are all guilty at this
point. When we are dealing with others we often do not realize
their true condition. We tend to become impatient with people
when they do not become Christians immediately. We do not see
that they are so much under the dominion of sin and of Satan,
they are so much the dupes of the devil, they are so twisted, and
perverted, and polluted—that is the word—inwardly by sin, that

they really are in a spiritual sense in this condition of dog and swine. They do not appreciate that which is holy; they do not attach any value to spiritual pearls; even God Himself is hateful to them. If we do not start by realizing that, we shall never be able to help them. And as we realize the truth about them we shall begin to understand why our Lord had a great compassion for the people, and a great sorrow in His heart as He looked upon them in pity. We shall never really help anybody until we have the same spirit and mind in us, and realize that in a sense they cannot help it. They need a new nature, they must be born again. The Sermon on the Mount just legal teaching for some Jews in the future? Out, out, upon the suggestion! Here is a doctrine that leads directly to the grace of God; nothing but the rebirth can ever enable any man to appreciate and receive the truth. Dead in trespasses and sins, we must be quickened by the Holy Spirit before we can ever give a true response to divine instruction. You see the number of profound doctrines that are hidden away in this one text.

Then there is a second matter; the nature of the truth. We have dealt with it to some degree, so we need only touch upon it now. Truth is very varied, truth is very full. It is not all exactly the same; there are different varieties, such as milk and strong meat. There is truth in the Scripture which is appropriate to the very beginner; but, as the author of the Epistle to the Hebrews says, we must also 'go on unto perfection'. He seems to say, 'We do not want to go back again and lay a foundation of first principles; we ought to have finished with that. If you but exercise yourselves I can take you on to this great Melchisedec doctrine; but I cannot do it now because you are slow to hear and to learn.' That shows us that there is this great composite character to the truth. The question we must ask ourselves is, am I growing in my knowledge? Am I hungering and thirsting after this higher doctrine, this wisdom that Paul has for them that are perfect? Do I feel that I am proceeding, as it were, from the Epistle to the Galatians to the Epistle to the Ephesians? Am I going on to these profounder truths? They are only for the children of God.

There are certain secrets in the Bible which only God's children can appreciate. Read the introduction to the Epistle to the Ephesians, just the first nine or ten verses, and there you will find doctrine that only the children of God can understand; indeed, only those children who are exercising their spiritual senses and growing in grace. People in spiritual ignorance may argue about the doctrines of God's calling and election, and questions like that, without having any understanding of them. But if we are growing in grace, these doctrines will become more and more precious. They are secrets which are given only to those who can receive them—'he that hath ears to hear, let him hear'. If you find that some of these great and mighty expositions of truth which you have in the Epistles say nothing to you, examine yourself, and ask yourself why you are not growing, and why you cannot take in these truths. There is a great distinction to be drawn between first principles and more advanced principles. There are people who spend their lifetime in the realm of apologetics and who never go on to deeper spiritual truths. They remain as babes in the Christian life. 'Let us go on unto perfection' and try to develop an appetite for these deeper aspects of truth.

Lastly, there is a question which we might ask here. And I deliberately put it in the form of a question because I admit quite frankly that I am not quite clear in my own mind what the answer should be. Is there, I wonder, a query, a question, perhaps a warning, in this verse regarding the indiscriminate distribution of the Scriptures? I am simply raising a question for you to consider and for you to discuss with others. If I am told that I have to discriminate in speaking to people about these things, if I have to differentiate between type and type and person and person, and about the particular truth I give to each, is it a good thing to put the whole Bible within the reach of people who can be described as spiritual dogs and swine? May it not sometimes lead to blasphemy and cursing and to behaviour and conduct of swinish character? Is it always right, I wonder, to put certain texts of Scripture on placards, especially those referring to the blood of Christ? I have often, myself, heard those very things leading to blasphemy. I simply put the questions. Think of the eunuch in Acts viii going back from Jerusalem. He had his Scriptures and was actually reading them, when Philip approached him and said: 'Understandest thou what thou readest?' And he replied, 'How can I, except some man should guide me?' Exposition is generally necessary, and you cannot do away with the human instrument as a general rule.

'But,' we protest, 'look at the wonderful effect of the distribution of the Scriptures.' If we could discover the exact facts, I wonder how many people we should find who have been converted apart from human agency? I know there are wonderful, exceptional cases. I have read stories of people who have been converted in that way. Thank God that kind of thing can happen. But I suggest that it is not the normal method. Does not the fact that we have to be careful in our choice of aspects of truth as we deal with different people raise a query in our minds? Sometimes, of course, we try to avoid the duty of speaking, by giving a Gospel or Scripture portion, but that is not God's normal way. The way of God has always been the presenting of the truth immediately through personality, man expounding the Scriptures. If you have a conversation with a man and are able to point out the truth to him, he may then ask for a copy of the Scriptures, or you may feel you should give him one. That is right and good. Give him your Scripture. The query I am raising has reference to the indiscriminate placing of the Bible where there is no-one to explain it, and where a man, in the condition described by our Lord in the verse of our text, is facing this great and mighty truth without a human guide.

This probably comes as a surprise to many, but I suggest that we need to think again carefully about some of these matters. We become slaves to custom and to certain habits and practices, and very often we become quite unscriptural as we do so. I thank God that we have this great written Word of God; but I have often felt that it would not be a bad thing to experiment for a while with the idea of not allowing anybody to have a copy of the Scriptures unless he showed signs of spiritual life. That may be going too far, but I have felt sometimes that doing this would impress upon people the precious nature of this Book, its wonderful character, and the privilege of being allowed to possess it and to read it. It might not only be a good thing for the souls of those who are outside; it would certainly give the Church a completely new conception of this priceless treasure that God has put into our hands.

We are the custodians and the expositors of the Bible; and if we gain nothing else as the result of our study, we must all feel that we have been lazy, that we have not prepared ourselves as we should have done for such a responsible, such a great task. It is not quite as easy as we sometimes seem to think, and if we take the Word of God seriously, we shall see the vital need of study and preparation and prayer. We must, then, consider this question; but above all, let us remember those other aspects of the truth which we have seen so clearly, and never forget the absolute need of regeneration for the reception and understanding of spiritual truth. The mere distribution of Scripture as such is not the key to the solution of the problem today. God still needs men and women like ourselves to expound, to explain the truth, to act as a Philip to those who have the Word but cannot understand it. Let us maintain a true balance and a due sense of proportion in these things, for the good of souls and in order that we may give a balanced, full-orbed representation of the truth of God.

CHAPTER EIGHTEEN

SEEKING AND FINDING

I CANNOT imagine a better, more cheering or a more comforting statement with which to face all the uncertainties and hazards of our life in this world of time than that contained in verses 7–11. It is one of those great comprehensive and gracious promises which are to be found only in the Bible. There is nothing that can be more encouraging as we face life with all its uncertainties and possibilities, our 'future all unknown'. In such a situation, this is the essence of the biblical message from beginning to end, this is the promise that comes to us: 'Ask, and it shall be given you; seek, and ye shall find; knock, and it shall be opened unto you.' In order that we might be quite certain about it, our Lord repeats it, and puts it in an even stronger form, for He says: 'Every one that asketh receiveth; and he that seeketh findeth; and to him that knocketh it shall be opened.' There is no doubt about it, it is certain; it is an absolute promise. What is more, it is a promise made by the Son of God Himself, speaking with all the fullness and authority of His Father.

The Bible teaches us everywhere that that is the one thing that matters in life. The biblical view of life, in contra-distinction to the worldly view, is that life is a journey, a journey full of perplexities, problems and uncertainties. That being the case, it emphasizes that what really matters in life is not so much the various things that come to meet us, and with which we have to deal, as our readiness to meet them. The whole of the biblical teaching with regard to life is in a sense summed up in that one man Abraham, of whom we are told, 'he went out, not knowing whither he went'. But he was nevertheless perfectly happy, at peace and at rest. He was not afraid. Why? An old Puritan who lived 300 years ago answers that question for us: 'Abraham went out, not knowing whither he went; but he did know with whom he went.' That is the thing that matters, he knew that he went out on that journey with Another. He was not alone, there was One with him who had told him that He would never leave him, nor forsake him; and though he was uncertain as to the events that were coming to meet him, and the problems which would arise, he was perfectly happy because he knew, if I may so put it, his Travelling Companion.

Abraham was like the Lord Jesus Christ Himself who, under the shadow of the cross, and knowing that even His most trusted disciples were suddenly going to leave Him and forsake Him in their fear and concern about saving their own lives, nevertheless was able to say this: 'The hour cometh, yea, is now come, that ye shall be scattered, every man to his own, and shall leave me alone: and yet I am not alone, because the Father is with me' (John xvi. 32). According to the Bible, that is the one thing that matters. Our Lord does not promise to change life for us; He does not promise to remove difficulties and trials and problems and tribulations; He does not say that He is going to cut out all the thorns and leave the roses with their wonderful perfume. No; He faces life realistically, and tells us that these are things to which the flesh is heir, and which are bound to come. But He assures us that we can so know Him that, whatever happens, we need never be frightened, we need never be alarmed. He puts all that in this great and comprehensive promise: 'Ask, and it shall be given you; seek, and ye shall find; knock, and it shall be opened unto you.' That is just one of the biblical ways of repeating this message which runs through the Scriptures as a golden cord from beginning to end.

If we are to derive the full benefit from such wonderful, gracious words, we must look at them a little more closely. It is not enough just to repeat a great phrase like this. The Bible must never be used as a form of psychological treatment. There are people who do that. There are people who think that the best way to go through life triumphantly is to read and repeat wonderful verses to oneself. Of course that can help you up to a point; but it is not the biblical message and the biblical method. That kind of psychological treatment gives only temporary ease. It is like the teaching which tells us that there is no such thing as disease, and that you cannot be ill, and that because there is no disease there is no pain. That sounds most helpful and may lead to a temporary improvement; but there *are* diseases, and diseases lead to death, as even the adherents of such cults eventually discover for themselves. That is not the biblical way. The Bible conveys truth to us, and wants us to consider this truth. So, when we come to a phrase like this, we do not just say, 'all is well'. We must know what it means, and we must apply it in detail to our lives.

As we come to analyse this great statement, we are reminded

again of that canon of interpretation which we have often had to heed which warns us of the danger of extracting a text from its context. We must avoid the terrible danger of wresting the Scriptures to our own destruction through not taking them in their setting, or failing to observe particularly what they say, or failing to note their qualifications as well as their promises. This is particularly important with a statement such as this. There are people who say, 'Scripture says, "Ask, and it shall be given you; seek, and ye shall find; knock, and it shall be opened unto you". Very well,' they go on; 'does not that say explicitly, and does it not mean of necessity, that whatever I want or desire, God is going to give to me?' And because they think that it does, and because they think that that is the scriptural teaching, they ignore all the other teaching and just go to God with their requests. Their requests are not granted, and then they are down in the depths of depression and despair. Their case is even worse than it was before. They say, 'God does not seem to be fulfilling His promise', and they are wretchedly unhappy. We have to avoid that. Scripture is not something that works automatically. It pays a great compliment to us by regarding us as intelligent people, and it presents truth to our minds by the Holy Spirit. It asks us to take it as it is, and as a whole, in all its promises. That is why, you notice, we are not looking at verses 7 and 8 only. We are considering verses 7–11 because we must take this statement as a whole if we are not to go seriously astray in considering its various parts.

There is no difficulty in showing that this statement, far from being a universal promise that God is pledged to do for us anything that we may ask of Him, is actually something very much bigger than that. I thank God—let me put it like this bluntly—I thank God that He is not prepared to do anything that I may chance to ask Him, and I say that as the result of my own past experience. In my past life I, like all others, have often asked God for things, and have asked God to do things, which at that time I wanted very much and which I believed were the very best things for me. But now, standing at this particular juncture in my life and looking back, I say that I am profoundly grateful to God that He did not grant me certain things for which I asked, and that He shut certain doors in my face. At the time I did not understand, but I know now, and am grateful to God for it. So I thank God that this is not a universal promise, and that God is not going to grant me my every desire and request. God has a much better way for us, as we shall now see.

The right way to look at this promise is this. First of all let us ask this obvious question. Why did our Lord utter these words at this particular point? Why do they come at this particular stage in the Sermon on the Mount? We have reminded ourselves that there are certain people who say that this seventh chapter of Matthew, this final portion of the Sermon on the Mount, is nothing but a collection of statements which our Lord just delivers one after another as they happen to occur to Him. But we have already agreed that that is a very false analysis, and that there is a theme running right through the chapter. The theme is that of judgment, and we are reminded that in this life we are always living under the judgment of God. Whether we like it or not, the eye of God is upon us, and this life is a kind of preparatory school for the great life that is awaiting us beyond death and time. So everything we do in this world is of tremendous significance, and we cannot afford to take anything for granted. That is the theme, and our Lord applies it immediately. He starts with the question of judging other people. We must be careful about that because we ourselves are under judgment. But, why then does our Lord utter this promise of verses 7–11 at this point? Surely the answer is this. In verses 1–6 He has shown us the danger of condemning other people as if we were the judges, and of harbouring bitterness and hatred in our hearts. He has also told us to see to it that we remove the beam out of our own eye before trying to extract the mote out of our brother's eye. The effect of all that upon us is to reveal us to ourselves and to show us our terrible need of grace. He has held us face to face with the tremendously high standard by which we shall be judged—'With what judgment ye judge, ye shall be judged: and with what measure ye mete, it shall be measured to you again.' That is the position at the end of verse 6.

Immediately we realize that, we are humbled and begin to ask, 'Who is sufficient for these things? How can I possibly live up to such a standard?' Not only that; we realize also our need of cleansing, we realize how unworthy and sinful we are. And the result of all this is that we feel utterly hopeless and helpless. We say, 'How can we live the Sermon on the Mount? How can anybody come up to such a standard? We need help and grace. Where can we get it?' Here is the answer: 'Ask, and it shall be given you; seek, and ye shall find; knock, and it shall be opened unto you.' That is the connection, and we should thank God for it, because standing face to face with this glorious gospel we must all feel undone and unworthy. Those foolish people who think of Christianity only in terms of a little morality which they themselves can produce have never really seen it. The standard by which we are confronted is that found in the Sermon on the Mount, and by it we are all crushed to the ground and made to realize our utter helplessness and our desperate need of grace. Here is the answer; the supply is available, and our Lord repeats it for the sake of emphasis.

As we look at this there are a number of questions which should be asked. Why are we all what we are in view of such promises? Why is the quality of our Christian living so poor? We are left entirely without excuse. Everything we need is available; why then are we what we are? Why are we not exemplifying this Sermon on the Mount more perfectly? Why are we not conforming more and more to the pattern of the Lord Jesus Christ Himself? All that we need is offered us; it is all promised us here in this comprehensive promise. Why are we not availing ourselves of it as we should? Again, fortunately, that question is also answered, and that is the real meaning of this verse. Our Lord analyses these words and He shows us why we have not received, why we have not found, why the door has not been opened to us as it should have been. He realizes what we are, and He encourages us to avail ourselves of the gracious promise. In other words, there are certain conditions which must be observed before we can rejoice in these great benefits that are offered us in Christ. What are they? Let us note them simply and briefly.

If we want to go through life triumphantly, with peace and joy in our hearts, ready to face whatever may come to meet us, and to be more than conquerors in spite of everything, there are certain things we have to realize, and here they are. The first is, we must realize our need. It is strange, but some people seem to think that all that is necessary is that the promises of God should be held before us. That is not enough, however, because the central trouble with the whole of mankind is that we do not realize our need. There are many who preach about the Lord Jesus Christ to no effect and we can see why. They have no doctrine of sin, they never convict or convince people of sin. They always hold Christ before men and say that that is enough. But it is not enough; for the effect of sin upon us is such that we shall never fly to Christ until we realize that we are paupers. But we hate to regard ourselves as paupers, and we do not like to feel our need. People are ready to listen to sermons which present Christ to them, but they do not like to be told that they are so helpless that He had to go to the cross and die before they could be saved. They think that that is insulting. We must be brought to realize our need. The first two essentials to salvation and to rejoicing in Christ are the consciousness of our need, and the consciousness of the riches of grace that are in Christ. It is only those who realize these two things who 'ask' truly, because it is only the man who says 'O wretched man that I am' who seeks for deliverance. The other man is not aware of his need. It is the man who knows that he is 'down and out' who begins to ask. And then he begins to realize the possibilities that are in Christ.

What our Lord emphasizes here at the beginning is the paramount importance of the realization of our need. He puts that by using these three terms—ask, seek, knock. When you consult the commentators you will find great discussions as to whether seeking is stronger than asking, and knocking stronger than seeking. They spend much of their time in dealing with such matters. And, as usual, you find that they tend to contradict each other. Some say that asking represents a faint desire, seeking a greater desire, and knocking something very powerful. Others say that the man who knocks is the man who is right outside and that the supreme thing is asking, not knocking. The unbeliever, they say, must knock at the door, and having entered in at the door he begins to seek, and at last face to face with his Lord and Master he can ask.

But, surely, all that is quite irrelevant. Our Lord is simply at pains to emphasize one thing, that is that we are to show persistence, perseverance, importunity. This comes out clearly when we notice the setting of this self-same passage in Luke xi. There we have the parable of the man upon whom a guest suddenly landed at midnight, and as he had no bread to set before him, he went and knocked at the door of a friend who was already in bed. And because of his importunity the friend gave him some bread. The same thing is taught in the parable of the importunate widow in Luke xviii. That is precisely what we have here. These three words emphasize the element of persistence. There are times of stocktaking in life when we pause for a moment and say: 'Life is moving on; I am moving on. What progress am I making in this life and world?' We begin to take stock of ourselves and say: 'I am not living the Christian life as I should; I am not as diligent in my reading of the Bible and in prayer as I know I should be. I am going to change all this. I see there is a higher level to which I must attain, and I want to get there.' We are honest; we are quite sincere; we fully intend to do it. And so, during the first few days of a new year, we read the Bible regularly, we pray and we ask God for His blessing. But—and this is surely true of all of us—we soon begin to slacken and to forget. At the very moment we thought of reading or praying something comes in, quite 'out of the blue', as we say, something we never anticipated, and our whole scheme and programme is upset. In a week or two we find that we have entirely forgotten our excellent resolve. That is what our Lord is concerned about. If you and I are really to obtain these blessings which God has for us, we must go on asking for them. 'Seeking' simply means going on asking; 'knocking' is just the same thing. It is an intensification of the word 'ask'. We go on, we persist; we are like the importunate widow. We keep on asking the judge, as it were, just as she did, and our Lord tells us that the judge said, 'I had better do something about this woman or else she is going to worry me with her persistence.'

The importance of this element of persistence cannot be exaggerated. You find it not only in biblical teaching, but also in the lives of all the saints. The most fatal thing in the Christian life is to be content with passing desires. If we really want to be men of God, if we really want to know Him, and walk with Him, and experience those boundless blessings which He has to offer us, we must persist in asking Him for them day by day. We have to feel this hunger and thirst after righteousness, and then we shall be filled. And that does not mean that we are filled once and for ever. We go on hungering and thirsting. Like the apostle Paul, leaving the things which are behind, we 'press toward the mark'. 'Not as though I had already attained', says Paul, 'but I follow after'. That is it. This persistence, this constant desire, asking, seeking and knocking. This, we must agree, is the point at which most of us fail.

Let us then hold on to that first principle. Let us examine ourselves in the light of these Scriptures and the pictures given of the Christian man in the New Testament. Let us look at these glorious promises and ask ourselves, 'Am I experiencing them?' And if we find we are not, as we all must confess, then we must go back again to this great statement. That is what I mean by the possibilities. While I must begin by asking and seeking, I must go on doing so until I am aware of an advance and a development and a rising to a higher spiritual level. We must keep on at it. It is a 'fight of faith'; it is 'he that endureth to the end' that will be saved in this sense. Persistence, continuance in well-doing, 'always to pray, and not to faint.' Not just pray when we want a great blessing and then stop; always pray. Persistence; that is the first thing. The realization of the need, the realization of the supply, and persistence in seeking after it.

Let us now look at the second principle, which is the realization that God is our Father. Our Lord talks about that in verse 9 and He puts it like this: 'Or what man is there of you, whom if his son ask bread, will he give him a stone?' This, of course, is the central principle of all—the realization that God is our Father. That is what our Lord is concerned to emphasize in all He says here. He is using His familiar method of arguing from the lesser to the greater. If an earthly father does so much, how much more so God? This is one of our main troubles, is it not? If you should ask me to state in one phrase what I regard as the greatest defect in most Christian lives I would say that it is our failure to know God as our Father as we should know Him. That is our trouble, not difficulties about particular blessings. The central trouble still is that we do not know, as we ought to, that God is our Father. Ah yes, we say; we do know that and believe it. But do we know it in our daily life and living? Is it something of which we are always conscious? If only we got hold of this, we could smile in the face of every possibility and eventuality that lies ahead of us.

How then are we to know this? It is certainly not something based on the notion of the 'universal Fatherhood of God' and the 'universal brotherhood of man'. That is not biblical. Our Lord says something here that ridicules that and proves such an idea to be nonsense. He says, 'If ye then, being evil'. You see the significance? Why did He not say, 'If *we* then, being evil'? He did not say it because He knew He was essentially different from them. The speaker is the Son of God; not a man who is called Jesus, but the Lord Jesus Christ, the only begotten Son of God. He does not include Himself in that 'ye'. But He does include the whole of mankind. 'Ye being evil' means that we not only do things which are evil, but that we *are* evil. Our natures are corrupt and evil, and those who are essentially corrupt and evil are not the children of God. There is no such thing as the universal Fatherhood of God in the generally accepted sense of that term. Christ says of certain people: 'Ye are of your father the devil, and the lusts of your father ye will do.' No; by nature we are all the children of wrath, we are all evil, we are all enemies of God; by nature we are not His children. So this does not entitle all men to say, 'Well now; I rather like this doctrine. I am rather afraid of all that lies ahead of me, and I like to be told that God is my Father.' But God is your Father only when you satisfy certain conditions. He is not the Father of any one of us as we are by nature.

How then does God become my Father? According to the Scriptures it is like this. Christ 'came unto his own, and his own received him not. But as many as received him, to them gave he power (i.e., authority) to become the sons of God' (John i. 11, 12). You become a child of God only when you are born again, when you receive a new life and a new nature. The child partakes of the nature of the Father. God is holy, and you and I are not children of God until we have received a holy nature; and that means we must have a new nature. Being evil, and even conceived in sin (Psalm li. 5), we do not have one; but He will give it to us. Now that is what is offered to us. And there is no contact and communion with God, nor are we heirs to any of these promises of God, until we become His children. In other words, we must remember that we have sinned against God, that we deserve the wrath and punishment of God, but that He has dealt with our sin and guilt by sending His Son to die on the cross of Calvary for us. And believing in Him, we receive a new life and nature and we become children of God. Then we can know that God is our Father; but not until then. He will also give us His Holy Spirit, 'the Spirit of adoption, whereby we cry, Abba, Father'; and the moment we know this we can be certain that God as our Father adopts a specific attitude with respect to us. It means that, as my Father, He is interested in me, that He is concerned about me, that He is watching over me, that He has a plan and purpose with respect to me, that He is desirous always to bless and to help me. Lay hold of that; take a firm grasp of that. Whatever may happen to you, God is your Father, and He is interested in you, and that is His attitude towards you.

But that does not exhaust the statement. There is a very interesting negative addition. Because God is your Father He will never give you anything that is evil. He will give you only that which is good. 'What man is there of you, whom if his son ask bread, will he give him a stone? Or if he ask a fish, will he give him a serpent?' Multiply that by infinity and that is God's attitude towards His child. In our folly we are apt to think that God is against us when something unpleasant happens to us. But God is our Father; and as our Father he will never give us anything that is evil. Never; it is impossible.

The third principle is this. God, being God, never makes a mistake. He knows the difference between good and evil in a way that no-one else does. Take an earthly father; he does not give a stone for bread, but he sometimes makes a mistake. The earthly father at his best sometimes thinks at the moment that he is acting for the good of his child, but discovers later that it was bad. Your Father who is in heaven never makes such a mistake. He will never give you anything which will turn out to be harmful to you, but which at first seemed to be good. This is one of the most wonderful things we can ever realize. We are the children of a Father who not only loves us but looks upon us and keeps His eye upon us. He will never give us anything evil. But beyond all, He will never lead us astray, He will never make a mistake in what He gives us. He knows everything; His knowledge is absolute. If we but knew we were in the hands of such a Father, our outlook upon the future would be entirely transformed.

Lastly, we must remember increasingly the good gifts which He has for us. 'How much more shall your Father which is in heaven give good things to them that ask him?' This is the theme of the whole Bible. What are the good things? Our Lord has given us the answer in that passage in Luke xi. There, you remember, it reads like this: 'If ye then, being evil, know how to give good gifts unto your children: how much more shall your heavenly Father give the Holy Spirit to them that ask him?' That is it. And in giving the Holy Spirit He gives us everything; every fitness we require, every grace, every gift. They are all given to us in Him. Peter summing it up says, 'his divine power hath given unto us all things that pertain unto life and godliness' (2 Peter i. 3). You see now why we should thank God that asking, and seeking and knocking, do not just mean that if we ask for anything we like we shall get it. Of course not. What it means is this. Ask for any one of these things that is good for you, that is for the salvation of your soul, your ultimate perfection, anything that brings you nearer to God and enlarges your life and is thoroughly good for you, and He will give it you. He will not give you things that are bad for you. You may think they are good but He knows they are bad. He does not make a mistake, and He will not give you such things. He will give you things that are good for you, and the promise literally is this, that if we seek these good things, the fullness of the Holy Spirit, the life of love, joy, peace, long-suffering, etc., all these virtues and glories that were seen shining so brightly in the earthly life of Christ, He will give them to us. If we really want to be more like Him, and like all the saints, if we really ask for these things, we shall receive; if we seek them, we shall find them; if we knock, the door will be opened unto us and we shall enter into their possession. The promise is, that if we ask for the good things our heavenly Father will give them to us.

That is the way to face the future. Find out from the Scriptures what these good things are and seek them. The thing that matters supremely, the best thing for all of us, is to know God, 'the only true God, and Jesus Christ, whom (he) hath sent'; and if we seek that above everything else, if we 'seek first the kingdom of God, and his righteousness', then we have the word of the Son of God for it that all these other things shall be added unto us. God will give them to us with a bounty that we cannot even imagine. 'Ask, and it shall be given you; seek, and ye shall find; knock, and it shall be opened unto you.'

CHAPTER NINETEEN

THE GOLDEN RULE

AS we approach the great statement of vii. 12, which is generally described as the 'Golden Rule for Life and Living', the first matter which must engage our attention is what we may describe as a question of mechanics, namely, the relationship of this statement to the rest of this Sermon on the Mount. Here at the beginning of this twelfth verse we meet the word 'therefore'. Why 'therefore'? Obviously, it tells us that it is not a detached statement, that it clearly has a connection with what has gone before. 'Therefore all things whatsoever ye would that men should do to you, do ye even so to them: for this is the law and the prophets.' In other words, our Lord is still dealing with the subject of our judgment of others. He has never left that. If we regard verses 7–11 as a parenthesis we must be careful to remember that they are there to remind us that we need this supply of grace because of this question of judgment. Having shown us how to be blessed and rendered capable of helping one another, and of living the Christian life in its fullness, He comes back again to the original subject and says 'Therefore', in this matter of judgment, in this whole question of your relationship to other people, let this be the rule. We are still looking at this general subject of our judgment of others. That justifies us in saying that there is this definite internal unity in this chapter; and, furthermore, it justifies us in the view we took of the instructions with regard to prayer. It is not a detached statement, but part of a great argument which is designed to bring us into this right position with regard to this subject.

But someone may say: 'If you argue that this verse is a continuation of the theme of our judgment of others, why did He not put this statement immediately after verse 6? Why did He introduce the subject of prayer and so on? Why not rather put it like this: "Give not that which is holy unto the dogs, neither cast ye your pearls before swine, lest they trample them under their feet, and turn again and rend you; therefore all things whatsoever ye would that men should do to you, do ye even so to them"?'

The answer, when you seek for it, is again not difficult. The statement at which we are now looking, which is the summing up

of this whole matter of judgment, comes with much greater force
and cogency when we look at it in the light of that brief statement about prayer. It is only after He has reminded us of what
God has done for us in spite of our sins, and of God's attitude
towards us and God's dealings with us, that the tremendous
argument of this exhortation really comes home to us. We shall
consider that point further when we come to study the exhortations in detail.

Here, then, we stand face to face with our Lord's final dictum
with regard to this whole matter of judging others and of our
relationship to them. It is well described as the 'golden rule'.
What an extraordinary and remarkable statement it is. It is
nothing, of course, but an epitome of the commandments which
our Lord has summed up elsewhere in the words, 'Love thy
neighbour as thyself'. He is really saying that, if you are in
trouble at all as to how you should deal with others, and behave
with respect to them, this is how you should act. You do not
start with the other person; you start by asking yourself, 'What is
it I like? What are the things that please me? What are the things
that help and encourage me?' Then you ask yourself: 'What are
the things I dislike? What are the things that upset me, and bring
out the worst in me? What are the things that are hateful and
discouraging?' You make a list of both these things, your likes
and dislikes, and you work them out in detail—not only in deeds,
but also in thoughts and in speech—with respect to the whole of
your life and activities. 'What do I like people to think about me?
What is it that tends to hurt me?'
    Our Lord goes right down into the details and, therefore, it is
essential that we also should deal with a matter like this in detail.
We all know how easy it is to read such a statement, or to listen
to an exposition of it, or to read an exposition of it in a book, or
to see some great picture which conveys it, and to say, 'Yes;
wonderful, marvellous,' and yet to fail completely to put it into
practice in actual life and living. So our Lord, the incomparable
moral and ethical Teacher, knowing that, teaches that the first
thing we have to do is to lay down a rule for ourselves about these
matters. And this is how we do so. Having drawn up this list of
all our likes and dislikes, when we come to deal with other people
we have nothing to do but to say quite simply: 'That other person
is exactly as I am in these matters'. We must put ourselves constantly in their position. In our conduct and behaviour with
respect to them we must be careful to do, and not to do, all the

things which we have found to be pleasing or displeasing to ourselves. 'Therefore all things whatsoever ye would that men should do to you, do ye even so to them.' If you only do that, says our Lord, you can never go wrong. You do not like unkind things said about you? Well, do not say them about others. You do not like people who are difficult, and who make your life difficult, and bring problems into your life, and constantly put you on edge? Well; in exactly the same way, do not let your behaviour be such that you become like that to them. It is quite as simple as that, according to our Lord. All the great textbooks on ethics and social relationships and morality, and on all the other subjects which deal with the problems of human relationships in the modern world can really be reduced to that.

This is something which is of urgent importance at the present time. All thinkers agree that the great problem of the twentieth century is after all the problem of relationships. Sometimes we foolishly tend to think that our international and other problems are economic, social or political; but in reality they all come down to this, our relationships with people. It is not money. Money does come into it, but it is only a kind of counter that is used. No; it is a question of what I myself want, and what the other person wants; and ultimately all the clashes and disturbances and unhappinesses in life are due to this. And our Lord here in this curious, laconic statement puts the whole truth concerning this matter: 'All things whatsoever you would that men should do to you, do ye even so to them.' That is the final statement about this question. If only we approached it like that, starting with self and then applying it to others, the entire problem would be solved.

But unfortunately we cannot leave it at that. There are people, as we shall see, who seem to think that this is all that is necessary. There are still people (and it is amazing that there can be such, but there are) who believe that all you have to do is just to hold up a standard before people and they will say: 'That is perfectly right; now we will proceed to do this.' But the world today is proving clearly that that is not the case, so we must go on with our consideration.

The gospel of Jesus Christ starts on the very basis which we have just been enunciating, that it is not enough merely to tell people the right way. That is not the problem; it is much deeper than that. Let us follow our Lord's way of putting it. You notice His comment on the golden rule; 'This', He says, 'is the law and the prophets'. In other words, that is a summary of the law and the prophets; it is their whole object and purpose. What does He mean by putting it like that? It is just another example of the way in which He calls attention, as He has done so frequently in this Sermon on the Mount, to the tragic manner in which God's law has been misunderstood. He still probably has His eye on the Pharisees and the scribes, the doctors of the law and the instructors of the people. You remember how at great length in the fifth chapter He took up many points of which He could say, 'Ye have heard that it was said by them of old time . . . but I say unto you'. His great concern there was to give these people the right view of the law; and He comes back to it here once more. Half our troubles are due to the fact that we do not understand the meaning of God's law, its true character and intent. We tend to think that it is just a number of rules and regulations which we are supposed to keep; we constantly forget the spirit. We think of a law as something which is to be observed mechanically, as something which is detached and almost impersonal; we regard it very much as if it were a series of regulations issued by a machine. You buy the machine, and you get your rules and regulations and all you have to do is to carry them out. Our whole tendency is to regard God's law with respect to life in some such way as that. Or, to put it in another form, the danger always is to regard the law as a thing in and of itself, and to think that all we have to do is to keep those regulations and that, if we do so and never deviate from them, or go beyond or stop short of them, all will be well. Now all those are entirely false views of the law.

Perhaps we can go further and say that our danger is to think of the law as being something negative, something prohibitive. Of course there are aspects of the law which are negative; but what our Lord is emphasizing here is—as He has said at great length in the fifth chapter—that the law which God gave to the children of Israel through the medium of angels and of Moses is a very positive thing, is a spiritual thing. It was never meant to be mechanical, and the whole fallacy of the Pharisees and the scribes, and all who followed them, was that they reduced something that was essentially spiritual and living to the realm of the mechanical, to something that was an end in itself. They thought that as long as they had actually not murdered somebody they had kept the law concerning murder, and that as long as they had not committed physical adultery they were all right in a moral sense. They were guilty of complete failure to see the

210 STUDIES IN THE SERMON ON THE MOUNT

spiritual intent, to see the spiritual character of the law, and above all to see the great end and object for which the law had been given.

Here, our Lord puts all that in this perfect summary. Why does the law tell us not to covet our neighbour's goods and possessions, or his wife, or anything else? Why does the law tell us 'Thou shalt not kill'; 'Thou shalt not steal'; 'Thou shalt not commit adultery'? What does it mean by all this? Is it designed simply that you and I should uphold these things as rules and regulations, or as sub-sections in Acts of Parliament which govern and control us and keep us within certain limits? No, that is not the object at all. The whole purpose and the real spirit behind it all is this, that we are to love our neighbour as ourselves, that we are to love one another.

Being the creatures that we are, however, it is not enough just to tell us to love one another; the matter has to be broken up for us. As the result of the Fall we are sinful; so it is not enough just to say, 'Love one another'. Our Lord breaks it up, therefore, and says: As you yourself value your life, remember that the other man also values his life, and that if your attitude towards that man is right, you will not kill that man, because you know he values his life as you do yours. The vital thing, after all, is that you love that man, that you understand him and desire the well-being of your neighbour even as you desire your own well-being. That is the law and the prophets. It all comes to that. All the detailed regulations given in the law in the Old Testament— what it tells you to do, for example, if you see your neighbour's ox straying, how you are to bring it back to him, or if you see anything going wrong in his farm, how you are to inform him at once and do your utmost to help him—are not just meant to lead you to say: 'The law says that if I see my neighbour's ox straying I am to take it back, therefore I must do so'. Not at all; it is rather that you may say to yourself: 'This man is like myself, and it will be a grievous matter and a loss to him if he is going to lose that ox. Well, he is a· man like myself, and how grateful I would be if someone returned my ox to me. Therefore I will do that for him.' In other words, you are to be interested in your neighbour, you are to love him, and to desire to help him, and to be concerned about his happiness. The object of the law is to bring us to that, and these detailed regulations are nothing but illustrations of that great central principle. The moment we cease to realize that that is the spirit of the law and the purpose of the law, we go hopelessly astray.

That, then, is our Lord's own exposition of it. It was very necessary in His own day; it is very necessary today. We so constantly forget the spirit of the law and of life as God meant us to live it.

We must now apply all this to the modern world and to ourselves. People hear this golden rule and they praise it as marvellous and wonderful, and as a perfect summary of a great and involved subject. But the tragedy is that, having praised it, they do not implement it. And, after all, the law was not meant to be praised, it was meant to be practised. Our Lord did not preach the Sermon on the Mount in order that you and I might comment upon it, but in order that we might carry it out. That will be impressed upon us later on when He says that the man who hears these sayings and does them is like a person who builds his house upon a rock, but the other man who 'hears and does not' is like one who builds his house upon the sand. The modern world is like that; it admires these wonderful statements of Christ but it does not put them into practice. That brings us to the crucial question. Why do men forsake this golden rule? Why do they not keep it? Why do they not live their lives in this way? Why are there troubles and disputes not only between nations, but also between different classes within the nations; yes, even in families; yes, even between two people? Why is it that there is any dispute or quarrelling or unhappiness? Why do we ever hear of two persons who do not speak to each other, and who avoid looking at each other? Why is there jealousy and backbiting, and all the other things which we know to be so true of life?

What is the matter? The answer is theological, and profoundly biblical. Foolish people, as we have seen, have so often said that they dislike theology, and especially the theology of the apostle Paul. They say that they like the simple gospel and especially the Sermon on the Mount, because it is practical and has no theology in it. Now this one verse proves how unutterably hollow the view is which says that all you have to do is to give people instruction, and tell them what to do, to hold before them the golden rule, and give them intelligent training, and that they will recognize it and rise up and put it into practice. The simple answer to that is that the golden rule has been confronting mankind for nearly two thousand years, and for the last hundred years in particular we have done everything we can by legislation and education to improve men, but still they are not obeying it.

Why is this so? It is just at this point that theology comes in. The first statement of the gospel is that man is sinful and perverted. He is a creature that is so bound and governed by evil that he cannot keep to the golden rule. The gospel always starts with that. The first principle in theology is the Fall of man and the sin of man. It can be put like this. Man does not implement the golden rule, which is a summary of the law and the prophets, because his whole attitude towards the law is wrong. He does not like the law; in fact he hates it. 'The carnal (natural) mind is enmity against God: it is not subject to the law of God, neither indeed can be' (Romans viii. 7). So it is useless to hold the law before such people. They hate the law, they do not want it. Of course, when they sit back in their armchair and listen to an abstract statement about life as it should be, they say that they like it. But if you apply the law to them, they immediately hate it and react against it. The moment it is applied to them they dislike and resent it.

But why should they be like this? According to the Bible we are all like this by nature because, prior to our dislike of the law, and prior to our wrong attitude to the law, is our wrong attitude towards God Himself who has given the law. The law is an expression of God's holy will; it is an expression in a sense of God's own person and character. And man dislikes the law of God because he is a natural hater of God. That is the New Testament argument: 'The natural mind is enmity against God'. The natural man, man as he is as the result of the Fall, is an enemy, an alien from God. He is 'without God in the world'; he dislikes God, and hates Him and everything that comes from Him. And why is this so? The ultimate answer is that his attitude towards himself is wrong. That is why all men do not by instinct and by nature hurry to carry out this golden rule.

The whole thing can be brought down to one word, 'self'. Our Lord expresses it by saying that we should 'love our neighbour as ourselves'. But that is the one thing we do not do, and do not want to do, because we love self so much in a wrong way. We do not do unto others as we would wish them to do unto us, because the whole time we are thinking only about ourselves, and we never transfer our thought to the other person. That is, in other words, the condition of man in sin as the result of the Fall. He is entirely self-centred. He thinks of nothing and no-one but himself, he is concerned about nothing but his own well-being. This is not my dictum; it is the truth, the simple, literal truth about everybody in the world who is not a Christian; and, alas, it very

often remains true even of Christians. Instinctively we are all
self-centred. We are resentful of what is said and thought of us,
but we never seem to realize that other people are the same,
because we never think of the other person. The whole time we
are thinking of self, and we dislike God because God is Someone
who interferes with this self-centredness and independence.
Man likes to think of himself as completely autonomous, but here
is Someone who challenges that, and man by nature dislikes
Him.

So the failure of man to live by, and to keep, the golden rule is
due to the fact that he is self-centred. That, in turn, leads to self-
satisfaction, self-protection, self-concern. Self is in the forefront
the whole time, for man wants everything for himself. In the last
analysis is not that the real cause of the trouble in your labour
disputes? It all really comes to that. One side says: 'I am entitled
to have more'. The other side says, 'Well, if he has more, I shall
have less'. And so they both object to each other and there is a
quarrel, because each one is thinking only of himself. I am not
entering into the particular merits of particular disputes. There
have been cases where men have been entitled to much more,
but the bitterness always comes in because of sin and self. If we
were only honest enough to analyse our attitude towards all these
questions, whether political, social, economic, national or international, we should find that it all comes back to that. You see
it in the nations. Two nations want the same thing, so each one
is watching the other. All nations try to see themselves simply
as the guardians and the custodians of the general peace of the
world. There is an element of selfishness in patriotism always. It
is 'my country', 'my right'; and the other nation says the same;
and because we are all so self-centred there are wars. All disputes and quarrelling and unhappinesses, whether between
individuals, or between divisions of society, or between nations
or groups of nations, all in the end come down to just that. The
solution for the problems of the world today is essentially theological. All the conferences and all the proposals about dis-
armament and everything else will come to nothing while there
is sin in the human heart controlling individuals and groups and
nations. The failure to implement the golden rule is due solely to
the Fall and to sin.

Let us now put that positively. How is it possible for anyone to
implement this golden rule? The question really is, how can our
attitude and conduct ever conform to what our Lord says here?

The answer of the gospel is that you must start with God. What is the greatest commandment? It is this: 'Thou shalt love the Lord thy God with all thy heart, and with all thy soul, and with all thy mind, and with all thy strength.' And the second is like unto it: 'Thou shalt love thy neighbour as thyself'. You notice the order. You do not start with your neighbour, you start with God. And relationships in this world will never be right, whether between individuals, or groups of nations, until we all start with God. You cannot love your neighbour as yourself until you love God. You will never see yourself or your neighbour aright until you have first of all seen both in the sight of God. We have to take these things in the right order. We must start with God. We were made by God and for God, and we can function truly only in relationship to God.

So then we start with God. We turn from all the quarrelling and disputes and problems and we look into His face. We begin to see Him in all His holiness and almightiness, and in all the power of His creatorship, and we humble ourselves before Him. He is worthy to be praised, and He alone. And, knowing that in His sight even nations are but as grasshoppers and like 'the small dust of the balance', we soon begin to realize that all the pomp and glory of man becomes as nothing when we truly see God. And, in addition, we begin to see ourselves as sinners. We see ourselves as such vile sinners that we forget that we ever had a right. We certainly see that we have no rights at all before God. We are wretched, foul and ugly. That is not only the teaching of Scripture; it is amply confirmed by the experiences of all who have come to know God in any real sense. It is the experience of every saint, and if you have not seen yourself as a worthless creature I should be very doubtful whether you are a Christian at all. No man can really come into the presence of God without saying, 'I am unclean'. We are all unclean. The knowledge of God humbles us to the dust; and in that position you do not think about your rights and your dignity. You have no need any longer to protect yourselves, because you feel you are unworthy of everything.

But, in turn, it also helps us to see others as we should see them. We see them now, no longer as hateful people who are trying to rob us of our rights, or trying to beat us in the race for money, or position or fame; we see them, as we see ourselves, as the victims of sin and of Satan, as the dupes of 'the god of this world', as fellow-creatures who are under the wrath of God and hell-bound.

We have an entirely new view of them. We see them to be exactly as we are ourselves, and we are both in a terrible predicament. And we can do nothing; but both of us together must run to Christ and avail ourselves of His wonderful grace. We begin to enjoy it together and we want to share it together. That is how it works. It is the only way whereby we can ever do unto others as we would that they should do unto us. It is when we are really loving our neighbour as ourselves because we have been delivered from the thraldom of self, that we begin to enjoy 'the glorious liberty of the children of God'.

And of course, finally, it works like this. When we look to God and realize something of the truth about Him, and ourselves in our relationship to Him, the one thing we are conscious of is that God never deals with us according to our deserts. That is not His method. That is what our Lord was saying in the previous verses: 'What man is there of you, whom if his son ask bread, will he give him a stone? Or if he ask a fish, will he give him a serpent? If ye then, being evil, know how to give good gifts unto your children, how much more shall your Father which is in heaven give good things to them that ask him?' That is the argument. God does not give us what we deserve; God gives us His good things in spite of our being what we are. He does not merely look at us as we are. Were He to do so we should all be condemned. If God saw us only as we are, every one of us would be utterly condemned for ever. But He is interested in us in spite of these externals; He sees us as a loving Father. He looks upon us in His grace and mercy. So He does not deal with us merely as we are. He deals with us in grace.

That is why our Lord kept back this argument and put it after that wonderful prayer. That is how God deals with us. 'Now', He says in effect, 'you deal like that with your fellow men. Do not merely see the offensive and the difficult and the ugly. See behind all that'. Let us then observe human beings in their relationship to God, destined for eternity. Let us learn to look at them in this new way, in this divine way. 'Look at them', says Christ in effect, 'as I have looked upon you, and in the light of the thing that brought Me from heaven for you, to give My life for you.' Look at them like that. The moment you do so you will find that it is not difficult to implement the golden rule, because at that point you are delivered from self and its terrible tyranny, and you are seeing men and women with a new eye and in a different way. You will be able to say with Paul, 'Henceforth know we no man after the flesh'. You see everybody in a spiritual way. It is only when we come to this, after having started with God and sin and self and others, that we shall indeed be able to implement this amazing summary of the law and the prophets: 'Whatsoever ye would that men should do to you, do ye even so to them'. That is the thing to which we are called in Christ Jesus. We are to implement it, we are to practise it. And as we do so we shall be showing the world the only way in which its problems can be solved. We shall at the same time be missionaries and ambassadors for Christ.

CHAPTER TWENTY

THE STRAIT GATE

THE remarkable and striking statement of verses 13 and 14 is, judged from every standpoint, a most important and vital one. In terms of the mechanics of an analysis of the Sermon on the Mount it is crucial, because anyone who analyses the Sermon must agree that at this point we reach one of its main divisions. Here we can safely say that our Lord really has finished the Sermon as such, and that from here on He is rounding it off, and applying it, and urging upon His listeners the importance and necessity of practising it and implementing it in their daily lives.

We have seen in our studies that the section of the Sermon occupying the seventh chapter has an essential unity, it has a common theme, namely the theme of judgment. Strictly speaking, the Sermon as such has come to an end at the close of verse 12. By the end of that verse our Lord has laid down all the principles which He was concerned to inculcate.

His object in this Sermon, as we have seen, is to bring Christian people to realize first of all their nature, their character as a people, and then to show them how they are to manifest that nature and character in their daily life. Our Lord, the Son of God, has come from heaven to earth in order to found and establish a new kingdom, the kingdom of heaven. He comes into the midst of the kingdoms of this world, and His purpose is to call out a people unto Himself from the world and to form them into a kingdom. Therefore it is essential that He should make it quite plain and clear that this kingdom He has come to establish is entirely different from anything that the world has ever known, that it is to be the kingdom of God, the kingdom of light, the kingdom of heaven. His people must realize that it is something unique and separate; so He gives them a description of it. We have been working through that description. We have looked at His general portrait of the Christian in the Beatitudes. We have listened to Him telling these people that, because they are that kind of person, the world will react to them in a particular way; it will probably dislike them and persecute them. Nevertheless they are not to segregate themselves from the world and become monks or hermits; they are to remain in society as salt and as light. They are to keep society from putrefaction and from falling to pieces, and they are to be its light; that light, apart from which the world remains in a state of gross darkness.

Having done that, He then comes to the practical application and outworking of it all. He reminds them at once that the kind of life they have to live is to be entirely different even from the best and most religious that was known at that time. He contrasts it with the teaching of the Pharisees and scribes and doctors of the law. They were considered to be the best people, the most religious people, and yet He shows His people that their righteousness is to exceed the righteousness of the scribes and Pharisees. And He proceeds to show how this is to be done by giving detailed instruction as to how we are to do our almsgiving, and how to pray and how to fast. Finally He deals with our whole attitude towards life in this world, and our attitude towards other people in the matter of judgment. He has been laying down all these principles.

'There', He says in effect, 'is the character of this kingdom which I am forming. That is the type of life I am going to give you, and I want you to live and manifest it.' He has not only laid down principles; He has worked them out for us in detail. Now, having done that, He pauses, as it were, and looks at His congregation and says, 'Well now; there is My purpose. What are you going to do about it? There is no point in listening to this Sermon, there is no purpose in your having followed Me through all this delineation of the Christian life, if you are only going to listen. What are you going to do about it?' He comes, in other words, to exhortation, to application.

Here once more we are reminded that our Lord's method must ever be the pattern and example for all preaching. That is not true preaching which fails to apply its message and its truth; nor true exposition of the Bible that is simply content to open up a passage and then stop. The truth has to be taken into the life, and it has to be lived. Exhortation and application are essential parts of preaching. We see our Lord doing that very thing here. The remainder of this seventh chapter is nothing but a great and grand application of the message of the Sermon on the Mount to the people who first heard it, and to all of us at all times who claim to be Christian.

So He proceeds now to test His listeners. He says, in effect, 'My Sermon is finished. Now at once you must ask yourselves a question, "What am I doing about this? What is my reaction?

Am I to be content to fold my arms and say with so many that it is a marvellous Sermon, that it has the grandest conception of life and living that mankind has ever known—such exalted morality, such wonderful uplift—that it is the ideal life that all ought to live?" ' The same applies to us. Is that our reaction? Just to praise the Sermon on the Mount? If it is, according to our Lord, He might as well never have preached it. It is not praise He desires; it is practice. The Sermon on the Mount is not to be commended, it is to be carried out.

Then He goes on and says that there is a further test, the test of fruit. There are many people who have praised this Sermon but who have not manifested it in their lives. Beware of such people, says our Lord. It is not what a tree looks like that matters; you test it by its fruit.

Then there is a final test, and that is the test applied to us by circumstances. What happens to us when the wind begins to blow, and the hurricane threatens, the rain descends and the floods come and beat upon the house of our life? Does it stand? That is the test. In other words, our interest in these things is quite useless and valueless unless it means that we have something that will enable us to stand in the darkest and most critical hours of our lives. That is the way in which He puts His application. Listening to these things, hearing them, praising them is not only not enough; according to our Lord, it is extremely dangerous. This Sermon is practical; it is meant to be lived. It is not merely an ethical idea; it is something that we are meant to implement and put into practice. We have been reminding ourselves of that as we have gone through it in detail; but the whole purpose of the remainder of this chapter is just to exhort us to do that in a most serious and solemn manner, and always in the light of judgment. And, of course, that is not only the teaching of the Sermon on the Mount; it is the teaching of the whole of the New Testament. Take a portion of Scripture such as the Epistle to the Ephesians, chapters iv and v. There you have exactly the same thing. The apostle gives them practical injunctions, tells them not to lie, and not to steal, to be loving and kind and tender-hearted. That is just a reiteration of this Sermon on the Mount. The Christian message is not some theoretical idea; it is something that really is to become characteristic of our daily life and living. That is the purpose of the remainder of this Sermon.

We must now examine particularly verses 13 and 14 in which our Lord begins this application of His own message. Let us look

at them like this. He tells us that the first thing we must do after
we have read this Sermon is to look at the type and kind of life to
which He calls us, and realize what it is. We have seen time and
again that the danger in dealing with the Sermon on the Mount
is to become lost in details, or to be side-tracked by particular
things that interest us. That is the false approach. So our Lord
exhorts us to wait a moment and to look at the Sermon as a whole
and to reflect upon it. What would we say is its outstanding
characteristic? What is the thing that emerges as being of
supreme importance? What is the one thing above all others that
we have to grasp as a principle? He answers His own question by
saying that the outstanding characteristic of the life to which He
calls us is 'narrowness'. It is a narrow life, it is a 'narrow way'.
He puts it dramatically before us by saying: 'Enter ye in at the
strait gate'. The gate is narrow; and we must also walk along a
narrow way.

His illustration is a very useful and practical one. He puts it in a
dramatic form and the scene is immediately conjured up in our
mind's eye. Here we are, walking along, and suddenly we find
two gates confronting us. There is one on the left which is very
wide and broad, and a great crowd of people are entering in. On
the other hand there is a very narrow gate which takes only one
person at a time. We see as we look through the wide gate that it
leads to a broad way and that a great crowd is surging along it.
But the other way is not only narrow at the beginning, it continues to be narrow, and there are but few to be seen walking
along it. We can see the picture quite clearly. That, says our Lord
in effect, is what I have been talking about. That narrow road is
the way along which I want you to walk. 'Enter ye in at the
strait gate.' Come on to this narrow way where you will find Me
walking before you. At once we are reminded of some of the outstanding characteristics of this Christian life to which our Lord
and Saviour Jesus Christ calls us.

The first thing we notice is that it is a life which is narrow or
strait at the very beginning. Immediately it is narrow. It is not a
life which at first is fairly broad, and which as you go on becomes
narrower and narrower. No! The gate itself, the very way of
entering into this life, is a narrow one. It is important to stress and
impress that point because, from the standpoint of evangelism,
it is essential. When worldly wisdom and carnal motives enter
into evangelism you will find that there is no 'strait gate'. Too
often the impression is given that to be a Christian is after all very

little different from being a non-Christian, that you must not think of Christianity as a narrow life, but as something most attractive and wonderful and exciting, and that you come in in crowds. It is not so according to our Lord. The gospel of Jesus Christ is too honest to invite anybody in that way. It does not try to persuade us that it is something very easy, and that it is only later on that we shall begin to discover it is hard. The gospel of Jesus Christ openly and uncompromisingly announces itself as being something which starts with a narrow entrance, a strait gate. At the very beginning it is absolutely essential that we should realize that. Let us look at this in a little more detail.

We are told at the very outset of this way of life, before we start on it, that if we would walk along it there are certain things which must be left outside, behind us. There is no room for them, because we have to start by passing through a strait and narrow gate. I like to think of it as a turnstile. It is just like a turnstile that admits one person at a time and no more. And it is so narrow that there are certain things which you simply cannot take through with you. It is exclusive from the very beginning, and it is important that we should look at this Sermon in order to see some of the things which must be left behind.

The first thing we leave behind is what is called worldliness. We leave behind the crowd, the way of the world. 'Wide is the gate, and broad is the way, that leadeth to destruction, and many there be which go in thereat: because strait is the gate, and narrow is the way, which leadeth unto life, and few there be that find it.' You must start by realizing that, by becoming a Christian, you become something exceptional and unusual. You are making a break with the world, and with the crowd, and with the vast majority of people. It is inevitable; and it is important that we should know it. The Christian way of life is not popular. It never has been popular, and it is not popular today. It is unusual, exceptional, strange, and it is different. On the other hand, crowding through the wide gate and travelling along the broad way is the thing that everybody else seems to be doing. You deliberately get out of that crowd and you start making your way towards this strait and narrow gate, alone. You cannot take the crowd with you into the Christian life: it inevitably involves a break.

We can put this best, perhaps, by emphasizing that it is something that is always intensely personal. Nothing, after all, is more difficult in this life than to realize that we are individual persons.

We are all of us so much slaves of 'the done thing'. We come into a world full of traditions and habits and customs to which we tend to conform. It is the easy and obvious thing to do; and it is true to say of most of us that there is nothing we hate so much as being unusual or different. There are exceptions of course, some who are eccentric by nature and others who affect eccentricity; but it is true of the vast majority of us that we all like to be the same. Children are like that. They want their parents to be the same as other parents; they do not want anything unusual. It is amazing to observe how people instinctively like to conform to pattern in custom, habit, and behaviour; and indeed, at times, it is even amusing. We hear certain people objecting to the tendency in modern legislation to regimentation. They voice their objections to it strongly, as they do their belief in individuality and freedom. Yet they themselves are often just typical representatives of the particular section or group in which they have been brought up, or to which they like to belong. You can tell almost at once the school or university they have attended; they conform to pattern.

We all tend to do this, with the result that one of the most difficult things that many people have to face when they become Christian is that it is going to involve them in being unusual and exceptional. But it has to happen. In other words, one of the first things that happens to a person who becomes alive to the message of the gospel of Christ is that he says to himself: 'Well; whatever may be happening to the majority, I myself am a living soul and I am responsible for my own life'. 'Every man shall bear his own burden.' So when a man becomes a Christian he first begins to see himself as a separate unit in this great world. Formerly he had lost his individuality and identity in the great crowd of people to whom he belonged; but now he stands alone. He had been rushing madly with the crowd, but he suddenly halts. That is always the first step in becoming a Christian. And he realizes, furthermore, that if his soul, his eternal destiny, is to be made safe, he must not only stand for a moment in the surge of that crowd, he must separate himself from it. He may find it difficult to extricate himself, but he must do it; and while the majority are going in one direction he must go in the other. He leaves the crowd. You cannot get a crowd through that turnstile all together, it only takes one person at a time. It makes a man realize that he is a responsible being before God, his Judge Eternal. The gate is strait and narrow, it brings me face to face with judgment, face to face with God, face to face with the question of life and my personal being, my soul and its eternal destiny.

But I not only have to leave the crowd, the world and the 'jollity' outside. Still more difficult, and still straiter and narrower, is the realization that I have to leave the *way* of the world outside. We are all familiar with this in practice and in our Christian lives. It is one thing to leave the crowd, but it is a very different thing to leave the *way* of the crowd. That, of course, is the ultimate and final fallacy of monasticism. Monasticism is really based upon the idea that if you leave people, you leave the spirit of the world. But you do not. You can leave the world in a physical sense, you can leave the crowd and the people; but there in your lonely cell the spirit of the world may still be with you. That is something that is equally true in connection with Christian life and living. There are people who have segregated themselves from the group to which they belonged, and yet you find the spirit of worldliness left in them still, perhaps even evident in their deportment. They have not left the spirit of the world and the way of the world. But we must. Living the way of the world and the life of the world in a different setting does not make us Christian. In other words, we must leave outside the gate the things that please the world. This cannot be evaded. We have only to read the Sermon on the Mount to come to the conclusion that the things that belong to and that please our unregenerate nature must be left outside that strait gate.

We can illustrate this. You remember that we have heard in this Sermon that we must check the spirit that demands 'an eye for an eye, and a tooth for a tooth', that we must not resist evil— 'whosoever shall smite thee on thy right cheek, turn to him the other also'. We do not do that sort of thing instinctively; it does not come naturally to us and we do not like it. 'If any man . . . take away thy coat, let him have thy cloke also.' 'Whosoever shall compel thee to go a mile, go with him twain.' 'Ye have heard that it hath been said, Thou shalt love thy neighbour, and hate thine enemy. But I say unto you, Love your enemies, bless them that curse you, do good to them that hate you, and pray for them which despitefully use you, and persecute you.'

To obey those injunctions is not instinctive, indeed it is something we do not like. The instinctive thing is to hit back, to defend our rights, to love those who love us, and to hate those who hate us. But our Lord has been telling us that if we are really to be His people and to live in His kingdom, we must leave outside the depraved, the instinctive, and the worldly, the things liked and done by our fallen nature. There is no room for such things. We should realize at the beginning that that kind of luggage cannot be admitted. Our Lord is warning us against the danger of an easy salvation, against the tendency to say: 'Just come to Christ as you are and all is going to be well'. No, the gospel tells us at the outset that it is going to be difficult. It means a radical break with the world; it is an entirely different type of life. So we leave not only the world, but also the way of the world outside.

Yes, but still narrower and still straiter; if we really want to come into this way of life, we have to leave our 'self' outside. And it is there of course that we come to the greatest stumbling-block of all. It is one thing to leave the world, and the way of the world; but the most important thing in a sense is to leave our self outside. Yet it is obvious, is it not? We are not to take our self with us on this way. That is not being foolish; it is typical New Testament language. Self is the Adamic man, the fallen nature; and Christ says that he must be left outside. 'Put off the old man', that is, leave him outside the gate. There is no room for two men to go through this gate together, so the old man must be left behind. Every illustration breaks down somewhere, and even this illustration used by our Lord Himself cannot cover the whole truth. There is a sense in which the Christian has not left the old man outside and so needs the exhortation of the apostle to 'put off the old man'. Nevertheless we are told at the very outset that self has no place in this kingdom.

The New Testament gospel is very humbling to self and to pride. At the beginning of the Sermon we are confronted by: 'Blessed are the poor in spirit'. No natural man born into this world likes to be poor in spirit. We are by nature the exact opposite to that; we are all born with a proud nature, and the world does its utmost to encourage our pride from our very birth. The most difficult thing in the world is to become poor in spirit. It is humbling to pride, and yet it is essential. At the entrance to that strait gate there is a notice that says: 'Leave yourself outside'. How can we bless them that curse us, and pray for them which despitefully use us, unless we have done this? How can we possibly follow our Lord, and be children of our Father which is in heaven, and love our enemies, if we are self-conscious and always defending and watching self and being concerned about it. We have gone through all this already in detail;

but we must look at it again in general, as our Lord calls upon us to do so in this invitation to enter the strait gate. Self cannot possibly exist in this atmosphere; all along it must be crucified. 'Judge not, that ye be not judged.' Do unto others as you would that all men should do unto you, and so on. Our Lord tells us that at the very beginning. Have no illusion about this. If you think it is a life in which you are going to make a great name, and be praised, and one in which you are going to be made wonderful, you may as well stop at this point and go back to the beginning, for he who would enter by this gate must say goodbye to self. It is a life of self-abasement, self-humiliation. 'If any man will come after me'—what happens? 'Let him deny himself (the first thing always), and take up his cross, and follow me.' But self-denial, denial of self, does not mean refraining from various pleasures and things that we may like; it means we deny our very right to our self, we leave our self outside, and go in through the gate saying: 'Yet not I, but Christ liveth in me'.

That then is the first thing. This gate is narrow; the very beginning of the Christian life is strait because we have to leave certain things outside.

But I would also emphasize that it is strait and narrow in another way, namely, that it is difficult. The Christian way of life is difficult. It is not an easy life. It is too glorious and wonderful to be easy. It means living like Christ Himself, and that is not easy. The standard is difficult—thank God for it. It is a poor kind of person who wants only the easy and avoids the difficult. This is the highest life that has ever been depicted to mankind, and because of that it is difficult, and it is strait and narrow. 'Few there be that find it.' Of course! There are always fewer consulting doctors of medicine than general practitioners; there are never as many experts as there are ordinary workers. It does not matter what realm or department of life you are thinking of, you will always find that the real experts are few in number. When you come to the topmost level in any walk in life the company is always smaller. Anybody can follow the ordinary; but the moment you want to do something unusual, the moment you want to reach the heights, you will find that there are not many trying to do the same. It is exactly the same with respect to the Christian life; it is such an exalted life and such a wonderful one, that there are but few who find it and enter it, simply because it is difficult. We need not emphasize this. Consider what we have been told as we have gone through the Sermon in detail. Look at this kind of life as our Lord has depicted it, and you will see that it must be narrow because it is so difficult. It is the highest, it is the acme of perfection in living.

In addition it is strait and narrow because it always involves suffering, and because, when it is truly lived, it always involves persecution. 'Blessed are ye, when men shall revile you, and persecute you, and shall say all manner of evil against you falsely, for my sake. Rejoice, and be exceeding glad: for great is your reward in heaven: for so persecuted they the prophets which were before you.' They have always done that, the world has always persecuted the man who follows God. You see it perfectly in the case of our Lord Himself. He was rejected by the world. He was hated by men and women because He was what He was. 'Yea,' says Paul, 'and all that will live godly in Christ Jesus shall suffer persecution.' But who likes being persecuted? We do not like to be criticized or to be dealt with harshly. We really do like all people to speak well of us, and it is very galling to us to know that we are being hated and criticized; but Christ has warned us that we will be, if we come into this narrow way. It is strait and difficult; and as we enter, therefore, we must be ready for suffering and persecution.

You must be ready to be misunderstood; you must be ready, perhaps, even to be misunderstood by your nearest and dearest. Christ has told us that He came 'not to send peace, but a sword', a sword that may divide mother from daughter, or father from son, and those of your own household may be your greatest enemies. Why? Because you have been set apart. You have been set apart from your family, and have entered by this strait gate that does not admit us by families, but one by one. It is very hard, it is very difficult. But the Lord Jesus Christ is honest with us; and if we see nothing else, God grant that we may see the honesty and the truthfulness of this gospel which tells us at the very outset that we may have to come apart from husband or from wife for the sake of becoming a Christian and following Christ. You are not called upon to separate actually and in fact, but spiritually. But you can only come one by one, for it is a strait and narrow gate.

So far we have seen how narrow and strait this life is at the beginning. But it is not only strait at the beginning; it continues to be strait. It is not only a strait gate, it is a narrow way also. The Christian life is narrow from the beginning to the end. There is no such thing as a holiday in the spiritual realm. We can take a holiday from our usual work; but there is no such thing as a holiday in the spiritual life. It is always narrow. As it starts, so it continues. It is a 'fight of faith' always, right to the end. It is the narrow way, and on each side there are enemies. There are things oppressing us and people attacking us all along to the very end. You will have no easy pathway in this world and in this life, and Christ tells us that at the beginning. If you have an idea that the Christian life is going to be difficult at the commencement and that later it becomes quite easy, you have an entirely false view of the teaching of the New Testament. It is narrow all the way; there will be foes and enemies attacking you right to the last minute.

Am I discouraging? Does anyone feel like saying: 'Well, if it is like that, I am going back'? But I would remind you before you decide to do that, that we are told something about the end to which this road leads. Yet apart from that, is it not the most glorious thing to go on following Him? Even so, let us be under no illusion; the wrestling against principalities and powers, against the darkness of this world, and the spiritual wickedness in high places, continues while man is in this life and world. There will be subtle temptations on the road of life, and you will have to watch and be on guard, from the beginning to the end. You will never be able to relax. You will always have to be careful; you will have to walk circumspectly, as Paul puts it; you will have to watch your every step. It is a narrow way, it starts as such and so it continues.

These then are the things that we have to bear in mind as we contemplate this Sermon as a whole. It is most dangerous, as well as being quite unscriptural, to fail to realize them at the very beginning. To divorce forgiveness of sins from the remainder of the Christian life and to regard it as if it were the whole is clearly heresy. True evangelism, as I understand it, is one that presents to men and women the Christian life as a whole, and we must be very careful about giving the impression that people can crowd, as it were, to Christ, can try to rush the strait gate without considering the narrow way to which it leads. It was our Lord Himself who spoke those parables about the foolish people who did not count the cost—the man who started to put up a tower, without counting the cost, and so had to leave his building unfinished. The same was true of the king who went to fight another king, without assessing the strength of the enemy. It is our Lord who tells us to count the cost and to face what we have to do before we start. He shows us the whole life. He has not merely come to save us from punishment and from hell; He has come to make us holy, and to 'purify unto himself a peculiar people, zealous of good works'. He came into this world to prepare the way of holiness, and His ambition and His purpose for us is that we shall walk in that way in His steps, in this high calling, in this glorious life, that we should live even as He Himself lived it, resisting even unto blood if necessary. That was His life, a straight and thorny road; but He trod it. And your privilege and mine is the privilege of coming out of the world and entering into this life, and following Him all the way.

> 'Christian! seek not yet repose,
>   Cast thy dreams of ease away;
> Thou art in the midst of foes:
>   Watch and pray.'

CHAPTER TWENTY-ONE

THE NARROW WAY

WE return to a further consideration of this statement in verses 13 and 14 because our Lord in these words does not ask us merely to contemplate the nature of the kingdom or the Christian life in general. It is not an invitation to come and view a wonderful prospect, to sit as it were in the gallery and look at the arena. We are meant to be participators in this; it is a call to action. You notice the words: 'Enter ye'; they are an invitation and an exhortation at one and the same time. Having contemplated it in general, we have to do something about it.

That then is the first principle which we must elaborate a little. It is a call to action. What does this mean? First, it means that the gospel of Jesus Christ, this enunciating of the principles of the kingdom, is something that demands a decision and a committal. This is quite unavoidable; it is something which is a part of the warp and woof of the New Testament presentation of the truth. It is not a philosophy that you look at and compare and contrast with other philosophies. You can never maintain a detached attitude to this; and if our concern about these things is a purely intellectual one, which has never affected our lives, then the New Testament says we are just not Christian. It is, of course, a wonderful philosophy, but the temptation is to regard it as just that, as something to be read about, and to be interested in. But the gospel refuses to be taken like that; it is essentially something that comes to us demanding to control our lives. It comes to us in much the same way as our Lord Himself approached men. You remember how, as He walked along, He came across a man like Matthew, and said to him, 'Follow me', and Matthew got up and followed Him. The gospel does something like that. It does not say: 'Consider Me; admire Me'. It says: 'Follow Me; believe Me'. It always calls for a decision, for a committal.

This is obviously something that is quite vital. There is no purpose in describing the glories and the wonders and the beauties of that narrow way if we are still going to look at it only from a distance. It is a road that is to be trodden; it is something we are to enter into. Nothing is more remarkable than the way in which we succeed in persuading ourselves for so long that an interest in the gospel without a decision and a committal is possible. But it is not.

So we ask ourselves a very simple question at this point. My ultimate test of myself, and of my profession of the Christian faith, can be put like this: Have I committed myself to this way of life? Is it the thing which controls my life? We have seen what it tells us to do; have we then put ourselves under its teaching? Is it dominating our lives? Is it governing and controlling us in our actual decisions and practice? This, of course, involves a very definite act of the will. It calls upon me to say: 'Recognizing this as God's truth and as the call of Christ, I am going to give myself to it, come what may. I am not going to consider the consequences. I believe it, I will act upon it; this henceforth is going to be my life.'

There was a time when some of our forefathers used to teach that it was a good thing for every Christian to make a covenant with God. Having considered the truth like this, they would sit down and solemnly write out on paper the covenant which they made with God, and they would put their signature to it and the date, exactly as if it were a business transaction. They would sign away themselves, and their right to themselves and all they had, and their right to live as they chose. They would henceforth give themselves to God, much as a man joining an army surrenders the right to himself and the control of his life. They would enter into a contract like that, a covenant with God, and they would sign, seal and settle it, and there it was. There is something to be said for that practice. Some of us suffer so much from the tendency just to contemplate the Christian life without doing anything about it, that it would be a good thing for us deliberately and definitely to make an act of committal such as this, and thus enter in at the strait gate. It demands a decision.

That in turn leads to the second principle. Having looked at the truth and having decided that I have to do something about it, I now begin to seek for this strait gate. You notice how our Lord puts it. He says, 'because strait is the gate, and narrow is the way, which leadeth unto life, and few there be that find it'. Why is this? It is because there are few that seek it. This is a gate which must be sought deliberately. In other words, the essence of wisdom in these matters is to move from the general to the particular. It is surely true of the experience of all of us to say that one of the greatest dangers confronting us is the danger of listen-

ing to the truth, or reading it, and nodding our head in agreement with it but of never doing anything at all about it. We do
not seek for the strait gate.

Seeking the strait gate means something like this. Having seen
the truth, and having expressed my agreement, I should then
say to myself, 'What exactly must I do to make this operative?'
That is seeking the strait gate. There is a way of seeking truly and
we must discover in detail exactly what it means for us. That is
seeking the strait gate—really to put the truth into operation. I
am concerned to impress the point that the gate really has to be
sought. It is not easy; it is difficult. You have to go out of your
way to find this gate. You will have to analyse yourself and be
very honest with yourself, and, having refused to hold back, say:
'I am going on with this until I discover exactly what I have to
do.' There are so many who do not find this way of life because
they have never sought the gate and entered in. If you read the
biographies of some of God's great saints in past times you will
find that they sought this strait gate for many a long day. Look at
Martin Luther. There he is in his cell, fasting, sweating and
praying. Read again about men like George Whitefield and John
Wesley. These men were seeking this strait gate. They did not
know what they had to do, they were wrong in their ideas, but at
long last, by diligent seeking they found it, and when they found
it they entered in. Now in some way or another we must all do
that. In other words, we must give ourselves no rest or peace
until we know for certain that we are on this way. That is
'entering the strait gate'. You enter it only after you have sought
and after you have found it.

The third step is that, having decided that you are going to
enter and having sought the gate and entered through it, you
then go right on; you commit yourself, and you say certain
things to yourself. It is surely true to say that the solution to many
of our problems in this Christian life is that we should talk more
to ourselves. We should constantly remind ourselves of who we
are and what we are. That is what is meant by not only entering
in but continuing along this way. The Christian man should
remind himself every morning as he wakes up, 'I am a child of
God; I am a unique person; I am not like everybody else; I
belong to the family of God. Christ has died for me and has
translated me from the kingdom of darkness into His own
kingdom. I am going to heaven, I am destined for that. I am but
passing through this world. I know its temptations and trials; I

know the subtle insinuations of Satan. But I do not belong to him. I am a pilgrim and a stranger; I am one who is following Christ along this road.' You remind yourself of that, you commit yourself, and you go on doing so. And the result will be that you will find yourself walking along this narrow way. That is the first general principle upon which we must act. When we have seen the truth we must do something about it; we must bring ourselves into a practical relationship to it.

The second principle stands out very clearly. It is the consideration of some reasons for doing this. Once more, as we have found so often in our study of this Sermon, our blessed Lord stoops to our weakness. We have found almost invariably that it is His method, His technique if you like, to lay down a principle or to give an injunction; and then, having done that, to give us some reasons for carrying it out. He need not have done so. There we see something of His great pastoral heart and His sympathy with us as His people. He is a High Priest who is able 'to sympathize with us'. He understands us. He knows that we are so fallible and imperfect as a result of sin that it is not enough merely to show us the way. We need to be supplied with reasons. 'Enter ye in at the strait gate: *for* wide is the gate, and broad is the way that leadeth to destruction, and many there be which go in thereat: *because* strait is the gate, and narrow is the way, which leadeth unto life, and few there be that find it.'

What then are the reasons? Let us just summarize them. The first reason He gives us for entering in at this strait gate is the character of the two types of life that are open to us and possible for us. There is the broad way which you enter through the wide gate, and there is the other way which is entered through the strait gate, a way which is narrow the whole time. If we only realized the truth concerning the character of these two ways there would be no hesitation. Of course, it is so difficult for us to detach ourselves from life in this world, and yet the essence of this matter is that we should do so. That is why, if one may say so, God in His infinite wisdom ordained that one day in seven should be set apart for the contemplation of these things, and that men should meet together in public worship. When we meet for worship we are stepping out of this world in which we live in order that we may look upon it all objectively. It is so difficult to do that when you are in it; but once you come out, and sit apart and look at it objectively, you really begin to see things as they are.

Look for a moment at that worldly life which those people live who are on the broad way. Look at it, for instance, as you see it in the newspapers. Take any one of them. They represent the typical worldly life at its best and at its worst. Look at that life which has such a fascination for so many people, that life which so fascinates them that they are prepared to risk their eternal soul for it, if they believe in the soul at all. What is it that holds them? Look at the life and analyse it. What is there in it ultimately with all its pomp and its glory and its luxury? Can you imagine anything that is so utterly empty finally? What real satisfaction is there in such a life? You remember those famous questions which the apostle Paul puts to the Romans, which, it seems to me, summarize this perfectly. At the end of Romans vi. 21, he asks, 'What fruit had ye then in those things whereof ye are now ashamed? for the end of those things is death.' Now that you have become a Christian, he says, as you look back across your life, you are ashamed of it. But what fruit did you have in it even then?

This is a question that all people should face, especially those who live from one round of pleasure to another, and who regard honest work as just a nuisance, or merely as a means of getting money in order to go back to have more pleasure. What is there in it? What is the gain? What is the satisfaction? What have they of ultimate value intellectually, apart from anything else? What is there uplifting and ennobling in dressing in a particular way and having their photographs in the so-called society papers, in being known for their fashionable attire or personal appearance, or for the figure they cut, and all the rest of it? What real value is there in the praise and adulation of man? Look at the people who live for such things, analyse their lives, and especially their end. That is not cynicism, it is realism. As the hymn puts it,

'Fading is the worldling's pleasure,
All his boasted pomp and show.'

How empty it is. The apostle Peter describes the same thing as 'vain conversation'. There is nothing in it, it is so superficial and empty. It is very difficult, apart from Christianity, to understand the mentality of people who live on such a level. They have minds and brains, but they do not seem to be much in evidence in this life of make-believe and delusion and folly and self-hypnotism. What an utterly empty life it is, even looked at as it is in and of itself, this life of pomp and show and shadow and appearance.

Then look at the other life and see how essentially different it is in every respect. The broad way is empty and useless, intellectually, morally, and in every other respect. It leaves man with a nasty taste in his mouth even at the time, and leads to jealousy and envy and all sorts of things that are unworthy. But look at the other, and immediately you see a striking contrast. Read the Sermon on the Mount again. What a life! Take this New Testament. What food for your intellect! Here is something to engage your mind. Read books about it. Can you imagine a higher intellectual occupation, apart from anything else? Here you have something to think about, something to grapple with intellectually, something that gives you real and lasting satisfaction. How ethical, how uplifting, how large and noble it is.

The trouble ultimately with all who are not Christian is that they have never seen the glory and the magnificence of the Christian life. How noble and pure and upright it is! But they have never seen it. They are blind to it. As the apostle Paul says, 'The god of this world hath blinded the minds of them which believe not' (2 Corinthians iv. 4). But once a man gets a glimpse of the glory and majesty and privilege of this high calling I cannot imagine that he would ever desire anything else. Let us be very practical and blunt about this. Anybody who calls this Christian life 'narrow' (in the usual sense of that term) and hankers after the other, is just proclaiming that he has never seen this truly. He is like those people who say that they find Beethoven rather boring, and that they prefer jazz music. What they are really saying is they do not understand Beethoven; they do not hear him, they know nothing about him. They are ignorant musically. As someone has said, they tell us nothing about Beethoven, but a great deal about themselves!

There, then, is the character and the nature of the two lives. The New Testament constantly presents this argument. This is to be found repeatedly in the Epistles. The writers describe the life, and then say, in effect: 'Surely, having seen that, you do not want to go back to anything else?' That is their argument. They remind you of these two lives; 'Wide is the gate, and broad is the way, that leadeth to destruction.' But 'strait is the gate, and narrow is the way, which leadeth unto life.' The man who does not consider his destination is a fool. The man who makes travelling an end in itself is illogical and inconsistent. That is the great argument of the Bible from beginning to end. 'Consider your latter end'; consider your destination and whither that sort of life leads. If only the world could be persuaded to ask that question, all would soon be changed. We have seen how the apostle Paul tells us that the broad way is certain to lead to shame and misery and destruction. 'The wages of sin is death'—spiritual death and separation from God as well as suffering, agony, despair and useless remorse; 'but the gift of God is eternal life through Jesus Christ our Lord' (Romans vi. 23). If ever, therefore, you feel that the Christian way of life is rather irksome, just remind yourself of the destination to which it leads. Then look at the world with its apparent joy and happiness; look at the people who are loving and enjoying it, and try to picture them when they will be decrepit with old age, and 'the last enemy' comes to meet them. Suddenly they are taken ill. They can no longer drink, and smoke, and dance, and gamble, and do the things on which they have lived. On their deathbed what have they? Nothing; nothing to look forward to except fear, and horror, and torment, and destruction. That is the end of that life. We know that well; it has always been true. Read the biographies of the world's great men, statesmen and others, who are not Christian, and notice again the eclipse which they experience. And remember that we are never given details of the actual end. How can it lead to anything else? It leads 'to destruction'.

But this other life leads to a life more abundant. It starts by giving new life, a new outlook, new desires, new everything; and as you go on it becomes greater and more wonderful. However much you may have to suffer in this life and world, you are destined for a glory which is indestructible. You are going on to an inheritance, according to the apostle Peter, which is 'incorruptible, and undefiled, and that fadeth not away', reserved in heaven by God for you.

Another argument our Lord uses is that not to enter in at the strait gate means that we are already on the broad way. It has to be one or the other. 'There is no mean between two opposites.' The Christian is confronted by two ways only, and if we are not on the strait and narrow way, we are on the wide and broad way. So indecision and a failure to commit ourselves means that we are not on the narrow way. Passive resistance is resistance; if we are not for Him we are against Him. That is a very powerful argument. Indecision is fatal, because it means wrong decision. There is no alternative. It is either the narrow or the broad way.

The greatest inducement of all, however, to enter in at the strait gate and to walk the narrow way, is this. There is Someone on that road before you. You have to leave the world outside. You may have to leave many who are dear to you, you have to leave yourself, your old self, and you may think as you go through that gate that you are going to be isolated and solitary. But it is not so. There are others on this road with you—'few there be that find it'. There are not as many as there are on the other way, but they are a very choice and separate people. But above all look at the One who is treading that road ahead of all, the One who said, 'Follow me', the One who said, 'Let him deny himself, and take up his cross, and follow me'. If there were no other inducement for entering in at the strait gate, that is more than enough. To enter this way means to follow in the footsteps of the Lord Jesus Christ. It is an invitation to live as He lived; it is an invitation to become increasingly what He was. It is to be like Him, to live as He lived whose life we read of in these Gospels. That is what it means; and the more we think of it in that way the greater will the inducement be. Do not think of what you have to leave; there is nothing in that. Do not think of the losses, do not think of the sacrifices and sufferings. These terms should not be used; you lose nothing, but you gain everything. Look at Him, follow Him, and realize that ultimately you are going to be with Him, and to look into His blessed face and enjoy Him to all eternity. He is on this way, and that is enough.

Before we leave this matter there is one other principle that we should consider. We have decided to enter, and we have found the reasons for entering. There are, however, certain problems that people constantly mention when they consider this text. One is that the theology of this teaching presents a stumbling-block to certain people. The first difficulty is this. Does our Lord teach here that there is a kind of neutral position in life? Here we are pictured as standing on a road with a wide and a narrow gate before us. Is there ever a time in a man's life when he is neither good nor bad? Are we all born in innocency and neutrality? Do we deliberately enter one or the other? It seems to teach that.

The answer, of course, is that we must always compare Scripture with Scripture, and take any particular Scripture in the light of the whole. Scripture teaches us plainly that we are all born into this world the children of sin and wrath. We are all, as descendants of Adam, born in guilt and shame, born in sin and shapen in iniquity, born, indeed, 'dead in trespasses and sins'. Actually, therefore, we are all born on the broad way. Why then did our Lord put it like that? For this reason. He is teaching here the importance of entering in upon His way of life, and He uses an illustration. He dramatizes and objectifies the situation and asks us to regard it as if we were confronted by the choice of one of two ways. In other words, He asks: Are you committed for ever to

that worldly life in which you were born, or are you going to
leave it and come into Mine? It is perfect teaching technique and
one cannot imagine a better illustration. Yet every illustration
has its limits. He is concerned about our committal of ourselves,
so He puts it like that. So there is no teaching here which contradicts the plain teaching of Scripture to the effect that we must all
be born again, that we all need a new nature, that we are all
children of this world, and the children of Satan, until we become
the children of God. Our Lord Himself teaches that, does He
not? He gives power to all who receive Him to 'become' the
children of God. That is the teaching everywhere in the Gospels,
as it is the teaching of all the Epistles also. So, as we look at it
like that, we see that it is an illustration to stress one great point
only.

But there is another question. Does our Lord teach that it is
our decision and action that saves us? 'Enter ye in at the strait
gate', He seems to say, 'and if you do so, and walk along the
narrow way, you will arrive at life; whereas if you enter in at the
other you will land in destruction.' Does this teach, then, that a
man saves himself by his decision and by his action?

Again we approach the problem in the same manner. We
must always compare Scripture with Scripture, and realize that
it never contradicts itself. And Scripture teaches that all are
justified by faith, and saved by the death of the Lord Jesus Christ
on our behalf. He came 'to seek and to save that which was lost.'
'There is none righteous, no, not one.' The whole world is guilty
before God. No man by his own action can save himself; his
righteousness is but as 'filthy rags'. We are all saved by the grace
of the Lord Jesus Christ and by nothing that we do. Then what
about this text? asks someone. The answer can be put in this
form. I do not save myself by entering in at the strait gate, but
by doing so I announce the fact that I am saved. The only man
who does enter in at the strait gate is the man who is saved; the
only people on the narrow way are those who are saved; otherwise they would not be there. 'The natural man receiveth not the
things of the Spirit of God'; 'The carnal (natural) mind is
enmity against God', and therefore against the narrow way. It
is 'not subject to the law of God, neither indeed can be.' So no
man, as he is, is ever going to choose to enter in at the strait gate
because it is foolishness to him. No; what our Lord is saying here
is this. It is not because I make myself 'poor in spirit' that I am
'blessed'; but when I become poor in spirit as the result of the
working of the Holy Spirit upon me, I am truly blessed. By being

and doing these things we proclaim what we are, we are announcing gladly and readily that we are His. It is only Christian people who are to be found along the narrow way, and you do not make yourself a Christian by entering in. You are entering in and walking upon it because you are saved.

We can put that the other way round; Does a failure to live the Christian life fully prove that we are on the broad way? We have spent time in considering the characteristics of the strait and the narrow way, and we have a clear picture of the Christian life everywhere in the Sermon on the Mount. But we fail in so many respects; we do not turn the other cheek, and so on. Does that mean, therefore, that we are still on the broad way? The answer is 'No'. No picture must be pressed in all its detail, otherwise, as we have seen so many times, it becomes ridiculous. The questions that have to be asked in the light of this text are these: Have you decided for this way of life? Have you committed yourself to it? Have you chosen it? Is this what you want to be? Is this what you are endeavouring to be? Is this the life you are hungering and thirsting after? If it is, I can assure you that you are in it. It is our Lord Himself who said, 'Blessed are they which do hunger and thirst after righteousness: for they shall be filled.' The man who hungers and thirsts after righteousness is not a man who is absolutely sinless and perfect. There is no such person in this life. What our Lord is saying in effect is, 'My people are the people who want to follow Me, those who are striving to do so.' They have entered in at the strait gate and are walking the narrow way. They often fail and fall into temptation but they are still on the way. Failure does not mean that they have gone back on to the broad way. You can fall on the narrow way. But if you realize that you have done so, and immediately confess and acknowledge your sin, He is 'faithful and just' to forgive you your sin and to cleanse you from all unrighteousness. John has put it all for us in the first chapter of his first Epistle: 'If we walk in the light, as he is in the light, we have fellowship one with another, and the blood of Jesus Christ his Son cleanseth us from all sin.' 'In him is no darkness at all'; but we stumble into sin and break the fellowship and communion. We are on the way still, but we have lost the communion. And we have nothing to do but to confess it, and at once the blood of Jesus Christ will cleanse us from that sin and every other unrighteousness. The communion is restored and we go on walking with Him. This picture of the narrow way is designed to stress and impress this one great principle—our desire, our ambition, our committal, our decision, our hungering and thirsting to be like Him, and to be walking with Him.

The last question is this. 'Wide is the gate, and broad is the way, that leadeth to destruction, and many there be which go in thereat: because strait is the gate, and narrow is the way, which leadeth unto life, and few there be that find it.' 'Does that mean,' says someone, 'that only a few are going to be saved? Are the vast majority of mankind to be damned?' I need do nothing by way of reply but give our Lord's answer to that question. People curious about theological problems, and who had often debated the question among themselves, came to our Lord one day (Luke xiii. 23), and asked, as their modern counterparts are so fond of asking, 'Are there few that be saved?' You remember our Lord's answer. He looked straight into the eyes of these philosophers, these speculative gentlemen, and said: 'Strive to enter in at the strait gate.' Leave a question like that to God; God, and God alone, knows how many are going to be saved. It is not your business or mine to discover how many are going to be saved. Our business is to strive to enter, to make certain that *we* are in it; and if we make certain that we are in it, one day in glory, and not until then, we shall find out how many companions we have. And it may very well be that we shall have a great surprise. But it is not our business now. Our business is to enter in, to strive to enter in, to make certain. Enter in, and you will find yourself amongst the saved, amongst those who are to be glorified, amongst all who look unto Jesus, 'the author and finisher of our faith'.

CHAPTER TWENTY-TWO

FALSE PROPHETS

IN verses 15 and 16, and to the end of this chapter, our Lord is concerned with just one great principle, one great message. He is emphasizing but one thing, the importance of entering in at the strait gate, and making quite certain that we are truly walking along the narrow way. In other words, it is a kind of enforcement of the message of verses 13 and 14. There He puts it in the form of an invitation or exhortation, that we are to enter in at this strait gate, and to walk and to keep on walking that narrow way. Here He elaborates that. He shows us some of the dangers, hindrances and obstacles that meet all who attempt to do that. But all along He keeps on emphasizing this vital principle, that the gospel is not just something to be listened to, or to be applauded, but ever to be applied. As James puts it, the danger is to look into the mirror, and immediately to forget what we have seen, instead of looking steadily into the mirror of that perfect law and remembering it and putting it into practice.

That is the theme our Lord continues to emphasize right until the end of the Sermon. First of all He puts it in the form of two particular and special dangers that confront us. He shows us how to recognize them and, having recognized them, how to deal with them. Then, having dealt with these two dangers, He winds up the argument, and the entire Sermon, by putting it in a plain, blunt, unvarnished statement in terms of the picture of the two houses, the one built upon the rock and the other upon the sand. But it is the same theme from beginning to end, and the thing that is common to the three divisions in the general statement is the terrible warning about the fact of judgment. That, as we have seen, is the theme right through this seventh chapter of Matthew's Gospel and it is most important that we should realize that. It is the failure to grasp this that accounts for most of our troubles and problems. It accounts for the light and superficial evangelism that is far too common today. It accounts also for the lack of holiness and sanctified living that is true of most of us. It is not that we need special teaching about these things. What we all seem to be forgetting is that the whole time the eye of God is upon us, and that we are all moving steadily and certainly in the direction of the final judgment.

So our Lord goes on repeating that. He puts it in different forms, but all along He emphasizes the fact of judgment, and the character of the judgment. It is not a superficial one, not a mere examination of the externals, but a searching of the heart, an examination of the whole nature. Above all He stresses the absolute finality of the judgment, and the consequences that follow upon it. He has already told us in verses 13 and 14 why we should enter in at the strait gate. The reason is, He says, that the other gate is a broad one which 'leadeth to destruction', the destruction that follows the final judgment upon the ungodly. Our Lord, clearly, was so concerned about this that He continually repeats it. This shows again the perfection of His method as a teacher. He knew the importance of repetition. He knew how dull we are, how slow we are, and how ready to think we know a thing, when in reality we do not, and how therefore we need to be reminded constantly of the same fact. We all know something of the difficulty of remembering these vital principles. People in past ages resorted to all sorts of means and methods to aid themselves in doing this. You find in many Anglican churches that the Ten Commandments were painted on the wall. It was their realization of the tendency to forget that led our forefathers to do that.

Our Lord, then, reminds us again of these things, first of all by putting before us two special warnings. The first is this one about the false prophets. 'Beware of false prophets, which come to you in sheep's clothing, but inwardly they are ravening wolves.' The picture which we should hold in our minds is something like this. Here we are, as it were, standing outside this strait gate. We have heard the Sermon, we have listened to the exhortation, and we are considering what to do about it. 'Now,' says our Lord in effect, 'at that point one of the things you have to beware of most especially is the danger of listening to false prophets. They are always there, they are always present, just outside that strait gate. That is their favourite stand. If you start listening to them you are entirely undone, because they will persuade you not to enter in at the strait gate and not to walk in the narrow way. They will try to dissuade you from listening to what I am saying.' So there is always the danger of the false prophet who comes with his particular subtle temptation.

The question that immediately arises for us is, What are these false prophets? Who are they, and how are they to be recognized? This is not as simple a question as it would appear to be. Its interpretation is one that is full of interest, indeed fascination. There have been two main schools of thought with regard to this statement about the false prophets, and some of the great names in the history of the Church are to be found on each side. The first is the school which says that this is a reference only to the teaching of the false prophets. 'Ye shall know them by their fruits', says our Lord, and the fruit, we are told, refers to teaching and doctrine, and to that alone. There are those who would confine the interpretation of the meaning of false prophets solely to that. Protestant expositors belonging to this group have generally thought of the Church of Rome as the supreme illustration of this.

The other group, however, disagrees entirely. It says that this reference to the false prophets really has nothing at all to do with teaching, that it is purely a question of the kind of life that these people live. A well-known expositor like Dr. Alexander Mac-Laren, for instance, says this: 'It is not a test to detect heretics, but rather to unmask hypocrites, and especially unconscious hypocrites.' His argument is, and there are many who follow him, that it has nothing to do with the teaching. The whole difficulty concerning these people is that their teaching is right, but their lives are wrong, and that they are not conscious that they are hypocrites.

There are, then, these two schools of thought, and obviously we have to face their different ways of explaining and expounding this statement. In the last analysis it does not matter very much which of the two we believe. Indeed, I suggest that they are both right and both wrong, and that the error is to say that the true exposition is either the one or the other. This is not to be guilty of compromise; but simply a way of saying that one cannot satis-factorily explain and expound this statement except by including the two elements. You cannot say that it is only a matter of teaching, and that it is a reference to heretical teaching only, for the reason that it is not really very difficult to detect such teaching. Most people who have any modicum of discrimination can detect a heretic. If a man came into a pulpit and seemed to be doubtful about the being of God, and denied the deity of Christ and the miracles, you would say that he was a heretic. There is not much difficulty about that, or anything very subtle about it. And yet, you notice, our Lord's picture suggests that there is a difficulty, and that there is something subtle about this.

You notice the very terms in which He puts it, this picture of the sheep's clothing. He suggests that the real difficulty about this kind of false prophet is that at first you never imagine that he is such. The whole thing is extremely subtle, so much so that God's people can be misled by it. You notice how Peter puts it in the second chapter of his second Epistle. These people, he says, 'creep in unawares'. They look like the right people; they have sheep's clothing on, and no-one suspects anything false. Now the Bible, in the Old Testament and in the New, always brings out that characteristic of the false prophet. It is his subtlety that really constitutes the danger. Any true exposition of this teaching, therefore, must give due weight to that particular element. For this reason, then, we cannot accept it as being merely a warning about heretics and their teaching. But the same thing applies to the other side. It is obviously not something outrageous in conduct. There again everybody could recognize it, and it would not be subtle, or constitute a difficulty.

The picture we need to have in our minds, therefore, should rather be this. The false prophet is a man who comes to us, and who at first has the appearance of being everything that could be desired. He is nice and pleasing and pleasant; he appears to be thoroughly Christian, and seems to say the right things. His teaching in general is quite all right and he uses many terms that should be used and employed by a true Christian teacher. He talks about God, he talks about Jesus Christ, he talks about the cross, he emphasizes the love of God, he seems to be saying everything that a Christian should say. He is obviously in sheep's clothing, and his way of living seems to correspond. So you do not suspect that there is anything wrong at all; there is nothing that at once attracts your attention or arouses your suspicion, nothing glaringly wrong. What then can be wrong, or may be wrong, with such a person? My suggestion is that finally this person may be wrong both in his teaching and in his type of life for, as we shall see, these two things are always indissolubly linked together. Our Lord puts it by saying, 'Ye shall know them by their fruits.' The teaching and the life can never be separated, and where there is wrong teaching in any shape or form it always leads to a wrong type of life in some respect.

How then can we describe these people? What is wrong with their teaching? The most convenient way of answering this is to say that there is no 'strait gate' in it, there is no 'narrow way' in it. As far as it goes it is all right, but it does not include this. It is a teaching, the falseness of which is to be detected by what it does *not* say rather than by what it *does* say. And it is just at this point that we realize the subtlety of the situation. As we have already seen, any Christian can detect the man who says outrageously wrong things; but is it unfair or uncharitable to say that the vast majority of Christians today do not seem to be able to detect the man who seems to say the right things but leaves out vital things? We have somehow got hold of the idea that error is only that which is outrageously wrong; and we do not seem to understand that the most dangerous person of all is the one who does not emphasize the right things.

That is the only way to understand rightly this picture of the false prophets. The false prophet is a man who has no 'strait gate' or 'narrow way' in his gospel. He has nothing which is offensive to the natural man; he pleases all. He is in 'sheep's clothing', so attractive, so pleasant, so nice to look at. He has such a nice and comfortable and comforting message. He pleases everybody and everybody speaks well of him. He is never persecuted for his preaching, he is never criticized severely. He is praised by the Liberals and Modernists, he is praised by the Evangelicals, he is praised by everybody. He is all things to all men in that sense; there is no 'strait gate' about him, there is no 'narrow way' in his message, there is none of 'the offence of the cross'.

If that is the description of the false prophet in general, let us put this question: What do we mean exactly by this 'strait gate' and 'narrow way'? What do we mean by saying that there is nothing offensive in his preaching? We can best answer this in terms of an Old Testament quotation. You remember how Peter argues in the second chapter of his second Epistle. He says, 'There were false prophets also among the people (the children of Israel in the Old Testament), even as there shall be false teachers among you.' So we must go back to the Old Testament and read what it says about the false prophets, because the type does not change. They were always there, and every time a true prophet like Jeremiah or someone else came along, the false prophets were always there to question him, and to resist him, and to denounce and ridicule him. But what were they like? This is how they are described: 'They have healed the hurt of the daughter of my people slightly (or lightly), saying, Peace, peace; when there is no peace.' The false prophet is always a very comforting preacher. As you listen to him he always gives you the impression that there is not very much wrong. He admits, of course, that there is a little; he is not fool enough to say that there is nothing wrong. But he says that all is well and will be well. 'Peace, peace,' he says. 'Don't listen to a man like Jeremiah,' he cries; 'he is narrow-minded, he is a heresy hunter, he is non-co-operative. Don't listen to him, it is all right.' 'Peace, peace.' Healing 'the hurt of the daughter of my people slightly, saying, Peace, peace; when there is no peace.' And, as the Old Testament adds devastatingly and with such terrifying truth about religious people then and now, 'my people like to have it so'. Because it never disturbs and never makes you feel uncomfortable. You carry on as you are, you are all right, you do not have to worry about the strait gate and the narrow way, or this particular doctrine or that. 'Peace, peace.' Very comforting, very reassuring always is the false prophet in his sheep's clothing; always harmless and nice, always, invariably, attractive.

In what way does this show itself in practice? I suggest that it does so generally by an almost entire absence of doctrine as a whole in its message. It always talks vaguely and generally; it never gets down to particularizing about doctrine. It does not like doctrinal preaching; it is always so vague. But someone may ask: 'What do you mean by this particularizing about doctrine, and where do the strait gate and the narrow way come in?' The answer is that the false prophet very rarely tells you anything about the holiness, the righteousness, the justice, and the wrath of God. He always preaches about the love of God, but those other things he does not mention. He never makes anyone tremble as he thinks of this holy and august Being with whom we all have to do. He does not say that he does not believe these truths. No; that is not the difficulty. The difficulty with him is that he says nothing about them. He just does not mention them at all. He generally emphasizes one truth about God only, and that is love. He does not mention the other truths that are equally prominent in the Scriptures; and that is where the danger lies. He does not say things that are obviously wrong, but he refrains from saying things that are obviously right and true. And that is why he is a false prophet. To conceal the truth is as reprehensible and as damnable as to proclaim an utter heresy; and that is why the effect of such teaching is that of a 'ravening wolf'. It is so pleasing, but it can lead men to destruction because it has never confronted them with the holiness and the righteousness and the justice and the wrath of God.

Another doctrine which the false prophet never emphasizes is that of the final judgment and the eternal destiny of the lost. There has not been much preaching about the Last Judgment in the last fifty or sixty years, and very little preaching about hell and the 'everlasting destruction' of the wicked. No, the false prophets do not like teaching such as you have in the second Epistle of Peter. They have tried to deny its authenticity because it does not fit in with their doctrine. They say that such a chapter should not be in the Bible. It is so strong, it is so blasting; and yet there it is. And it is not an isolated case. There are others. Read the Epistle of Jude, read the so-called gentle apostle of love, the apostle John, in his first Epistle, and you will find the same thing. But it is here also in this Sermon on the Mount. It comes out of the mouth of our Lord Himself. It is He who talks about the false prophets in sheep's clothing that are ravening wolves; it is He who describes them as rotten, evil trees. He deals with the judgment in exactly the same way as did Paul when he preached to Felix and Drusilla of 'righteousness, temperance, and judgment to come'.

In the same way the false prophet's teaching does not emphasize the utter sinfulness of sin and the total inability of man to do anything about his own salvation. It often does not really believe in sin at all, and certainly does not emphasize its vile nature. It does not say that we are all perfect; but it does suggest that sin is not serious. Indeed, it does not like to talk about sin; it talks only about individual or particular sins. It does not talk about the fallen nature, or say that man himself in his totality is fallen, lost and depraved. It does not like to talk about the solidarity of the whole of mankind in sin, and the fact that we have 'all sinned and come short of the glory of God'. It does not emphasize this doctrine of the 'exceeding sinfulness of sin' as you find it in the New Testament. And it does not emphasize the fact that man is 'dead in trespasses and sins', and utterly helpless and hopeless. It does not like that; it does not see the necessity of doing that. What I am emphasizing is that the false prophet does not say these things, so that an innocent believer listening to him assumes that he believes them. The question that arises concerning such teachers is, do they believe these things? The answer, obviously, is that they do not, otherwise they would feel compelled to preach and to teach them.

Then there is the expiatory aspect of the atonement, and the

substitutionary death of the Lord Jesus Christ. The false prophet
talks about 'Jesus'; he even delights to talk about the cross and the
death of Jesus. But the vital question is, What is his view of that
death? What is his view of that cross? There are views being
taught which are utterly heretical and a denial of the Christian
faith. The one test is this: Does he realize that Christ died on the
cross because it was the only way to make expiation and propitiation for sin? Does he really believe that Christ was there
crucified as a substitute for him, that He was bearing 'in his own
body on the tree' his guilt and the punishment of his guilt and
sin? Does he believe that if God had not punished his sin there in
the body of Christ on the cross, I say it with reverence, then even
God could not have forgiven him? Does he believe that it was
only by setting forth His own Son as a propitiation for our sins on
the cross that God could be 'just, and the justifier of him which
believeth in Jesus' (Romans iii. 25, 26)? Merely to talk about
Christ and the cross is not enough. Is it the biblical doctrine of
the substitutionary penal atonement? That is the way to test the
false prophet. The false prophet does not say these things. He
talks around the cross. He talks about the people round the cross
and sentimentalizes about our Lord. He does not know anything
about Paul's 'offence of the cross'. His preaching of the cross is
not 'foolishness to the Greeks', it is not a 'stumbling block to the
Jew'. He has made the cross 'of none effect through his philosophy'. He has made it a rather beautiful thing, a wonderful
philosophy of love and heart-break because of a world that is not
interested. He has never seen it as a tremendous, holy transaction
between the Father and the Son in which the Father has 'made'
the Son to be 'sin for us', and has laid our iniquity upon Him.
There is none of that in his preaching and teaching, and that is
why it is false.

In the same way it does not emphasize repentance in any real
sense. It has a very wide gate leading to salvation and a very
broad way leading to heaven. You need not feel much of your
own sinfulness; you need not be aware of the blackness of your
own heart. You just 'decide for Christ' and you rush in with the
crowd, and your name is put down, and is one of the large
number of 'decisions' reported by the press. It is entirely unlike
the evangelism of the Puritans and of John Wesley, George
Whitefield and others, which led men to be terrified of the
judgment of God, and to have an agony of soul sometimes for
days and weeks and months. John Bunyan tells us in his *Grace*

Abounding that he endured an agony of repentance for eighteen months. There does not seem to be much room for that today. Repentance means that you realize that you are a guilty, vile sinner in the presence of God, that you deserve the wrath and punishment of God, that you are hell-bound. It means that you begin to realize that this thing called sin is in you, that you long to get rid of it, and that you turn your back on it in every shape and form. You renounce the world whatever the cost, the world in its mind and outlook as well as its practice, and you deny yourself, and take up the cross and go after Christ. Your nearest and dearest, and the whole world, may call you a fool, or say you have religious mania. You may have to suffer financially, but it makes no difference. That is repentance. The false prophet does not put it like that. He heals 'the hurt of the daughter of my people slightly', simply saying that it is all right, and that you have but to 'come to Christ', 'follow Jesus', or 'become a Christian'.

Finally, therefore, we can put it like this. The false prophet does not emphasize the absolute necessity of entering this strait gate and walking along this narrow way. He does not tell us that we must practise this Sermon. If we only listen to it without practising it we are damned; if we only comment on it, without carrying it out, it will rise in judgment against us and condemn us. The false teaching is not interested in true holiness, in biblical holiness. It holds on to an idea of holiness such as the Pharisees had. You remember that they picked out certain sins of which they were not guilty themselves, as they thought, and said that as long as you were not guilty of those you were all right. Alas, how many Pharisees there are today! Holiness has just become a question of not doing three or four things. We no longer think of it in terms of 'love not the world, neither the things that are in the world . . . the lust of the flesh, and the lust of the eyes, and the pride of life' (1 John ii. 15, 16). 'The pride of life' is one of the greatest curses in the Christian Church. The false teaching desires a holiness like that of the Pharisees. It is just a question of not doing certain things that we ourselves have agreed upon because they do not happen to appeal to us in particular. Thus we have reduced holiness into something that is easy, and we crowd into that broad way and try to practise it.

Those are some of the characteristics of these false prophets that come to us in sheep's clothing. They offer an easy salvation, and an easy type of life always. They discourage self-examination; indeed, they almost feel that to examine oneself is heresy. They tell you not to examine your own soul. You must always 'look to Jesus', and never at yourself, that you may discover your sin. They discourage what the Bible encourages us to do, to 'examine' ourselves, to 'prove our own selves', and to face this last section of the Sermon on the Mount. They dislike the process of self-examination and mortification of sin as taught by the Puritans, and those great leaders of the eighteenth century—not only Whitefield and Wesley and Jonathan Edwards, but also the saintly John Fletcher, who put twelve questions to himself every night as he retired to bed. It does not believe in that, for that is uncomfortable. It is an easy salvation and easy Christian living. It knows nothing about Paul's feeling, when he says 'we that are in this tabernacle do groan, being burdened'. It does not know anything about fighting 'the good fight of faith'. It does not know what Paul means when he says that 'we wrestle not against flesh and blood, but against principalities, against powers, against the rulers of the darkness of this world, against spiritual wickedness in high places' (Ephesians vi. 12). It does not understand that. It does not see any need for the whole armour of God, because it has not seen the problem. It is all so easy.

We do not like this kind of teaching against false prophets today. We are living in days when people say that, as long as a man claims to be a Christian at all, we should regard him as a brother and go on together. But the reply is that our Lord said, 'Beware of false prophets.' These awful, glaring warnings are there in the New Testament because of the very kind of thing to which I have been referring. Of course, we must not be censorious; but neither must we mistake friendliness and affability for saintliness. It is not a question of personalities. We must not despise these people. Indeed, Dr. Alexander MacLaren is right when he says that they are unconscious hypocrites. It is not that they are not nice and pleasing; they are. In a sense that is their greatest danger, and that is what makes them such a source of danger. I am emphasizing this matter because, according to our Lord, we should always be facing it. There is a way that leads to 'destruction', and the false prophet does not believe in 'destruction'.

Is it not true to say that the explanation of the present state of the Christian Church is this very thing we have been considering? Why has the Church become so weak and ineffective? I have no hesitation in answering and saying that it is due to the type of preaching that came in as the result of the higher critical movement of the last century, and which utterly condemned doctrinal preaching. Its advocates preached morality and general uplift. They took their illustrations from literature and poetry, and Emerson became one of the High Priests. That is the cause of the trouble. They still talked about God; they still talked about Jesus; they still talked about His death on the cross. They did not stand out as obvious heretics; but they did not say those other things that are vital to salvation. They gave this vague message that never upsets anybody. They were so pleasant and 'modern' and up to date. They suited the popular palate, and the result is not only the empty churches about which we are hearing so much at the present time, but, as we shall see, the poor quality of Christian living of which most of us are so guilty. These things are distasteful and unpleasant, and whether you believe me or not, in honesty I have to confess that if I had not pledged myself to preach like this through the Sermon on the Mount, I would never have chosen these words as a text. I have never preached on it before. I have never heard a sermon on it. I wonder how many of you have done so? It is not liked; it is unpleasant; but our business is not to choose what we like. It is the Son of God who said this, and He puts it into the context of judgment and of destruction. So, at the risk of causing myself to be known as a heresy hunter, or as a peculiar person who is sitting in judgment on his brethren and everybody else, I have tried honestly to explain the Scripture. And I ask you to consider it again prayerfully in the presence of God as you value your own immortal soul and its eternal destiny.

CHAPTER TWENTY-THREE

THE TREE AND THE FRUIT

OUR previous examination of this difficult paragraph vii. 15–20 emphasized particularly the element of subtlety in the false prophets, those men who come to us in sheep's clothing, but who inwardly are ravening wolves. To many people this is a difficult section because of its context, because it comes after those words: 'Judge not, that ye be not judged. For with what judgment ye judge, ye shall be judged.' Yet these words were uttered by our Lord Himself. The false prophets are always unhappy about certain statements of our Lord. They are never happy about Matthew xxiii, for example, where our Lord described the Pharisees as 'whited sepulchres'. Our modern false prophets try to find nice things to say even about the Pharisees. The sheep's clothing prophet teaches that we must never say anything which is at all critical or severe. But the words are uttered by our Lord Himself, therefore we must face them. Again, let us repeat, we must avoid censoriousness; but we cannot expound the Sermon on the Mount fully unless we face them, and try to deal with them quite honestly, realizing as we do so that we are setting up a standard by which we ourselves shall be judged.

Our Lord, clearly, was concerned to emphasize this matter. He has said that the false prophets are to be known by their fruits, and then He goes on to elaborate this by drawing this further picture. He says, 'Do men gather grapes of thorns, or figs of thistles? Even so every good tree bringeth forth good fruit; but a corrupt tree bringeth forth evil fruit. A good tree cannot bring forth evil fruit, neither can a corrupt tree bring forth good fruit. Every tree that bringeth not forth good fruit is hewn down, and cast into the fire. Wherefore by their fruits ye shall know them.' You notice He starts and ends with 'Ye shall know them by their fruits', and 'Wherefore by their fruits ye shall know them'— repetition for the sake of emphasis.

First we must be quite clear on one purely technical point, and that is the meaning of this word 'corrupt'. 'Every good tree bringeth forth good fruit; but a corrupt tree bringeth forth evil fruit.' 'Corrupt', of course, does not mean rotten, because a decayed or rotten tree does not bring forth fruit at all. That is very important, because if we fail to notice it we shall again be missing this element of subtlety which is the main thing in our Lord's emphasis. He is calling attention to the fact that trees which resemble each other in that they look perfectly all right, do not of necessity produce the same kind of fruit. One tree may produce good fruit, the other tree may produce poor fruit. What is called 'evil fruit' does not mean entirely 'rotten' either; it means it is poor in quality, it is not good fruit. So the contrast which our Lord brings out is between two types of tree which to look at may be almost identical, but which, when you come to judge the fruit, you find to be entirely different. One you can use, and the other you cannot. Clearly there is very profound teaching here. Having considered the question of the doctrine we can now come to the matter of the life, the conduct and the behaviour.

Before, however, we come to the details we must emphasize the great principle which our Lord is here inculcating. It is that to be a Christian is something central to personality, something vital and fundamental. It is not a matter of appearance on the surface either with regard to belief or life. In using this picture of the character, the nature, the real essence of these trees and the fruit which they produce, our Lord is placing very great emphasis upon that. And surely this is the point which we must always be looking for in ourselves and in others. He seems to be drawing attention to the danger of being misled by appearances. It is precisely the same as in that other figure of the false prophets which come to us in sheep's clothing. In other words, it is the danger of appearing to be Christian without really being so. We have already seen that that can happen in the matter of teaching and doctrine. A man may appear to be preaching the gospel when, in reality, and as judged by the true tests, he is not doing so at all. It is exactly the same with regard to conduct and life. The danger here is to try to make ourselves Christian by adding certain things to our lives, instead of *becoming* something new, instead of receiving life within, instead of the very nature which is within us being renewed after the image of the Lord Jesus Christ Himself.

The whole emphasis in our Lord's teaching here is upon the man himself, and He is really saying that what matters in the last analysis is just that. A man may speak in the right way, he may apparently live in the right way, and yet, according to our Lord, he may be a false prophet the whole time. He may be assuming the appearance of the Christian life without really being Chris-

tian. This has been a constant source of trouble and of danger in
the long history of the Christian Church. But our Lord has
warned us right at the beginning that we must grasp this principle, that to be a Christian means a change in a man's very life
and nature. It is the doctrine of the rebirth. No man's service is of
any value unless his nature is changed. We shall presently be
dealing with that statement: 'Many will say to me in that day,
Lord, Lord, have we not prophesied in thy name? and in thy
name have cast out devils? and in thy name done many wonderful works?' There we are looking at a man who has been doing
many things in his life; but he himself is not changed. He was
saying and doing the right things, but they are of no value.

Exactly the same thing can happen with life and conduct.
Christianity is unique in this respect, that it is concerned
primarily about the state of the heart. And in Scripture the
heart is generally not the seat of the emotions, but the centre of
the personality. Take, for instance, Matthew xii. 33-37. There,
surely, our Lord puts it quite clearly and specifically: 'Either
make the tree good, and his fruit good; or else make the tree
corrupt, and his fruit corrupt: for the tree is known by his fruit.'
The emphasis is again upon the character or the nature of the
tree. 'It is that', He says in another place, 'which cometh out of
the heart that defiles a man'. It is not merely the things you do on
the surface; it is not a question of washing the outside of the cups
and the platters; it is not that which goes in, it is that which
comes out; it is the man himself that really counts. Our Lord is at
great pains to emphasize in this picture that what is in the centre
of the heart is certain to proclaim itself. It will proclaim itself in
its beliefs, in its teaching and doctrine. It will proclaim itself also
in its life. It is not always easy to see that, but our Lord tells us
that if we have eyes illuminated by the teaching of the New
Testament, we shall always be able to recognize it. We saw about
doctrine, for instance, that if you only watch to see whether a
man is going to say things that are outrageously wrong you will
probably never detect the false prophets because they do not say
such things. But if you realize that there are certain things a true
Christian must always emphasize, and if you watch for them,
then you will discover that they are omitted, and you will see that
the man you thought was a Christian is really a false prophet, and
therefore a grievous danger. It is exactly the same with regard to
the life. We can show this in a number of principles.

The first principle is that there is an indissoluble link between belief and life—the nature will out. That which a man is ultimately in the depths is always going to reveal and manifest itself, and it does so in belief and life. The two things are indissolubly linked together. As a man thinks, so eventually he is. As a man thinks, so he does. In other words, we inevitably proclaim what we are and what we believe. It does not matter how careful we are, it is bound to come out. Nature must express itself. You do not get 'grapes of thorns' or 'figs of thistles'; 'a good tree cannot bring forth evil fruit, neither can a corrupt tree bring forth good fruit.' You are not in the realm of appearances; you are now examining in a more critical manner. Our Lord lays these things down as absolutes; and if we observe ourselves and others, and the whole of life carefully, we must agree that this is perfectly true.

We may be deceived for a while. Appearances can be very deceptive, as we all know; but they do not last. The Puritans were very fond of dealing at great length with what they called 'temporary believers'. They meant by that, people who seemed to come under the influence of the gospel, and who gave the appearance of being truly and soundly converted and regenerate. Such people said the right things and there was a change in their lives; they appeared to be Christian. But the Puritans called them 'temporary believers' because those people gave clear, unmistakable evidence afterwards that they had never truly become Christian at all. That kind of thing often happens during revivals. Whenever there is a religious awakening, or any religious excitement, you generally find people who are, as it were, carried along by the flood. They do not know quite what is happening, but they come under the general influence of the Holy Spirit and are clearly affected for the time being. But, according to this teaching, they may never become truly Christian.

There is a discussion of this in 2 Peter ii where the apostle describes such cases clearly and graphically. He talks about certain people who had come into the Church and had been accepted as Christians, but who had gone out. He describes them in these terms. 'The dog is turned to his own vomit again, and the sow that was washed to her wallowing in the mire.' You see what has happened. To use his illustration, even the sow can be washed, and can appear to be clean on the surface; but there is no change in nature. This becomes yet clearer when we compare it with what the apostle Peter says in verse 4 of chapter i of that same Epistle. He says that the Christian has been 'delivered from the corruption that is in the world through lust'. But when he comes to these temporary believers in the second chapter he says that they have been washed from—not 'the corruption', but 'the pollution'. There is a kind of superficial cleansing which does not change the nature. Washing is of real value, but it can be very misleading. A man who has washed on the surface only may give all the appearance of being a Christian. But our Lord's argument is that what really decides whether he is one or not is the nature within. And that nature within is bound to express itself.

You may have to wait before you can see any true evidence. God sees it from the beginning, but we are very slow to see these things. But what a man is, he is bound to show. He will show it in his teaching for certain, he will show it in his life also. It is quite inevitable. We can say, therefore, that true Christian belief must of necessity produce that characteristic type of living. That is, surely, the meaning of this question: 'Do men gather grapes of thorns, or figs of thistles?' These things can never be separated; the inner nature is bound to express itself. A man's final belief is bound to manifest itself, sooner or later, in his life. We must be careful, therefore, that we do not mistake for the real thing that which looks like true Christianity, but which is in reality merely sham and only outward appearance. The exhortation is that we should teach and discipline ourselves always to look carefully for the fruit.

We must now consider in detail the nature or the character of the good fruit. We must look for it in ourselves and in others. We must be very careful because there are people standing outside the narrow and strait gate, who say to us, 'You need not do all that. This is the way'. And we can be misled by them. Therefore we must learn to discriminate; and once more, as we come to examine the fruit, we must bear this element of subtlety in mind. There are types of life which can closely simulate true Christianity, and they are obviously the most dangerous of all. It seems more and more clear that the greatest enemies of the true Christian faith are not those who are right out in the world militantly persecuting Christianity, or flagrantly ignoring its teaching; but rather those who have a false and spurious Christianity. They are the people who will receive the condemnation which our Lord pronounces here on the false prophet. If you look at the history of the Church throughout the centuries you will find that this has always proved to be the case. It is a false and counterfeit Christianity that has always been a hindrance to, and the greatest enemy of, true spirituality. And surely the greatest trouble at this present moment is the worldly state of the Church. We should be much more concerned about the state of the Church herself than about the state of the world outside the Church. It seems increasingly evident that the explanation of the present state of Christendom is to be found inside the Church and not outside. We must bear in mind the question of the subtlety of this whole matter, and therefore we must apply certain delicate tests.

The tests can be both general and particular. Here we are, as it were, looking at someone who makes a profession of Christianity. He does not say anything obviously wrong, and appears to be living a good Christian life. How do we test such a person? You can have good, ethical, moral people with a high code and standard of personal life and living, who look remarkably like Christians but who may not be Christian at all. How do you tell the difference? Here are some of the questions for which you must seek an answer. First of all, why is the man living this sort of life? Take the case of a modern good man who makes no pretence of Christianity, or that of a man who attends a place of worship regularly but who, as judged by New Testament standards, is not a Christian. Why do they live as they do? There are many reasons for this. It may be purely a matter of temperament. There are certain people who have been born nice. They have an equable temperament and character; they are quiet, there is nothing naturally vicious or offensive about them. They have to make no effort to be like this; they were born like that, it is the kind of person they are. It is something purely physical and natural.

Secondly, does this man live this kind of life because he holds certain beliefs or subscribes to certain moral teaching? There are men, in other words, who are what may be called good pagans. They are admirably delineated and analysed in a book called *The Failure of the Good Pagan*, by Rosalind Murray. Such men have very high standards, and they live up to them in their daily practice. A man may do all that quite apart from Christianity. So if you are going to judge merely by the general appearances of a man's life and living then obviously you may well be deceived. It is often said that there are better Christians outside the Christian Church than inside. What that means is that you may find good morality outside the Church. But good morality may have nothing to do with Christianity. It has no essential connection with it. Greek pagan philosophers propounded their great moral teaching before Christ came. Still more significantly, Greek philosophers were sometimes the most bitter opponents of the Christian gospel; they were the very men who regarded the preaching of the cross as 'foolishness'.

So you do not merely look at the man and his life in general. You must try to discover reasons and motives for his actions. From the Christian standpoint there is only one vital test at this point. Does this man give the impression that he is living this sort of life because he is a Christian and because of his Christian faith? If he does not live this life because he is a Christian there is no value in it; it is what our Lord calls corrupt fruit. The Old Testament puts it very strongly when it says: 'All our righteousnesses are as filthy rags'. It was righteousness in the world's eyes, but it was as filthy rags in the sight of God. It is only that which is the outcome of Christian character, and springs from the new nature, which is of any value ultimately in the sight of God.

There then is our general test. Let us now look at certain particular tests. Here we must be careful lest again we expose ourselves to the charge of censoriousness, and we must be fully aware that what we are saying is a judgment upon ourselves. The particular tests of this life are both negative and positive. By negative we mean that if a man is not a true Christian, and if he has not the true Christian doctrine, we shall inevitably find somewhere in his life a certain slackness, a certain failure to conform to the true Christian character. He does not do anything outrageously wrong. We cannot convict him of drunkenness or murder, etc. But unless a man believes those essential tenets of the Christian faith which we emphasized earlier we shall find a slackness somewhere in his life. If a man is not conscious of the utter, absolute holiness of God and the exceeding sinfulness of sin, if he does not see that the real message of the cross of Calvary is that all man's righteousness is worthless and that he is an utter, helpless, foul sinner, he is going to show this in his life. It is bound to show, and in fact it does, though he may conform to a general moral code. There is always somewhere in a man who rejects this high doctrine of salvation a failure to walk the narrow way, and a conformity at some point or other to the world and its outlook. His way of life may look remarkably like the Christian's, but if you watch and observe it in detail you will find that it fails. It is very difficult to put this in a clear and explicit manner. There are certain people about whom all you can say is that, while you find nothing wrong with them in particular, you nevertheless feel that they are wrong centrally. You cannot find anything specific to condemn but at the same time you feel that their outlook is secular and not spiritual, that though they never do anything that is outrageously worldly, their whole attitude is worldly. There is in them a lack of tone and an absence of that peculiar 'aura' which is always present in the man who is truly spiritual.

But, to put it positively, what we look for in anybody who claims to be Christian is evidence of the Beatitudes. The test of fruit is never negative, it is positive. Certain apples may look all right, but you begin to eat them and you will find that they are sour. Now that is the positive kind of test. A true Christian must exemplify the Beatitudes, because you do not get grapes from thorns or figs from thistles. A good tree must bring forth good fruit; it cannot help itself, it is bound to. A man who has the divine nature within himself must produce this good fruit, the good fruit which is described in the Beatitudes. He is poor in spirit, he mourns because of sin, he is meek, he hungers and thirsts after righteousness, he is a peacemaker, he is pure in heart, and so on.

These are some of the tests, and they are tests which always exclude the 'good pagan'. They also always exclude false prophets and temporary believers, because these are the tests of a man's ultimate nature and his real being. Or it can be put in terms of the fruit of the Spirit described in Galatians v. The fruit that is formed in us and manifests itself is love, joy, peace, long-suffering, gentleness, goodness, meekness, temperance, faith— that is the fruit, and that is what we must look for in a man's life. It is not found in the man who is just morally good: this is the fruit that only a good tree produces. A Christian can generally be known by his very appearance. The man who really believes in the holiness of God, and who knows his own sinfulness and the blackness of his own heart, the man who believes in the judgment of God and the possibility of hell and torment, the man who really believes that he himself is so vile and helpless that nothing but the coming of the Son of God from heaven to earth, and His going to the bitter shame and agony and cruelty of the cross could ever save him, and reconcile him to God—this man is going to show all that in his whole personality. He is a man who is bound to give the impression of meekness, he is bound to be humble. Our Lord reminds us here that if a man is not humble, we are to be very wary of him. He can put on a kind of sheep's clothing, but that is not true humility, that is not true meekness. And if a man's doctrine is wrong, it will generally show itself at this point. He will be affable and pleasant, he will appeal to the natural man, and to the things that are physical and carnal; but he will not give the impression of being a man who has seen himself as a hell-bound sinner, and who has been saved by the grace of God alone. Truth within must of necessity affect a man's appearance. The New Testament man is a sober man, he is grave and humble, he is a meek man. He has the joy of the Lord in his heart, yes, but he is not effusive, he is not boisterous, he is not carnal in his life. He is a man who says with Paul, 'We that are in this tabernacle do groan, being burdened' (2 Corinthians v. 4). To say and to believe that is bound to affect the whole man, even his very dress as well as his demeanour. He is not interested in pomp and show and externalities, he is not interested in making an impression; he is meek and concerned about God and his relationship to Him, and the truth of God.

The ultimate test of all, however, is humility. If we have the pride of life and of the world in us, of necessity we do not know much about the truth; and we should examine ourselves again to make sure that we have the new nature within us. What is within is going to show itself. If I am a worldly-minded person, though I may preach a great doctrine, though I may have given up certain things, it will come out in my 'idle speech'. Our Lord says that we shall be judged by our 'idle words' (see Matthew xii. 36). It is when we are off guard that we really show what we are. We can make ourselves appear to be Christian; but it is what comes out suddenly that reveals our real nature. So everything about this man is going to proclaim what he is. The way in which a man preaches is often much more significant than what he says, because the way in which he speaks displays what the man really is. A man's methods sometimes deny the message that he is preaching. A man who preaches judgment and salvation and yet laughs and jokes is denying his own doctrine. Self-confidence, self-assertion, reliance upon human ability and 'personality', proclaim that the man has a nature within him which is far removed from that of the Son of God who was 'meek and lowly in heart'. Such a man is unlike the apostle Paul, who when he was preaching in Corinth did not come to them with self-confidence and self-assertion, but 'in weakness, and in fear, and in much trembling'. How we give ourselves away, how we proclaim by our unguarded actions what we really are!

Finally we must remember that whatever we may think of these things, and however wrongly we may judge, and however much we may be deceived by false prophets, God is the Judge, and God is never deceived. 'Every tree therefore which bringeth not forth good fruit is hewn down, and cast into the fire.' God have mercy upon us. May He awaken us to these vital principles, and enable us to exercise this discrimination with regard to ourselves, and with regard to all others who may be a danger to our souls, and who are grievously misrepresenting the cause of our blessed Lord in this sinful and needy world. Let us concentrate upon being certain that we have the divine nature, that we are partakers of it, that the tree is good; because if the tree is good, the fruit also must of necessity be good.

CHAPTER TWENTY-FOUR

FALSE PEACE

WE consider now the section vii. 21–23. These, surely, are in many ways the most solemn and solemnizing words ever uttered in this world, not only by any man, but even by the Son of God Himself. Indeed, were any man to utter such words we should feel compelled not only to criticize but even to condemn him. But they are words spoken by the Son of God Himself, and therefore demand our most earnest attention. How often, I wonder, have we considered them, or heard a sermon on them? Must we not all plead guilty to the fact that, though we claim to believe the whole of Scripture, in practice we frequently deny much of it by ignoring it, simply because it does not pander to the flesh, or because it disturbs us. But if we really believe that this is the Word of God, we must consider it all; and especially must we be careful to avoid those specious arguments by which certain people endeavour to avoid the plain teaching of Scripture. These words are extremely solemn, and the only way in which we can consider them truly is to do so in the light of the fact that a day is coming 'when all earthly scenes shall pass away'. It is a word addressed to men and women who are conscious of the fact that they will have to stand before God in final judgment.

It is clear that in this paragraph our Lord is continuing the theme with which He dealt in the previous paragraph, where He warned the people against false prophets. To our Lord this is such a desperately serious matter that He comes back to it again. He is not content with one warning. He has really finished the teaching of the Sermon, and has worked it out in great detail. Now He is applying it. He began the application in the exhortation about entering in at the strait gate, and walking in the narrow way. But He is so concerned that none should be misled about this matter that He repeats the warning time and again.

Having shown us the subtlety of the false prophets in His two remarkable analogies, our Lord now makes His warning concerning that matter still more explicit. This time it is even more blunt than the previous one, and our Lord undoubtedly puts it like this because of the desperate seriousness of the matter and the terrible danger that confronts us at this point. His method, you observe, is the same as it has been right through the Sermon on the Mount. He starts always by making a blunt assertion, then He takes it up and illustrates, elaborates and amplifies it. That is exactly what we have in this particular paragraph. First of all He says, 'Not every one that saith unto me, Lord, Lord, shall enter into the kingdom of heaven; but he that doeth the will of my Father which is in heaven.' That is the proposition. But then He goes on to illustrate and elaborate it. 'Many will say to me in that day, Lord, Lord,' etc.

The most important thing from the standpoint of exposition is that we should take these two parts together, that we should not isolate verse 21 from verses 22 and 23, as some have been tempted to do, but that we take all these verses together and regard them as the laying down of the proposition, and the demonstration of its implication. The importance of doing so is seen when we are reminded that certain people, taking verse 21 on its own, have argued that what our Lord is really teaching there is that, in the last analysis, what matters is not so much what a man believes as what he does. It is a quotation often used by people who like to put up faith and works as opposites. They ask: 'Did not He say, "Not every one that saith unto me, Lord, Lord, shall enter into the kingdom of heaven; but he that doeth the will of my Father which is in heaven"?' The emphasis, they maintain, is upon the doing. And then they propound their whole doctrine of salvation by works. 'Some people', they say, 'are always concerned about doctrine, and everlastingly talking about it; but it is not a man's doctrine, but what he does, that really matters'. They misuse verse 21 in that way because they isolate it from verses 22 and 23. But the moment you put them together you see that the object of the statement cannot be to contrast belief and works, because our Lord says about the works in verses 22 and 23 precisely what He says about the belief in verses 21 and 22. It is important, therefore, to take the text in its context and not to isolate it.

No, the message here is not to emphasize works at the expense of belief; it is something much more serious than that. It is, rather, to open our eyes again to the terrible danger of self-deception and self-delusion. That is what our Lord is concerned about here. It was the same general theme in the previous paragraph. There the danger was considered in terms of our being misled by the false prophets because of their sheep's clothing, and the attractive character of their doctrine which is so deceiving,

and so subtle. Here, our Lord proceeds to show us the same
thing, not now in the false prophets, but in ourselves. It is the
danger, the terrible danger of self-deception and self-delusion.
Or, to put it positively, our Lord is emphasizing once more that
nothing avails in the presence of God but true righteousness, true
holiness, the 'holiness, without which no man shall see the Lord'
(Hebrews xii. 14). And if our idea of justification by faith does not
include that, it is not the scriptural teaching, it is a dangerous
delusion. Scripture, it must be repeated again, must be taken as a
whole, and our Lord at this point is simply warning us that whatever we may say or do, we cannot stand in the presence of God if
we are not truly righteous and holy. It is what Scripture teaches
from beginning to end. It is the teaching of the Lord Himself; it
is not human legalism. He is showing once more what true faith
really means, and He does so in a new way.

We can put it like this. Our Lord shows us some of the false and
wrong things on which men tend to rely. He gives us a list of
them. First we shall work through this list; then later we can
consider the general lessons and principles which can be deduced
from this detailed teaching. But we are bound to face squarely
the things which our Lord puts before us for our consideration.
The general principle behind the teaching is that self-deception
with regard to the soul and its relationship to God is generally
due to our relying upon false evidences of salvation. Or, to put it
in another way, our Lord shows us what is actually possible in the
experience of a man who is finally reprobate and damned. That
is the alarming thing. He shows us that a man can get so far and
yet be altogether wrong. It is certainly one of the most astounding
statements that is to be found anywhere in the Scriptures.

The first piece of false evidence on which some people tend to
rest is rather surprising. It is none else than a correct belief. 'Not
every one that saith unto me, Lord, Lord, shall enter into the
kingdom of heaven; but he that doeth the will of my Father
which is in heaven.' There are certain people, says our Lord in
effect, who say to Me, 'Lord, Lord', and yet they shall never enter
the kingdom of heaven. We must handle this very carefully. He
is not criticizing people for saying: 'Lord, Lord'. Everybody
should say: 'Lord, Lord'. He is referring to people who are right
in their doctrine concerning His nature and about His Person,
to people who have recognized Him, and who come to Him, and
say 'Lord, Lord'. They say the right things to Him, they believe
the right things about Him. Our Lord is not criticizing them for

that. What He is saying is that not everyone who does say that shall enter the kingdom of heaven.

The negative is very important at this point. A man who does not say 'Lord, Lord' shall never enter the kingdom of heaven. That is, of course, the starting-point in this whole question of salvation. No man is a Christian unless he says 'Lord, Lord' to the Lord Jesus Christ. Paul says that no man can say that apart from the Holy Spirit (1 Corinthians xii. 3). Orthodoxy, in other words, is absolutely essential. So what we have here is not a criticism of orthodoxy; it cannot possibly be. But it is a statement of the fact that, if you rely only upon your orthodoxy, you may be damned. Orthodoxy is absolutely vital and essential. Unless we believe that Jesus of Nazareth is indeed the Son of God, unless we recognize Him as the eternal Son, 'substance of the eternal substance', made flesh and dwelling amongst us, unless we believe the New Testament doctrine that He was sent by God to be the Messiah, the Saviour of the world, and that because of that He has been exalted and is Lord of all, to whom every knee shall eventually bow, we are not Christian at all (see Philippians ii. 5–11). We *must* believe that. To be a Christian is primarily a matter of believing certain truths concerning the Lord Jesus Christ; in other words, believing on Him. There is no such thing as Christianity apart from that. To be a Christian means that we rest our entire case, our whole salvation, our whole eternal destiny entirely upon the Lord Jesus Christ. That is why a true Christian says, 'Lord, Lord'; that is the content of the statement. It does not just mean saying the right words, it indicates that we mean those things when we say them.

But the alarming and terrifying thing which our Lord says is that not everyone who does say 'Lord, Lord', shall enter into the kingdom of heaven. Those who do go in say it; anyone who does not say it can never enter into the kingdom of heaven; but not all who do say it shall enter in. This is clearly something that should arrest us and cause us to pause. James, in his Epistle, puts the very same point. He warns us to be careful against merely relying upon our belief of certain things, and he puts it like this in a rather startling manner by saying, 'The devils also believe, and tremble' (James ii. 19). An instance of this is found in the Gospels where we read that certain devils recognized Him and said 'Lord, Lord', but remained devils. We are all in danger of being content with an intellectual assent to the truth. There have been people throughout the centuries who have fallen into this trap. They have read the Scriptures and accepted their teaching.

They believed the teaching, and sometimes they have been exponents of the truth, and have argued against heretics. And yet their whole character and life have been a denial of the very truth they have claimed to believe.

It is a terrifying thought and yet Scripture so often teaches us that it is a dreadful possibility. A man who is unregenerate and not born again may accept the scriptural teaching as a kind of philosophy, as abstract truth. Indeed, I would not hesitate to say that I always find it very difficult to understand how any intelligent man is not compelled to do that. If any man comes to the Bible with an intelligent mind and faces its evidence, it seems almost incredible that he should not arrive at certain inevitable logical conclusions. And a man may do that and still not be a Christian. The historical evidence for the Person of Jesus Christ of Nazareth is beyond question. You cannot explain the persistence of the Christian Church apart from Him; the evidence is overwhelming. So a man may face that and say: 'Yes, I accept that argument'. He may subscribe to the truth and say: 'Jesus of Nazareth was none other than the Son of God'. He may say that and still be unregenerate, and not a Christian. He may say 'Lord, Lord', and yet not enter the kingdom of heaven. Our forefathers, in days when they realized these dangers, used to emphasize this tremendously. Read the works of the Puritans and you will find that they devoted not only chapters but volumes to the question of 'false peace'. Indeed, this danger has been recognized throughout the centuries. There is the danger of trusting your faith instead of Christ, of trusting your belief without really becoming regenerate. It is a terrible possibility. There are people who have been brought up in a Christian home and atmosphere, who have always heard these things, and in a sense have always accepted them, and have always believed and said the right thing; but still they may not be Christians.

The second possibility is that these people may not only be believers of the truth, but also fervent and zealous. You notice the repetition of the word 'Lord', they do not merely say 'Lord', they say 'Lord, Lord'. These people are not intellectual believers only; there is an element of feeling; emotion is involved. They seem keen and anxious and they are full of fervour. Yet our Lord says that even that may be quite false, and that there are many who thus zealously and fervently say the right things about Him, and to Him, who still shall not enter into the kingdom of God. How is this to be explained?

It is to be explained in the following manner. One of the most difficult things, all Christians must surely admit, is to differentiate between a truly spiritual fervour and a carnal, fleshly, animal zeal and enthusiasm. Natural animal spirits and temperament may very well make a man fervent and zealous. A man may be born with an energetic nature and a fervent enthusiastic spirit—some of us have to be more careful at this point than others. There is nothing of which a preacher needs to be more sure than that the zeal and fervency in his preaching is not produced by his natural temperament or his sermon, but by real belief in Christ. It is a very subtle matter. A man prepares a message and, having prepared it, he may be pleased and satisfied with the arrangement and order of the thoughts and certain forms of expression. If he is of an energetic, fervent nature, he may well be excited and moved by that and especially when he preaches the sermon. But it may be entirely of the flesh and have nothing at all to do with spiritual matters. Every preacher knows exactly what this means, and anybody who has ever taken part in public prayer knows the same. You can be carried away by your own eloquence and by the very thing you yourself are doing and not by the truth at all. There are some people who seem to think it is their duty to be fervent and emotional. Some people never pray in public without crying, and some tend to think that they feel more than others. But it does not follow for a moment. The emotional type of person is always more liable to weep when he prays, but it does not mean of necessity that he is more spiritual.

Our Lord, then, is emphasizing that though they say 'Lord, Lord', and are fervent and zealous, it may be nothing but the flesh. Great enthusiasm in these things does not of necessity imply spirituality. The flesh may account for that; it can counterfeit almost everything. We can perhaps emphasize this point best by quoting something which was written by Robert Murray McCheyne. That man of God, when he merely entered the pulpit, caused people to break down and weep. People felt that he had come straight from an audience with God, and they were humbled by his very appearance. This is what he said in his diary one day: 'Today, missed some fine opportunity of speaking a word for Christ. The Lord saw that I would have spoken as much for my own honour as for His, and therefore He shut my mouth. I see that a man cannot be a faithful, fervent minister until he preaches just for Christ's sake, until he gives up trying to attract people to himself, and seeks to attract them to Christ. Lord', he ends, 'give me this.' Robert Murray McCheyne there recognizes this terrible danger of doing things in the flesh and imagining that we are doing them for Christ's sake.

That, then, is the first part of our Lord's analysis. Nothing is more dangerous than to rely only upon a correct belief, and a fervent spirit, and to assume that, as long as you believe the right things and are zealous and keen and active concerning them, you are therefore of necessity a Christian.

In the verses which follow He goes further and includes works also—that is what makes the supposed antithesis between faith and works so foolish and ridiculous. What then are the works, which, according to the Lord, a man may perform and still be outside the kingdom? It is really an alarming and terrifying list. The first thing He says is: 'Many will say to me in that day, Lord, Lord, have we not prophesied in thy name?' To prophesy means to deliver a spiritual message. You find much about prophecy in the New Testament. Paul discusses it at some length in 1 Corinthians, in connection with the various gifts that were exercised in the Church. Those were the days before the New Testament was written, when certain members of the Church were given messages and the ability to speak them by the Holy Spirit. That is what is meant by prophesying; and our Lord says that there will be many people who will come to Him in the day of judgment and say that they have prophesied in His name—not in their own name, but in His name—but He will say unto them: 'I never knew you: depart from me, ye that work iniquity'. We can interpret that for our own age in this way. It is possible for a man to preach correct doctrine, and in the name of Christ, and yet himself remain outside the kingdom of God. That is the statement, nothing less. If anyone other than the Lord Jesus Christ had said this we would not believe it. Moreover, we would feel that he was a censorious, narrow-minded person. But it is the Lord Himself who says it.

This is something that is taught frequently in the Scriptures. Was not that, for example, the exact position of a man such as Balaam? He delivered the right message, and yet he was a hireling prophet and a reprobate. He gave, in a sense, the right message and teaching, yet he himself was outside. Did not God use Saul in this kind of way? The spirit of prophesy came upon him from time to time, yet Saul, too, was outside. When you come to the New Testament, you find these things stated still more explicitly. Paul, knowing these terrible dangers, says: 'I keep under my body ... lest that by any means, when I have preached to others, I myself should be a castaway' (1 Corinthians ix. 27). When he talks about 'keeping under the body' he is not only thinking, as people often imagine, about certain sins of the flesh, he is referring to the whole of his life. A man has to keep under his body in a pulpit as well as on the street. To keep under the body means to keep curbing and controlling everything that the flesh is anxious to do. The flesh thrusts itself into the forefront. The apostle Paul tells us, in this very context of preaching, that he pounded and pummelled his body and bruised it, in order that, having preached to others, he might avoid becoming a castaway himself.

Or take the marvellous statement of this truth which we have in 1 Corinthians xiii. 1–3. 'Though I speak with the tongues of men and of angels, and have not charity, I am become as sounding brass, or a tinkling cymbal'. Or again: 'Though I have the gift of prophecy, and understand all mysteries, and all knowledge; ... and have not charity, it profiteth me nothing.' The apostle Paul says in effect, 'I may preach like an angel, I may produce the most wonderful eloquence and oratory; I may be considered by people to be the greatest speaker the world has ever heard, and I may speak about the things of God; and yet I may be outside the kingdom. All is useless if I lack these qualities that really make a man a Christian.' So a man can prophesy and be outside. Think also of his statement in Philippians i. 15 where he says of certain people that they 'preach Christ even of envy and strife'. Their motive is wrong, their thoughts are wrong; but they are preaching Christ, they are saying the right things about Him. Paul glories in their right preaching, but they themselves are wrong because they are doing it in a wrong spirit moved by envy and desiring to score over the apostle. We must realize, then, that it is actually possible for a man to be preaching correct doctrine and yet to be outside the kingdom. Our Lord said on one occasion to the Pharisees, 'Ye are they which justify yourselves before men; but God knoweth your hearts: for that which is highly esteemed among men is abomination in the sight of God'. It is a very terrifying thought, and I understand it to mean this, that at the day of judgment we shall all have great surprises. We shall find men who have been lauded and praised as preachers outside the kingdom. They said the right things, and said them marvellously; but they never had the life and truth within them. It was all carnal.

But not only do these people prophesy, they even cast out devils. Again you notice the repetition of 'in thy name'—'and in thy name have cast out devils'. It is possible for a person to do even that and still to be outside the kingdom! To prove this is simple. Is it not clear from the New Testament that even Judas had this power? Our Lord sent òut His disciples to preach and to cast out devils, and they came back and said to Him in great elation on one occasion, 'Even the devils are subject unto us'. It is quite clear that that applied equally to Judas. Our Lord may give power to a man, and yet the man himself may be lost. There are other powers also that can enable us to do remarkable and astounding things. You remember on one occasion when the people charged our Lord with doing miracles by the power of Beelzebub, He retorted by saying, 'If I by Beelzebub cast out devils, by whom do your sons cast them out?' They were Jewish exorcists. In Acts xix you will find certain people described as sons of Sceva who had the self-same power. We see, then, that people may even drive out devils in Christ's name and yet be outside the kingdom.

Finally our Lord comes to the climax which He puts in this form. These people will be able to say to Him that in His name they have done 'many wonderful works'—works of power, miracles, amazing things, almost incredible things. They have done many wonderful works in His name, and yet they are outside the kingdom. How do we prove that this is possible? Part of the proof undoubtedly is found in the case of the magicians of Egypt. You remember when Moses was sent to deliver the children of Israel and to work his miracles, the magicians of Egypt were able to counterfeit and repeat them up to a certain point. They did many marvellous works. But we need not rely only upon that. Our Lord says in Matthew xxiv. 24: 'For there shall arise false Christs, and false prophets, and shall shew great signs and wonders; insomuch that, if it were possible, they shall deceive the very elect.' These are the words of Christ. But take Paul's words in 2 Thessalonians ii. 8: 'And then shall that Wicked be revealed, whom the Lord shall consume with the spirit of his mouth, and shall destroy with the brightness of his coming: even him, whose coming is after the working of Satan with all power and signs and lying wonders'. These things are prophesied.

In other words, a man may be able to point to great results such as healings and so on, and yet they may signify nothing. And we should not be surprised at this. Are we not learning more and more in these days about the powers that are innate in man even in a natural sense? There is such a thing as a natural gift of healing; there is a kind of natural, almost magical power in certain people. For instance the whole question of electricity in the human frame is most interesting. We are merely beginning to understand it. There are people such as water-diviners who possess certain curious gifts. Then there is the whole question of telepathy, transference of thought and extra-sensory perception. These things are just coming into our ken. As the result of such gifts and powers many can do marvellous and wondrous things, and yet not be Christian. The natural power of man can simulate the gifts of the Holy Spirit, up to a point. And, of course, we are reminded by Scripture that God, in His own inscrutable will, sometimes decides to give these powers to men who do not belong to Him in order to bring to pass His own purposes. He raises up men for His own particular purpose, but they themselves remain outside the kingdom. It was God who called and used the pagan Cyrus.

Above all we must remember the power of the devil. The devil, as Paul teaches in 2 Corinthians xi. 14, can transform himself even into an angel of light, and the devil as an angel of light sometimes persuades people that they are Christian when they are not. If the devil can keep a man outside the kingdom by making him say 'Lord, Lord', he will certainly make him do so. He will do anything to keep a man outside the kingdom; so if a false belief or a true belief held in the wrong way will do this, he will make him have it, and he will give him power to work signs and wonders.

It has all been prophesied, it is all in the Bible; and that is why our Lord warns us so solemnly to pay heed to it. He once summed it up to His disciples like this: 'In this', He says, 'rejoice not, that the spirits are subject unto you; but rather rejoice, because your names are written in heaven'. They had been sent out to preach and to cast out devils, and had been highly successful. They came back full of pride because of the things that had happened, and our Lord said to them in effect: 'Did I not tell you in the Sermon on the Mount that people who are outside the kingdom can preach in My name, and cast out devils and do many wonderful works? Do not be misled by these things; make certain of yourself. It is your heart that matters. Is your name written in heaven? Do you really belong to Me? Have you this holiness, this righteousness which I am teaching? "Not every one that saith unto me, Lord, Lord, shall enter into the kingdom of heaven; but he that doeth the will of my Father which is in heaven".' The way to test yourself, the way to test any man, is to look below the surface. Do not look at the apparent results, do not look at the wonders and the marvels, but discover whether he conforms to the Beatitudes. Is he poor in spirit; is he meek; is he humble; does he groan in his spirit as he sees the world; is he a holy man of God; is he grave; is he sober; does he say with Paul, 'We that are in this tabernacle do groan, being burdened'? Those are the tests, the tests of the Beatitudes, the tests of the Sermon on the Mount—the man's character, the man's nature. Not the appearances only, but the reality itself alone counts with God.

Let us remember again that it is the Lord who says these things, and it is He who will judge. The words 'Many will say to me in that day' refer to the day of judgment, when He will be the Judge, so do not be deceived. 'Ye are they', He says again of this type, 'which justify yourselves before men; but God knoweth your hearts: for that which is highly esteemed among men is abomination in the sight of God.' The New Testament Christian is a definite type of character; he is unmistakable. Read your New Testament, put down the marks of the New Testament man, put them on paper, learn them, meditate upon them, apply them to yourself and to everybody else. Do that, says our Lord, and you will never be led astray, you will not be left outside that strait gate and narrow way. These then are the tests and they may all be summed up in the phrase, 'he that doeth the will of my Father which is in heaven'.

May God grant us honesty as we face this terrifying truth, this truth we shall have to answer for when 'all earthly scenes have passed away', and we stand before Christ and face Him. If you feel you are condemned, confess it to God, hunger and thirst after righteousness, turn believingly to the Lord Jesus Christ, ask Him to give it you, cost what it may, whatever its effects and results, and He will give it to you, for He has said: 'Blessed are they which do hunger and thirst after righteousness: for they shall be filled.'

CHAPTER TWENTY-FIVE

UNCONSCIOUS HYPOCRISY

WE have already considered the general message conveyed by these solemn and solemnizing verses. As we return to them it is important that we should bear in mind that in this little paragraph our Lord is dealing with those who are orthodox. It is not a statement about those who are heterodox, those who hold false teaching or doctrine. Here, the teaching is correct. They prophesy in His name; it is in His name that they cast out devils; and it is in His name that they do many wonderful works. And yet He tells us that they are finally reprobate. So much then is possible for one who is nevertheless finally lost. That is why these words in many ways are more solemnizing and, indeed, alarming than anything we find in the whole extent of Holy Writ.

After that preliminary survey, we can now proceed to draw certain lessons and deductions from it. Surely nothing can be more important than that we should do so. Our Lord goes on repeating these warnings as He exhorts men and women to enter in at the strait gate and to walk in the narrow way, and here again He warns us of the terrible dangers and possibilities that confront us. The one great lesson to be learnt from this passage is the danger of self-deception, and this is emphasized in several ways. For instance our Lord uses the word 'Many'. 'Many will say to me in that day, Lord, Lord, have we not done this and that?' We must not exaggerate the force and strength of this word 'many', but it is a word that carries a very definite meaning. He does not say 'an odd person here and there', but 'many'— self-deception is a danger to the 'many', and His warnings against it are frequent. It is there in the picture that follows about people who build their houses upon the sand. It is the same warning that we find also in the parable of the ten virgins. The five foolish virgins are a straightforward case of self-deception, nothing more. It occurs again in that final picture in Matthew xxv, where Christ portrays the final judgment and speaks of those who will confidently come and tell Him of the things they have done for Him. The same warning is being given in all these cases; it is the warning against the terrible danger of self-deception. In other words, as we read what He says here, we are given the impression that these people to whom He is referring will be amazed and astonished at the day of judgment—'that day'. As we have seen, the whole paragraph is spoken with the day of judgment clearly in mind. Indeed, the whole chapter, as we have constantly seen, is concerned to enforce the fact that the Christian must live his whole life in the light of that coming day. Read through the New Testament and observe how frequently 'that day' is spoken of. 'The day will declare it', says Paul, as if to say: It is all right. I am going on with my ministry, I am doing everything with my eye on that day; people may criticize and say this or that about me, but I shall not allow that to worry me. I have delivered myself and my whole eternal future into the hand of the Lord my Judge, and the day of His judgment is going to make everything manifest.

It is clear from the words in this passage that these people, according to our Lord, are going to be astonished at the day of judgment. They have assumed that they are safe, and seem quite sure of their own salvation. Upon what grounds? Because they were saying, 'Lord, Lord'. They were orthodox; they said the right things; they were fervent; they were zealous. They prophesied in His name; they cast out devils; they did many wonderful works. And they were praised of men; they were in fact regarded as outstanding servants. So they were perfectly happy about themselves, quite assured about their whole position, and they never suspected for a second that there was any fault to find in them. They could turn to our Lord in the day of judgment and say: 'Surely, Lord, You know our record? Don't You remember all we said and did in Your name?' They had no doubt about themselves; they were perfectly happy; they were quite assured. It had never crossed their minds even to contemplate the possibility that they could be anything but Christians and saved people, heirs of glory and of eternal bliss. And yet what our Lord says to them is that they are lost. He will 'profess' to them—He plays upon words here, they make their profession, He too will make a profession—He will profess unto them: 'I never knew you, I never had anything to do with you. Though you were always saying "Lord, Lord", and doing things in My name, I never recognized you, there was never any contact between us. You have been deceiving and fooling yourselves the whole time. Depart from Me, ye that work iniquity.'

There can be no doubt about it, the day of judgment is going to be a day of many surprises. How often does our Lord tell these people, His contemporaries, and tell us through them, that He does not judge as they judge. 'Ye are they which justify yourselves before men; but God knoweth your hearts: for that which is highly esteemed among men is abomination in the sight of God.' That kind of false judgment is found at times in the Church, as well as in the world. So often our judgments are carnal. Listen to the comments people make as they go from a place of worship. So often they are about the man, about his very physical appearance, or what they call 'personality', rather than about the message. Those are the things that attract. Our judgments are so carnal. Thus our Lord teaches us to beware of this terrible, alarming possibility of deceiving ourselves. We are all quite clear about conscious hypocrisy. The conscious hypocrite is not a problem; he is obvious and self-evident. What is so much more difficult to discern is unconscious hypocrisy, when a man not only misleads others but also deceives himself, when a man not only persuades others wrongly about himself, but persuades himself wrongly about himself. That is the very thing with which our Lord is dealing here, and we must repeat again, that if we believe the New Testament is true, then there is nothing more important than that we should examine ourselves in the light of a statement such as this.

If, then, what we are describing is unconscious hypocrisy, does it not follow that we can do nothing about it? Is it not by definition something with which a man cannot deal? If it is a condition in which a man is deluding himself, how can he possibly safeguard himself against it? The answer is that, on the contrary, a great deal can be done. The first and most important thing is to consider the causes of self-deception. That is the way to discover it in ourselves. If we can arrive at a list of the causes of self-delusion and self-deception, and then examine ourselves in the light of these causes, we shall be in a position to deal with them. And the New Testament is full of instruction with respect to that. That is why it is always exhorting us to test and to examine ourselves; that is why it is always exhorting us to prove and try the spirits, and indeed to prove all things. It is a great book of warning. That is not popular today. People say that that is being negative; but the New Testament always emphasizes the negative aspect of truth as well as the positive.

What, then, are the common causes of self-deception in this matter? First: there is a false doctrine of assurance. This is the tendency to base our assurance only upon certain statements which we ourselves make. There are those who say, 'Scripture says, "He that believeth on him is not condemned" but shall receive "everlasting life"; "Believe on the Lord Jesus Christ, and thou shalt be saved"; "Whosoever believeth in his heart and confesseth with his mouth shall be saved".' They interpret such statements as meaning that as long as they acknowledge and say certain things about the Lord Jesus Christ, they are automatically saved. Their error is surely this: the man who is truly saved and who has a genuine assurance of salvation does make, and must make, these statements, but the mere making of these statements does not of necessity guarantee, or assure, a man of his salvation. The very people with whom our Lord is dealing *do* say: 'Lord, Lord,' and they seem to put the right content into that statement; but, as we have seen, James reminds us in his Epistle that 'the devils also believe, and tremble'. If we read the Gospels, we discover that the evil spirits, the devils, recognize the Lord. They refer to Him as 'the Holy One of God'. They know who He is; they say the right things about Him. But they are devils and they are lost. So we must be wary of that very subtle temptation, and remember the way in which people wrongly persuade themselves. They say: 'I do believe, and I have said with my mouth that I believe Jesus of Nazareth was the Son of God, and that He has died for my sins, therefore . . .'—but the argument is incomplete. The believer, the Christian, does say these things, but he does not stop at merely saying them. That is what is sometimes described as 'fideism' or 'believeism', which means that a man is really putting his final trust in his own faith and not in the Lord Jesus Christ. He is relying on his own belief, and on his mere assertion of it.

The whole object of this paragraph, surely, is to warn us against the terrible danger of basing our assurance of salvation upon a repetition of certain statements and formulae. We can think of other illustrations of this danger of being a merely formal Christian. What in fact is the difference between what we have just described and basing our assurance of salvation upon the fact that we are members of a church, or that we belong to a certain country, or that we were christened when we were infants? There is no difference. It is possible for a man to say all the right things and yet to live such an evil life that it is quite plain that he is not a Christian. 'Be not deceived', says the apostle Paul in writing to the Corinthians; 'neither fornicators, nor idolaters, nor adulterers . . . shall inherit the kingdom of God.' It is therefore quite possible for a man to say the right

276 STUDIES IN THE SERMON ON THE MOUNT

things and yet to be living an evil life. 'Let no man deceive himself.' The moment we begin to rest our faith solely upon repeating a formula, without being sure that we are regenerate and that we have evidence of the life of God within us, we are exposing ourselves to this terrible danger of self-delusion. And there are many who state and defend their doctrine of assurance in that way. They say: Do not listen to your conscience. If you have said that you believe, that is enough. But it is not enough, for 'many will say . . . Lord, Lord'. But He will say: 'I never knew you: depart from me, ye that work iniquity.' A superficial doctrine of assurance, therefore, or a false doctrine of assurance, is one of the most common causes of self-delusion.

The second cause of this condition follows inevitably from the first. It is the refusal to examine oneself. Self-examination is not popular today, especially, strangely enough, amongst evangelical Christians. Indeed, one often finds that evangelical Christians not only object to self-examination, but occasionally even regard it as almost sinful. Their argument is that a Christian should look only to the Lord Jesus Christ, that he must not look at himself at all, and they interpret this as meaning that he should not examine himself. They regard examining oneself as looking to oneself. They say that, if you look at yourself, you will find nothing but blackness and darkness; therefore you must look not at yourself, but to the Lord Jesus Christ. So they look away from themselves and refuse to examine themselves.

But that is not scriptural. Scripture constantly exhorts us to examine ourselves, to 'prove to our own selves whether we are in the faith' or whether we are 'reprobate'. And it does so for the very good reason that there is the terrible danger of drifting into antinomianism; that is, into holding that as long as a man believes on the Lord Jesus Christ it does not matter what he does; that if a man is saved it does not matter what kind of a life he lives. Antinomianism holds that the moment you begin to concentrate on behaviour, you are putting yourself back under the law. Believe on the Lord Jesus Christ, it says, and all is well. But that, again, is surely the very thing against which our Lord is warning us in this paragraph; the fatal danger of trusting only in what we say, and forgetting that the essential thing about Christianity is that it is a life to be lived, that it is 'the life of God in the soul of man', that the Christian is a 'partaker of the divine nature', and that this must of necessity be manifest in his life.

Or let us look at the first Epistle of John, which was written to correct this very danger. It has in mind those people who were very ready to say certain things, but whose lives were a blatant contradiction of what they professed. John produces his famous tests of spiritual life. He says: 'He that saith, I know him, and keepeth not his commandments, is a liar, and the truth is not in him.' 'If we say that we have fellowship with him, and walk in darkness, we lie, and do not the truth.' There were people who were doing just that; they were saying, 'I am a Christian, I am in fellowship with God, I am a believer on the Lord Jesus Christ'; but they were living in sin. That is a lie, says John; it is transgression of the law, it is disobedience to God and His holy commandment. However much a man may *say* he believes on the Lord Jesus Christ, if the habit of his life is persistently sinful he is not a Christian. And clearly the way to discover this is to examine ourselves. We must look at ourselves and examine ourselves in the light of the commandments, in the light of scriptural teaching, in the light of this Sermon on the Mount, and we must do so honestly. And, furthermore, when we come to this question of the works which we do, whether prophesying or casting out devils and doing 'many wonderful works', we must examine our motives. We must ask ourselves honestly, 'Why am I doing this, what is the real urge behind it all?'; because a man who does not realize that he may be doing the right things for a thoroughly wrong motive is a mere tyro in these matters. It is possible for a man to preach the gospel of Christ in an orthodox manner, to mention the name of Christ, to be right in doctrine and to be zealous in the preaching of the Word, and yet really to be doing it the whole time for his own self-interest and his own glory and self-satisfaction. The only way to safeguard ourselves against that is to examine and scrutinize ourselves. It is painful and unpleasant; but it has to be done. It is the only way of safety. A man has to face himself squarely and ask: 'Why am I doing it? What is the thing that, in my heart of hearts, I am really out for?' If a man does not do that he is exposing himself to the terrible danger of self-delusion and self-deception.

But let us now consider another cause of this self-same condition, which is the danger of living on one's activities. We need to be quite clear about this, for there is no doubt that one of the greatest dangers of all in the Christian life is that a man may live on his own activities. I once had a letter from a lady who had been a very active Christian worker for some forty years or so.

Then she was taken seriously ill and for six months was unable to leave her house. She was honest enough to tell me that she had found it to be a very severe and trying discipline. I know exactly what she meant. I have seen it in others and, alas, know something about it in my own experience. I have seen men who have been indefatigable in the work of the kingdom suddenly laid aside by illness, and scarcely knowing what to do with themselves. What is the matter? They have been living on their own activities. You can be so busy preaching and working that you are not nurturing your own soul. You are so neglecting your own spiritual life that you find at the end that you have been living on yourself and your own activities. And when you stop, or are stopped by illness or circumstances, you find that life is empty and that you have no resources.

This is not confined, of course, to the Christian life. How often have we heard of business or professional men who have been highly successful and perfectly healthy all their lives. They then decide to retire, and everybody is astounded when, in six months or so, they hear that they have suddenly died. What is the matter? Often the real explanation is that the thing which kept them going, which provided the stimulus to living and the purpose to life, is suddenly withdrawn, and they collapse. Or think of the way in which so many people today are kept going solely by entertainments and pleasures. When they are suddenly cut off from these they do not know what to do with themselves; they are utterly bored and helpless. They have been living on their own activities and pleasures. And the same thing can happen in the Christian life. That is why it is a good thing for all of us from time to time to stop and take a rest, and to examine ourselves, and ask 'What am I living on?' What if the meetings you attend so frequently and so regularly were suddenly prohibited to you, how would you find yourself? What if your health broke down and you could not read, or enjoy the company of other people, and you were just left alone? What would you do? We must take time to ask ourselves these questions, for one of the greatest dangers to the soul is just to be living on our own activities and on our own efforts. To be over-busy is one of the high-roads to self-deception.

Another fruitful cause of this trouble is the tendency to balance our lives by putting up one thing against another. For instance, if our conscience condemns us about the life we are living, we put over against it some good work we are doing. We recognize that certain things count against us, but then we make a list of the good deeds we are doing, and the account balances with a little credit at the end. We have all done that. Do you recall the classic example of it in the case of Saul, the first king of Israel? Saul had been commanded to exterminate the Amalekites; and he had done so up to a point. But he kept King Agag alive, and he also kept the best of the sheep and oxen and so on. You notice how clever he was when upbraided by Samuel. He said, 'I have kept them in order that we might make a sacrifice unto the Lord.' That is a perfect instance of balancing. And we are all prone to this. Instead of allowing our consciences to do their work, we immediately put positive things over against the negative. A man who judges the condition of his life in that way can have only one end. A man who does that sort of thing in business will soon be bankrupt, and a man who does it in the Christian life will soon be spiritually bankrupt, and in the end will be dismissed by the Lord Himself. We must apply this lesson to ourselves. We must allow conscience to deal with us. We must not excuse ourselves, but listen to its dictates and obey them.

That brings us to the vital principle which underlies all the causes of self-deception. In many ways the root trouble, even among good Evangelicals, is our failure to heed the plain teaching of Scripture. We accept what Scripture teaches as far as our doctrine is concerned; but when it comes to practice, we very often fail to take the Scriptures as our only guide. When we come to the practical side we employ human tests instead of scriptural ones. Instead of taking the plain teaching of the Bible, we argue with it. 'Ah, yes,' we say, 'since the Scriptures were written, times have changed.' Dare I give an obvious illustration? Take the question of women preaching, and being ordained to the full ministry. The apostle Paul, in writing to Timothy (1 Timothy ii. 11–15), prohibits it directly. He says quite specifically that he does not allow a woman to teach or preach. 'Ah, yes,' we say, as we read that letter, 'he was only thinking of his own age and time; but you know times have changed since then, and we must not be bound. Paul was thinking of certain semi-civilized people in Corinth and places like that.' But the Scripture does not say that. It says, 'Let the woman learn in silence with all subjection. But I suffer not a woman to teach, nor to usurp authority over the man, but to be in silence.' 'Ah, but that was only temporary legislation,' we say. Paul puts it like this: 'For Adam was first formed, then Eve. And

Adam was not deceived, but the woman being deceived was in the transgression. Notwithstanding she shall be saved in child-bearing, if they continue in faith and charity and holiness with sobriety.' Paul does not say that it was only for the time being; he takes it right back to the Fall and shows that it is an abiding principle. It is something that is true, therefore, of the age in which we live. But thus, you see, we argue with Scripture. Instead of taking its plain teaching, we say that times have changed—when it suits our thesis we say it is no longer relevant.

Another way in which we do the same thing is this. The Scripture lays down quite plainly not only that we are to preach the gospel, the true message, but also *how* we are to do so. It tells us that we are to do so with 'sobriety' and with 'gravity', in fear and trembling, in 'demonstration of the Spirit and of power', and not with 'enticing words of man's wisdom'. But today evangelistic methods which are a flagrant contradiction of these words are justified in terms of results. 'Look at the results', men say. 'Such and such a man may not conform to the scriptural method, but look at the results!' And because of 'the results' the plain dictates of Scripture are put on one side. Is that believing the Scriptures? Is that taking the Scriptures as our final authority? Is not that repeating the old error of Saul, who said, 'Yes, I know, but I thought it would be good if I did so and so.' He tries to justify his disobedience by some result he is going to produce. We Protestants, of course, hold up our hands in horror at the Roman Catholics, especially the Jesuits, when they tell us that 'the end justifies the means'. It is the great argument of the Church of Rome. We repudiate it in the Roman Catholic Church, but it is a common argument in evangelical circles. The 'results' justify everything. If the results are good, the argument runs, the methods must be right—the end justifies the means. If you want to avoid terrible disillusionment at the day of judgment, face Scripture as it is. Do not argue with it, do not try to manipulate it, do not twist it; face it, receive it and submit to it whatever the cost.

A further common cause of self-deception is our failure to realize that the one thing that matters is our relationship to Christ. He is the Judge, and it is what He thinks of us that matters. It is He who will say to these people, 'I never knew you', and that word 'knew' is very strong. It does not mean that He was not aware of their existence. He knows all things, He sees everything; everything is naked and open to Him. 'Know' means 'taking a special interest in', 'being in a particular relationship to'. 'You only have I known of all the families of the earth,' said God to the children of Israel through Amos. That means that He is in this peculiar relationship to Israel. What our Lord will say on the judgment-day to these self-deceived people is that they have done all these things in their own power and energy. He never had anything to do with it. So the most important thing for all of us is not to be interested primarily in our activities or in results, but in our relationship to the Lord Jesus Christ. Do we know Him, and does He know us?

Finally, therefore, we must realize that what God wants, and what our blessed Lord wants, above all, is ourselves—what Scripture calls our 'heart'. He wants the inner man, the heart. He wants our submission. He does not want merely our profession, our zeal, our fervour, our works, or anything else. He wants *us*. Read again the words uttered by the prophet Samuel to Saul, king of Israel: 'Hath the Lord as great delight in burnt offerings and sacrifices, as in obeying the voice of the Lord? Behold, to obey is better than sacrifice, and to hearken than the fat of rams' (1 Samuel xv. 22). To Saul's argument: 'We kept the best of the sheep and the oxen in order that we might sacrifice them, in order that we might offer them to the Lord,' this is the answer: God does not want our offerings; He does not want our sacrifices; He wants our obedience, He wants *us*. It is possible for a man to say right things, to be very busy and active, to achieve apparently wonderful results, and yet not to give himself to the Lord. He may be doing it all for himself, and he may be resisting the Lord in the most vital place of all. And that is finally the greatest insult we can offer to God. What can be a greater insult than to say: 'Lord, Lord,' fervently, to be busy and active, and yet to withhold true allegiance and submission from Him, to insist upon retaining control of our own lives, and to allow our own opinions and arguments, rather than those of Scripture, to control what we do and how we do it? The greatest insult to the Lord is a will that is not completely and entirely surrendered; and whatever else we may do—however great our offerings and sacrifices, however wonderful our works in His name—it will avail us nothing. If we believe that Jesus of Nazareth is the only begotten Son of God and that He came into this world and went to the cross of Calvary and died for our sins and rose again in order to justify us and to give us life anew and prepare us for heaven—if you really believe that, there is only one inevitable deduction, namely that He is entitled to the whole of our lives, everything without any limit whatsoever. That means that He must have control not only in the big things, but in the little things also; not only over what we do, but how we do it. We must submit to Him and His way as He has been pleased to reveal it in the Bible; and if what we do does not conform to this pattern, it is an assertion of our will, it is disobedience, and as repellent as the sin of witchcraft. Indeed, it belongs to the type of conduct that makes Christ say to certain people: 'Depart from me, ye that work iniquity'. Workers of iniquity! Who are they? The people who said: 'Lord, Lord,' the people who prophesied in His name and in His name cast out devils and in His name did many wonderful works. He calls them 'workers of iniquity' because, in the last analysis, they were doing it to please themselves and not in order to please Him. Let us then solemnly examine ourselves in the light of these things.

CHAPTER TWENTY-SIX

THE SIGNS OF SELF-DECEPTION

W E have already considered twice the momentous and
alarming words of vii. 21–23; but because of their vital
importance we must do so once again. This matter of
self-deception is a very large subject. If you are interested in so-
called Manuals of Devotion, whether Roman Catholic or
Protestant, you will find that they always devote a good deal of
attention to this particular question. All wise physicians of the
soul have always concentrated attention on it. We are called to
do so by the Bible itself. It is full, not only of exhortations on this
matter, but also of practical illustrations of people who have
deluded and deceived themselves. But apart from all that, as we
value our souls, and as we realize that we are all passing through
this world in the direction of a final judgment, and shall all have
to stand before the judgment-throne of Christ, this kind of self-
examination becomes quite inevitable. As the apostle John put
it: 'Every man that hath this hope in him purifieth himself, even
as he is pure' (1 John iii. 3). And you cannot purify yourself
without examining yourself. Some people devote the season of
Lent in particular to this question of self-examination. Others of
us believe that it should be done throughout the whole year, and
that we should be examining ourselves and disciplining ourselves always. We need not enter into that, however. What is
important is to recognize the need of self-examination. It is
taught constantly in the Bible.

We have seen that the first step to take if we are anxious to
avoid deceiving ourselves is to consider the causes of self-
deception, and we have dealt with some of the more common
ones. Having thus laid down principles, we now come to deal
with a few practical details; these are designed to warn us of the
subtle way in which we can deceive ourselves. We start by
reminding ourselves that we do not live our Christian life in a
kind of vacuum. Quite apart from the fact that we live in society
among men and women, we have also to contend with the devil
and 'the principalities and powers, the rulers of the darkness of
this world, and spiritual wickedness in high places.' Nothing
according to Scripture teaching will enable us to stand in that

conflict except the putting on of the whole armour of God. One of the ways in which we put on that armour is to beware of the subtlety of the attack. And that, because of its very nature, will have to be considered in some detail. I am a little fearful as I proceed to do this, because I know that to do so exposes one to the risk of being misunderstood. If one uses illustrations attention becomes concentrated on the illustrations and not on the principles.

The first big principle is that there is a sense in which everything in connection with the Christian life can be dangerous. I am not maintaining that everything *is* dangerous but that it can be. The devil in his subtlety, as an angel of light, comes to us and takes hold of things which are legitimate and good, and given to us by God, and he so influences us as to make us turn those very things into the instrument of our own self-deception. The things themselves are all right, but we can abuse them. That is the theme which we must elaborate. In a sense, even the means of grace with which God has provided us can prove to be a source of trouble. I trust I am making this clear. Obviously I am not denouncing the means of grace; I am simply pointing out the terrible danger of turning the means of grace which God Himself has appointed, and given us, into something that may be harmful to our souls. I am concerned with the *abuse* of what is good, and not with the *use* of what is good. It is always a great comfort to any man who preaches to know that even such a great master preacher as the apostle Paul could be misunderstood when he taught and preached. Take, for instance, 2 Corinthians xi with its superb sarcasm. The apostle deals there with the grievous, childish way in which so much of his teaching had been misunderstood in Corinth.

Here, then, are the controlling principles. Things that are good in and of themselves, unless we are careful, may be the very things that will deceive us about the state of our souls. But how can we know whether we are tending to depart from the simplicity that is in Christ, and getting into this terrible false position that is described in this verse? Here are some of the answers. One clear indication of this tendency reveals itself in the following way. If, when we examine ourselves to discover what our main interest is, we find that it is in attending meetings, we are entering into a dangerous condition. Obviously I believe in attending Christian meetings; but when a man gets into the condition in which he lives on meetings, and they become his primary interest, he is in a very dangerous condition. And there are many people in that position. They are kept going by meetings, and when they are suddenly cut off from them they begin to discover a terrible barrenness in their soul and in their Christian experience.

Another symptom of the same condition is an undue interest in phenomena. There are many phenomena in connection with the Christian life for which we can thank God, certain things that come as blessings in connection with the gospel, such as exalted feelings, guidance, physical healing, and so on. These things are part and parcel of the Christian message, but if we find that our main interest is in these phenomena we are in a position that may lead to self-deception. We must never be more interested in what we may call the by-products of the faith than in the faith itself. We must examine ourselves concerning each of these things. We betray our fundamental interest, of course, by what we say. As we listen to other people we discover their main and their real interests. And the same applies to us. We must ask: 'What is my main interest?' Or, perhaps, it would be wise to get someone else to examine and observe us. I suggest that if we discover in ourselves or in others this tendency for the interest to be absorbed by the means of grace and phenomena rather than by our relationship to the Lord, we are already on the way that ultimately leads to this dread self-deception.

Another sign of this is an undue interest in organizations, denominations, particular churches, or some movement or fellowship. We all know exactly what this means. Man is a social being, and we all like to have some outlet for our social instinct and the social part of our make-up. It is the simplest thing in the world to find an outlet for that natural, social, gregarious instinct in the realm of things Christian. The danger lies in our assuming that because of our interest in these things we are, of necessity, Christian. That is the very thing our Lord is saying. Here is a man who says, 'Lord, Lord'; he casts out devils, he does many wonderful works in the name of Christ, in the realm of the Church, and because of that he assumes that he is a Christian. Yet Christ says he may not be. How easily this can be done! There are people who by nature prefer to be in moral rather than immoral societies, but who are not Christian at all. As natural human beings they like moral, ethical people, and their natural desire to have a social outlet, or an outlet for their active moral nature, is provided by some type of organization in connection with Christianity. Self-deception comes in, because they assume that, as they are doing it in a Christian realm, they must be Christian. But their real interest is in the activity and in the organization, not in the Lord, nor in their own relationship to the Lord. This is a terrible possibility. There are people whose real and ultimate interest is in their particular church, not in Christian salvation, not in the Lord at all. They like the church, they like the people, they have been brought up in that atmosphere, and that is the thing that really holds them—that particular church, that particular denomination, or that particular alignment of people. Again it is always revealed by their talk. You will find that they are greatly interested when you talk about the organization, or the people, or the preacher, but that they become strangely silent if you try to have a spiritual talk with them about their soul or about the Lord. We must examine ourselves by that test. What are we really interested in? Are we interested in our relationship to Him and in His glory, or only in one of these other things?

Another, and a very common, danger at this present time is to be interested in the social and general rather than in the personal aspects of Christianity. This has been particularly important in the present century. Many people today, confronted by the problems of this country and of society, are saying more and more that what is needed is biblical teaching and a Christian attitude towards these national and social problems. Watch the statesmen, and the politicians—even some of the leading ones. Although one is given to understand that they practically never attend a place of worship on Sunday they are using increasingly the words 'religion' and 'Christian'. They seem to think vaguely that Christian teaching can help to solve the problems of State. Though they are not active and practising Christians themselves (and I am referring only to these and not to the Christians among them), and are not giving any personal obedience to the Lord, they seem to think that Christianity can be of help in a general way. We are always on dangerous ground when we begin to talk about 'Christian civilization' and 'Christian' or 'Western' values. This is surely much in evidence at the present time; and it is one of the major dangers confronting the Christian Church. I refer particularly to the tendency to regard Christianity as if it were nothing more than anti-communist teaching. This can be seen in the way in which Christian organizations sometimes advertise, and in their use of slogans such as 'Christ or Communism?', etc. It is not surprising that the Roman Catholic Church should think in such terms, but it is sad to see innocent evangelical people being gradually drawn into that net. It works in a very subtle way. A man persuades himself that, because he is an anti-communist, he must be a Christian. But it by no means follows. We thus persuade and deceive ourselves. We judge ourselves by these general criteria, and assume that we are Christians. The substitution of the social and general for the particular and personal in Christian matters is always a terrible danger. Christendom has often been the greatest enemy of spiritual religion. If I find my interest tends to be more and more general, or social, or political, if that is increasingly my main interest in Christianity, then I am in an extremely dangerous state because I have probably ceased to examine myself.

The next danger is that of those whose main and primary interest is in what we may call apologetics, or the definition and defence of the faith, instead of in a true relationship to Jesus Christ. This is a danger of which every preacher should be particularly aware. Many a man who has persuaded himself that he is a Christian is in reality only interested in apologetics. He spends the whole of his time arguing about the Christian faith, defending it, denouncing evolution, denouncing psychology and various other things that seem to be attacking the very vitals of the faith. This is a very subtle danger because such a man may be completely neglecting his own soul, his own personal holiness and sanctification and his personal relationship to the Lord. But he feels quite happy about himself because he is denouncing evolution and is defending the faith against this or that attack. He may not only be putting this to his own account for righteousness, he may even be using it to evade the task of honest self-examination. Apologetics have their essential place in the Christian life, and it is a part of our business as Christians earnestly to contend for the faith; but if we find ourselves doing nothing but that, we are in a dangerous condition. I knew a man who was much used as an evangelical preacher, perhaps second to none at one time. But he began to spend the time every Sunday in his pulpit attacking the Church of Rome and Modernism, and he ceased to preach a positive gospel. Apologetics had taken the place of central gospel truth. It is a special temptation to those who can reason and argue and debate; and it is one of the most subtle attacks to which the soul can ever be subjected. This is the question, therefore, which some of us should constantly be putting to ourselves. Do I find that most of my time is taken up in arguing with people about the outposts of the Christian position? Do I find that I practically never talk to people about their souls and about Christ and about their experience of Him? Am I always, as it were, going round the outposts of the Citadel? How much of my time is spent in the centre itself? 'Let every man examine himself.'

The next danger is a purely academic and theoretical interest in theology. These dangers are not confined merely to one or two types of Christian; not only are they real to the man who is excessively interested in activities and meetings; but also to the man whose only interest is in theology. His position is just as dangerous as that of the other. It is the simplest thing in the world to be interested in the body of Christian truth, in doctrine as such, merely as an intellectual matter; and it is a particular danger to some of us. There is no view of life and the world today which is in any way comparable to Christian theology; there is nothing more exciting or more interesting as an intellectual pursuit than to be reading theology and philosophy. But, valuable as it is, and wonderful as it is, it may become one of the most subtle dangers and temptations to the soul. A man can be so absorbed in the intellectual apprehension that he forgets that he is alive, and forgets other people. He spends the whole of his time reading and enjoying it, he never makes contact with anybody, and he is useless to everybody. In the history of the Church we find again that this has happened frequently. First there is a great revival. Then there follows a stage which is generally described as that of 'consolidation'. People very rightly feel the need of a state of consolidation after revival. The converts must be built up, so they are taught theology and doctrine. Yet we often find that that has led to a state of intellectual religiosity and spiritual aridity. The classical instance of this is to be found in the sixteenth and seventeenth centuries, after the great Protestant revival and Reformation. After the Reformation in England came the era of the Puritans, with its great teaching of theology. But that was followed by a period of barren intellectualism which continued until the evangelical awakening broke out in the thirties of the eighteenth century. Something similar happened in the Reformed and Lutheran Churches. So, again, while we believe that theology is vital and essential, we must remember that the devil may so press us that our interest in it becomes inordinate and unbalanced, with the result that we are 'puffed up' rather than 'edified'. As I look back across some thirty years and more in the Christian ministry I have seen many instances of that. I have watched such people, and have seen a kind of intellectual pride, a pride of knowledge coming in. I have seen the tendency to compromise on the ethical and moral side, I have seen the note of urgency disappearing from their prayers. Though the original interest was right and good, gradually it mastered them. They lost their balance and became intellectualists who were no longer concerned about the idea of holiness and the pursuit of a true and living knowledge of God.

Let us now come to another danger. What we have to say concerning it is particularly liable to be misunderstood, so we must be careful. I have, as the result of much observation, come to the conclusion that one of the most dangerous signs in connection with this matter of self-deception is an over-interest in prophetic teaching. The Bible contains a great deal of prophetic teaching, and it is our business to acquaint ourselves with it; but there is nothing that can be so dangerous as an undue interest in prophetic teaching, and especially at a time like this with the world in its present condition. Gradually this interest seems to absorb and to master certain people and they think and talk and preach of nothing but prophecy. There is scarcely anything more dangerous to the spiritual condition of the soul than this over-absorption in prophetic teaching. One can so easily be spending all one's time in thinking about Russia and Egypt and Israel and other countries, and in working out times and seasons in terms of Ezekiel xxxvii, xxxviii, Daniel vii–xii, and other prophetic passages that one's whole life is given to that. In the meantime you are becoming hard and neglectful of yourself and of other people, in a spiritual sense. You are so interested in the 'times and seasons' that you have forgotten your own soul. Of course prophetic teaching is a vital part of the biblical message, and we should be vitally interested in it; but we must recognize the terrible danger of having such an interest in future world events that we forget that we have a life to live here and now and that at any moment we may die and have to stand before God in judgment. At all points our chief danger is to lose a sense of balance and proportion.

There is a further group of dangers connected with the Bible itself. All Christians should believe in reading the Bible and in studying it diligently and regularly. And yet even the Bible, unless we are very careful, can become a danger and a snare in our spiritual lives. Let me illustrate what I mean. If you ever find yourself approaching the Bible in an intellectual rather than a spiritual manner, you are already on the wrong road. To approach the Bible in a purely intellectual manner, to take it as a text-book, to divide up its chapters exactly as if you were analysing a play by Shakespeare, is a very interesting pursuit. Indeed, nothing can be more exciting to a certain type of person. And yet if you once begin to approach it intellectually only, and not spiritually, it can become the cause of your damnation. The Bible is God's Book and it is a Book of Life. It is a Book that speaks to us a word from God. If, therefore, you find yourself looking down at the Bible instead of looking up at it, you had better examine yourself urgently. If it is a Book which you handle as a master, then it is probably the case that you are being mastered by the devil, who as 'an angel of light' is using the very Word of God to rob you of certain spiritual blessings to your soul. Beware then of becoming a student of the Bible in a wrong sense. Personally, I have always disapproved, for these reasons, of all examinations in biblical knowledge. The moment you begin to approach the Bible as a 'subject', you are already in trouble. We should never approach the Bible theoretically; the Bible should always preach to us, and we must never allow ourselves to come to it in any way but that. Nothing is more dangerous than the expert's or preacher's approach to the Bible. This is so in the case of the preacher because his greatest temptation is to regard the Bible as just a collection of texts on which to preach. So he tends to go to his Bible simply to look for texts and not to feed his soul. The moment a man does that he is in a dangerous condition.

But what is true about reading the Bible is equally true of listening to the preaching of the Bible. Some people simply look for 'points' in sermons, and at the end they make comments about this or that. Let us always be careful not to regard ourselves as experts. Let us ever seek to come under the power of this Word, whether we are reading it or listening to it. When a man comes to me at the close of a service and talks about preaching as such, and as an expert, I know I have failed completely as far as he is concerned. The effect of true preaching should be to make us fear and tremble; it should make us examine ourselves and think more about the Lord Jesus Christ. Beware of becoming interested in the mere letter of the Word. It is something that can happen very easily. Beware of becoming over-interested in the mechanics—jumping from text to text, working out comparisons, etc. Of course we are to be interested in everything in the Bible, but we are not to be mastered by the mechanics. It is good to be interested in figures, in biblical numerics for instance; but you can easily spend the whole of your life working at such problems, and thereby forget the true interests of your soul. In particular, beware of too great an interest in the various translations of the Bible. I remember a man, an intelligent man, who was converted by the gospel of Jesus Christ. It was wonderful to see the change in him and to observe his development. Then he came under the influence of a certain teaching, and the first evidence I had of his having been influenced by that teaching was that, when he wrote to me, he began to put as a postscript references to certain passages of Scripture. But he did not just write them as he had done formerly. He now put Matthew vii. 21 (Weymouth). Then the next time somebody else, Moffatt or Way. (Now probably it would also be Phillips, Knox, etc.) Thus the poor man became more and more interested in translations and in the mechanics. I remember another man of this type coming to me once at the end of a service which had been highly spiritual and very moving. One of the speakers in stressing a point had read a passage, but from a translation other than the Authorized or Revised Versions. This man's one remark about the meeting was to ask the question: 'Whose translation was that?' The particular translation had nothing to do with the message. The passage was equally clear in all versions; but he was interested in translations. Translations, as such, can be most valuable and helpful; but once you become absorbed by an interest in them you have probably become more concerned with the mechanics of the Bible than with the spiritual food which it imparts.

The last danger is the terrible one of playing grace against law and thereby being interested only in grace. There is no saving doctrine at all apart from the doctrine of grace; but we must beware lest we hide ourselves behind it in a wrong way. Again I remember a man who had been converted, but who then fell into sin. I was very ready to help him until I found that he was much too ready to help himself. In other words, he came and confessed his sin, but immediately he began to smile and said: 'After all, there is the doctrine of grace'. I felt he was too healthy; he was healing himself a little too quickly. The reaction to sin should be deep penitence. When a man is in a healthy spiritual condition he does not find relief quite as easily as that. He feels he is hopeless and vile. If therefore you find that you can heal yourself easily, if you find you can jump lightly to the doctrine of grace, I suggest you are in a dangerous condition. The truly spiritual man, while he believes in the doctrine of grace, when he is truly convicted of sin by the Holy Spirit, feels at times that it is almost impossible that God can forgive him. I have put that sometimes in this form by saying that I do not quite understand the Christian who can sit through a truly evangelistic sermon without feeling convicted again. Surely, our feeling should be: 'I almost felt that I went through it once more; I felt I was being put through the whole process again'. That is the true reaction. There is always a convicting aspect to the message; and once we find that we are not reacting in that way because we fly at once to grace, we are in the condition which leads to this tragic self-deception.

In other words, the final question is this—what of the soul? You remember the famous story about William Wilberforce and the woman who went to him at the height of his campaign against slavery and said 'Mr. Wilberforce, what about the soul?' And Mr. Wilberforce turned to the woman and said, 'Madam, I had almost forgotten that I had a soul'. This poor woman came to Wilberforce and asked her vital question, and the great man said that he was so concerned about the liberation of the slaves that he had almost forgotten his soul. But, with all due respect to him, the woman was right. Of course, she may have been a busy-body; but there is no evidence that she was. Probably the woman saw that here was a good and fine Christian man, doing a most excellent work. Yes, but she also saw and realized that the danger confronting such a man was that of being so absorbed in the question of anti-slavery that he might forget his own soul. A man can be so busy preaching in pulpits that he forgets and neglects his own soul. After you have attended all your meetings, and denounced Communism until you can scarcely speak, after you have dealt with your apologetics, and displayed your wonderful knowledge of theology and your understanding of the times, and your complete map of the next fifty years, and after you have read all the translations of the Bible, and have shown your proficiency in a knowledge of its mechanics, I still ask you: 'What about your relationship to the Lord Jesus Christ?' You know a great deal more than you did a year ago; but do you know Him better? You denounce many wrong things; but do you love Him more? Your knowledge of the Bible and its translations has become quite astounding, and you are an expert in apologetics;

but are you obeying the law of God and of Christ increasingly?
Is the fruit of the Spirit more and more manifest and evident in
your life? Those are the questions. 'Not every one that saith unto
me, Lord, Lord' (and does many wonderful works), 'but he that
doeth the will of my Father which is in heaven.'

Let us all examine ourselves and let us take time to do it
thoroughly. Do we really desire to know Him? Paul says in effect
that he had virtually forgotten everything else. He had no other
care: 'That I may know him, and the power of his resurrection...'
(Philippians iii. 10). Forgetting all the past, and pressing on to
that—to 'know' Him, and to 'be like' Him. If anything takes the
place of that, we are on the wrong road. All these other things are
means to bring us to a knowledge of Him, and if we stay with
them they are robbing us of Him. God deliver us from the danger
of allowing the means of grace to hide the blessed Saviour from
our eyes.

CHAPTER TWENTY-SEVEN

THE TWO MEN AND THE TWO HOUSES

WE have suggested many times, while studying the words in the previous paragraph, that they are amongst the most solemnizing in the whole range and realm of Scripture. Yet verses 24–27, which we are now considering, seem even more solemn and awe-inspiring. They are words with which we are all familiar. Even in a day like this, when there is such ignorance of the Scriptures, most people are familiar with this particular picture. Our Lord has finished His Sermon on the Mount and has given His detailed instruction, He has laid down all His great and vital principles, and He is now applying the truth. He is confronting His followers with the two possibilities; they must all go in at one or other of the two gates, either at the narrow gate or at the broad gate, and they will walk either the narrow way or the broad way. His purpose has been to help them as they face this choice. To that end He has shown them how to recognize and avoid the subtle temptations and dangers which invariably confront those who are in that situation. In these verses our Lord continues with the same theme. Notice the connection. It is not something new; rather it is a continuation and final clinching of His earlier argument. It is the same warning about the danger of a lack of obedience, of being content with listening to the gospel and not putting it into practice. In other words, it is once more the danger of self-deception. The Scriptures, as we have seen, are full of warnings against this; and we have it here pictured, in a most arresting fashion, in the greatness of the fall of the house that was built upon the sand. We have seen it already in the case of the unconscious hypocrites—these people who were so sure that they were Christian, but who will be so sadly disillusioned in the day of judgment, when the Lord says to them, 'I never knew you: depart from me, ye that work iniquity'. It is, then, the same theme, but with an added lesson. Our Lord never drew a new picture merely for the sake of doing so. There must be some new aspect of the matter, which He is anxious to present; and this arresting picture shows clearly what that new emphasis is.

The best way to approach this particular picture is to look at it as the third in a series. The first, in verses 15–20, concerning the false prophet, was designed to warn us against the danger of being deceived by appearances. Affable men come to us in sheep's clothing who inwardly are ravening wolves. How easily we can be deceived by such people because we are so superficial in our judgments. Our Lord said on one occasion, 'Judge not according to the appearance.' He said that God does not judge by the appearance, but by the heart. That is the first warning. We must not assume, as we stand there outside these two gates, that any man who comes to talk to us, and who is pleasant and affable, and who seems to be a Christian, is of necessity a Christian. We must not judge him by appearances; we must apply another test—'By their fruits ye shall know them.'

The second picture is one of people who assume that everybody who says 'Lord, Lord' shall enter into the kingdom of heaven. This is a picture designed to warn us against the danger of deceiving ourselves in terms of what we believe, or in terms of our zeal and fervour, and our own activities. 'Many will say to me in that day, Lord, Lord, have we not prophesied in thy name? and in thy name have cast out devils? and in thy name done many wonderful works?' They were resting on these things; but they were quite wrong. He had never had anything to do with them; He had never known them. They were just deceiving and deluding themselves.

We are now going to look at the third and last picture. I suggest at once, in order to concentrate attention, that our Lord's chief concern in this picture is to warn us against the danger of seeking and desiring only the benefits and the blessings of salvation, and resting upon our apparent possession of them. Clearly the words are addressed to those who are professing Christians. They are not addressed to people who have no interest whatsoever in the kingdom; they are addressed to people who have been listening, and who like listening, to teaching concerning it. These words are obviously addressed to members of churches, to those who make the claim of being Christian, who profess discipleship, and who are seeking the benefits and blessings of salvation. Everything about the picture emphasizes that, and we see that it, again, is meant to show us the difference between the false and the true profession of Christianity; the difference between the Christian and the seeming Christian; between the man who really is born again and is a child of God, and the man who only thinks he is.

In order to bring out this distinction our Lord presents us with a comparison; indeed, there is a kind of double comparison in the picture. There are two men and two houses. Obviously, therefore, if we are to arrive at the spiritual truth which is taught here, we must examine the picture in detail. There are similarities and differences to be observed.

First of all let us look at the similarities in the case of the two men. To begin with, they had the same desire. They both desired to build a house, a house in which they could live with their families, dwell at ease and enjoy themselves. They wanted the same thing, they thought about the same thing, and they were interested in the same thing. There is no difference at all at that point. Not only so, but they desired a house in the same locality; indeed, they built their houses in the same locality, for our Lord points out clearly that the two houses were subjected to precisely the same tests and stresses. A strong impression is thus given that the two houses were quite near to one another, and were subject to precisely the same conditions. This is a most important point. But we can go one step further and say that they obviously liked and designed the same kind of house. We deduce that from the fact that our Lord makes it clear that there was no difference between these two houses except in the foundation. Looked at externally and on the surface there was no difference. The doors, the windows and the chimneys were in the same position; they had the same design, the same pattern—the two houses were apparently identical apart from just this one difference beneath the surface. So we are entitled to deduce that these two men liked the same kind of house. Not only did each want a house; they wanted the same kind of house. Their ideas on the subject were absolutely identical. They had much in common.

In saying that, we have incidentally brought out the similarities in the two houses. We have seen that the two houses look absolutely identical if we merely examine them superficially. Everything seems to be in exactly the same position in the one as in the other. Furthermore, we must remember that they are subject to precisely the same tests. Up to this point, therefore, as we look at the two men and the two houses we find nothing but similarity. Yet we know that the whole point of the picture is to show the difference and the dissimilarity. Indeed, our Lord is concerned to show that the difference is a fundamental and vital one.

As we concentrate our attention therefore upon the differences, we can divide up the matter once more into the difference between the men, and the difference between the houses. Before we come to the details, let us look at the difference in general. The first point is that it is not an obvious one. We need to be reminded of this constantly because there is no point at which the devil in his subtlety seems to trap us so frequently. We cling to the notion that the difference between the true Christian and the pseudo-Christian is obvious. Our Lord's whole point, however, is that this is a most subtle matter. It is not obvious either in the case of the men or the houses. If we do not stress that point we miss the whole purpose of His teaching in the Sermon on the Mount. Our Lord emphasizes this element of subtlety everywhere. It was there in the first picture of the men in sheep's clothing—the false prophets. The whole difficulty about the false prophet, as we saw, was that on the surface he was so extraordinarily like the true prophet. The false prophet is not of necessity a man who says there is no God and that the Bible is just the product of human thinking, and who denies the miracles and the supernatural. The false prophet can be detected only when you examine him very carefully with a sense of discrimination given only by the Holy Spirit. His condition is such that he deceives himself as well as others. It was precisely the same in that second picture: and it is so here also. The difference is not obvious; it is very subtle. Nevertheless to those who have eyes to see it is perfectly clear. If you interpret this picture by saying that the difference between the two houses and the two men is discovered only when the trials come, when the floods descend and the winds blow, then not only is your exposition wrong, it is of no value. By then it is too late to do anything about it. So if our Lord were teaching that, He would in effect be mocking us. But that is not the case; His whole object is to enable us to detect the difference between the two, so that we may safeguard ourselves against the consequences of the false position while there is still time. If we have our eyes anointed with the eye-salve which the Holy Spirit can give, if we have 'that anointing from the Holy One', and the unction which enables us to discriminate, we shall be able to detect the difference between the men and the houses.

Look first at the difference between the two men. At this point the record as given at the end of Luke vi is particularly helpful. There we are told that the wise man digged deep and laid a foundation for his house, whereas the foolish man did not dig at all, and did not trouble to lay a foundation. In other words, the

298   STUDIES IN THE SERMON ON THE MOUNT

way to discover the difference between these two men is to make a detailed analysis of the foolish man. The wise man is just the exact opposite. And, of course, the key to the understanding of that man is the word 'foolish'. It describes a particular outlook, a characteristic type of person.

What are the characteristics of the foolish man? The first is that he is in a hurry. Foolish people are always in a hurry; they want to do everything at once; they have no time to wait. How often does Scripture warn us against this! It tells us that the godly, righteous man 'shall not make haste'. He is never subject to flurry and excitement and hurry. He knows God and he knows that the decrees and purposes and plan of God are eternal and immutable. But the foolish man is impatient; he never takes time; he is always interested in short cuts and quick results. That is the chief characteristic of his mentality and his conduct. We are all familiar with this kind of person in ordinary life and quite apart from Christianity. He is the type of man who says, 'I must have a house at once, there is no time for foundations.' He is always in a hurry.

At the same time, because he has that mentality, he does not trouble to listen to instruction; he does not pay any attention to the rules that govern the construction of a house. The construction of a house is a serious matter, and a man who is anxious to build one should never think merely in terms of having some kind of roof over his head. He should realize that certain principles of construction should be observed if he is to have a satisfactory and durable edifice. That is why men consult architects; and the architect draws up plans and specifications and makes his calculations. The wise man is anxious to know the right way to do things; and so he listens to instruction and is prepared to be taught. But the foolish man is not interested in such things; he wants a house; he cannot be bothered about rules and regulations. 'Put it up,' he says. He is impatient, contemptuous of instruction and teaching, saying that he wants 'to get on with it'. That is the typical mentality of the foolish person, both in ordinary life and in connection with things spiritual.

Not only is he in too much of a hurry to listen to instruction, but this foolish man also considers it unnecessary. In his opinion his ideas are the best. He has nothing to learn from anybody. 'Everything is all right,' he says. 'There is no need to be so cautious and to bother so much about these details.' 'Let us get the house built' is his slogan. He does not care what has been done in the past, but simply follows his own impulses and ideas. I am not

caricaturing this type of person. Just think of people you have
seen and known going into business, or getting married, or
building houses, or anything similar, and you will agree that that
is a true picture of this foolish mentality which thinks it knows all,
is satisfied with its own opinion, and is always in a hurry to put it
into effect.

Finally, it is a mentality that never thinks things right through,
it never stops to envisage and consider possibilities and eventualities. The foolish man who built his house without a foundation, and on the sand, did not stop to think or to ask himself,
'Now what may happen? Is it possible that the river which is so
pleasant to look at in the summer may, in the winter, suddenly
become very swollen as the result of heavy rain or snow and I
may be flooded out?' He did not stop to think of that; he just
wanted a pleasant house in that particular position, and he put
it up without considering any one of these things. And if someone
had come along and said, 'Look here, my friend, it is no use
putting up a house like that on the sand. Don't you realize what
may happen in this locality? You don't know what that river is
capable of doing. I have seen it like a veritable cataract. I have
known storms here that bring down the best-built houses. My
friend, I suggest that you dig deep. Get down to the rock'—the
foolish man would have dismissed it all and persisted in doing
what he considered best for him. In a spiritual sense, he is not
interested in learning from Church history; he is not interested in
what the Bible has to say; he wants to do something, and he
believes it can be done in his way, and away he goes and does it.
He does not consult the plans and specifications; he does not try
to look to the future and envisage certain tests that must inevitably come upon the house that is being built.

The wise man, of course, presents us with a complete contrast
to that. He has one great desire, and that is to build durably. So
he starts by saying, 'I do not know much about this; I am not an
expert in these matters; wisdom dictates therefore that I should
consult people who do know. I want to have plans and specifications, I want some guidance and some instruction. I know men
can build houses quickly, but I want a house that will last. There
are many things that may happen, which will test my ideas of
construction and my house.' That is the essence of wisdom. The
wise man takes trouble to find out all he can; he holds himself
in check, and does not allow his feelings and emotions or his
enthusiasm to carry him away. He desires knowledge, truth and
understanding; is ready to respond to the exhortation of the book

of Proverbs which urges us to seek and to covet wisdom, for 'the gain thereof (is better) than fine gold. She is more precious than rubies'. He is not prepared to take risks, and does not rush off in a hurry; he thinks before he acts.

Turning our attention now to the difference between the two houses, there are but two matters calling for comment. The first is that the time for examination has already passed. When the house is built it is already too late. The time for examination is at the very beginning. These two men and their operations must be watched when they are prospecting and planning and choosing the site and location. The time to watch your jerry-builder is at the beginning, to see what he does as regards laying a foundation. It is not enough just to look at the house when it is completed. Indeed, it may look better than the other. That, in turn, leads to the second point which is that, though the difference between the two houses is not obvious, it is nevertheless vital, for ultimately the most important thing about a house is the foundation. This is a truth which is frequently emphasized in the Bible. The foundation, which seems so insignificant and unimportant because it is out of sight, is nevertheless the most vital and important thing of all. If the foundation is wrong, everything else must be wrong. Was not that Paul's great argument when he said, 'Other foundation can no man lay than that is laid, which is Jesus Christ'? The foundation, the first principles, are more important than anything else. Another reason for the vital significance of this one difference between the houses is brought out by the coming of the tests later. They are certain to come sooner or later. We shall not stay with the application of that to our lives now; but as certainly as we are in this life the tests are going to come for every one of us, and we shall have to face them. They are inexorable and unavoidable; and in view of that nothing matters more than the foundation.

Our Lord drew this graphic and dramatic picture of the difference between the two men and the two houses because it is all of vital importance in the spiritual realm. Everything we have been saying provides us with the means of analysing the difference between the Christian and the pseudo-Christian. Is it not significant that we hear so very little today about what the Puritans called the 'false professor'? Read the history of the Church in this land, and you will find that in great periods such as the Puritan era and the Evangelical Revival they paid great attention to this subject. It is seen in the way in which Whitefield and Wesley and others examined the converts before they admitted them to membership of their classes. The same is seen in the great days of the Church in Scotland, and in the first hundred years of the story of the Presbyterian Church of Wales. Indeed it has always been the most prominent feature among all who think of the Church as 'the gathered saints'.

How are we to exercise this discrimination in practice? Let us adopt exactly the same technique as we have already employed. The first thing we have to say about the Christian and the pseudo-Christian is that they have certain points in common. As there were certain similarities between the two builders and the two houses, so there are certain similarities between these two people. The first is that you tend to find them in the same place. The two men in the picture put up their houses in the same locality, they wanted to be near each other and near the river. It is exactly the same in the realm of religion. The true Christian and his false counterpart are generally to be found in the same sphere. You generally find them both in the Church, as members together. They sit and listen to precisely the same gospel; and both seem to like doing so. They are to all appearance in exactly the same position, having the same general outlook and interested in the same activities. The man who is deluded by the counterfeit is not outside the Church; he is inside it. He likes being connected with the Church and he may be an active member of it. These two men are, on the surface, as like each other as were the two builders and their houses in the picture.

But they are not only found in the same place. As we saw, the two men appear to have the same general desires. And in the spiritual application the essence of the difficulty lies in the fact that the nominal Christian has the same general desires as the true Christian. What are these? He desires forgiveness and wants to believe that his sins are forgiven. He wants peace. He went to a meeting in the first place, because life had made him restless. He was unhappy and could not find satisfaction, so he went to the meeting and began to listen. It is a great mistake to think that the only person who desires peace within and the 'quiet heart' is the true Christian. The world today is hungering and thirsting for this peace, and is searching for it. Many people come into the sphere of Christianity because they desire it, as others turn to the various cults.

The same thing is true, also, of the desire for comfort and consolation. Life is hard and difficult and we all tend to be weary and sad, so the world is longing for comfort. The result is that there are many people who come to the Church just, as it were, to be drugged. They sit in the service and do not even listen to what is said. They say that there is something about the atmosphere of the building which is soothing. They are longing for comfort and consolation. The true and the false share that in common.

The same applies in the matter of guidance and the desire to find a way out of our troubles and difficulties. It is not only the true Christian that is interested in guidance. There are unbelievers who have made great mistakes in life, and who are unhappy as a result. They say, 'I always seem to do the wrong thing; I try to work things out but my decisions are always wrong.' Then suddenly they hear someone speaking about guidance, someone who claims an infallible guidance, who says that if you do what he tells you things can never go wrong, and they jump at the teaching with avidity. We must not blame them; it is very understandable. We all know this longing for guidance, for infallible guidance, so that we may cease from making mistakes and always do the right thing and make the right decision. The 'false professor' desires that quite as much as the true Christian.

In exactly the same way he may have a desire to live a good life. You need not be a true Christian in order to desire to live a better life. There are highly moral, ethical men outside the realm of Christianity who are very concerned to live a better life. That is why they read philosophy and study ethical systems. They want to live a good and moral life. Emerson's teaching is still popular. We cannot hope to discriminate between these two men by these tests alone.

Dare we go further and say that the 'false professor' may be very interested in and desirous of spiritual power? Read again that account in Acts viii of Simon the sorcerer in Samaria. That man saw Philip working miracles, and he was impressed. He had been doing that kind of thing too, but not with this ease and power; and he joined himself to the Christians. Then when he saw that Peter and John by laying their hands on people gave them the gift of the Holy Ghost, Simon became covetous, and offered them money for the possession of that power. He coveted it, and his spiritual descendants in these days may likewise covet and desire spiritual power. He sees a man preaching with spiritual power, and says, 'I would like to be like that.' He pictures himself standing in a pulpit and apparently exercising great power, and it appeals to his carnal nature. There are many examples of men who were blind to spiritual truth but who nevertheless were most desirous of possessing spiritual power. It is as subtle as that.

Finally, the 'false professor' also desires to get to heaven. He is a man who believes in heaven and hell, and he does not want to go to perdition. He very definitely desires to go to heaven. Have you not known such people? Many can be found outside the Church altogether. They most certainly want to go to heaven, and say that they have always believed in God. If that is true of the man obviously outside, how much more is it true of this nominal Christian who is inside the realm and sphere of Christian interest?

So we find these strange similarities between these two persons. They seem to believe the same things and desire the same things. They are similar also in that not only do they desire the same things, they even seem to have the same things. That is the most alarming thought of all, but the two previous pictures have emphasized that truth quite as much as this one does. The 'false professor' believes he is safe. The people who had cast out devils and done many wonderful works in the name of Christ were quite sure of their salvation. They had no vestige of doubt about it. They believed that they were forgiven; they seemed to be at peace and to be enjoying the comforts of religion; they seemed to have spiritual power and were living a better life; they said, 'Lord, Lord'; and they wanted to spend their eternity with Him. Yet He said to them: 'I never knew you: depart from me, ye that work iniquity.' Do you realize that it is possible to have a false sense of forgiveness? Do you realize that it is possible to have a false peace within you? You say, 'I have not worried about my sins for years.' I can well believe that, if you are only a nominal Christian. The fact that you have not thought about these things for years is an indication in itself that there is something wrong about your sense of security and peace. The man who never knows what it is to have certain fears about himself, fears which drive him to Christ, is in a highly dangerous condition. You can have false peace, false comfort, false guidance. The devil can give you remarkable guidance. Telepathy, and all sorts of occult phenomena and various other agencies can do so too. There are powers that can counterfeit almost everything in the Christian life. And, as we have already seen in the previous paragraph, these people can have a certain spiritual power. There is no doubt about it. They can have power to 'cast out devils' and to do 'many wonderful works'. There was no evident difference between Judas Iscariot and the eleven other disciples, though he was 'the son of perdition'.

According to our Lord's teaching, therefore, the similarities between the true and the false can include such matters and extend even as far as that. Nevertheless our Lord's teaching is that though there are these many similarities between these two men and the two houses in the parable, and in the realm of Christian profession, yet there is a vital difference. It is not obvious on the surface, but if you look for it, it is perfectly clear and unmistakable. If we take the trouble to apply our analysis, we cannot fail to see it. We have already indicated the nature of the tests in our analysis of the foolish man. All we need to do is to apply them to ourselves—this hurry, this mentality that does not listen to warnings, that is not concerned about plans and specifications, that thinks it knows what it wants and what is best and goes all out for it. Let us examine ourselves in the light of these criteria, and then we shall see very clearly to which category we belong. I can sum it up in the form of a question: What is your supreme desire? Are you out for the benefits and blessings of the Christian life and salvation, or have you a deeper and profounder desire? Are you out for the fleshly carnal results, or do you long to know God and to become more and more like the Lord Jesus Christ? Are you hungering and thirsting after righteousness?

CHAPTER TWENTY-EIGHT

ROCK OR SAND?

SO far we have dealt mainly with the mechanics of our Lord's picture of the two men and the two houses. Obviously, with a picture like this, the first thing to do is to look at the picture itself, and discover its meaning. Then that can be applied to the spiritual condition under consideration. We have already begun to do this, but we must now proceed with it in detail.

What are the characteristics of the merely nominal or pseudo-Christian? We can divide them into general and particular. In general, they are obviously the very things which we observed in the foolish man who built his house upon the sand. That is to say, he is foolish, hasty and superficial. He does not believe very much in doctrine, or in understanding the Scriptures; he wants to enjoy Christianity without much trouble. He cannot be bothered with all these doctrines and definitions, he is in a great hurry, and he is always impatient of instruction, and experience and guidance. He is, indeed, generally impatient of all true knowledge; that is his chief characteristic according to our Lord's picture of him. So far we have considered his mentality; and before going on to our next consideration, I want to stress the importance of that. There is nothing which provides such a true index of what a man really is as his general mentality. It is a mistake to ignore this and to concentrate only on his actions in detail.

But turning now to the particulars—what are the characteristics of the 'false professor'? The first thing about him is that, like the man in the picture, he is a man who is out to please himself. Analyse all he does, and listen to what he says, and you will find that it all revolves around himself. That is really the key to everything he does and everything he says; self is at the centre of his life, and self controls his outlook and all his actions. He desires ease and comfort and certain benefits. That is why he is to be found in the realm of the Church. He is anxious to obtain certain blessings, and in this he differs from the man who is right out in the world, and who does not claim to have any beliefs at all. This man has discovered that there are certain blessings offered in Christianity. He is interested in them, and wants to know something about them and how to obtain them. He is always thinking in terms of: What can I get? What will it give me? What benefits are likely to accrue to me if I go in for it? That is the kind of motive that animates him. And because this is his attitude, he does not really face the full teaching of the gospel, nor want to know the whole counsel of God.

Let us consider this in detail. We saw, in looking at the picture earlier, that the trouble with the man who builds his house hurriedly and without foundations upon the sand, is that he does not believe in consulting manuals on architecture and house building, he does not believe in going to an architect, he does not want plans and specifications. Indeed, all such details seem to him an unnecessary fuss, and he has no interest in them. It is exactly the same with the false believer. He does not really trouble to study the Word of God; he is not a true student of the Bible. He may indeed have a certain interest in the grammar or the mechanics of Scripture, but he is not really concerned to know the message of the Book; he has never really allowed himself to face its full teaching. Paul was able to return to the elders of the church at Ephesus and to say to them that he was very happy about one thing, that he had delivered unto them 'all the counsel of God'. He did not keep anything back. The message he had been given by the risen Lord he had given to them. There were parts of it that hurt; parts that perhaps he would rather not have given, but it was not his message; it was the whole counsel of God, and he had given it to them as from God. The superficial false believer is not interested in that.

Secondly, he picks out what he likes, and concentrates on what appeals to him. For instance, he likes the doctrine of the love of God, but not the doctrine of the justice of God. He does not like the idea of God as a holy God, and a righteous God. The idea of the holiness of God is repellent to him, so he does not read about it. He knows that there are certain great passages in the Bible that manifest the love of God, and he can recite them by heart because he reads them so often. He thinks he knows all about John iii. 16, but he does not even read that properly. He emphasizes a portion of it, but he does not like the idea of 'should not perish'. He does not go to the end of that same third chapter where it says, 'The wrath of God abideth on him'—that he does not believe and does not like. He is interested in the love of God, and in forgiveness. He is interested, in other words, in everything that gives him the feeling of comfort, and happiness, and joy and peace within. So, whether consciously or unconsciously, he picks and chooses as he reads the Bible. There are many people who do that. There was quite a vogue in that kind of thing in the early part of this century. There were people who never read the Epistles of the apostle Paul; they read only the Gospels. And they did not read the whole of the Gospels because they felt that there were things that were offensive, so they narrowed it down to the Sermon on the Mount. But even here, in the same way, they did not read the Beatitudes, they simply read about 'loving your enemies', etc. They were pacifists and idealists who did not believe, they said, in striking back, but in turning the other cheek. That is the typical false believer. He extracts and picks out that which pleases him, and ignores the rest. You see it so clearly in the picture of the man who built his house upon the sand, and it is exactly the same in the spiritual realm.

We should examine ourselves constantly in the light of the Word. And if we are not reading it in such a way as to be examined by it, we are not reading it correctly. We must face these things. Do I take the whole message of the Scriptures? Am I taking the whole counsel of God? Do I accept the teaching concerning the wrath of God as I do that concerning the love of God? Am I as ready to believe in the righteousness of God as in His mercy; in the justice and holiness of God as well as in His compassion and longsuffering? That is the question. The characteristic of the false believer is that he does not face it all; he just picks out what he wants and likes, and ignores the rest. In other words, his outstanding characteristic always is that he never faces completely and honestly the nature of sin, and the effects of sin, in the light of the holiness of God. The trouble with him is that he never wants to feel unhappy, he never wants to feel a sense of dissatisfaction with himself, or a sense of discomfort. The thing he wants to avoid at all costs is being unhappy or being made to feel uncomfortable. He does not like the people who make him feel uncomfortable, nor the passages in the Bible that do the same, so he picks and chooses. He is always out for ease and comfort and happiness; and he never faces properly the biblical doctrine of sin, because it disturbs him and causes him disquiet.

But in so doing he is evading a vital part of the great message of the Bible. The Bible in the first instance is a terrible exposition and a graphic delineation of the effects of sin. That is why it gives all that history in the Old Testament; why, for instance, it shows a man like David, one of its greatest heroes, falling into gross sin, committing adultery and murder. Why does it do that? It is to impress upon us the effects of sin, to teach us that there is something in all of us that can drag us down to that, that we are all by nature false and foul and vile. The false believer does not like such teaching. He dislikes it so much that he even objects to the distinction which the Bible draws between sin and sins. I knew a man who used to attend a place of worship, but now no longer does so. His main reason for staying away is that he did not like the preacher's constant talk about sin. He did not object to hearing about sins, because he was prepared to admit that he was not absolutely perfect. But when the preacher said that man's very nature was vile and foul, he felt that that was going too far. He was not as bad as that! But the Bible talks about the sinful nature and says of us that we are 'shapen in iniquity, and in sin did my mother conceive me', that we are all 'by nature the children of wrath', that we must say, if we speak truthfully, that 'in me (that is in my flesh) dwelleth no good thing', and that nothing will suffice for us but to be born again and to be given a new nature. The nominal and formal Christian hates that doctrine and avoids it.

In other words, the trouble with him ultimately is that he does not really desire to know God. He wants God's blessing, but he does not want God. He does not really desire to serve God and to worship Him with the whole of his being, he simply wants certain things that he believes God can give him. To sum it up, his real trouble is that he does not know the meaning of the expression 'hungering and thirsting after righteousness'. He is not interested in righteousness; he is not interested in holiness. He really does not want to be like Christ; he simply wants to be made comfortable. He is like the man in the picture who wants to build a house hurriedly, so that he can sit in his armchair and enjoy himself. He wishes all to be well with him in this life and in the life to come, but he wants it on his own terms and in his own way. He is impatient, and dislikes all teaching and instruction that warn him that this is not sufficient if he really wants to have a satisfactory and durable edifice.

What, then, are the characteristics of the true Christian? Put positively, it is that he 'doeth the will of my Father which is in heaven'. Our Lord says: 'Not every one that saith unto me, Lord, Lord... but he that doeth the will of my Father which is in heaven.' 'Therefore whosoever heareth these sayings of mine, and doeth them, I will liken him unto a wise man.' What does this mean?

The first part of the answer is to make clear what it does not mean. That is most important. Obviously it does not mean 'justification by works'. Our Lord is not saying here that the man who is truly Christian is the man who, having listened to the Sermon on the Mount, puts it into practice and thereby makes himself a Christian. Why is that interpretation impossible? For the good reason that the Beatitudes make it quite impossible. At the very beginning we emphasized that the Sermon on the Mount must be taken as a whole, and so it must. We start with the Beatitudes, and the first statement is: 'Blessed are the poor in spirit.' We can try from now until we are dead, but we shall never make ourselves 'poor in spirit', and we can never make ourselves conform to any of the Beatitudes. That is a sheer impossibility, so it cannot mean justification by works. Then take that great climax at the end of the fifth chapter: 'Be ye therefore perfect, even as your Father which is in heaven is perfect.' That again is quite impossible to man in his own strength, and proves further that this passage does not teach justification by works. Were it to do so it would contradict the whole message of the New Testament which tells us that what we have failed to do, God has sent His Son into the world to do for us—'with men this is impossible, but with God all things are possible'. No man shall be justified by the deeds of the law, but only by the righteousness of Jesus Christ.

Neither is it a teaching of sinless perfection. Many people read these pictures at the end of the Sermon on the Mount, and say that they mean that the only man who is allowed or able to enter into the kingdom of heaven is the man who, having read the Sermon on the Mount, puts each detail into practice, always and everywhere. This again is obviously impossible. If that were the teaching, then we could be quite certain that there never has been and there never will be a single Christian in the world. For 'all have sinned, and come short of the glory of God'. We have all failed. 'If we say that we have no sin, we deceive ourselves, and the truth is not in us.' It cannot be sinless perfection, therefore, which is advocated here.

What then is it? It is none other than the doctrine which James, in his Epistle, summarizes in the words, 'Faith without works is dead.' It is simply a perfect definition of faith. Faith without works is not faith, it is dead. The life of faith is never a life of ease; faith is always practical. The difference between faith and intellectual assent is that intellectual assent simply says, 'Lord, Lord', but does not do His will. In other words, though I may say 'Lord, Lord' to the Lord Jesus Christ, there is no meaning in it unless I regard Him as my Lord, and willingly become His bondslave. My words are idle words, and I do not mean 'Lord, Lord', unless I obey Him. Faith without works is dead.

Or, to put it another way, true faith always shows itself in the life; it shows itself in the person in general, and it also shows itself in what he does. Mark the double emphasis—faith shows itself in the person in general, as well as in what he says and does. There must be no contradiction between a man's appearance and general demeanour and what he says and does. The first thing we are told about the Christian in the Sermon on the Mount is that he must be 'poor in spirit', and if he *is* 'poor in spirit', he never *looks* as if he were proud and self-satisfied. Another thing we are told about him is that he mourns because of his sin, and that he is meek. The man who is meek never looks pleased with himself. We are talking of what he looks like before he has said or done anything. True faith always shows itself in a man's general appearance, in the total impression he gives, as well as in what he says and does in particular. You have sometimes seen men saying, 'Lord, Lord,' who almost give the impression that they are patronizing God as they say it, so full of themselves are they, so pleased with themselves, so self-confident. They do not know what Paul meant when he said to the church at Corinth, 'I was with you in weakness, and in fear, and in much trembling.' He preached the gospel with a sense of awe upon him because it was the message of God, and he was aware of his own unworthiness and the seriousness of the situation. So we must not forget that faith shows itself in a man's general bearing as well as in what he says and does.

Faith always shows itself in the whole personality. We can summarize it all in the words we find in the first and second chapters of John's first Epistle, where we read, 'If we say that we have fellowship with him, and walk in darkness, we lie, and do not the truth.' 'He that saith, I know him, and keepeth not his commandments, is a liar, and the truth is not in him.' We can see where those have gone astray who hold that the Sermon on the Mount cannot apply to us, but only to the disciples of our Lord's own day, and to the Jews of some future kingdom which is yet to come. They say it must be so, otherwise we are put under the law and not under grace. But the words just quoted from the first Epistle of John were written 'under grace', and John puts it like that specifically: If any man says, 'I know him'—that is your faith, believing in the grace of Christ and the free forgiveness of sin—if any man says, 'I know him, and keepeth not his commandments, (he) is a liar.' That is simply repeating what our Lord says here about those who shall enter the kingdom of heaven: 'Not every one that saith unto me, Lord, Lord, . . . but he that doeth the will of my Father which is in heaven.' And it is the message of the whole of the New Testament. He 'gave himself for us', says Paul to Titus, 'that he might . . . purify unto himself a peculiar people, zealous of good works.' We have been saved 'unto holiness'. He set us apart in order to prepare us for Himself, and 'every man that hath this hope in him purifieth himself, even as he is pure'. That is the doctrine of the Bible.

But we must apply all this in a yet more detailed manner. What is implied by putting into operation the Sermon on the Mount? How can I know whether I am a 'wise' man or a 'foolish' man? Again let me start with a few simple negatives. One of the best tests is this. Do you resent this Sermon on the Mount? Do you dislike it? Do you object to hearing preaching on it? If you do, you are a 'foolish' person. The foolish person always dislikes the Sermon on the Mount when it is presented as it is, in all its parts. Do you feel it is making things impossible for you? Do you become annoyed at its standard? Do you say it is quite impossible? Do you say, 'It is grim, this preaching is grim, it is making everything hopeless'? Is that your reaction to it? It is always the reaction of the false believer. He is impatient with the Sermon on the Mount; he resents being examined, he hates being examined because it makes him feel uncomfortable. The true Christian is entirely different; he does not resent it, as we shall see. He does not resent the condemnation of the Sermon on the Mount, and he never defends himself against it. We can put it like this. We know that we betray ourselves by our idle remarks, and we can often tell a man by his immediate reaction. We are all so subtle and clever, that when we take second thoughts and begin to think about a thing, we are a little more guarded and careful in what we say. What really shows what we are is our instinctive answer, our immediate reaction. And if our reaction to the Sermon on the Mount is one of resentment, if we feel it is hard and difficult and makes things impossible, and that it is not the nice sort of Christianity we thought it was, we are not true believers.

Another characteristic of the false believer at this point is that, having heard it, he forgets all about it. He is a forgetful hearer who listens to the message and immediately forgets it. He is interested for a moment, then it goes from his mind, perhaps as the result of a conversation in the vestibule on the way out of church.

Another feature of the false professors is that while, in general, they may admire the Sermon and praise its teaching, they never put it into practice. Or they will approve certain parts of it and ignore others. So many people seem to think that the Sermon on the Mount simply says one thing, such as 'love your enemies'. They do not seem to understand all these other things. But we must take it as a whole, chapters v, vi and vii, the Beatitudes, the law, instruction, everything, it is all one Sermon.

But let us turn to the positive characteristics of the true believer. He is a man who does face this teaching, and he faces the whole of it. He does not pick and choose, he allows every part of the Bible to speak to him. He is not impatient. He takes time to read it, he does not rush to a few favourite Psalms and use them as a kind of hypnotic when he cannot sleep at night; he allows the whole Word to examine him and to search him. Far from resenting this searching, he welcomes it. He knows it is good for him, so he does not object to the pain. He realizes that 'no chastening for the present is joyous, but grievous'; but he knows that 'afterward it (invariably) yieldeth the peaceable fruit of righteousness to them that are exercised thereby'. In other words the true Christian humbles himself under the Word. He agrees that what it says of him is true. Indeed, he says, 'it has not said enough about me'. He does not resent its criticism, nor that of other people, but rather he says to himself, 'They do not say the half, they do not know me.' He humbles himself under the Word and all its criticism. He admits and confesses his utter failure and his complete unworthiness. You see, the man who is right with respect to this Sermon is a man who, having humbled himself, submits himself to it, becomes poor in spirit, becomes a mourner for his sins, becomes meek because he knows how worthless he is. He immediately conforms to the Beatitudes because of the effect of the Word upon him, and then, because of that, he desires to conform to the type and pattern set before him. Here is a very good test. Would you *like* to live the Sermon on the Mount? Is that your true desire? Is that your ambition? If it is, it is a very good and healthy sign. Any man who desires to live this type and kind of life is a Christian. He hungers and thirsts after righteousness; that is the big thing in his life. He is not content with what he is. He says, 'O that I might be like the saints I have read about, like Hudson Taylor, or Brainerd, or Calvin. If only I were like the men who lived in caves and dens and sacrificed and suffered everything for His sake. If only I were like Paul. O that I were more like my blessed Lord Himself.' The man who can say that honestly is a man who is building on the rock. He is conforming to the Beatitudes. Observe the nature of the test. It is not asking whether you are sinless or perfect; it is asking what you would like to be, what you desire to be.

Then, of course, the true believer is a man who accepts our Lord's teaching concerning the law. You remember how, in the fifth chapter, our Lord interpreted the ancient law spiritually with regard to certain things. The believer accepts that and believes it is right; he is not content with simply refraining from committing adultery as an act, he does not want to *look* at a woman to lust after her. He says, 'That is right; one must be clean in heart, and not only in actions, and I want to be clean like that.' He accepts fully our Lord's teaching about the law.

In the same way he accepts the teaching about doing our alms in secret. He does not advertise his good deeds—neither does he draw attention to the fact that he does not advertise! His left hand really does not know what his right hand is doing. He also remembers the teaching about prayer, and about not setting our affections on the things of the world, about having a 'single' eye. He remembers that we are not even to worry about our daily bread, but are to leave it all to our Father who feeds the sparrows and will certainly not neglect His children. He remembers the instruction about not judging or condemning our brother, and about taking the beam out of our own eye before dealing with the mote in our brother's eye. He recalls that we are taught to do unto others as we would that they should do unto us; he accepts the whole teaching in its fullness. But not only that, he bemoans his failure to live it out. He wants to, he desires to, he tries to, but he realizes that he fails. But then he believes the next portion of the teaching, and he asks, he seeks, he knocks. He believes the message that tells him that by the Holy Spirit these things are possible, and he remembers that Christ has said in this Sermon, 'Ask, and it shall be given you; seek, and ye shall find; knock, and it shall be opened unto you.' And he goes on until he obtains. That is what is meant by 'doing these things'. It means that a man's supreme desire is to do these things and to be like the Lord Jesus Christ. It means he is a man who not only wants forgive-

ness, not only wants to escape hell and to go to heaven. Quite as
much, in a sense, he wants positive holiness in this life and in this
world. He wants to be righteous, he sings from his heart that
hymn of Charles Wesley's—

> O for a heart to praise my God,
> A heart from sin set free;
> A heart that always feels Thy blood
> So freely shed for me.

That is the man who builds upon the rock. He is a man who
desires and prays for holiness and who strives after it. He does his
utmost to be holy, because his supreme desire is to know Christ.
Not only to be forgiven, not only to go to heaven, but to know
Christ now, to have Christ as his Brother, to have Christ as his
Companion, to be walking with Christ in the light now, to enjoy
a foretaste of heaven here in this world of time—that is the man
who builds upon the rock. He is a man who loves God for God's
sake, and whose supreme desire and concern is that God's name
and God's glory may be magnified and spread abroad.

There, then, are the details of this matter. That is what is
meant by 'doing' these things. That is what is meant by practising the Sermon on the Mount. It is to agree with the Shorter
Catechism that 'the chief end of man is to glorify God and to
enjoy Him for ever'. You know that you will never bring yourself
to perfection, but your desire, your effort, is to that end, and all
the time you are relying upon the Holy Spirit who has been given
you to enable you to do so. That is the doctrine, and anyone who
can face these tests, the negative and the positive, in that way can
be happy and certain and sure that his house is being built upon
the rock. If, on the other hand, you find you cannot answer these
tests satisfactorily, there is but one inevitable conclusion: you
have been building upon the sand. And your house will collapse.
It will do so for certain on the day of judgment; it may well do so
before that, when the next war comes, perhaps when the hydro-
gen bomb is let loose, or when you lose your money, your goods,
your possessions. You will see, then, that you have nothing. If you
see that now, admit it, confess it to God without a second's delay.
Confess it and humble yourself 'under the mighty hand of God'.
Acknowledge it and cast yourself upon His love and mercy, tell
Him that, at last, you desire to be holy and righteous; ask Him to
give you His Spirit and to reveal to you the perfect work of Christ
on your behalf. Follow Christ, and He will lead you to this true
holiness, 'without which no man shall see the Lord'.

CHAPTER TWENTY-NINE

THE TRIAL AND THE TESTS OF FAITH

WE come now to some final considerations about the picture which is contained in verses 24–27 and also about the two previous pictures which we have already studied. We remind ourselves that the teaching in general is designed to warn us against the terrible and subtle danger of self-deception. It is astonishing to note how much space is given in the New Testament to warnings. How slow we are to observe that and to heed it. There are constant warnings against a light and superficial belief, against the tendency just to say, 'Lord, Lord,' and do no more, warnings against the danger of trusting to works and to our own activities. We have been reminded of that very forcibly in the second picture. It is something that is to be found throughout the New Testament Scriptures; it is seen frequently in the teaching of our Lord Himself, and in the teaching of the apostles afterwards.

But it includes at the same time the danger of trusting to feelings, especially to false feelings. There is nothing that is so surprising to the natural mind as the New Testament expositions on the subject of love. For some reason or other we tend to think of love as being a mere matter of sentiment and feeling; we tend to regard it as simply an emotion. And we tend to carry this over into our thinking concerning the New Testament's great gospel of love, and the announcement of the love of God to offending sinners. Yet think for a moment of John's Gospel and his first Epistle in which so much is said about love, and also of 1 Corinthians xiii. You will see that their whole emphasis is upon the fact that love is something which is very practical. How often does our Lord say in various ways, 'He that hath my commandments, and keepeth them, he it is that loveth me.'

That is the precise teaching at this point. All this warning at the end of the Sermon on the Mount is simply designed to emphasize the one thing, that 'not every one that saith unto me, Lord, Lord, shall enter into the kingdom of heaven, but he that doeth the will of my Father'. The recurring emphasis on this point is designed to save us from deluding ourselves into thinking that all is well with us because of some vague, general feeling which we may possess. Our Lord says that it is useless to talk about loving Him unless we keep His commandments. 'He that loves Me truly', He seems to say, 'does what I tell him to do'. Nothing is so fallacious as to substitute feelings and sensibilities for definite obedience. That is something that is stressed very emphatically in this great final word of warning, and that is why we have considered in detail what is meant by doing the will of our Father which is in heaven. The wise man is the man who, having heard these sayings, does them.

But we still have to consider why our Lord put His teaching in this particular form. There is in each one of these pictures, as you observe, a note of warning. We have been making casual reference to that as we have been considering each one. But, clearly, we cannot complete this series of considerations without taking up the question of judgment which He announces in every one of the pictures from verse 13. You remember that it is in the verse where He speaks of entering in at the strait gate that He begins to apply the message of the entire Sermon and to enforce its doctrine; and from there onwards the note of judgment comes in. 'Enter ye in', He says, 'at the strait gate: for wide is the gate, and broad is the way, that leadeth to destruction'. There is the note of warning at once. It is to be found again in exactly the same way in connection with the second picture, where He likens the true Christian to the good tree and the false Christian to the corrupt tree. He tells us that 'every tree that bringeth not forth good fruit is hewn down, and cast into the fire'. In the next picture we get it in the words: 'Many will say to me in that day, Lord, Lord, have we not done these various things in thy name. Then will I profess unto them, I never knew you: depart from me, ye that work iniquity.' And here it is, strikingly, in the last picture of the two houses and the two men, because He tells us that a day came when the houses were tested and that one of them fell, and 'great was the fall of it'. So we are forced to consider this great question of judgment. Indeed, we have seen that not only is it the prominent note in these pictures at the end of the Sermon, it has been the dominant note right through this chapter, beginning with 'Judge not, that ye be not judged . . .', in verse 1. The note that runs right through this final exhortation is the tremendous note of judgment.

In a sense the message can be put thus: apart from any other consideration, false religion is useless. It is wrong, of course, just as anything that is false is always wrong; but apart from its being wrong, it is in the last analysis of no value at all. It leads in the end to nothing. It may give temporary satisfaction; but it fails to stand the real tests. That is the thing that is emphasized here. That broad way seems safe enough; that corrupt and evil tree in general looks healthy, and you even imagine its fruit to be good until you examine it and find that it is not. In the same way the house that the foolish man built upon the sand appears to be perfect; it looks sound and durable. But the fact is that in the end none of these things are of any value at all; they fail to stand up to the test. That is surely something about which there can be no disagreement. The real thing we need to know about any view of life, or any situation in life that we may hold, is whether it will stand the test. Is it going to help us and be of value to us in the hour of our greatest need? There is little value in a house, however luxurious and comfortable it may be, if when the storms come and the floods begin to beat upon it, it suddenly collapses. That is what we call living in 'a fool's paradise'. It seemed so wonderful when the sun was shining, and when, in a sense, we had no need of its protection and might have been quite satisfied with a tent. But we need a house that can stand up to the storms and the hurricanes. A house built upon the sand cannot do so and is obviously of no value at all.

The Bible makes much of this. It has some very alarming pictures of the apparent success and affluence of the ungodly, spreading himself 'like a green bay tree', when everything is going well. But it always shows that in the time of trouble, when all his prosperity has gone, he has nothing to fall back upon. The Bible is at pains to show the utter folly of the man who is not a Christian. Apart from anything else, what a foolish man he is, living for, and trusting to things that cannot help him in the hour of his greatest need. Think of our Lord's picture of that rich fool who had his barns bursting with goods and who was thinking of building greater ones, when God suddenly said to him, 'Thou fool, this night thy soul shall be required of thee; then whose shall those things be?' The Bible is full of that kind of teaching.

But this teaching that what is false is worthless is not confined to the Bible; human experience through the centuries confirms and establishes this. We can study that in the light of this particular picture. Our Lord says that everything we build in this world, everything that we are relying upon, every preparation that we make, our whole view of life, is going to be subjected to tests. He pictures the tests in the form of the rain descending and the floods coming and the winds blowing. It is something

universal; it is something that is going to happen to the wise and
to the foolish alike. Nowhere does the Bible tell us that immediately you become a Christian all your troubles end, and that
the remainder of the story is that 'all lived happily ever after'.
Nothing of the kind. 'The rain descended, the floods came, the
winds blew' on the one house, just as they did upon the other.
The whole of humanity is subjected to these tests.

The question as to what our Lord meant exactly by the
details in this picture is full of interest. Some teach that they refer
only to the day of judgment; but that is a totally inadequate
understanding of the picture. It certainly includes the day of
judgment; but what our Lord says here applies to life in this
world as well as to what will happen to us after death and beyond
the grave.
It is a dangerous thing, of course, to press the details of any
picture too far, and yet, surely, our Lord did not take the trouble
to differentiate between the rain and the flood and the wind to
no purpose. Obviously He was anxious to convey certain definite
ideas, and we can discover something of what is represented by
these pictures. Think of the rain, for instance. This rain that He
speaks of is something that is going to meet us all. We are all in
one of two positions; we are either like the wise man or the
foolish one; we are either, as we saw earlier, doing our utmost to
put into practice the teaching of the Sermon on the Mount, or
else we are not; either we are Christians, or we are deluding ourselves into thinking that we are Christians, and picking and
choosing the things that please us out of the gospel, and saying,
'This is quite enough. You need not take these things too
seriously; you must not become narrow. All is well as long as you
believe things in general.' But our Lord teaches here that if we
are in the wrong position our supposed belief will not help us at
all; indeed, it will let us down completely when we need it most.
What does He mean by the rain? I think He means things like
illness, loss or disappointment, something going wrong in your
life; something on which you were banking suddenly collapsing
before your eyes; perhaps being let down by somebody else, or
experiencing some grievous disappointment, a sudden change
for the worse in your circumstances, or overwhelming grief and
bereavement. These are the things that, at some time or another,
come to all of us. There are certain things in life which are
unavoidable; try as we may to evade them, we have to face them
in the end. It is very difficult for those who are young and

bounding with health and vigour to think of themselves as old people, finding it difficult to move from one room to another, or even from one chair to another. But that is the sort of thing that does happen. Age advances, health and vigour go, illness comes. These things, as our Lord shows here, are inevitable, and when they come they test us. It is no small trial to spend weeks and months in the same room; it tests one to the very foundations. The rain, then, covers things of that kind, and includes these tests that search and try us to the very depths.

But not only did the rain descend; our Lord tells us that the floods came and beat upon the house. I always think that this represents, in general, the world, using that term in its biblical sense, as meaning the worldly outlook, the worldly type of life. Whether we like it or not, and whether we are true believers or false, the world comes beating against this house of ours, hurling itself in its full flood-tide against us. We all have great trouble with the world—'the lust of the flesh, and the lust of the eyes, and the pride of life'. As surely as we put up our building in this world, as indeed we are all doing, the world itself will come and test it and try it. Worldliness in its subtlety seeps in everywhere. It comes sometimes with mighty power; at other times it will do equal damage by flooding in silently, unobserved and unsuspected. There is literally no end to the forms it may assume. We all know something of this. Sometimes it comes as an enticement, something that draws us and appeals to us and pleads with us; it paints a glowing picture to attract us. At another time it will come as persecution. The world does not care ultimately what method it uses as long as it attains its object. If it can entice us from Christ and the Church it will do so, but if enticement fails, it will show its teeth and try persecution. Both ways test us, and one is quite as subtle as the other—'the floods came . . . and beat upon that house'.

We all know something of what it is to feel the house almost rocking at times. It is not so much that the Christian wants to forsake his faith, but the power of the world can be so great that he wonders at times whether his foundation is going to hold. He has a wonderful belief in Christ when he is young, but sooner or later, perhaps in middle life, he begins to think of his future, and his career, and his whole position in life; and he begins to hesitate and to wonder. The slowing down process of age comes in, and a kind of slackness enters—that is the world beating against your house, trying and testing it.

Then there is the wind—'the rain descended, the floods came, and the winds blew'. What does He mean by this—'and the winds blew'? I tend to agree with those who would interpret the wind as being definite Satanic attacks. The devil has many different ways of dealing with us. According to the Word of God, he can transform himself into an angel of light and quote Scripture. He can tempt us through the world. But sometimes he attacks us directly; he may hurl doubts and denials at us. He will bombard us with foul, evil and blasphemous thoughts. Read the lives of godly men of old, and you will find that they have been subjected to this kind of thing. The devil makes violent attacks, trying to blow the house over, as it were, and the saints throughout the centuries have suffered from the power of this form of attack. You may have known good men who have been subject to this, fine Christians, who have lived godly lives; then, somewhere before the end, perhaps on their deathbed, they go through a period of darkness, and the devil attacks them violently. Indeed, 'we wrestle not against flesh and blood, but against principalities, against powers, . . . against spiritual wickedness in high places.' In Ephesians vi the apostle Paul says that the only way to stand is to put on the whole armour of God. And here our Lord says in the same way that nothing but the solid foundation He advocates will enable our house to stand.

These things come to us all. But, finally, of course, certain and inevitable, comes death itself. Some have to endure the rain, others the flood, and others the wind and the hurricane; but we all have to meet and to face the fact of death. It will come to each of us in some shape or form, and will test to the very foundation all we have ever built. What a tremendous thing death is! We have not been through it, so we know nothing about it, although we may sometimes have watched others dying and heard them speak of it. Whether it comes suddenly or gradually, we have to meet it. I say it must be a tremendous thing to pass through that moment when you realize you are going out of this world, and leaving all you have always known, and crossing into that land beyond the veil. There is nothing that so profoundly tests a man as to his foundations as the mighty fact and moment of death.

The real question is, how do we stand up to these things? In many ways the prime business of the preaching of the gospel is to prepare men to stand up to these things. It matters not what your view of life may be, nor what your feelings; if you cannot stand up to those tests which I have enumerated you are an utter failure. Whatever a man's gifts or calling may be, and however noble and good his character, if his view and philosophy of life have not catered for these certainties, he is a fool, and all he has will fail him and collapse beneath his feet just when he most needs help. We have already experienced some of these tests. Here are the questions we must ask ourselves. Do we always find God when we need Him most of all? When these tests come and we turn to Him, do we know He is there? Are we agitated and alarmed? Do we dread His presence, or do we turn as a child to his father, and always know He is there, and always find Him? Are we conscious of His nearness and presence at these critical points, and moments? Have we a deep unshakeable confidence in Him, and an assurance that He will never leave us nor forsake us? Are we able to rejoice in Him at all times, even in tribulation? What is our view of the world at this moment, what is our attitude towards the world? Are we in any hesitancy or doubt as to which of these lives we want to live? Have we any uncertainty? Have we not found the utter uselessness of that worldly life that does not put God and His Christ in the centre? What is death to us? Are we horrified at the thought of it; are we so afraid of it that we are always doing our best to banish it out of our thoughts?

The Bible shows clearly what we should be like in all these respects if we are truly Christian. Psalm xxxvii. 37 says: 'Mark the perfect man, and behold the upright: for the end of that man is peace'. There is nothing so wonderful in this world as the death of a good man, the Christian man. 'Mark him', says Scripture. The psalmist was an old man when he wrote that—'I have been young, and now am old', he says—and this is his experience, this is his advice to young people: 'Mark the perfect man . . . for the end of that man is peace'. Many a man seems to have a good time in this world, but his end is not very peaceful. Poor creature! he has not prepared for it, he is not aware that he is going, he is clutching at anything, and he does not die peacefully. Or listen to this extract from Psalm cxii. 7: 'He shall not be afraid of evil tidings: his heart is fixed, trusting in the Lord'. He is not afraid of pestilences, he is not afraid if wars should arise, he is not afraid of evil tidings. He does not say: 'What are we going to do tomorrow morning?' Not a bit—'his heart is fixed, trusting in the Lord'. Again, take this magnificent word in Isaiah xxviii. 16: 'He that believeth shall not make haste' or, if you prefer it, 'He that believeth shall not be confounded', he that believeth shall not be 'taken unawares'. Why? Because he has been paying heed, he has been preparing, so that whatever comes to meet him he has a foundation. He is not in a hurry, he never makes haste. Our Lord Himself has taught it perfectly in the parable of the sower. He tells us that the false believer 'had no root in himself'. He endured for a while, but when persecution came he was finished. 'He also that received seed among the thorns is he that heareth the word; and the care of this world, and the deceitfulness of riches, choke the word, and he becometh unfruitful.' The teaching of Scripture is endless on this theme.

This is something that is taught positively in Scripture and is confirmed by Christian experience. Read again the account of those first Christians who, when they were being persecuted, even being put to death, thanked God that He had counted them worthy to suffer for His name's sake. We have those great stories of the first martyrs and confessors, who though thrown to the lions in the arena, yet praised God. Far from complaining, Paul, as he writes to the Philippians from prison, gives thanks to God for his imprisonment, because it gives him an opportunity to preach the gospel. He could even endure the treachery of false friends. He was perfectly happy, and quite serene through it all, and could even look into the face of death and say that it was kind, because it meant going 'to be with Christ; which is far better'. He tells the Corinthians that 'our light affliction, which is but for a moment, worketh for us a far more exceeding and eternal weight of glory'. Read 2 Corinthians iv; read the list of his trials and tribulations; despite it all he can say that. And then listen to him, in his old age, facing death again, knowing it was coming; 'For I am now ready to be offered, and the time of my departure is at hand. I have fought a good fight, I have finished my course, I have kept the faith.' What a way to die! It has been the same throughout the centuries ever since the days when Paul wrote these words. Christian men have been repeating these experiences in their lives. Read the stories of the saints, read the stories of the martyrs and the confessors, read about those men who advanced to the stake smiling, preaching from the stake as the flames were encircling them. It is the most glorious story in the whole of history. Read again the stories of the Covenanters, of the great Puritans and many others.

The teaching, therefore, comes to this; it is only the men who have done these things of which our Lord speaks in the Sermon on the Mount who have these experiences. The pseudo-Christian finds that when he needs help, what he regarded as his faith does not help. It forsakes him when he needs it most. There is no question about this. The one common factor in the lives of all those who have been able to face the trials of life triumphantly and gloriously, is that they have always been men who have given themselves to living the Sermon on the Mount. That is the secret of the 'perfect' man, the 'righteous' man, the 'good' man, the 'Christian' man. So if you want to be able to face these things as Paul faced them, you must try to live as Paul lived. There is no other way for it; they all conformed to the same pattern.

But beyond all these things which we meet in this life, there is the certain approach of the day of final judgment. This is a constant theme in the teaching of the Bible. Here it is: 'Many will say to me in that day'. The Bible has a great deal to say about 'that day'. There were people who disagreed with Paul as to how the gospel should be preached, and as to how the Church should be built up. 'All right', says Paul in effect, 'I am not going to argue with you; the day will declare it.' 'We must all appear before the judgment seat of Christ.' It is mentioned everywhere in the Bible. Read in Matthew xxv about the ten virgins, and the talents, and the nations. All things come before Him in the final judgment. But remember that 1 Peter iv. 17 teaches that 'judgment must begin at the house of God'. What is the book of Revelation but a great announcement of this judgment that is coming, when the books will be opened, and all shall be judged everywhere. All will come to judgment. The Bible is full of this, and it tells us that the day of judgment is certain. It tells us that it will be searching, that it will be inward. Everything is known to Him. These men said, 'Have we not done this and that?' And He said, 'I never knew you'. The whole time He has His eye upon them. They do not belong to Him, and He always knew it. Everything is known to Him. 'All things are naked and opened unto the eyes of him with whom we have to do'. He 'is a discerner of the thoughts and intents of the heart'. Nothing can be hid from His sight. Above all we are told that this judgment is final. There is no teaching in Scripture about a second chance, about a further opportunity. Try to produce the evidence, if you can. It is not there. You can perhaps produce two or three highly debatable statements of whose exposition no-one can be certain. But are you going to bank on that while the weight of Scripture everywhere is on the other side? It is final judgment; there is no going back.

How then can we make certain of these things? How am I to live my life here on earth with peace and certainty and assur-

II—21*

ance? How can I make certain that I am building my house upon the rock? How do I really put these things into practice? It is the greatest question in this world. Nothing is more vital than that we should daily remind ourselves of these things. At the risk of being misunderstood, let me put it like this. I sometimes think that there is nothing more dangerous in the Christian life than a mechanical devotional life. I hear people talking glibly about 'having their Q.T.' in the morning. They do not even say 'Quiet Time', they say 'Q.T.' That attitude, as I understand these things, is absolutely fatal. It means that this person has been taught that it is a good thing for a Christian first thing in the morning to read a certain amount of Scripture and then to offer a prayer, before going to his daily work. You observe your 'quiet time' and off you go. Of course, it is a good thing to do; but it can be most dangerous to one's spiritual life if it becomes purely mechanical. I suggest, therefore, that what we should do is this. Certainly read your Scripture, and certainly pray; but not in any mechanical sense, not because you have been told to do it, not because it is 'the done thing'. Do it because the Bible is God's Word, and because He is speaking to you through it. But having read and prayed, stop and meditate, and in your meditation remind yourself of the actual teaching of the Sermon on the Mount. Ask yourself if you are living the Sermon on the Mount, or really trying to do so. We do not talk to ourselves sufficiently; that is our trouble. We talk too much to other people and not enough to ourselves. We must talk to ourselves, and say 'Our Lord said, in effect, I preach this Sermon to you, but it will be of no value to you if you do not do what I say.' Test yourself by the Sermon on the Mount. Remember these pictures at the end of the Sermon. Say to yourself: 'Yes, I am here now; I am young. But I have to die sometime, and am I ready for it?' What would happen to you if you suddenly lost your health, or lost your good looks, or your money or your possessions? What would happen to you if you became disfigured by some disease? Where are you, what are you going to rest upon? Have you faced the inevitability of judgment beyond death? That is the only safe way. It is not really enough just to be reading the Bible and praying; we have to apply what we learn; we have to face ourselves with it, and hold it before us. Do not rely upon activities. Do not say: 'I am so active in Christian work, I must be all right.' Our Lord said that you may not be all right, though you think you are doing it for Him. Just face these things one after another, and test your life by them; and then make certain that you are really keeping this teaching in the forefront and at the very centre of your life. Make quite sure that you are able to say honestly that your supreme desire is to know Him better, to keep His commandments, to live for His glory. However enticing the world may be, say, 'No; I know that I, as a living soul, have to go to meet Him face to face. At all costs that must come first; everything else must fall into the background.' It seems to me that that is the whole purpose of our Lord's picture at the end of this mighty Sermon, namely, that we should be warned against and made aware of the subtle danger of self-delusion, and that we should avoid it by thus examining ourselves daily in His presence, in the light of His teaching. May He grant us grace so to do.

CHAPTER THIRTY

CONCLUSION

IN the last two verses of this chapter we are told by the sacred
writer what effect this famous Sermon on the Mount produced
upon its auditors. They thus provide us at the same time with
the opportunity of considering in general what effect this
Sermon should always produce upon those who read and
consider it.

These two verses are by no means an idle or useless kind of
epilogue. They are of great importance in any consideration of
the Sermon. I have no doubt that that was the reason why the
writer was led by the Holy Spirit to record the effect of the
Sermon, because we are directed here to the Preacher rather
than to the Sermon. We are asked, as it were, having considered
the Sermon, to look at the One who delivered it and preached it.
We have spent much time in considering in detail the teaching
of the Sermon, and in the later chapters, especially, we have been
considering the urgent appeal which our Lord addressed to those
who had been listening. He besought them to put it into practice.
He issued a terrible warning against self-deception, against
merely admiring the Sermon and commending certain things in
it, and failing to realize that, unless we are indeed practising it,
we are outside the kingdom of God, and shall find that all on
which we have been resting will suddenly be taken from us on the
day of judgment.

But the question many may be tempted to ask is: Why should
we practise this Sermon? Why should we pay heed to this
terrible warning? Why should we believe that, unless we are
indeed making our lives conform to this pattern, we shall be
without hope as we come face to face with God? The real answer
to all that is the subject to which we are directed by these last
two verses. It is the Person Himself, the Person who uttered these
sayings, the One who has delivered this teaching. In other words,
as we consider the Sermon on the Mount as a whole, having gone
into its various parts, we must realize that we must not concentrate only upon the beauty of the diction, the perfect structure of
the Sermon, the impressive pictures, the striking illustrations
and the extraordinary balance which we find in it, both from the

standpoint of material and the way in which it is presented. Indeed, we can go further. When we consider the Sermon on the Mount, we are never to stop even with the moral, ethical, spiritual teaching; we are to go beyond all these things, wonderful though they are, and vital as they all are, to the Person of the Preacher Himself.

There are two main reasons for saying that. The first is that, ultimately, the authority of the Sermon derives from the Preacher. That is, of course, what makes the New Testament such a unique book, and gives uniqueness to the teaching of our Lord. With all other teachers that the world has ever known, the important thing is the teaching; but here is a case in which the Teacher is more important even than what He taught. There is a sense in which you cannot divide and separate them from one another; but if we are to give priority to one, we must always put the Preacher first. So these two verses coming at the end of the Sermon direct our attention to that fact.

If any man asks: Why should I pay heed to that Sermon, why should I put it into practice, why should I believe that it is the most vital thing in this life? the answer is, because of the Person who preached it. That is the authority, that is the sanction behind the Sermon. In other words, if we are in any doubt as to the Person who preached this Sermon, that is obviously going to affect our view of it. If we are in doubt about His uniqueness, about His deity, about the fact that here was God in the flesh speaking, then our whole attitude towards the Sermon is undermined. But, conversely, if we do believe that the Man who spoke these words was none other than the only begotten Son of God, then they have an awful solemnity and added authority, and we must take the teaching as a whole with all the seriousness which must ever be given to any pronouncement that comes from God Himself. There, then, we have a very good reason for considering this matter. The ultimate sanction behind every expression in the Sermon is to be found there. When we read it, therefore, and are tempted perhaps to argue against it or to explain certain things away, we must remember that we are considering the words of the Son of God. The authority and the sanction are derived from the Speaker, from the blessed Person Himself.

But quite apart from such a general deduction, our Lord Himself insists upon our paying attention to it. He calls attention to Himself in the Sermon. He repeats tests which are obviously

designed to focus our attention upon Himself. That is the point
at which so much that passes for gospel differs from the real
gospel. There is a tendency for some people to create a division
between the teaching of the New Testament and the Lord
Himself. That is an essential error. He is always calling attention
to Himself, and we find that abundantly illustrated in this particular Sermon. The ultimate trouble, therefore, with people
who emphasize the teaching of the Sermon on the Mount at the
expense of doctrine, and at the expense of theology, is that they
never realize that point. We have often referred, in passing, to
the case of those who say they like the Sermon on the Mount, and
who put the Sermon on the Mount over against the teaching
about the atonement and the death of Christ and all the high
doctrines of the Epistles, because, they say, the Sermon on the
Mount is something practical, something that can be applied to
life and become the basis of the social order, and so on. The real
trouble with such people is that they have never truly read the
Sermon on the Mount, for, if they had done so, they would have
found that they were being directed continually to this Person.
And immediately that raises crucial doctrine. In other words, the
Sermon on the Mount, as we have seen so many times, is really a
kind of basic statement out of which everything else comes. It is
full of doctrine; and the idea that it is moral, ethical teaching and
nothing else, is an idea that is quite foreign to the teaching of the
Sermon, and particularly to the point which is emphasized here
in these last two verses.

We see, then, that our Lord Himself calls attention to Himself,
and, in a sense, there is nothing in the Sermon which is quite so
remarkable as the way in which He does that. So, having looked
at the whole Sermon, we find that all the instructions He gave
become focused together in Him. We look at Him in a special
way in the Sermon on the Mount; and any study of it should
always lead us to that. Here in these two verses we have a very
wonderful way of doing so. We are told about the reaction of
these people who had the great and high privilege of looking at
Him and listening to the Sermon. And we are told that their
reaction was one of astonishment. 'It came to pass, when Jesus
had ended these sayings, the people were astonished at his doctrine (or at his teaching): for he taught them as one having
authority, and not as the scribes.'

Let us try to recapture this if we can, for there is nothing that
we should enjoy—I use the term advisedly—so much as looking

at Him. There is no value in all other teaching if we are not right about Him. Essentially the vital point of all teaching, of theology, and of the whole Bible is to bring us to a knowledge of Him and into relationship with Him. So we look at the blessed Person, and we must try to picture this scene. Here is a great crowd of people. First of all it was just our Lord and His disciples when He sat down to teach; but by the end it is obvious that there was a great crowd. Here, sitting before all these people on that mountain, is this young Man, apparently just a carpenter from a little place called Nazareth in Galilee, an artisan, a common, ordinary person. He had had no training in the schools, He was not a Pharisee, or a scribe; He had not been sitting at the feet of Gamaliel or any of the great authorities or teachers. Apparently He was just a very ordinary person, who had lived a very ordinary life. But suddenly He bursts forth upon the countryside in an extraordinary ministry, and here He sits and begins to teach and to preach and to say the things we have been considering together. It is not surprising that these people were astonished. It was all so unexpected, so unusual in every way, so different from everything they had ever known. How difficult it is for us, because of our sheer familiarity with these facts and details, to realize that these things actually happened nearly two thousand years ago, and to realize what the effect must have been upon our Lord's contemporaries. Try to imagine their utter astonishment and amazement as this carpenter from Galilee sits and teaches and expounds the law, and speaks in this extraordinary manner. They were amazed and astonished and dumbfounded.

The thing for us to discover is exactly what caused the astonishment. The first thing, clearly, is the general authority with which He spoke—this Man who talked to them with authority and not as the scribes. That negative is very interesting —that His teaching was not after the manner of the scribes. The characteristic of the teaching of the scribes, you remember, was that they always quoted authorities and never uttered any original thoughts; they were experts, not so much in the law itself, as in various expositions and interpretations of the law which had been put forward since it was first given to Moses. Then, in turn, they were always quoting the experts on these interpretations. As an illustration of what this means, we have but to think of what so often happens in the Law Courts when a case is being heard. Various authorities are quoted; one authority has said this and another authority has said that; other textbooks are

produced and their expositions are given. That was the manner
or practice of the scribes, and so they were always arguing; but
the chief feature was the endless string of quotations. It is something that still happens today. You can read or hear sermons
that seem to be nothing but a series of quotations from various
writings. That kind of thing gives the impression of learning and
culture. We are told that the scribes and Pharisees were very
proud of their learning. They dismissed our Lord with derision,
and said, 'How hath this man learning, never having learned?'
That points to the fact that the outstanding characteristic of His
method was the absence of the endless quotations. In other words,
the surprising thing about Him was His originality. He keeps on
saying 'I say unto you'; not 'So-and-so has said', but 'I say unto
you'. There was a freshness about His teaching. His whole
method was different. His very appearance was different. His
whole attitude towards teaching was different. It was characterized by this originality of thought and of manner—the way in
which He did it as well as what He did.

But, of course, the most astonishing thing of all was the confidence and certainty with which He spoke. That appeared at the
very beginning, even as He was uttering those great Beatitudes.
He begins by saying: 'Blessed are the poor in spirit' and then,
'for theirs is the kingdom of heaven.' There is no doubt about it,
and no question; this is no mere supposition, or possibility only.
This extraordinary assurance and authority with which He
spoke was something that was manifested from the very beginning.

I imagine, however, that what really astonished these people
over and above His general authority was what He said, and in
particular what He said about Himself. That, most surely, must
have amazed and astonished them. Think again of the things
which He said, first of all about His own teaching. He keeps on
making remarks which call attention to His teaching, and to His
own attitude towards it. Take, for instance, the frequency with
which in the fifth chapter He said something like this: 'Ye have
heard it said by them of old time . . . but I say unto you'. He does
not hesitate to correct the teaching of the Pharisees and their
authorities. 'They of old time', you remember we saw, stood for
certain Pharisees and their exposition of the Mosaic law. He
did not hesitate to put that aside and to correct it. This artisan,
this carpenter who had never been to the schools, saying: 'I say
unto you'! He claims that authority for Himself and for His
teaching.

Indeed, He does not hesitate to assert in that phrase, that He, and He alone, is able to give a spiritual interpretation of the law that was given through Moses. His whole argument is that the people had never seen the spiritual intent or content of the law given by Moses, they were mis-interpreting it and reducing it to the physical level. As long as they did not actually commit physical adultery, they thought it did not matter. They did not see that God was concerned about the heart, the desire, the spirit. So He stands before them as the only true interpreter of the law. He says that His interpretation alone brings out the spiritual intent of the law; indeed, He does not hesitate to speak of Himself and to regard Himself as the law giver: 'I say unto you.'

Then you remember how at the end of the Sermon He puts this in a still more explicit manner. 'Therefore', He says, 'whosoever heareth these sayings of mine, and doeth them, . . .' You notice the significance He attaches to His own sayings. As He says that, He is saying something about Himself. He is using this terrifying picture of the two houses. He has already spoken about judgment, and He puts it all in terms of 'these sayings of mine'. He says in effect: 'I want you to listen to these, and I want you to practise them—"these sayings of mine"; do you realize who I am and the importance, therefore, of what I say?' Thus we find that in what He said about His teaching He is making a tremendous pronouncement about Himself. He claims this unique authority.

But we are not left simply with inferences and implications; His references to Himself are not only indirect. Have you ever contemplated the direct references which He makes to Himself in this Sermon on the Mount? Let us take them in the order in which they appear. First, in v. 11, when He has just finished the Beatitudes, He goes on to say: 'Blessed are ye, when men shall revile you, and persecute you, and shall say all manner of evil against you falsely, for my sake.' What an astonishing and amazing thing that is. He does not say, 'Blessed are ye when men shall revile and persecute you for the teaching's sake', or 'Ah, blessed are you people if, in your desire to implement this high and exalted teaching, you suffer persecution and perhaps death itself.' He does not say: 'If you suffer like this for the name of God your Father in heaven, you are blessed.' No, He says 'for my sake'. What unutterable folly it is for people to say that they are interested in the Sermon on the Mount as ethical and moral and social teaching only. Here, before He comes to 'turning the other cheek' and the other things they like so much, He tells us that we ought to be ready to suffer for His sake, and that we are to endure persecution for His sake, and that we may even have to be ready to die for His sake. This tremendous claim comes at the very beginning of the Sermon.

Then He goes on to do the same thing by implication immediately afterwards. 'Ye are the salt of the earth', and 'ye are the light of the world'. Do you see the implication of that? He says in effect, 'You people who are My disciples and My followers, you who have given yourselves to Me even to the extent of enduring persecution for My name's sake, and if necessary death for My sake, you, who are listening to Me and are going to repeat My teaching and propagate it throughout the world, you are the salt of the earth, and the light of the world.' There is only one real deduction to draw from that, that they are going to be a very special and unique people who, because of their relationship to Him, become the salt of the earth and the light of the world. It is the whole doctrine of the rebirth. They are not just people who listen to teaching and then repeat it and so have the effect of salt and light. No, they themselves are going to become salt and light. We have here the doctrine of the mystical relationship to and union of His people with Him, He dwelling in them and imparting His nature to them. Therefore, they in turn become the light of the world as He is the light of the world. So it is again a tremendous statement about Him. He is here asserting His unique deity and His Saviourhood. He is asserting that He is the long expected Messiah.

So, as we look at these two striking statements before we come to His detailed teaching, we are driven to ask, as these people must have asked, Who is this Person who talks like this? Who is this man, this carpenter from Nazareth, who asks us to be ready to suffer for Him, and tells us we shall be blessed indeed of God if we do; who says, 'Rejoice, and be exceeding glad: for great is your reward in heaven' if you suffer injustice and persecution 'for my sake'? Who is this? And who is this who says He can make us the salt of the earth and the light of the world? He gives the answer to the question in v. 17, where He says: 'Think not that I am come to destroy the law, or the prophets: I am not come to destroy, but to fulfil.' Look for a moment at this extraordinary expression, 'I am come'. He speaks of Himself and of His life in this world as being different from that of anybody else. He does not say: 'I have been born, therefore this or that.' He says: 'I am come.' Where Has he come from? He is One who has arrived in this world; He has not only been born, He has come into it from somewhere. He has come from eternity, from heaven, He has come from the bosom of the Father. The law and the prophets had said that He was to come. They said, for instance, 'The Sun of righteousness (shall) arise with healing in his wings.' They were always talking of someone who was to come from the outside. And, here, He says of Himself, 'I am come.' It is not surprising that these people as they sat and listened said: What does He mean; and who is this man, this carpenter who looks like ourselves?

He is always saying: 'I am come.' He is telling them that He does not belong to this realm, but that He has come into this life, and into this world, from glory, from eternity. He is saying: 'I and the Father are one.' He is referring to the incarnation. What tragic folly to regard this Sermon as just a social manifesto, and to see nothing but ethics and morality in it. Listen to what He says about Himself: 'I am come.' This is no human teacher; this is the Son of God.

But furthermore He says that He has come to fulfil, and not to destroy the law and the prophets; which means that He has come to fulfil and to keep God's holy law, that He is also the Messiah. He is claiming here that He is sinless, absolutely perfect. God gave His law to Moses, but not a single human being had ever kept it—'all the world may become guilty before God', 'there is none righteous, no, not one'. All the saints of the Old Testament had broken the law; none had succeeded in observing it. Yet here is One who stands and says: I am going to keep it; not one jot or one tittle of this law will I break; I am going to fulfil it, I am going to keep and to honour it perfectly. Here is One who claims to be sinless, to be absolutely perfect. Not only that. He does not hesitate to claim for Himself what Paul puts in the words: 'Christ is the end of the law for righteousness to every one that believeth.' In other words, He fulfils the law by carrying it out, He honours it by absolute perfection in His own life. Yes; but He bears the punishment it metes out upon transgressors also. He has satisfied every demand of the law of God, He has fulfilled the law for Himself and others.

But He claims that he is fulfilling the prophets also. He claims that He is the One to whom all the Old Testament prophets pointed. They had been talking about the Messiah; He says, I am this Messiah. He is the One who fulfils in His own Person all the promises. Again the apostle Paul sums it up by putting it like this: 'For all the promises of God in him are yea, and in him Amen.' God's promises are all fulfilled in this wonderful Person who here says of Himself that He is the fulfiller of the law and the prophets. Everything in the Old Testament points to Him; He is the centre of it all. This is the coming One, the One expected. He says all that in the Sermon on the Mount, this Sermon which we are told has no doctrine, and which people like because it is not theological! Can there be a more tragic blindness than that which causes men to speak in such a foolish manner? The whole doctrine of the incarnation of Christ, His Person and His death, is all here. We have seen it as we have gone through the Sermon, and we are looking at it again now.

Another great statement pointing in the same direction is the one we found in vii. 21: 'Not every one that saith unto me, Lord, Lord, shall enter into the kingdom of heaven.' He does not hesitate to say that people will address Him as Lord, and that means that He is Jehovah, that He is God. He says here quite calmly that people are going to say to Him, 'Lord, Lord.' They are saying it now, in a sense, and on that great day they will say, 'Lord, Lord', to Him. But the emphasis is upon the fact that they will say that to 'me'—not to the Father who is in heaven, but to 'me', the One speaking there on the mountain. He does not hesitate to ascribe to Himself, and to take to Himself, the highest term used in the whole realm of Scripture for the eternal, absolute, blessed God.

He even went a step further, and announced at the end of the Sermon that He is to be the Judge of the world. 'Many will say to me in that day, Lord, Lord,' etc. Notice the repetition—'And then will I profess unto them, I never knew you: depart from me, ye that work iniquity.' Yes, judgment is being committed to the Son. He is claiming that He is to be the Judge of all men, and that what matters is our relationship to Him, His knowledge of us, His concern about us and His interest in us. As someone once put it very well: 'The One who sat there on the Mount to teach, is the One who at the end will sit on the throne of His glory and all the nations of the world shall appear before Him, and He will pronounce the judgment upon them.' Was ever anything more astounding, more astonishing, uttered in this world? Try again to capture the scene. Look at this apparently ordinary Person, this carpenter, sitting there and saying, in effect: 'As I am sitting here now I shall sit on the throne of eternal glory, and the whole world and the nations and all people will appear before Me, and I will pronounce judgment.' He is indeed the Judge eternal.

Thus we have gathered together the main statements He makes about Himself in this famous Sermon on the Mount. As we leave it, therefore, I ask you this simple yet profound question: What is your reaction to it all? We are told that these people 'were astonished at his doctrine: for he taught them as one having authority, and not as the scribes'. We are not told that their reaction went any further than that; but we are told that they were astonished and amazed because of His manner, because of the very form of His teaching, and because of the astounding teaching itself, and especially some of these things which He said about Himself. There are many people who are not even astonished by this Sermon. God forbid that that should be true of any of us. But it is not enough that we should merely be astonished; our reaction must go beyond astonishment. Surely our reaction as He speaks to us should be to recognize that this is none other than the Son of God Himself who has been speaking to us in the words we have considered; the very incarnate Son of God. Our first reaction should be that we recognize again the central truth of the gospel, that God's only begotten Son has entered into this world of time. We are not concerned here with a mere philosophy or outlook upon life, but with the fact that the preacher was the Son of God Almighty here in the flesh.

Why did He come, why did He preach the Sermon? He has not just come to give another law. He was not merely telling people how to live, because the Sermon on the Mount (we say it with reverence) is infinitely more impossible to practise than even the law of Moses, and we have already seen that there had not been a single human being who had been able to keep that. What then is the message? It must be this. In this Sermon our Lord condemns once and for ever all trust in human endeavour and natural ability in the matter of salvation. He is telling us, in other words, that we all have come short of the glory of God, and that however great our efforts and striving from now until our death, they will never make us righteous, or fit us to stand in the presence of God. He says that the Pharisees have been reducing the real meaning of the law, but that the law itself is spiritual. He is saying what Paul came to see and to say later: 'I was alive without the law once; but when the commandment came, sin revived, and I died' (Romans vii. 9). In other words, He is saying that we are all condemned sinners in the sight of God, and that we cannot save ourselves.

Then He goes on to say that we all need a new birth, a new nature, and a new life. We cannot live a life like this as we are by nature; we must be made anew. And what He is saying in this Sermon is that He has come in order to give us this new life. Yes, in relationship to Him, we become the salt of the earth and the light of the world. He has come not merely to outline the teaching. He has come to make it possible. In this Sermon, beginning with the Beatitudes, He has given an account of His people. He has stated what they will be like in general, and given a more detailed account of how they will act. The Sermon is a description of Christian people, people who have received the Holy Spirit; not of natural man striving to make himself right with God, but of God making His people anew. He has given us the gift of the Holy Spirit, the promise made to Abraham, 'the promise of the Father', and having received this promise, we become people conformable to this pattern. The Beatitudes are true of all who are living the Sermon on the Mount, of all who are Christian. That does not mean that we are sinless or perfect; it means that if we look at the general tenor of our life it corresponds to this, or as John puts it in his first Epistle: 'He that is born of God does not continue the practices of sin.' There is this difference. Look at a man's life in general. As you look at the believer he conforms to the Sermon on the Mount. He wants to live it and he does his utmost to do so. He realizes his failure, but prays to be filled with the Spirit; he hungers and thirsts after righteousness, and he has the blessed experience of the promises being realized in his daily life.

This is the true reaction to the Sermon on the Mount. We realize that this was none other than the Son of God, and that in the Sermon He has been saying that He has come to start a new humanity. He is 'the first born among many brethren'; He is 'the last Adam'; He is God's new Man, and all who belong to Him are going to be like Him. It is astounding doctrine, it is astonishing, amazing doctrine; but, thank God, we know it is the truth. We know that He died for our sins, that our sins are forgiven; 'we know that we have passed from death unto life, because we love the brethren'; we know that we belong to Him, because we do indeed hunger and thirst after righteousness. We are conscious of the fact that He is dealing with us, that His Spirit is working within us, revealing to us our shortcomings and imperfections, creating longings and aspirations within us, 'working in us both to will and to do of his good pleasure'. Above all, in the midst of life, with all its trials and problems and tests, indeed amidst all the uncertainties of life in this 'atomic age' and the certain fact of death and the final judgment, we can say with the apostle Paul, 'For the which cause I also suffer these things: nevertheless I am not ashamed: for I know whom I have believed, and am persuaded that he is able to keep that which I have committed unto him against that day' (2 Timothy i. 12).

> 'In every high and stormy gale
> My anchor holds within the veil.
>
> When all around my soul gives way,
> He then is all my hope and stay.
>
> On Christ, the solid Rock, I stand;
> All other ground is sinking sand.'

'For other foundation can no man lay than that is laid, which is Jesus Christ' (1 Corinthians iii. 11). 'Nevertheless the foundation of God standeth sure, having this seal, The Lord knoweth them that are his. And, Let every one that nameth the name of Christ depart from iniquity' (2 Timothy ii. 19).